The Frederick Chopin Singing Society of Buffalo, New York, 1899 - 2024

The Frederick Chopin Singing Society of Buffalo, New York, 1899 – 2024

Gregory L. Witul

The Frederick Chopin Singing Society

www.chopinsingingsociety.com

Contents

Foreword

Author Greg Witul shares his extensive knowledge, research, writing skills and wit to present the rich history of a legendary Western New York organization, the Chopin Singing Society, now celebrating 125 years. When other such organizations have gone by the wayside, this one continues and thrives as a cultural resource. Founded in 1899, suffering through the Depression, two world wars, and two pandemics, its longevity prevails. Beginning as a refuge for scores of Polish immigrants on Buffalo's East Side and beyond, it provided an opportunity to bask in their cultural heritage even though their homeland had been divided and conquered. Through world wars and the near half century of communist oppression, it worked to assist Poland financially and spiritually. Its three emotionally charged trips to Poland lifted the spirits of Poland's downtrodden population through song, while secretly assisting Solidarity's struggle for freedom. Celebrating the election and legacy of Pope St. John Paul II until today, it embodies his call to "Keep alive this heritage! Intensify this heritage! Impart it to the next generations!" (Gniezno, Poland June 3, 1979)

Through the years, the Society has left a formidable mark on this city and its people. From its gift of the Chopin monument which now stands proudly by Kleinhans Music Hall, to its support of the Buffalo Philharmonic Orchestra and scholarships to young pianists, to its concerts, radio broadcasts, and television performances which have delighted audiences over the years, to its presentations at the Oath of Citizenship ceremonies aboard the USS Little Rock welcoming Buffalo's newest citizens, to its inauguration of the celebration of Dyngus Day which now, thanks to promoter Eddy Dobosiewicz, draws scores of visitors from across North America, to its role as Buffalo's ambassador to Poland, Italy, Brazil, and all the corners of the US, the Society has enriched the life of the region. From accolades in the 1960s when Mrs. Joseph Varge wrote in a letter to a local newspaper: "What a boost (Buffalo) received…with the first concert of the Chopin Singing Society of Buffalo. Here surely is a vocal group that ranks with the best. A delight to hear, even though one understands no word of the language, a charming sight to see in colorful folk costumes, this is a group to enhance the musical and cultural life of Buffalo" and A. Brown's Letter to the Editor writing, "Buffalo can well be proud of its

Polish citizens! What they are contributing to the culture and art of our great city was vividly revealed at last Saturday's evening of song and dance..." to the accolades given by Mayor Byron Brown at the kickoff to the 2024 Dyngus Day celebration, ordinary citizens, and even the mayor, have acknowledged the contributions of the Chopin Singing Society.

In this delightful and meticulously researched survey of the life of one of the longest serving organizations of Buffalo, Greg Witul gives us a reason to celebrate our past and challenges us to continue the legacy and cultural vibrancy of this storied institution. Dziekuje Greg!

Gary A. Bienkowski and Mary Lou T. Wyrobek, President and Vice President, Chopin Singing Society.

Acknowledgements

This book would not have been possible without the generous contributions of the following organizations and individuals:

The Permanent Chair of Polish Culture at Canisius University provided a significant Grant which allowed this endeavor to succeed.

Platinum Sponsors

Gary A. Bienkowski, President of the Chopin Singing Society
Frances J. Cirbus, Treasurer of the Chopin Singing Society
Robert J. Fronckowiak – "Grateful for your Preserving and Promoting Polish Culture in Song"
Mary Lou T. Wyrobek, President of the Polish Singers Alliance of America and Vice President of the Chopin Singing Society offered in memory of Michaeline A. Wyrobek (1944-2002)

Silver Sponsors

Paul Walker Chodkowski
Witul and Szymborski Families

Bronze Sponsors

Am-Pol Eagle – The Voice of WNY Americans of Polish Origin
The Bucki Family
The Chopin Singing Society Auxiliary: President Christine Witkowski
Vice President Irene Kmiotek
Robert M. Ciesielski, Esq., Board Member of the Chopin Singing Society
Greater Buffalo Friends of Music (buffalofom.com)
The Honorable Ann T. Mikoll, President Emeritus of the Chopin Singing Society
Nadolny/VanderHorn/Ellis Family
The Polish Arts Club of Buffalo

Introduction

In Buffalo's Polonia there are a handful of pillars that connect the community's past to the present day. The grandeur of the Roman Catholic churches of the East Side and Black Rock, the legacy of Dr. Francis Fronczak, the surviving art of Joseph Mazur, the endurance of the Broadway Market, the flexibility of the Adam Mickiewicz Library and Dramatic Circle, and the music of the Chopin Singing Society have kept all of these symbols of Polonia relevant in the minds of Western New Yorkers. But of all these pillars Chopin has had the furthest reach and left the most enduring mark on not just Buffalo but the nation as a whole.

From their humble beginnings at St Adalbert's parish hall the singing society would grow and touch every aspect of life in Buffalo. They would work for better education for Polish youth, press America to go to war for Polish independence, see their members elected to political office, and with the donation of the Chopin Monument leave a permanent mark of the Polish colony in the Queen City. All this while entertaining thousands with music, dance, and festivities. For the last 125 years the singers would thrive in boom times, survive through depression and war, and pivot when change was needed. Where other organizations closed due to the old guard unable to give up power, influence, and control to the next generation, the men of Chopin stepped aside so the choir they invested so much in could thrive for decades to come. It would be this willingness to pass the torch that would open the doors to younger members, allow women to join the ranks of the singers, and expand the social aspect of the society with the inclusion of non-singing members.

With this younger, social, and expanded membership the Chopins would inadvertently create what has become one of the defining Polish American festivals, Dyngus Day. What started off as just another party on an expansive social calendar has grown to a party that is now celebrated in just about every corner of Polish North America. By transforming the traditional Polish festival into an Americanized party, the Chopins created an event that acts as a cultural ambassador where everyone is Polish on Dyngus Day, just as everyone is Irish on St. Patrick's Day or German during Oktoberfest.

While Dyngus Day became the public face of the Chopinites to the outside world, within Polonia and in Poland they were true ambassadors. They would represent Polonia to presidents, perform for a Pope on behalf of America, and be treated as dignitaries both at home and abroad. In time they would become one of the defining Polish singing groups in Buffalo and nationally with their winning of the Hlond Trophy.

When the second great wave of organization closings happened in the 1990s the Chopins were able to adapt again by moving out of the city and into the suburbs. From their new home they would reinforce their importance as a cultural touchstone and set a pace of concerts, events, and appearances that would keep them relevant to this day.

Just how did the Chopin Singing Society survive for 125 years when so many others have fallen? The answers are both simple and complex. They always stayed true to their mission of spreading and preserving Polish culture in America through music, they adapted to the realities of a changing world, and the members and their families had a deep desire to see the society thrive. From the very beginning it would be generations of families that would guide Chopin. From the Brockis and Nadolnys at the founding of the society to the Kujawas, Kedzierskis, Mikolls, and Wyrobeks, it would be families of members who kept the organization going through thick and thin. It would be the foresight and the founding families' ability to put ego aside that allowed the society to change with the world. The death of many organizations starts when there is no change of leadership at the top. This leads to comfort, then complacency, atrophy, and death. By allowing younger members to take over, the older members ensured that the society stayed relevant. Most importantly, the Chopin Singing Society has survived by staying true to its mission of spreading Polish culture through music. Sometimes that mission looks like a performance in an arts festival, participating in a parade, or providing music at a religious service, and sometimes it looks like hosting a Dyngus Day party, but till the very end they are working to keep the traditions of Poland alive and well in the New World.

Appreciation

A work like this is never possible without the help and assistance of a near countless number of individuals and organizations. The following is only the briefest list of those I own a debt of gratitude to

Mary E. Lanham, Edward Witul, Mary Lou Wyrobek, Gary Bienkowski, Fran Cirbus, Ann Mikoll, Thomas Witakowski, Michael Szafranski, Paul Walker, Peter Sloane, Maureen Gleason, Monica Rzepka, Andrew Golebiowski, Steven, Erin, Teddi, Sammy, and McTavish Jacobson, Larry and Deb Witul, Daniel Kij, Adeline Wujcikowski, Cynthia Van Ness and the Buffalo History Museum, Renee Harzewski and Roger Puchalski of the Am-Pol Eagle Newspaper, Mark Kohan of the Polish American Journal, the librarians at the Grosvenor Room of the Buffalo & Erie County Public Library, and the Permanent Chair of Polish Culture at Canisius University to name a few. My greatest apologies to those I have missed.

Chapter 1

Buffalo's Early Polish Community

As it is in every Polonia across the globe, it would be the events in Poland that dictated the lives of her Diaspora. From the November Uprising, to Imperial repression, cultural suppression, unemployment, the First and Second World Wars, and the rise of Communism, what happened in Poland would encourage Poles to leave their homeland and settle in Western New York.[1]

The Niagara Frontier's first Pole was an exile who took part in the 1830 armed rebellion against the Russian Empire. Henry I. Glowacki was born in Poland in 1816 to a family of standing with noble lineage. Because of his station, Henry received a military education and earned the rank of major. When the November Uprising began, Glowacki quickly fell in with the partisans and engaged the Russian forces. He was captured and after some diplomatic wrangling, exiled to America by 1834. Heading west to Illinois, Henry and his party stopped in the city of Batavia, where after a conversation with Davis Evans of the Holland Land Company, he was offered a job. Glowacki quickly rose through Batavia society, becoming a citizen in 1839, a lawyer by 1842, and following the American Civil War, a village trustee. He married American Mary Redfield and his 1895 passing was considered to be a great loss to the city.[2]

In Buffalo, it was the Jews who spoke the first Polish words in the Queen City. Barnard (Barnett) Lichtenstein arrived in Buffalo from Poland in 1838, settling in the nascent German-Jewish community east of the city center. A hat maker by trade he married the American-born Eliza, and in 1841 the couple welcomed their first daughter Sarah. Sarah Lichtenstein was the first Jewish-American born in Buffalo.[3] More Polish-Jews followed, including Posen-born Mark Moritz, who along

---

[1] "The Nation of Polonia:Polish/Russian: Immigration and Relocation in U.S. History: Classroom Materials at the Library of Congress: Library of Congress." The Library of Congress

[2] Barnes, Larry D. *A Polish Revolutionary in Batavia, His Wife and Descendants, and a House Divided: The Story of Henry Glowacki and His Family*. Larry D. Barnes, 2008.

[3] Adler, Selig, and Thomas Edmund Connolly. *From Ararat to Suburbia; the History of the Jewish Community of Buffalo*. Jewish Publication Society of America, 1960.

with their German brethren started Temple Beth El in 1847, the city's first synagogue.[4]

As the burgeoning Jewish community grew so too did Buffalo. In the middle of the nineteenth century Western New York was a hub of westward expansion. Thousands of Germans, Irish, Swedes, and Poles, stopped off in the city before heading out to Wisconsin, Iowa, and Michigan. But some that stopped in the city as a layover, found that the burgeoning metropolis had all that they needed and decided to stay. The first Polish couple to do this was Charles and Elizabeth Barnicki.

Leaving their home in Poznan by way of Hamburg, the couple arrived in Buffalo in late 1852. With a desire to head further west, a heavily pregnant Elizabeth put a stop to their journey. Finding an apartment in Buffalo's German East Side, Charles quickly began working as a cobbler. Not many of the Polonias spread across the world can pinpoint the exact moment their community was founded, but Western New York can. It would be the labor grunts of Elizabeth Barnicki and a midwife yelling *drücken* and *mach weiter* that heralded the birth of Buffalo's Polonia in the form of Katarzyna Barnicki.[5] Her February 27, 1853, nativity would make her the first of the city's soon to be tens of thousands of American born Poles.

Being Catholic, the Barnickis had their child baptized at the parish they had been attending, St. Mary German Roman Catholic Church on Broadway. Knowing enough of the language and customs, these Polish pioneers adapted to their new living situation and integrated into the German community as much as they could, while still holding to their own Polish traditions in their home and heart.

As more Poles moved into Buffalo, they, like the Barnickis, began to attend St. Mary's. Not as affluent as the Germans that came before them, and distinctively Slavic, the Poles had to stand at the rear of the church during Mass. But as the 1860s wore on their numbers grew and soon, they had overtaken the narthex and began filling up the aisles. The Polish parishioners were soon approached by Father James Nagel of St. Michael Church and asked if they wanted to have a side chapel for their own Masses. Arranged by the Jesuit Fathers, Jan Arent, a layman, read the gospel in his native tongue for the services,

---

[4] Garfinkel, Marvin H. *Temple Beth El's First Century; Centennial Souvenir Book, 1847-1947.* 1947.

[5] Kaszubik, Keith. "Buffalo's Polonia Marks 157th Anniversary as North America's Oldest Polish Settlement." *Am-Pol Eagle*. N.p., 3 Mar. 2010. Web. 26 Jan. 2016.

while the congregation sang some of the first Polish hymns in Western New York.

The Polish population of Buffalo continued to grow, which brought them to the attention of Father J. M. Gartner, the Procurator of the Slavonic Catholic Churches in the United States. With his help the Polish Catholics of St. Michael's formed the Society of St. Stanislaus on December 12, 1872, with the mission to establish a Roman Catholic Church for themselves.

Half a world away, Jan Pitass was a seminarian attending the Collegium Romanum in Rome. While at school, Pitass made the acquaintanceship of Father Gartner and was told about the desire of the Buffalo Poles to establish a parish. At first Pitass was intrigued, but when Gartner gave him a gift of $124 in gold, Jan boarded a ship and headed off to America. In Western New York Jan finished his education at Niagara University where he was ordained. On June 8, 1873, Father Pitass met with the society, celebrated Mass, and the parish of St. Stanislaus Bishop & Martyr was born.[6]

As the congregation began looking for a home, real estate developer Joseph Bork approached them with an offer. Bork would gift St. Stanislaus a parcel in east Buffalo if they promised to build their church on it. Pitass graciously accepted the land, and soon a wooden church, and Bork-built homes, began rising around Peckham and Townsend Streets.

With a Catholic church, more Poles stopped passing through Buffalo and started to stay. The "Mother Church" of St. Stanislaus would become the cradle of Buffalo's Polonia and the Polish colony would spread out from it. The early years saw slow and steady growth, but by the end of the decade the population exploded. At the start of 1879, 2,500 Poles lived in the shadow of St. Stanislaus, by the end of the year there were over 3,500 residents.

As word spread in Poland of the abundance that could be found in the New World, more Poles flooded into the Queen City. Another two thousand Slavs packed into the area around Broadway and Fillmore in the following year, and four thousand more were to join them in 1881. Over the next decade twenty thousand Poles resided in the East Side spreading out over a mile to the north, east, and south of St. Stanislaus.

---

6 "St. Michael's Roman Catholic Church." *Polonia Trail*, Polish-American Congress WNY, 29 June 2016

Now a city within a city, fissures began to appear among the populace. As more Poles from Krakow, Warsaw, Lodz, Poznan, and Gdansk moved in, formerly disparate regions found themselves living together in which a cultural clash ensued. On top of that, some in the community began to chafe under the leadership of Father Pitass.[7] As the dissent grew, efforts began to establish a second parish in the neighborhood. After an intervention from the Holy See, this would be accomplished, and St. Adalbert Parish was formed in 1886.

With religious music firmly established at St. Stanislaus, Bernard J. Pitass and George Ignatius Nowak wanted to establish a patriotic singing society, like the ones in Poland and spreading across America.[8] To meet this end the two, along with a handful of other men from St. Stanislaus, organized the Moniuszko Singing Society on September 16, 1890.[9]

Not only did they have a strong commitment to musical endeavors, the Moniuszkos also became the prototype of the singing society that served as a venerable who's who of Polonia.[10] Some of the illustrious names that could be found on the membership rolls included Fillmore Avenue tobacconist Joseph Jankowski,[11] brewer Anthony Schreiber,[12] wholesaler Stanislaw K. Lipowicz,[13] and community pillar Dr. Francis E. Fronczak.[14]

As the Moniuszkos mastered their sound, St. Adalbert's began to flourish a world away from Father Pitass. But that distance slowly shrank and within a decade the influence of the Polish pastor was felt again. Upset by this growing control, many parishioners left to form

---

[7] "St. Stanislaus, B. & M. Church." *Polonia Trail*, Polish-American Congress WNY, 29 June 2016

[8] Blejwas, Stanislaus A. *The Polish Singers Alliance, 1888-1998: Choral Patriotism.* University of Rochester Press, 2005.

[9] "50 Years Old." *Buffalo Courier-Express*, 29 Apr. 1940, p. 20.

[10] "Jubilant Poles." *Buffalo Courier*, 19 June 1894, p. 5.

[11] "Jozef Jankowski." *Album Pamiatkowe I Przewodnik Handlowy: Osady Polskiej W Miescie Buffalo, Z Dolaczeniem Okolicznych Miejscowosci Ze Stanu New York* , Wydane Staraniem i Nakladem Polskiej Spolki Wydawniczej, 1906, p. 137-140.

[12] "Antoni Schreiber." *Album Pamiatkowe I Przewodnik Handlowy: Osady Polskiej W Miescie Buffalo, Z Dolaczeniem Okolicznych Miejscowosci Ze Stanu New York* , Wydane Staraniem i Nakładem Polskiej Spolki Wydawniczej, 1906, p. 282-297.

[13] "Stanislaw K. Lipowicz." *Album Pamiatkowe I Przewodnik Handlowy: Osady Polskiej W Miescie Buffalo, Z Dolaczeniem Okolicznych Miejscowosci Ze Stanu New York* , Wydane Staraniem i Nakladem Polskiej Spolki Wydawniczej, 1906, p. 142-146.

[14] "Dr. Francis E. Fronczak." *Album Pamiatkowe I Przewodnik Handlowy: Osady Polskiej W Miescie Buffalo, Z Dolaczeniem Okolicznych Miejscowosci Ze Stanu New York*, Wydane Staraniem i Nakladem Polskiej Spolki Wydawniczej, 1906, p. 102-107.

the Holy Mother of the Rosary Cathedral of the Polish National Catholic Church. Even with this loss of congregants, St. Adalbert grew to be a large and significant church.[15]

As the epicenter of Buffalo's Polonia moved from Townsend and Peckham to Broadway, more institutions developed to care for the growing populace on the major thoroughfare. After St. Adalbert was carved out of St. Stanislaus's territory, St. John Kanty in 1891 and Transfiguration in 1893 soon followed. As branches of the Polish Union formed and a Polish Falcons nest was established, a number of men living along Broadway moved to start a second singing society for Polonia. Led by John M. Chrzanowski, Peter Piotrowski, and Wladyslaw Nowak the Polskie Kolo Spiewackie or Polish Singing Circle was created on September 5, 1897, with Leon Olszewski as conductor.[16]

After much practice, the newly formed choir of 64 gave its first public performance on February 18, 1898. The success of the venture brought in more members, and soon the Kolo Spiewackie became one of the first Buffalo singing groups to join the Polish Singers Alliance. The society was also dedicated to supporting local cultural and educational ventures such as the Polish Reading Room. As the popularity of the male singers grew, women soon petitioned to join and in time the Kalina Singing Society was formed.

It would be under this backdrop that Father Thomas Flaczek at St. Adalbert would hire Boleslaus Michalski as the church organist in 1898. Little did Michalski know that taking the position at the parish named after Poland's patron saint of music, he would start a musical legacy that would span centuries and touch America's Polonia in ways he could never imagine.

---

15 "St. Adalbert's Basilica Complex." *Polonia Trail*, Polish-American Congress WNY, 29 June 2016

16 "Polish Singing Circle." *Polonia Trail*, Polish-American Congress WNY, 29 June 2016

Chapter 2

Birth of the Chopin Singing Society

Winter was still nipping at the faces of the eight men who gathered at St. Adalbert Church in late March of 1899. The threat of rain, snow, and subfreezing weather was tempered by their passion for Polish song and the respect of the parish organist who called for them to attend. One by one the parish choir members bundled in long winter coats, gloves, and hats arrived in the shadow of the brick monolith that dominated Stanislaus Street. Francis Poltowicz, the harness maker, made the trip down Sweet Avenue to the church hall in less than twenty minutes. Brothers Ignatius and Stanislaw Nadolny would be accompanied by Joseph Brocki of Rother Avenue and his son Ignatius. Tailor Paul Rupocinski had the furthest to travel, walking nearly a mile in the cold East Side. Finally, Michael Stefanski and Michal Bilicki arrived at the future basilica, and waiting for them all was the maestro of the parish, Boleslaus Michalski.[1]

The men were all familiar with one other, singing together in the choir or chatting after Mass. As the popularity of other singing groups rose in Little Poland, all gathered wanted a secular outlet that was based at St. Adalbert. It took little discussion for them to agree that their choir would be named in honor of Poland's greatest composer, Frederic Chopin. Mr. Michalski who presided over the meeting, assured the group that he could secure practice space in the parish hall and would also serve as choir master. The group agreed to the terms and selected him as their society's first leader.

Headquartered at St. Adalbert's Hall the new choir practiced and performed sporadically. The members of the Society weren't looking for their names in the headlines as grandiose vocalists but were amateur performers who enjoyed the opportunity to sing together. By the time of their first annual meeting on March 26, 1900, the formerly informal group decided to become a real organization. The members agreed that monthly dues were needed and set the rate at 10 cents a month. The $1.10 that was gathered allowed the group to purchase a

---

[1] *Towarzystwo Spiewu Fryderyka Chopina 1899-1949*. Buffalo, NY: Tow. Spiewu Fryderyka Chopina, 1949. Print.

ledger and account book to keep track of the dues and to take the minutes of their future meetings. The notes from that day record that Michal Bilicki was elected president, Francis Poltowicz as vice president, Ignatius Nadolny as secretary, and new member Francis Urbanski as cashier.[2] Boleslaus Michalski continued to lead them musically as their conductor. They earmarked the money raised from their March 17 performance as a donation to the parish, agreed to hold a May Ball on March 29, and finally, moved to purchase a painting of their patron Chopin to decorate their club room. Six months after their annual meeting, the members of Chopin voted after a performance to join Polish Singers Alliance of America. In time they would be known as Choir #34.

Over the next few years, the number of Chopin Singers swelled as new members joined from everywhere and from every social standing. From Leon Olszewski, the director general of the Polish Singers Alliance of America, and grocer Francis Szelmeczko to John Zaklekowski a frame worker and Jan Gaca, the Lovejoy carpenter, the ranks of the society grew.[3] Whole families would lend their voices to the choirs like when brothers Stanislaw and Theophilus Kujawa joined. More names of this era who would make their mark on the Society included John Zelechowski, Anthony Budniak, Kazimierz Nowak, Boleslaus Radka, and Martin Marczynski. Stanislaw E. Mrugowski, and Constantine Nowakowski.[4] Marczynski, Nowak, and Zelechowski would add greatly to the organization when they worked with Michael Stefanski and Francis Poltowicz in drafting a constitution for the Society. Other important members of this era included Leon J. Nowak,[5] Alexander Cwiklinski and Ignacy Romaszkiewicz.[6] Leon, son of Albert Nowak who made his fortune in cereal, grain, hay, and feed, was part of Polish Buffalo's still burgeoning intelligentsia. A Columbia and University of Buffalo trained lawyer, Nowak had already worked in Washington for a while before returning to Buffalo and joining Chopin.[7] With his family's wealth and brother's business prowess Leon would open the Broadway National Bank, the Amherst

2 Chopin Singing Society. "Meeting Minutes." Buffalo, NY, 1900.
3 "Nowi Czlonkowie." *Harmonia* [Buffalo, NY] 21 Dec. 1901: 6. Print.
4 "Nowi Czlonkowie." *Harmonia* [Buffalo, NY] 15 May 1902: 7-8. Print.
5 ibid
6 "Nowi Czlonkowie." *Harmonia* [Buffalo, NY] 15 Mar. 1902: 8. Print.
7 "Leon J. Nowak." Album pamiatkowe i Przewodnik Handlowy: Osady Polskiej w miescie Buffalo, z dolaczeniem Okolicznych miejscowosci Ze Stanu New York, Wydane Staraniem i Nakladem Polskiej Spoki Wydawniczej, 1906, pp. 121–122.

National Bank, the Clinton Street State Bank, the American Bank of Lackawanna, and the Falls National Bank of Niagara Falls.[8] Later in life Leon moved to Chicago to practice law. For his part, Cwiklinski was another major industrialist in Buffalo's East Side. Born in Poland and raised in Buffalo, Alex went from grade school to trade school before graduating from an industrial college. Starting off as a builder and contractor,[9] Cwiklinski's fortune and influence grew when he opened his Sycamore Lumber & Mill Co. on Lathrop Street.[10] Romaszkiewicz was a bit of an outlier in the group, not because he was famous for being a Broadway-based photographer, but because he was Lithuanian. Ignacy was born in Kaunas and moved to Buffalo in 1898, where he set up his studio at 1017 Broadway. Romaszkiewicz's real rise to prominence came after he opened his Fillmore Studios and Buffalo's Polish elite would sit for a portrait by his camera.[11] These three men epitomized the increasing influence Chopin was starting to develop with its expanding membership. To communicate efficiently to this fast-growing group, the locally owned *Echo* newspaper was chosen to carry their official announcements.

With Buffalo serving as the host city of the 1901 Pan-American Exposition, the "United" branch of the Polish Singers Alliance of America decided to hold their twelfth national conference in the City of Light. Over one thousand singers from Chicago, Bay City, Detroit, Nanticoke, Baltimore, Philadelphia, and Polonias the country over descended on the Niagara Frontier and assembled at Fillmore Hall. In the middle of all the action were the Chopin Singers. Members of Chopin could be found mingling at the official opening of the convention on August 18, chatting up singers from across the country, and listening to the formal welcoming addresses given by Dr. Francis E. Fronczak, Mayor Conrad Diehl, former congressman Rowland B. Mahany, and their own member Leo Olszewski. The next day the choir paraded down Fillmore with the rest of the attendees to Transfiguration Church for a special High Mass in honor of the conference, returning to the hall for business sessions before warming up for their part of that

---

[8] Witul, Gregory L. "Buffalonian Memorialized in Krakow." *Am-Pol Eagle*, 6 Sept. 2012, p. 9
[9] "Alexander Cwiklinski." Album pamiatkowe i Przewodnik Handlowy: Osady Polskiej w mieście Buffalo, z dołączeniem Okolicznych miejscowosci Ze Stanu New York, Wydane Staraniem i Nakladem Polskiej Spolki Wydawniczej, 1906, pp. 147–148.
[10] "Among Buffalo's Most Prominent Polish Citizens, Who Will Be Among Patrons of The Polish Night Travelogue." *Buffalo Evening News*, 1 Oct. 1913, p. 16.
[11] Witul, Gregory L. "Behind the Camera of Ignacy Romaszkiewicz." *Am-Pol Eagle*, 24 Jan. 2013, p. 11.

evening's concert.

Starting at 8:30 in the evening, singers and choirs from across Polonia graced the stage of the Fillmore Hall to entertain not just each other, but the public at large. For the opening, the anthems of the Polish Singers Alliance and Polish National Alliance were played. Then under the direction of Olszewski all the men of the Alliance gave a rendition of Schubert's "Gott der Weltschopfer." After this and a vocal selection from the women of the alliance, individuals, and groups performed. The Paderewski Choir of Chicago sang Jan Czubski's "Modlitwa Jagielly przed bitwa pod Grunwaldem," Mme. Antoinette Zaremba of Bay City Michigan gave a solo rendition of "Queen of the Night" and closing out the groups for the evening was Choir #34, the Chopin Singing Society. Still under the baton of their friend and member Leo Olszewski, Chopin's choice of song is only listed as "Fiolki Polskie." Following their performance, the men were accompanied again by the rest of the alliance as they closed out the show with Polish composer, conductor, pianist, and organist Ludwik Grossman's "Krakowiaczek."

During the business sessions of the convention the men of Buffalo and Chopin spoke with passion and conviction about the important role Polish music played in America and rallied enough votes to assume leadership positions within the alliance. Jan M. Chrzanowski, a founding member and president of the Polish Singing Circle, was elected president of the Alliance, while Paul Nowicki of Chopin was selected for vice-general secretary. Friend and member of both groups Leo Olszewski was reelected as director general of the Alliance and was given the responsibility of editor of their newspaper *Harmonia*. In the closing days of the congress, the members of Chopin and the other Western New York choirs played host to their visiting brethren by arranging an excursion to Niagara Falls with a luncheon at Alt Nurnberg and the Streets of Mexico on the Pan-Am's Midway.

The year 1902 would bring monumental changes to the still young organization. The first would be the election of John Zelechowski as president. Unlike the previous two administrations, Zelechowski was not present at the founding of the Singing Society in 1899. But the far greater change would be the resignation of Boleslaus Michalski as choir master. Interested in starting a family and expanding his business interest into real estate and insurance, Michalski stepped aside as conductor of Chopin, leaving a musical void in his wake. Luckily for the Society, the Chopinites already had Polonia's leading maestro on its roster. After a meeting of the board, Leon T. Olszewski was selected as the Singing Society's next conductor. The selection of Olszewski made Leon the head of three of Buffalo's leading singing societies, the Polish Singing Circle, Kalina, and now Chopin. This overlapping leadership role led to more coordination and harmonization between all three groups. One of the earliest examples of this cooperation was the Chopin Singing Society being given a leading role in the elaborate fifth anniversary celebration of the founding of the Polish Singing Circle held in the autumn of 1902.[12] But even with this new unity, the choir still stood on their own feet receiving high praise for their renditions of "Chlopek Ci Ja Chlopek" and "Do Piesni" by Dembinski at their own October concert.

The tumultuous changes of 1902 carried over into 1903. With Michalski's departure the Society was no longer tied to St. Adalbert Parish or its hall where their headquarters was. This dilemma turned out to be a blessing in disguise as they were able to strike a deal with John Patrzykowski and rent the rooms above his distillery and wholesale liquor center at 1119-1123 Broadway. With this move, Chopins moved off the byway of Stanislaus Street and into the heart of the East Side on Broadway. With their new headquarters the members purchased a cabinet to keep their records, songsheets, and music library in. The second major move by the Society was the adoption of "Gora Piesn" as their slogan. For the annual meeting of the Polish Singers Alliance, that year in Chicago, Francis Szelmeczka, John Zelechowski, Martin Marczynski, and Stanislaw Kujawa were among the men sent to represent Choir #34. Closer to home, the Chopinites did a bit of traveling, holding a picnic in Cascade Park near Springville, taking a boat tour of Dunkirk, and making several appearances with the Polish Singing Circle and Kalina. The Society also faced the first test of its constitution with the resignation of President Stanislaw Mrugowski and the installation of Vice President Constantine Nowakowski. Although there were some hard feelings surrounding the affair at the time, all was forgiven by the next election.[13]

With a growing membership and swelling treasury, the Society purchased its first piano for the clubrooms in 1905. That same year Stanislaw Nadolny was elected president while interim president

---

[12] "Singing Circle's 5th Anniversary." *Buffalo Courier*, 20 Oct. 1902, p. 6.

[13] *Towarzystwo Spiewu Fryderyka Chopina 1899-1949*. Buffalo, NY: Tow. Spiewu Fryderyka Chopina, 1949. Print.

Nowakowski became the club's cashier. The singers also awarded a special honorary diploma to Mrs. Rose Kwasigroch, daughter of Peter Kiolbassa of Chicago, setting a precedent that would be followed for years to come.[14] Many of the members of Chopin witnessed the monumental opening of the Dom Polski that summer, even though the choir was not selected to perform at the ceremony. The Society would perform at the Polish Home at Playter and Broadway later that year in a concert with the Polish Singing Circle, Kalina, and the Lirnik Singing Society of Buffalo's Black Rock neighborhood.[15] That year members Leon Olszewski and Kazimierz Nowak attended the Congress of the Polish Singers Alliance in Milwaukee which united the two warring factions of the organization, leading once again to a unified Polish Singers Alliance.[16]

As would often happen in the Society's early years, the presidency fell within a small handful of members for a single term. But 1906 marked a change as John A. Zelechowski was elected for a second consecutive term of the 50-voice organization.[17] His second year would hold several major highlights for the singers. The first was their assistance with the golden jubilee of Father Valentine Swinarski, chaplain to the Felician Sisters and chaplain-director of the Immaculate Heart of Mary Orphan's Home. The choir, as well as the Polish Falcons, were close to Swinarski's heart, and the feelings were mutual. The group demonstrated their love for the priest by making a sizable donation to the Orphan's Home that year, and his appreciation for them would be choosing them to hold the honor of being the only group to sing at his 1914 funeral, which saw over 5,000 mourners in attendance.[18] It is little surprise that the second grand celebration the Society took part in during 1906 was the 15th Anniversary of the founding of the Polish Tailors Society Group 194 of the Polish National Alliance. Many of the founding members and leaders of Chopin were on the rolls of both organizations. The last major event of the year for the members of Chopin involved a trip to Niagara Falls where they sang at the cornerstone laying for Holy Trinity Roman Catholic

---

14 Busyn, Helen. "Peter Kiolbassa: Maker of Polish America." Polish American Studies, vol. 8, Dec. 1951, pp. 65–84.

15 "A Concert Will Be Given This Evening by The United Polish..." Illustrated *Buffalo Express*, 22 Oct. 1905, p. 26. Chapter 2

16 *Towarzystwo Spiewu Fryderyka Chopina 1899-1949*. Buffalo, NY: Tow. Spiewu Fryderyka Chopina, 1949. Print.

17 "Tuning Up for Polish Singing Society Contest." *Buffalo Courier*, 2 Sept. 1906, p. 29.

18 "Poles Do Honor at Bier of Loved Asylum Chaplain." *Buffalo Courier*, 2 Jan. 1914, p. 6.

Church. The Chopinites were part of a large delegation of Buffalo Poles that were present for the red-letter day in the history of the Mother Church of Niagara Falls's Polonia.[19]

The Society continued to see widespread growth under its seventh elected president, Stanislaus F. Kujawa. Kujawa's tenure would be highlighted by the group's purchase of a new piano, having a large presence at the General Assembly of the Polish Singers Alliance held in Cleveland, Ohio and singing at a mass rally in Buffalo opposing the Germanization of Prussian occupied Poland.[20] At the end of the first decade of the twentieth century, the members of Chopin were preparing for the biggest celebration in their history so far, their 10th anniversary concert.

Under the leadership of President Jan Nowak, the members of Chopin remodeled and redecorated their clubrooms at 1119 Broadway and began practicing for the concert. Among the items they added to their collection was a bust of their patron sculpted by Casimir Chodzinski.

The original date was set for the founding month of March. However, it had to be pushed back to August 12, but this didn't diminish the importance of the community celebration. One organization that got particularly involved with the preparation of the celebration was the Kolko Polek.[21] The ladies, well-known as ardent fundraisers, worked diligently to ensure the party went off without a hitch.

The members of Chopin kicked off their second decade by electing Kazimierz Nowak as president and taking part in the 15th anniversary celebration of the Adam Mickiewicz Library & Dramatic Circle. In greater Polonia, they participated in a grand celebration of the January Uprising of 1863. Under the auspices of the local Polish National Alliance branches, and held at the Dom Polski, the singing society gave a performance under the baton of Olszewski for a crowd of hundreds. The performance was part of a program that also included a history of the uprising, speeches by Father Sobieniowski an assistant at St. Stanislaus, lawyer Alexander Ruszkiewicz, and a reading by school children. The money raised from the event went toward the

---

[19] *Towarzystwo Spiewu Fryderyka Chopina 1899-1949*. Buffalo, NY: Tow. Spiewu Fryderyka Chopina, 1949. Print.

[20] "Buffalo Polish Citizens Ask U.S. To Halt Prussia." *Buffalo Courier*, 16 Mar. 1908, p. 7

[21] "Increasing Activities of the Kolko Polek Charity Circle." *Buffalo Express*, 25 Mar. 1909, p. 8

Copernicus College project.[22]

The educational venture would be the beneficiary of another fundraiser a month later. Now under the guidance of the Copernicus College Association, a concert was held again at Dom Polski Hall by a coalition of local Polish singers and singing societies. For their part the members of Chopin performed a rendition of "Zaby," while the Moniuszko Singing Society sang "Krakowiak," Lutnia performed "Nowa Wiosna," and Kalina Singing Society brought down the house with "Drumka Wieczorna." Individual vocalists included Pani Blazewicz and ten-year-old Walerya Krzyzykowska who sang Chopin's "Zyczenie." In total, the 20-song program, all conducted by Olszewski, raised one thousand dollars.[23] Over the next year more money would be raised for the college, and preparations were made to use space in the Dom Polski for classrooms,[24] though there was still not enough money to get the school off the ground.[25] In the end, the association would be reorganized and the funds raised would go towards scholarships for local Polish American students to attend a college or a conservatory.[26]

As part of the 120th Anniversary of the May 3 Constitution, the members of Chopin would take the stage of Dom Polski again, this time with the Polish Singing Circle. The two choirs traded songs following speakers, Anthony Schreiber, W. H. Zawadzki, John Maternowicz, and Anthony Malik.[27] The May 3 festivities extended out for almost a week with the Society singing again on May 14, this time in North Buffalo. As part of the closing ceremonies of the anniversary the men of Chopin, as well as members of Polish societies from across the city, descended on the Black Rock neighborhood to partake in a grand parade down Amherst Street. After the parade ended, the largest gathering of the month filled the school at Assumption parish to hear speeches, watch a program put on by the school children, and hear the songs of the Chopin Singing Society.[28] The Society wrapped up the

---

22 "Anniversary Of Uprising Celebrated." *Buffalo Courier*, 23 Jan. 1911, p. 7.

23 "Copernicus College Fund Gets $1,000 out of Concert." *Buffalo Courier*, 27 Feb. 1911, p. 7.

24 "Copernicus College Will Be Erected; $6,000 Given as Starter for Institution." *Buffalo Courier*, 18 Aug. 1911, p. 7.

25 "Copernicus Association to Aid Needy Students." *Buffalo Courier*, 1 Feb. 1912, p. 8.

26 "Copernicus College Aid Society Meets." *Buffalo Evening News*, 23 May 1913, p. 17.

27 "First Of Polish Festivities Is to Be Held Tonight." *Buffalo Courier*, 3 May 1911, p. 7.

28 "Two Thousand Polish Residents in Celebration." *Buffalo Courier*, 8 May 1911.

year by traveling to Erie, PA to perform at Holy Trinity Parish.[29]

The singers celebrated the May 3 Constitution again at the Dom Polski the next year, but this time with Kalina.[30] That same year, the Chopinites took home first prize at a singing competition in Erie, PA, and played the debut concert of the Philharmonia Musical Association. Made up of musicians mostly from Transfiguration Church, the mission of Philharmonia was to unite the many bands and mini orchestras the parish members played in and form a larger organization that could serve as an orchestra for Polonia. At the May 12 concert, the voices of Chopin joined the 35-instrument association under the baton of Leon Olszewski, leader of both societies, and performed a selection of songs.[31] In the clubhouse, Helena Nowak and Helena Urbanska took up the maintenance responsibility while the treasury reached $310.

For the 1913 anniversary of the January Uprising, the Society was accompanied by the Lutnias, Moniuszkos, Kalina, and the Polish Singing Circle on stage, but the real star of the show that year was Mayor Fuhrmann. Preceded by a parade of 10,000 marchers to the Broadway Auditorium,[32] and a letter read from New York State Governor William Sulzer,[33] Stanislaus Adamkiewicz, president of the Polish Roman Catholic Union of America, and Marian Steczynski, rector of the Polish National Alliance College in Cambridge Springs, PA were the main speakers of the day. Commissioner of Public Health for the City of Buffalo Dr. Fronczak, Leon J. Nowak, Zdzislaw F. Krysztafkiewicz, and Thaddeus Sowinski gave their speeches before making way for the music selections. In a rare exception, Chopin, the other singing societies, and the many church choirs that joined them were not overseen by conductor Leon Olszewski but by Chopin founder Boleslaus Michalski.[34] Michalski as well as Frank Majerowski the organist at St. Casimir in Kaisertown,[35] and St. Stanislaus parish music director Tadeusz G. Balucinski traded places on the podium

---

[29] *Towarzystwo Spiewu Fryderyka Chopina 1899-1949*. Buffalo, NY: Tow. Spiewu Fryderyka Chopina, 1949. Print.

[30] "Poles Celebrate 121st Anniversary of Constitution." *Buffalo Courier*, 6 May 1912, p. 7.

[31] "Philharmonia Musical Association's Concert." *Buffalo Courier*, 14 Apr. 1912, p. 45.

[32] "Great Day for The Poles." *Buffalo Express*, 16 Feb. 1913.

[33] "Buffalo Poles Pay Splendid Tribute to Heroes of '63 Revolt." *Buffalo Evening News*, 10 Feb. 1913, pp. 1–11.

[34] "Polish Citizens to Commemorate Uprising Of '63." *Buffalo Courier*, 15 Jan. 1913, p. 55.

[35] Pamietnik Zlotego Jubileuszu Kosciola Sw. Kazimierza, Buffalo, N.Y. Druk Dziennika Dla Wszystkich, 1940.

over the course of the show.[36] It could have been from this gathering that the Circle, Kalina, Chopin, and the Adam Mickiewicz Library decided to get together and discuss jointly funding a single building for the disparate organizations.[37] This large project never came to fruition and the Mickiewicz Library would add an addition to its building in 1914.[38]

Other celebrations the Chopinites would take part in were the 10th Anniversary of the Women's Auxiliary of Polish Falcons Nest 6,[39] and a commemoration of the November Uprising at the Dom Polski.[40]

By this time, the membership of Society had grown large enough that politicians began speaking before them to court their vote. One of the earliest candidates to address the group was John Lord O'Brian, the 1913 Citizens' Committee nominee for mayor.[41] While he didn't win the mayorship, even with an endorsement from Chopin,[42] he did become the first special assistant attorney general for the Department of Justice's War Emergency Division. He would go on to argue before the Supreme Court to uphold the constitutionality of the Tennessee Valley Authority and won. When O'Brian died, Chief Justice Warren E. Burger said, "[t]he death of John Lord O'Brian, the dean of the Supreme Court Bar, at 98, marks the end of an era in a sense...he epitomized the highest standards of the legal profession."[43]

If the Society were to celebrate a second birthday, it would be February 6. On that day in 1914, club secretary Joseph Dulski, father of future member of Chopin Congressman Thaddeus J. Dulski, legally incorporated the organization as the Frederick Chopin Singing Society of Buffalo. The listed directors were Leon Olszewski, Vincent Kwiecikowski, John Bojanek, Frank Urbanski, Joseph Dulski, Joseph Siudzinski, Felix Kulwicki and Bernard Laute.[44] Five months later on

---

36 "Tadeusz G. Balucinski." Album pamiatkowe i Przewodnik Handlowy: Osady Polskiej w miescie Buffalo, z dolaczeniem Okolicznych miejscowosci Ze Stanu New York, Wydane Staraniem i Nakladem Polskiej Spoki Wydawniczej, 1906, pp. 307.

37 "Polish Singing Bodies Plan on Amalgamation." *Buffalo Courier*, 15 Feb. 1913, p. 7.

38 "Adam Mickiewicz Library and Dramatic Circle." Polonia Trail, Polish-American Congress WNY , 29 June 2016,

39 "Polish Woman Observe Anniversary of Nest 6." *Buffalo Evening News*, 26 May 1913, p. 8.

40 "Poles Unite in Recalling Great Battles of Old." *Buffalo Courier*, 30 Nov. 1913, p. 84.

41 "Citizens' Committee Issues Schedule of Meetings." *Buffalo Courier*, 12 Oct. 1913, p. 52.

42 "Polish Society Endorses Mr. O'Brian's Candidacy." *Buffalo Express*, 15 Oct. 1913.

43 "John Lord O'Brian Dies at 98; Dean of the Supreme Court Bar." *New York Times*, 11 Apr. 1973, p. 51.

44 "Society Incorporates." *Buffalo Courier*, 7 Feb. 1914, p. 6.

July 13, New York State issued the certificate of incorporation.

Becoming incorporated added a little spring to the step of the Society, it made the organization a little more real in both the eyes of the members and the community. One of the first events covered by the English language media for the newly incorporated group was a recital by Leon Wyszatycki at the Polish Falcons Hall on Playter Street under the auspices of the singing society. Wyszatynski, a member of Chopin and Buffalo native was visiting from Chicago where he was a student at a conservatory. The *Buffalo News* reviewed the tenor saying his performance was, "executed with delightful color and tone."[45] The singers followed up the recital with their annual Easter banquet held in their clubrooms at 1125 Broadway. Over seventy members and their families were present for the post-Lenten celebration, hearing speeches from Postmaster William F. Kasting, President Nowak, Secretary Kwiecikowski, and Choir Master Olszewski.[46] In November, the Society closed out their incorporation year with a large joint concert at the Dom Polski with the Kalina and Philharmonia singing societies all under the direction of Olszewski.[47] The following month they commemorated the 1831 Uprising.[48] The Chopin members also took part in the twenty-fifth anniversary of the Polish Reading Room and the fifteenth anniversary of Kolko Polek Charity Organization that year.

In the election of 1915 Casimir Nowak was once again selected as president, Vincent Kwiecikowski as recording secretary, John Bojanek as financial secretary, Stanislaus Urbanski as treasurer, and Stephen Mikolajczak was placed in charge of the Society library. The rest of the board was filled out with Edward Czuprynski, Felix Kulwicki, Bernard Lauta, and heading them all was Leon Olszewski as chairman. The formal installation of the board was held on January 10, with a grand celebration and entertainment by the Philharmonia Orchestra.[49] That June, members of Chopin were part of a concert supporting the American Committee for Polish Relief held at the Elmwood Music Hall to assist those in Poland suffering from the Great War.[50]

On August 29, 1915 the group took part in one of the most

---

45 "Tenor Gives Recital." *Buffalo Evening News*, 19 Feb. 1914, p. 3.

46 "Polish Singing Society Gives Annual Banquet." *Buffalo Courier*, 20 Apr. 1914, p. 6.

47 "Concert at Dom Polski." *Buffalo Evening News*, 16 Nov. 1914, p. 14.

48 "Uprising of 1831 Recalled by Poles." *Buffalo Courier*, 7 Dec. 1914.

49 "Chopin Singing Society Holds Its Installation." *Buffalo Courier*, 11 Jan. 1915, p. 7.

50 "Polish Societies Pick Voices for Relief Concert." *Buffalo Courier*, 24 May 1915, p. 7.

momentous days of Buffalo's Polonia, the dedication and opening of the Polish Union of America building on Fillmore Avenue.[51] Designed by Wladyslaw H. Zawadzki, 10,000 spectators packed the streets of the East Side to watch a parade of 8,000, led by Chief Marshal Joseph Knaszak,[52] march from Rother Avenue at Broadway to Corpus Christi Church, St. Stanislaus, and Transfiguration until ending at the new building.[53] Once there, PUA President Anthony Wisniewski, Chairman Frank Burzynski, and Secretary John Wisniewski spoke, and Father Boleslaus Kwiatkowski blessed the building. For their part the members of Chopin took the stage and under Director Olszewski's hand presented a special selection of songs for the occasion. When they were done, they gifted a portrait of Fredrick Chopin to be hung in the new home. The Society was formally affiliated with the union later in the year.[54]

In November the singers returned to the Union Hall, this time to celebrate the November Insurrection. The men sang patriotic songs and heard addresses from Father Stanislaus Bidacz, John Dobinski, [55] and Miss Mary Malachowski.[56] The year concluded with the election of officers for 1916. John Zelechowski was chosen for the presidency, and John Domachowski was a new face to the board with Felix Kulwicki, John Bojanek, and Vincent Kwiecikowski being reelected to their previous roles.[57]

The Sons of the Queen of Poland, Branch 4 of the Polish Union of America celebrated their silver anniversary in February of 1916. The branch organized by Father Jan Pitass of St. Stanislaus church boasted a membership of 1,775 men from across Buffalo's Polonia and a few from beyond it. The program for the evening included an address by Branch President Anthony Wisniewski, a history of the branch by Secretary Francis Zandrowicz, and musical selections by the

---

51 "Polish Union of America Building." Polonia Trail, Polish-American Congress WNY, 29 June 2016,

52 "Polish Union in New Home." *Buffalo Express*, 30 Aug. 1915.

53 "Poles Parade to Union's New Home for Dedication and Jubilee Celebration." *Buffalo Courier*, 30 Aug. 1915, p. 7

54 "Chopin Singing Society Is Affiliated with Polish Union." *Buffalo Evening News*, 25 Oct. 1915, p. 8.

55 "Polish Community Will Honor Heroes of Insurrection." *Buffalo Courier*, 21 Nov. 1915, p. 76.

56 "Four Celebrations Mark Anniversary of Poles' Revolt." *Buffalo Courier*, 29 Nov. 1915, p. 6.

57 "Polish Societies Elect Officers." *Buffalo Courier*, 12 Dec. 1915, p. 59.

Chopin, Lutnia, and Moniuszko Singing Societies.[58] The Polish Union hosted another event where the members of Chopin sang, a week-long bazaar to raise money for the Polish Relief Fund.[59] The Society shared the stage with the Orchestra of Polish Falcons Nest 313 on the closing Friday of the fair, which raised hundreds of dollars for the widows and war orphans of Poland.[60]

One of the largest celebrations for all the singers of Buffalo's Polonia that year was the fifteenth anniversary of the Kalina Singing Society.[61] Held in May at the Dom Polski, this program included addresses by Frank A. Olszanowski, Leon Wyszatycki, Director Leon Olszewski, a violin solo by Henry Jankowski, and songs by Kalina, the Polish Singing Circle, and Chopin Singing Society. The three societies would later join voices with the Harmonia, Lirnik, and Jutrzenka choirs at a grand May 3 event held at the Broadway Auditorium.[62]

It may have been this concert that prompted the Chopin Singing Society, the Polish Singing Circle, and other singers to meet at Chopin's clubrooms in late May to discuss uniting the Polish singing societies of Buffalo. To explore this option a committee consisting of Leon Olszewski, Vincent E. Kwiecikowski, John Domachowski, Stanislaus Kujawa, Joseph Siudzinski, Frank Szelmeczki, John Gaca, and John Zelechowski was formed.[63] That summer, the Polish Singing Circle purchased two lots on Fillmore before changing their mind and bought a Wladyslaw H. Zawadzki designed building at the corner of Rother and Broadway. With the new edifice it was thought that Chopin and a few others would join the circle at 1170 Broadway.[64] In time, Harmonia[65] and Kalina would be the only other singing societies to call that building home.[66]

Much of the board stayed the same as America entered the First World War with Kujawa, Urbanski, Czuprynski, Kalinowski,

---

[58] "Sons of Queen of Poland Celebrate Their Twenty-Fifth Anniversary Today." *Buffalo Courier*, 20 Feb. 1916, p. 70.
[59] "Polish Relief Bazar Draws Large Crowds to Union Home." *Buffalo Evening News*, 5 May 1916, p. 24.
[60] "Trunk Mystery in Benefit Bazaar." *Buffalo Courier*, 5 May 1916, p. 9.
[61] "Kalina Singing Society Celebrates Anniversary." *Buffalo Courier*, 8 May 1916, p. 6.
[62] "300 To Sing U.S. Anthem At Poles' Constitution Day." *Buffalo Courier*, 14 May 1916, p. 75.
[63] "Initiate Plan to Unite Polish Singing Societies." *Buffalo Courier*, 24 May 1916, p. 8.
[64] "Polish Singers Purchase Building for Club House." *Buffalo Courier*, 1 Aug. 1916, p. 5.
[65] "Harmonia Society Holds Reception to Alliance." *Buffalo Evening News*, 22 May 1916, p. 4.
[66] "Club House Is Bought for The Polish Singers." *Buffalo Evening News*, 1 Aug. 1916, p. 2.

Domachowski, Kulwicki, Bojanek, and Kwiecikowski maintaining leadership roles.[67] With the war, membership declined as men prepared to fight for a free Poland. That same year saw the passing of former president and stalwart supporter of Chopin, Kazimierz Nowak.[68]

The ongoing war in Europe, and the number of possible outcomes it could produce, was on the minds of many in Polonia. Due to this uncertainty, the Society, along with the Polish Singing Circle, the Corpus Christi Club, Moniuszkos, and other Polish organizations began running ads in Polish language newspapers pledging their loyalty to America and encouraging alien Poles, especially those from the German-occupied regions of Poland, to become American citizens. The societies' fear was that once the U.S. entered the war, the loyalty and status of these Polish immigrants would be questioned. The ads said in part,

> Those who are not as yet citizens of this country ought to apply for naturalization papers without delay as the war with Germany hangs on a hair and it is not known what will happen to non-citizens. For that reason Polish Citizens' Protective association urges all Poles who are not already possessors of such papers to enroll as members of the organization. The association obtained citizenship papers already for 600 men and as heretofore so in the future it will aid in obtaining them free of charge."[69]

The ads ran with the patriotic headers, "[w]e are on the eve of war, a war of incalculable results," "[f]ellow countrymen: The country of Washington became a second fatherland to all of us. Here we found liberty, opportunity for unhampered national and cultural development and protection of the law," "[t]oday the chief national executive rose in defense of the honor of the United States and at a minute's notice may call all for the protection of the nation's borders and against the enemy," "[w]e exhort you to remember that your duty is to respond to the call of the Star Spangled Banner and to defend it," and "[l]ong Live America."[70] The conclusion of the war was also speculated on, especially by Ignace M. Morawski who told Polonia to prepare for a

[67] "Societies Elect Officers for Year." *Buffalo Courier*, 17 Dec. 1916, p. 75.
[68] "Death Claims Founder of Chopin Singing Body." *Buffalo Courier*, 20 Jan. 1917, p. 5.
[69] "Polish Residents at Meeting Tell of Their Loyalty." *Buffalo Courier*, 5 Feb. 1917, p. 5.
[70] ibid

great influx of Poles at the close of the conflict. While Morawski was preaching this to the Library Association, Vincent Kwiecikowski presented "History of Song and Music" covering Chopin, Moniuszko, and other Polish composers to the members of Chopin.[71]

After the U.S. entered the war, many men from Chopin enlisted and the numbers began to dip even more. Some of the first to sign up for military service were Victor B. Wylegała, John Mikolajczak, Michael Domalski, M. Szelmeczka, Stanislaw Dylowski, and T. Poplawski. To keep up morale, raise some funds, and entertain the community during the long winter, Chopin began holding big Sunday card parties in their clubrooms which would soon be shared with Harmonia.[72] Some of the big card winners that year were J. Bojankowski, F. Szelmeczka, and A. Widzinski[73].

As the war raged, membership of Chopin dropped by 67%, but the remaining singers worked diligently to support the war effort. As part of the Fourth Liberty loan drive, the members of Chopin performed on the second day of a two-day concert that opened with John Philip Sousa's 303 piece band. The concert, which also included the Singing Circle, Harmonia, and Kalina, was much needed as the loan drive had fallen behind due to the social restrictions brought on by the Great Influenza Pandemic.[74] Beyond the concert, the choir personally raised $1,700 according to Chopin Liberty Loan Chairman Edward Czuprinski.[75] This amount was on top of the efforts of the 27 members who sold over $4,600 worth of war stamps earlier in the summer.[76]

This fundraising effort was doubly impressive considering that the members of Chopin were also preparing to be one of the host choirs for the 20th National Convention of the Polish Singers Alliance. Held at the Statler Hotel from August 25 to 30, members of Chopin, the Polish Singing Circle, the Moniuszko Singers, Harmonia, and Kalina planned to host over three hundred delegates from across the country. Overseeing the preparations were Walter K. Missall, Chairman of the Pre-Convention Committee, Chopin board member Vincent E. Kwiecikowski serving as secretary, John M. Chrzanowski head of information, and Chopin founder Boleslaus Michalski as concert

---

71 "Sees Influx of Poles When Great War Ends." *Buffalo Courier*, 2 Apr. 1917, p. 76.

72 "Polish Convention Ends." *Buffalo Express*, 29 Aug. 1918.

73 "Society Holds Party." *Buffalo Courier*, 12 Dec. 1917, p. 5.

74 "Sousa's Band Sailor Lads Boost Loan." *Buffalo Evening News*, 14 Oct. 1918, pp. 1–2.

75 "Seek Lodges' Help in Big War Measure." *Buffalo Evening News,* 5 Oct. 1918, p. 13.

76 "Will Play Ball to Boost Sale of War Stamps." *Buffalo Evening News*, 18 July 1918, pp. 1–2.

chair.[77]

For their part, the members of Chopin gave tours of the region, including a visit to Camp Kosciuszko, the Polish Army training facility in Niagara-On-The-Lake,[78] and most importantly hosted the closing reception of the convention at their clubrooms at 1125 Broadway.[79] The closing event saw the last actions of the delegates for the convention. At that point the convention had already adopted plans to increase membership, establish more local branches and bring into the alliance every Polish singing society not already associated with them. The motions approved in the clubrooms of Chopin included electing a wholly Buffalo board with Frank A Olzanowski as president, John Chrzanowski as first vice president, Ludwiga Kaminska second vice president, Paul Myszka secretary, and Mrs. John Rutkowska as treasurer, moving the headquarters of the alliance to Buffalo for a term of three years, and selecting Schenectady as the host city of the 1919 convention. [80] Finally the group sent a telegram of support to President Woodrow Wilson on his war attitude and praising him for his peace proposal, the Fourteen Points. The members were particularly grateful for his Thirteenth Point which called for "An independent Polish state should be erected which should include the territories inhabited by indisputably Polish populations, which should be assured a free and secure access to the sea, and whose political and economic independence and territorial integrity should be guaranteed by international covenant."[81] The members of Chopin, and the rest of Polonia, would see that great feat accomplished November 11, 1918 with the end of the Great War and the establishment of a free Polish nation.

As the decade ended, the membership of Chopin swelled with returning veterans and new faces joining the ranks. Much like the rest of Polonia, the men of Chopin were ready to party in post-war Buffalo. The returning military members were given boxes of cigars and singers who had 15 years with the choir were given diplomas. That spring the young men of the organization hosted a huge post-Lenten ball attended by 400 at the Dom Polski on April 28, a week and a day after

---

[77] "Polish Singing Alliance Will Convene Here." *Buffalo Evening News*, 3 Aug. 1918, p. 14.
[78] "200 Polish Singers Here for Convention." *Buffalo Evening News*, 28 Apr. 1918, p. 6.
[79] "Polish Singers Alliance Holding Annual Meeting." *Buffalo Evening News*, 27 Aug. 1918, p. 5.
[80] "Buffalonians Are Elected Polish Alliance Officers." *Buffalo Evening News*, 29 Aug. 1918, p. 12.
[81] President Wilson's Message to Congress, January 8, 1918; Records of the United States Senate; Record Group 46; Records of the United States Senate; National Archives.

Easter.[82] But as these youths, full of manly pride and friendship drank in life, a pillar of Chopin was crumbling. Sitting in his bed on East Parade Ave., Leon T. Olszewski, the maestro of Chopin for over a decade, worked feverishly to set a course for Polonia he knew he would not live to see. Cancer was eating away at his body, but his soul was set on establishing the Broadway National Bank. A project he hoped would help Poles become "more prosperous and better citizens." On July 17, 1919, Leon Olszewski died with a sense of peace and a bit of joy knowing that his work was done, his era was over, and Poland was free.

The loss of a giant such as Olszewski was blunted by the leadership of newly elected president Joseph Siudzinski, the younger singers joining on, and all the activity that was happening in Polonia. In November the Society gave the opening night concert at the Dom Polski as part of the Second Great Sejm of the Poles in America, also known as the All Polish Convention. The mission of this convention was to marshal American support for the young Polish nation with Dr. Francis E. Fronczak giving the keynote address.[83]

To close out 1919, the members of Chopin celebrated their twentieth anniversary with a large blow-out party that saw 50 new members join. The master of ceremonies was stalwart member Dr. Fronczak, but the speakers that evening also included the young pastor of St. John Gualbert Church, Peter Adamski, and the newly elected congressman from the 42nd district, James Mead.[84] As America and Polonia were evolving at the dawn of the new decade, so too was Chopin by electing a new board. Vincent E. Kwiecikowski would see 1920 as president but it would be his secretary, Zdzislaw F. Krysztafkiewicz that ushered in a new epoch to the Chopin Singing Society.[85]

---

[82] "Dom Polski Scene of Enjoyable Ball by Young Men's Club." *Buffalo Courier*, 29 Apr. 1919, p. 4.

[83] "Second All-Polish Convention Named Fronczak Leader." *Buffalo Courier*, 11 Nov. 1919, p. 8.

[84] "Chopin Society Concert." *Buffalo Express*, 4 Jan. 1920, p. 8.

[85] "Polish Societies Choose Officers For 1920." *Buffalo Express*, 21 Dec. 1919, p. 8.

Chapter 3

Milestones and Monuments

In late 1919 the men of Chopin began working to fill the hole in the organization left by the passing of Leon Olszewski. While a serious search was underway, Franciszek Majerowski and Antoni Grzegorzewski tested for the position, but neither could finesse the baton the way Olszewski had.[1] The choir would choose Jan Nadolny that winter to lead them.[2] To assist Nadolny as he began his tenure with the singers, President Vincent E. Kwiecikowski stepped in and directed the choir in a rendition of the French National Hymn for a concert under the auspices of the Adam Plewacki Post in early 1920.[3]

In November of 1919, Nadolny began preparing for one of the grandest productions Chopin would put on, Maude Elizabeth Inch and William Rhys-Herbert's operetta *Sylvia.* The pastoral story, which tells the tale of the aristocratic Sylvia and farm girl Betty trading places for the day,[4] had already proven to be popular with audiences along the East Coast, and the Society believed it would do well in Buffalo. While the male parts would be sung by the men of Chopin, the ladies of Kalina would come on to fill in the female parts. The lead role of Sylvia's sweetheart, Sir Bertram de Lacey, was played by tenor Antoni Figiel, while Betty's betrothed Franek was portrayed by Teofil Kujawa. The female leads of Sylvia and Betty were sung by Stanislawa Mazurowska and Klara Schenk respectively. Misters J.A. Siudzinski and Anthony Adamczak filled out the other male roles while the ladies, Wlad. Chrzanowska, Helena Ruschke, Cecylia Szelazkiewicz, St. Michalowski, Br. Gruchala, and B. Greniewiecki rounded out the rest of the cast with Dabrowski's 16-piece orchestra providing all the music.[5] By spring, the performers were working out

---

[1] Towarzystwo Spiewu Fryderyka Chopina 1899-1949. Tow. Śpiewu Fryderyka Chopina, 1949.

[2] "Operetka Sylvia W Domu Pol." *Dziennik Dla Wszystkich*, 7 May 1920, p. 7.

[3] "Kin of Soldier Dead Receive French Tribute." *Buffalo Evening News*, 24 Feb. 1920, p. 16.

[4] J. Fischer & Bro., New York. "Sylvia." A Nautical Knot or The Belle of Barbstapoole, 1911, p. 112.

[5] Operetka Sylvia Chor Chopina z Udzialm Choru Kalina Poniedzialek 10 Maja 1920. Chopin Singing Society, 1920.

their final kinks and Chopin's president Vincent Kwiecikowski opened up rehearsals for some limited previews.[6] On May 1 tickets went on sale and were sold from over a half dozen locations, including florist Thaddeus Puchalski's Shop and Joseph Dombrowski's Music Store on Broadway, tobacconist Leon Sliwinski and Walter Mandziak's Menswear on Sycamore, and J. Frost's Pharmacy on Clinton Street.[7]

On May 6, the staff of the *Dziennik Dla Wszystkich* was invited to view and review the operetta for the following day's paper. The cultural critics praised the performance calling it, "full of the best singing, both solo and choral." Figiel earned accolades being described as "one of the best tenors in Buffalo" while Ms. Mazurowska's performance was "greatly appreciated." The writers further encouraged everyone to purchase tickets before they were all sold out.[8] The early review sparked the masses and the show was soon oversold, forcing the box office to spend the afternoon and evening leading up to the Monday night performance issuing refunds.[9]

At 8:00 in the evening, draped with bunting and flags, the curtain of the Dom Polski stage rose, and the debut performance of *Sylvia* began. The two-act operetta was praised by the audience for being sung with understanding and feeling. The cast, crew, guests, and audience enjoyed a post-performance ball well into the early morning.[10] Word spread like wildfire across Polonia about the show and the encore performance on May 19 quickly sold out and was equally praised.[11] With defining direction, public accolades, and the production of the year under his belt, any doubt public or personal, of Jan Nadolny's ability to fill Olszewski's shoes were firmly put to rest. The men of Chopin had found a conductor that could lead them with the passion and vigor they needed.

While many of the members of Chopin were taking part in *Sylvia*, others were preparing for the Society's other major performance of the year, the *Festival of the Bells* in late May at the Broadway Auditorium.[12] Under the direction of Harry Barnhart, Chopin joined other societies in the Buffalo Community Chorus to create a 700-voice

---

6 "Z Tow, Spiewu Chopin." *Dziennik Dla Wszystkich*, 1 May 1920, p. 3.
7 "Bilety Na Operetke Sylvia." *Dziennik Dla Wszystkich*, 1 May 1920, p. 3.
8 "Operetka Sylvia W Domu Pol." *Dziennik Dla Wszystkich*, 7 May 1920, p. 7.
9 "Chopini Wystawiaja 'Sylvie.'" *Dziennik Dla Wszystkich*, 18 May 1920, p. 3.
10 "Sylvia" *Dziennik Dla Wszystkich*, 11 May 1920, p. 5.
11 "Chopini Wystawiaja 'Sylvie'." *Dziennik Dla Wszystkich*, 18 May 1920, p. 3.
12 "2000 To Appear in Festival of Bells." *Buffalo Evening News*, 19 Mar. 1920.

choir, performing a rendition of Bach's "Sleepers Wake."[13] Kwiecikowski closed out his only year as president by securing a new home for the Society at 1212 Broadway on the corner of Lathrop Street in 1920. The process took over a year, but after some negotiations and remodeling, the new clubrooms were opened with a grand party on November 1.

The year 1921 would begin a new era for the Society with the election of Zdzislaw F. Krysztafkiewicz as president. A member of Chopin for only three years, Krysztafkiewicz was able to ascend to the leadership position based on his years of experience with the Polish Falcons and the endorsement of Kwiecikowski. Zdzislaw would prove to be such an effective leader that he would helm the choir for nearly two decades.

In the first year of his presidency, the Society had two major accomplishments. The first was hosting an evening with Adam Didur a Polish-born bass singer that was popular with the East Side community and a member of the Metropolitan Opera Company. Having Didur as the headliner of a spring concert that included the 120 voices of Chopin and special guest Leon Wyszatycki, was an opportunity the group couldn't pass up. Since Adam was so well known, the Society decided that they could get some exposure to the English-speaking music fans of Buffalo as well.[14] To achieve this they ran several advertisements for the show in the *Buffalo Courier* that April.[15] The second feat of the year was raising $500 in coordination with Dr. Francis Fronczak in support of the Polish war orphans. Beyond the two highlights of the year, 1921 also proved that the members of Chopin had maintained their political importance as Buffalo Mayor George S. Buck appealed to the group as part of his re-election campaign against F.X. Schwab.[16] The Society concluded the year by participating in the Shelton Square Christmas Eve concert that included the Guido Chorus, Rubenstein Club, the Women's Choral Club, and the Liederkranz Saengerbund.[17] The status of the Society as one of the premier singing groups in greater Polonia was affirmed when they were chosen to provide the music for a number of silver jubilee celebrations. The first

---

13 "Festival of Bells Pretentious Effort." *Buffalo Evening News*, 22 May 1920.

14 "Polish Society Concert." *Buffalo Courier*, 9 Apr. 1921, p. 7

15 Chopin Singing Society. "Adam Didur." *Buffalo Courier*, 11 Apr. 1921.

16 "North Jefferson Ave. To Greet Mayor Buck." *Buffalo Evening News*, 7 Oct. 1921, p. 34.

17 "Municipal Christmas Tree at Lafayette Square; Ready Friday." *Buffalo Courier*, 21 Dec. 1921, p. 5.

was for the Polish Falcons Nest 6 where they sang at St. Luke's church,[18] while the second was for the Sons of Poland branch 380 of the Polish National Alliance, also at St. Luke.[19] Lastly, they sang at the 25th anniversary banquet of their compatriots, the Polish Singing Circle held at the Dom Polski in the fall of 1922.[20]

One big undertaking the Society tried at this time was the organization of a boys' choir. The members reached out to local parishes, families, members with children, and the community, but when only a handful of children showed interest, the project was abandoned.[21]

As the 25th anniversary of the Chopin Singing Society approached, the membership wanted to do something special to mark the occasion. After much discussion it was decided that they would give the citizens of Buffalo a statue of their patron. It would serve as a permanent marker of the Society and a physical embodiment of the importance the Poles were to the fabric of Western New York, just as the Mozart monument did for the Germans[22] and the bust of Sandor Petofi was doing for the Hungarians.[23] The Society formed a committee consisting of Felix Kulwicki, John Zelechowski, Vincent Widzinski, and Thaddeus Puchalski to head the effort and oversee its progress.[24] To raise funds they earmarked some of the receipts from the annual concert that featured Polish singer Leonia Ogrodzka for the project.[25] Ogrodzka, a graduate of the Lviv Conservatory where she studied under Walery Wysocki, was a large draw for the year's event. The popular opera singer had been garnering rave reviews as part of her U.S. tour where she gave stellar performances as Cio-Cio-San in *Madama Butterfly* and Halka in *Halka*.[26] With this national attention Buffalo's Polish press made Leonia's appearance a lead story for three months, leading to a box office smash for the Society. The singers held a subscription drive among the members and dipped into the treasury to

---

[18] "Falcons To Observe Their 25th Birthday." *Buffalo Evening News*, 15 Oct. 1921, p. 22.
[19] "Sons of Poland Celebrate Twenty-Fifth Anniversary." *Buffalo Courier*, 10 July 1922.
[20] "To Observe Its 25th Anniversary." *Buffalo Courier*, 3 Sept. 1922.
[21] Towarzystwo Spiewu Fryderyka Chopina 1899-1949. Tow. Spiewu Fryderyka Chopina, 1949.
[22] Witul, Gregory "A Century Later, the Notes of the Buffalo Liedertafel Still Linger." The German Citizen, 2015, p. 11
[23] "Hungarians Will Erect Statue of Poet-Hero July 4." *Buffalo Courier*, 19 June 1924, p. 87.
[24] Commemorating the Unveiling of the Chopin Memorial by the Chopin Singing Society: Humboldt Park, Buffalo, New York, June Seventh, Nineteen Twenty Five. The Society, 1925.
[25] "Dla Lubownikow Spiewu i Muzyki." *Dziennik Dla Wszystkich*, 13 Mar. 1923, p. 9.
[26] Encyklopedia teatru polskiego. "Leonia Ogrodzka." *Encyklopedia Teatru Polskiego*, 2016.

complete financing of the statue.

With the monument underway, the singers took part in the celebration of the Aleksander Fredro Library and Singing Society's 20th anniversary. This concert had a bit of bitter sweetness to it as the Chopin's conductor John F. Nadolny was transitioning from leading them to heading up the Fredros. By the autumn of the year Nadolny's replacement had been found in the form of Seth C. Clark. One of Clark's first performances with Chopin would be a monumental one, when he directed the group for General Joseph Haller's visit to Buffalo. Held at the Majestic Theater, they sang patriotic songs, including the "Star-Spangled Banner" for the General, Mayor Francis Schwab, Rev. Fudzinski, Dr. Fronczak, and the packed theater of 1,500 Buffalonians.[27]

Like America, Poland, and Polonia, the choir, too, mourned the passing of President Woodrow Wilson in early 1924. The man whose Thirteenth Point that called for an independent Polish state as part of the conclusion of the First World War made him a hero to Polish people everywhere. At the memorial service for the late president at the Polish Union, Chopins were the featured singers who performed a rendition of "In a Dark Tomb."[28]

By the time of the U.S. president's passing, planning was well under way for the silver jubilee of Chopin. Led by event chairman Victor B. Wylegala and a planning committee that included Vice President Tadeusz Puchalski, former President John A. Mikolajczak, Waclaw Staniewicz, Joseph Poczekaj, John Dulski, John Bojanek, and fourteen others,[29] the men selected Sunday, May 18 as the day they would celebrate the club's birthday.[30] Securing the Polish Union Hall, the 60 singers began incorporating the planned program into their weekly rehearsals. As the day approached, invitations were sent out to the full 200 membership, dignitaries, societies, groups, and clubs. On May 15 a special Mass was celebrated at Transfiguration Church in honor of the anniversary with W. Galantowicz and K. Banaszak performing solos as part of the service.

Finally on the big day, guests from Niagara Falls, Rochester and as far as Cleveland arrived at the Fillmore Hall with the members

---

27 "Buffalo Pours Out Glowing Greeting to Gen. Haller, Poland's 'Man of The Hour.'" *Buffalo Courier*, 26 Nov. 1923, p. 3. Chapter 3

28 "Polish Citizens Honor Wilson." *Buffalo Courier*, 18 Feb. 1924, p. 3.

29 "Srebrny Jubileusz Tow. Spiewu Chopin." *Dziennik Dla Wszystkich*, 18 May 1924, p. 3.

30 "Chopin Society to Unite Polish Choirs in Recital." *Buffalo Courier*, 27 Apr. 1924, p. 102.

of Chopin waiting to greet them. To a fully packed building, Buffalo Mayor F.X. Schwab opened the evening with a few words, saying, "[m]usic is the heart's delight. Those of us who have listened to lullabies sung by loving mother always will be lovers of music. If there were more song in life there would be less misery." Jacob Rozen then spoke on the life of Frederic Chopin with former President John Zelechowski giving a history of the Society. President Krysztafkiewicz and Secretary Kulwicki made a few quick remarks before the singers took to the stage. The Polish Singing Circle, the Moniuszko Singing Society, and the Kalina Singers each gave renditions of some of Chopin's most popular songs, with an evening that concluded with gifts. Mieczyslaw Karpinski, president of the Polish Singing Circle presented Chopins a silver cup in honor of their silver anniversary on behalf of its members, many of whom were in attendance that evening. Harmonia of Buffalo and the Harmonia-Chopin Choir of Cleveland also presented silver goblets to the singers while Polish National Alliance Group 194, the Fredro Singers, donated money for the forthcoming monument.[31]

Following their anniversary event, the choir had performances inside and outside Polonia. At the Polish Union Hall, Chopins brought in Warsaw-born opera tenor Ignacy Dygas conducted by Clark and assisted by Clark's other chorus, the Guidos.[32] The Society also had the honor of singing at the silver jubilee Mass for Kolko Polek held at Transfiguration that October.[33] Outside of Polonia they entertained the Buffalo Lion's Club in the mahogany room of the Lafayette Hotel with renditions of "Wisla" and "The Song of Peace."[34]

While the Society was finishing its own silver celebration, the rest of Polonia was preparing for the Polish Jubilee Week. The jubilee was a celebration in commemoration of the fiftieth anniversary of the Polish settlement of Buffalo and in recognition of the thriving, 130,000 strong Polish community that developed following the establishment of St. Stanislaus parish on Buffalo's Peckham Street in 1873. Led by a committee of Dr. Francis Fronczak, Walter K. Missall, the Polish Manufacturers and Traders, Business Men's Association, the Polish

---

[31] "Podniosly Obchod Jubileuszowy Tow. Spiewu Chopina." *Dziennik Dla Wszystkich*, 19 May 1924, p. 7.

[32] Howard, Mary M. "Music and Musicians." *Buffalo Express*, 7 Sept. 1924, p. 10.

[33] "Kolko Polek Celebrates Its Silver Jubilee." *Buffalo Express*, 10 Oct. 1924, p. 7.

[34] "Lions Club." *Buffalo Express*, 8 June 1924, p. 3.; "Tells Lions' Club How Scout Training Helps Develop Boy." *Buffalo Courier*, 3 June 1924, p. 4.; "Singing Society Entertains." *Buffalo Courier*, 10 June 1924, p. 2.

Union of America, the Polish National Alliance, the Polish Central Allied organization, Polish Roman Catholic organization, Polish Literary Circle, The Joseph Conrad Literary Club, the College Club, the singing societies, and a handful of other organizations, the members started to plan for the weeklong event in late spring. By June 8, the groups had settled on the week of September 22, 1924, for the festival that would be highlighted with products from Poland.[35] After working on the event for a month and a half,[36] Felix A. Wisniewski of the Polish Business Men's Association announced that the program would be delayed until May of 1925, citing supply chain issues related to the imports from Poland. Not wanting the year to pass without a celebration, Wisniewski further stated that a mini festival of the Polish events, including a concert at the Broadway Auditorium, would be held. The groups already secured for the event were Polish Singing Circle, Kalina, Harmonia, Lutnia, Lirnik, Moniuszko, and the Frederick Chopin Singing Society.

With Vice President Puchalski as part of the committee overseeing the event, the members of Chopin began rehearsing promptly for their opening night performance.[37] Soon more events were added to the program and the festival was expanded to include athletic demonstrations, a harvest festival, and orators.[38] Finally on October 2, five thousand people crammed into the blue and red decorated auditorium for the official opening of the Polish Jubilee Week. The rally was formally opened by Mayor Schwab and the members of Chopin as part of the grand choir that sang the "Star-Spangled Banner," the "Polish National Anthem," and Chopin's "Military Polonaise." Alternating between singing groups and speakers, Polish consul Stanislaus Manduk talked on the history of Poland and its place in the new post war world, Professor Thurman W. Stoner of the University of Buffalo's law school spoke on the ideals and principles of the Polish people and their love of liberty and democracy, while Secretary of State of New York James A. Hamilton gave some historical facts of the Polish American experience and the contributions they were making to society.[39] The evening concluded with the reading of letters from Governor Smith,

---

35 "Polish Jubilee Week." *Buffalo Courier*, 8 June 1924, p. 53.

36 "Postpone Polish Jubilee Week." *Buffalo Courier*, 22 July 1924, p. 7.

37 "Polish Jubilee Festivities to be Opened Thursday." *Buffalo Courier*, 28 Sept. 1924, p. 75.

38 "Buffalo's Polish Colony to Mark 50th Anniversary." *Buffalo Courier*, 21 Sept. 1924, p. 86.

39 "5,000 Persons Attend Opening Ceremonies of Polish Jubilee Week." *Buffalo Express*, 3 Oct. 1924, p. 5.

President Coolidge, and commanding performances from the singing societies. As Polonia had left its mark on Buffalo, Chopin left its own mark on Polish Jubilee Week.

The Society went on to close the year with an evening dedicated to Henryk Sienkiewicz at Dom Polski Hall. This event was part of an international celebration called for by Wojciech Trampczynski, the Marshal of the Polish Senate. The celebration was called for in recognition of the repatriation of Sienkiewicz's remains to Poland from Switzerland. Jacob Rozen, Father Kasprzak of Transfiguration, and Father Krayan of Queen of the Most Holy Rosary all spoke with Waclaw Gasiorowski, author and Dean of Alliance College in Cambridge Springs, as the keynote. In addition to Chopins, the Polish Singing Circle performed, and a requiem was sung by Mrs. Sophia Zakrzewska.[40]

The Chopin Singing Society became acquainted with Joseph Mazur when his fellow artist and friend, Mr. Kaninski, passed away. With no relatives nearby, Mazur was charged with making the funeral arrangements for the veteran of the Great War. Not wanting his passing to go unnoticed, Mr. Mazur contacted Chopins to let them know that their member Kaninski had passed away and asked if they could sing at the poor artist's service. Always ready to honor a fallen member, the men of Chopin arrived in force for what would have otherwise been a paltry showing. As a thank you gift, Mazur gave the group a wooden bust of Chopin that Kaninski had carved, which surprised the members as they never knew Kaninski had any artistic talents beyond his singing skills at practice.[41] As the artist was well-known to Chopins, it was no surprise to of Felix Kulwicki, John Zelechowski, Vincent Widzinski and Thaddeus Puchalski when Mazur submitted his proposal to the Chopin Monument Committee.

Jozef C. Mazur, also known as Joseph Mazur, was born in Buffalo's East Side at the very end of the nineteenth century. Mazur began demonstrating his artistic acumen while still attending St. Adalbert's parochial school. From there he attended Masten Park High School where he received a scholarship to the Albright Art School, a rare honor at that time for a Buffalonian of Polish heritage. Mazur then attended the Art Students League of New York and worked as a muralist during the First World War. Returning to Buffalo in 1922, he created a

---

[40] "Pay Homage to Poland's Humanitarian." *Buffalo Express*, 17 Nov. 1924.

[41] "Chopin Society to Unite Polish Choirs in Recital." *Buffalo Courier*, 27 Apr. 1924, p. 102.

memorial stained glass window for Grace Episcopal Church at Lafayette Avenue and Congress Street, while landing his most important commissions, the redecoration of St. Stanislaus Bishop & Martyr Church on Peckham and St. Adalbert Basilica on Stanislaus Street a short time later. Working on such high-profile projects on the Polish East Side, Mazur was an easy choice to go with for the monument committee.[42]

As Mazur moved from drafting the bust of Chopin, to making models, and finishing the project, the men of the Society began practicing for their first radio appearance of 1925.[43] On the evening of April 24, the choir took to the waves of WGR and gave an hour-long performance under the direction of Seth Clark. They opened with Olszewski's "The Power of God," went into "The Spanish Knight" by Kotte and closed the night with "Wine, Women and Song" by Strauss. In between, Norbert Kujawa played "Polish Dance Op. 3 No.1" by Scharwenka on the piano, tenor K. Banaszak sang "Speak to Me Again" by Rutkowski, and violinist Tad Przybycien performed "Kujawiak" by Lewandowski.[44]

By early 1925 the plaster model of Mazur's Chopin was cast in bronze and the fourteen-foot granite pedestal was receiving its final polish. In late May the Monument Committee announced that the dedication of the Chopin Monument would be in the afternoon of June 7. They also received word that while the flowers and soil from the grave of Chopin would be arriving, regretfully Maestro Paderewski would not be able to book passage to Buffalo in time to make it to the dedication.[45] The dignitaries who did arrive were Buffalo Mayor Frank X. Schwab, Buffalo Park's Commissioner John H. Meahl, Congressman S. Wallace Dempsey, C. Pascal Franchot from the French Consul, and Sylvester Gruszka Polish Consul General of New York.[46]

June 7 was a warm spring day in Buffalo. The pleasant weather and historic nature of the event brought out 10,000 members of Polonia to the post-Mass parade that kicked off dedication day. Gathering at the clubhouse at 1212 Broadway, grand marshal Steven

---

42 Commemorating the Unveiling of the Chopin Memorial by the Chopin Singing Society: Humboldt Park, Buffalo, New York, June Seventh, Nineteen Twenty Five. The Society, 1925.

43 "St Adalbert's Church Adorned by Polish Artist's Works." *Buffalo Courier*, 5 Apr. 1925, p. 73.

44 "Radio." *Buffalo Courier*, 24 Apr. 1925, p. 9.

45 "To Present Chopin Monument June 7." *Buffalo Courier*, 31 May 1925, p. 83.

46 "Will Unveil a Monument to Composer." *Buffalo Morning Express*, 3 June 1925, p. 5.; "Chopin Statue Unveiled and Presented to City." *Buffalo Evening News*, 8 June 1925.

Ryszkowski, a veteran of Haller's Blue Army,[47] led the line of Polish organizations, societies, and clubs, ranging from the Boy Scouts to the Polish Legion, down Broadway, turning onto Fillmore and then right into Humboldt Park. Draped along the route were American flags and red and white bunting for Poland. By the time the crowd reached the entrance of the park, the number of attendees had swelled to 25,000.[48]

Once the crowd had positioned itself around the monument, hidden under a draping of the Polish and America flag, little Amelia Puchalski pulled a cord, releasing the flags into the waiting hands of the Haller's Army veterans, uncovering the statue for all of Buffalo to see.[49] A collection of Polish American choruses sang the national anthems of both countries, Monsignor Kasprzak gave the invocation, and then President Krysztafkiewicz formally presented the monument of Chopin to the city. Mayor Schwab, representing a half million Buffalonians gratefully accepted the monument on their behalf. In receiving the gift, the mayor said Buffalo was proud of its Polish colony because of both its culture and its high attainments. After the speeches by the dignitaries on the dais and the reading of telegrams from those who could not attend, the members of Chopin, Moniuszko, the Polish Singing Circle, Fredro, Harmonia and a small orchestra gave a concert under the direction of Seth Clark. The urn of French soil, flowers, copies, of that day's newspapers, and an event program were sealed in a copper box and entombed in the monument for future generations to find.[50]

With the warm welcome Mayor Schwab received from the Singing Society and the 25,000 Polish attendees at the monument dedication, Francis decided to launch his 1925 primary campaign with the choir at their Broadway headquarters on September 20.[51] This would be the beginning of a busy political season for Chopins that year. Candidate for City Court Judge David Diamond would address the club at 1212 later in the year, campaigning for himself and his running mate Frank V. Hanavan, stating that the Democrats have "sympathy with

---

[47] "Polish Army in France Recruitment Records - Page 32, R." Foundation for East European Family History Studies, Polish Genealogical Society of America, feefhs.org/resource/poland-army-recruitment-32

[48] "25,000 See Chopin Statue Unveiling in Humboldt Park." *Buffalo Courier*, 8 June 1925, p. 3.

[49] "Chopin Statue Unveiled and Presented to City." *Buffalo Evening News*, 8 June 1925.

[50] "Chopin Bust Unveiled in Buffalo Park." *Buffalo Morning Express*, 8 June 1925, p. 4.

[51] "Schwab Fires First Big Gun of Campaign." *Buffalo Morning Express*, 21 Sept. 1925, p. 4.

the problems and needs of the masses of the people."[52] At the same time Society member Alexander A. Patrykowski worked the clubrooms drumming up support for his chance to serve on Buffalo's District Council.[53] At the end of the year, of the four candidates, the mayor was successful with his endeavor while Diamond, Hanavan, and Patrykowski were not.[54]

In celebration of Zdzislaw F. Krysztafkiewicz's fifth year as president, the members of Chopin held a testimonial dinner in his honor. Victor Wylegala acted as toastmaster as the men of the club sang Zdzislaw's praises in the packed clubrooms.[55] Almost as soon as the dinner concluded the men of Chopin had to freshen up for their annual concert and what would be the biggest musical event of the year, the silver anniversary of the Kalina Singing Society.

The ladies of Kalina began their April 11 celebration with a special morning Mass at Transfiguration. That evening at Dom Polski, after some refreshments and speeches, the Polish Singing Circle and the Chopin Singing Society took the stage to entertain the 800 guests in attendance.[56] Kalina would hold events for the anniversary all spring long, but in the meantime the members of Chopin had their own annual concert to prepare for.

For their yearly celebration, the choir debuted tenor Eugene Stebelski to Western New York at the Polish Union Hall. Stebelski gave renditions of the "Song of the Midnight Wanderer" by Zarzycki, "Dance of the Skeletons" by Studzinski, and the "Soldiers Chorus" from *Faust*. For their part of the performance Chopins sang arias from *Halka*, *Tosca,* and a version of "Krakowiak" by Moniuszko.[57]

Back with Kalina, the members of Chopin concluded the celebration not as singers, but as audience members at the closing concert. The featured performers for the night were soprano Jadwiga Sliwinska, pianist Agatha Plewacka-Dombrowska, a quartet, and an octet of Kalina singers.[58] At the conclusion the full 60-voice choir gave an impassioned performance under the direction of Jan F. Nadolny that was

---

52 "Urge Election of Diamond, Hanavan to City Bench." *Buffalo Courier*, 21 Oct. 1925, p. 5.
53 "Economy, Not Parsimony, Slogan of Patrykowski, Councilmanic Candidate." *Buffalo Courier*, 6 Oct. 1925, p. 3.
54 "Schwab Sweeps in on High Vote; Moore, Love Elected to Council." *Buffalo Courier*, 4 Nov. 1925, p. 1.
55 "Singers to Honor Chief." *Buffalo Courier*, 31 Jan. 1926, p. 80.
56 "800 Pay Tribute to Kalina Singing Society at Jubilee." *Buffalo Courier*, 12 Apr. 1926, p. 2.
57 "News and Notes of Music in Buffalo." *Buffalo Evening News*, 15 May 1926, p. 8.
58 "Kalina Singing Society Ends Jubilee with Concert." *Buffalo Courier*, 30 May 1926, p. 86.

remembered as "a concert which will rank as one of the best musical feasts presented by the organization."[59]

The members of Chopin ended 1926 with a live Tuesday evening performance on radio station WMAK. The chorus produced over an hour's worth of entertainment, which included "Wisla Mazurka Nowakowski," "The Clock," and "The Bells of St. Mary's," with interludes of solos and piano performances.[60]

The day before spring 1927 began, the Polish singing societies of Buffalo held a tribute to Chopin in recognition of the completion of Waclaw Szymanowski's Frederic Chopin Monument in Warsaw, which was unveiled three months earlier.[61] Headed by President Krysztafkiewicz, the evening included piano, violin, and vocal solos with a speech on the life of Chopin by Polish Vice Consul Edmund Kalenski. In his speech the vice consul said approvingly of the statue, "[i]t was appropriate, in my opinion, to have the statue in Warsaw represent the composer under a weeping willow tree, for nature provides the inspiration for all great art." Afterward, the stars of the evening took to the stage of the Polish Union Hall to the roaring approval of the at capacity crowd. Opening the evening were the Fredro Singers under the baton of Anthony Wierzbicki, followed by the Buffalo's oldest Polish singing group, the Moniuszko Singing Society led by Zygmant A. Nowacki, with the ladies of Kalina bringing their voices guided by Frank Narkon. Jan Nadolny led the Lirnik Singers while Chopins and the Polish Singing Circle closed out the show, both directed by Seth Clark.

With a short turnaround, the 40 voices of Chopin returned to the stage at 761 Fillmore on April 11 for their annual concert.[62] Special guest pianist Zygmunt Stojowski played selections from Beethoven, Chopin, and Kjerulf, while Walter Bakos and Theophile Kujawa gave resounding solo performances.[63] The entire choir closed the show with "Worship of God in Nature" by Beethoven and the "Finale" from *The Gondoliers* by Gilbert and Sullivan.[64] The members relaxed for much of the rest of the season, holding a dance in mid-May,[65] and a

---

[59] "Singers End Jubilee with Big Concert." *Buffalo Courier*, 31 May 1926, p. 22.
[60] "Tuesday's Programs." *Buffalo Evening News*, 7 Dec. 1926, p. 23.
[61] "Chopin Eulogized by Polish Singers." *Buffalo Evening News*, 21 Mar. 1927, p. 20.
[62] "Singers to Give Concert." *Buffalo Evening News*, 6 Apr. 1927, p. 40.
[63] "Chopin Society." *Buffalo Evening News*, 16 Apr. 1927, p. 2.
[64] "Stojowski Plays at Concert of Chopin Singing Society." *Buffalo Evening News*, 25 Apr. 1925.
[65] "Events Saturday." *Buffalo Evening News*, 17 May 1927, p. 14.

picnic at Liberty Park at William and Union in Cheektowaga.[66]

While the singers of Chopin slowed down a bit for 1927, their hall at the corner of Broadway and Lathrop saw plenty of action. The Polish Women's National Alliance held "meet the candidates" events,[67] card parties,[68] and their local branch meetings as well.[69] The Deotyma Society of the Polish National Alliance[70] and the Polish College Club also made great use of the space that year.[71] The women of Chopin were also busy, organizing the Ladies' Auxiliary that May.[72]

As the year ended, the choir held a Halloween party in their clubrooms headed up by Stanley Jendrasiak.[73] The members switched out the ghost and witch cutouts for turkeys and horns of plenty as they held a Thanksgiving celebration on the evening before the holiday.[74] The final event for the year was the election for the board of directors at which five new members were voted in. Stanley Jendrasiak, Stanley Domolski, Theophile Kujawa, Frank Michalski, and Silvester Dzimian who would each serve for the next three years.[75] This group would continue to be led by Albert L. Widzinski when he was re-elected president of Chopin for a second year, starting in 1928.

For his second term, Widzinski, a contractor by day, began an effort to extensively renovate and redecorate the Chopin clubrooms at 1212 Broadway. Having been at the address for almost a decade, the building needed some freshening up and a much-needed library was to be added to the premises. In early 1928 the rooms were closed off to public use while they were being upgraded.

While work was being done on their home, the members of Chopin were excitedly waiting for what would be the musical event of the year, the March 16 concert by I.J. Paderewski at the Buffalo Consistory Auditorium. While every music lover in Buffalo was queuing up to buy tickets for the show, the members of Polonia's four major singing groups were working on a way to honor the gifted maestro. The members of Polish Singing Circle, Chopin, Kalina, and Lirnik

---

66 "Frederick Chopin Singing Society will..." *Buffalo Evening News*, 13 July 1927, p. 26.
67 "Candidates to Take to Firing Line Tomorrow." *Buffalo Evening News*, 16 Oct. 1927, p. 2.;
68 "Party Chairman Named." *Buffalo Evening News*, 19 Oct. 1927, p. 17.
69 "Gabriela Zapolski Branch, Polish..." *Buffalo Evening News*, 14 Nov. 1927, p. 29.
70 "The Deotyma Society of the Polish National Alliance..." *Buffalo Evening News*, 10 Sept. 1927, p. 5.
71 "Annual Smoker Held." *Buffalo Evening News*, 9 Nov. 1927, p. 38.
72 "Chopin Society Meeting." *Buffalo Evening News*, 9 Jan. 1929, p. 12.
73 "To Celebrate Hallowe'en." *Buffalo Evening News*, 28 Feb. 1927.
74 "Falcons to Celebrate Thanksgiving Tonight." *Buffalo Evening News*, 22 Nov. 1927, p. 19.
75 "Chopin Singing Society Elects." *Buffalo Evening News*, 15 Dec. 1927, p. 15.

Singing Societies all agreed on a bespoke plaque that they could present to the musician. Contracting with Military Road jeweler Charles Bieda, the groups called for a shield styled plaque of polished ebony with a laurel wreath encircling a lyre all made of solid gold. Inscribed on it in Polish would be, "[i]n homage to the Master I.J. Paderewski by the Buffalo Polish Singing Societies" with a second inscription that included the names of the four presenting societies.[76]

After an evening of playing Beethoven, Schubert, Liszt, Chopin, and a few of his own melodies, Paderewski returned to the stage to meet his old friend Dr. Francis Fronczak.[77] There, the doctor along with Vincent P. Zawadski, president of the Polish Singing Circle; Albert Widzinski, president of Chopin; Victoria Bilska, president of Kalina; and president John Hotlos of the Lirnik Singing Society presented the plaque to Paderewski.[78] The composer thanked the groups for the gift and Dr. Fronczak gave a short speech.

While Chopins kept things light that Easter, many of the members joined Kalina and the Philharmonic Society to perform a special high Easter Mass under the baton of Jan Nadolny at Transfiguration Church.[79] The one thing the group was able to do that Easter was sponsor the Polish Singing Circle's benefit concert for the Kosciuszko Foundation.[80] Along with the Adam Mickiewicz Library & Dramatic Circle, Echo Singing Society, Polish Army Veterans Association, and dozens of other sponsors, Chopins helped the Polish Singers meet the last of the $50,000 goal the community set to help the foundation.[81]

By April 21 the renovations at 1212 were completed and the next day a members-only party was held in the rooms. As part of the celebration, Father Joseph Winnicki held a *bigos* ceremony, described as a tradition of eating blessed foods while Councilman Wylegala served as the toastmaster.[82] The speakers for the day were Health Commissioner Fronczak, Music Director Clark, Joseph S. Kaszubowski, Paul P. Myszka, B.S. Kamienski, and several Chopin

---

[76] "Paderewski Tribute Prepared by Poles." *Buffalo Evening News*, 15 Mar. 1928, p. 24.

[77] Slawinska, Wanda M. "Dr. Francis Eustace Fronczak and Ignacy Jan Paderewski: The Enduring Friendship." The Polonian Legacy of Western New York: Stories of the Lives, Accomplishments, and Contributions of Four Prominent Polish-Americans, edited by Edward R. Szemraj, Canisius College Press, Buffalo, NY, 2005, pp. 119–155.

[78] Duney, Edward. "Paderewski Piano Recital." *Buffalo Evening News*, 27 Mar. 1928, p. 4.

[79] "Music at Transfiguration Church." *Buffalo Courier*-Express, 1 Apr. 1928, p. 11.

[80] "60 Sponsors Added for Easter Concert." *Buffalo Evening News*, 4 Apr. 1928.

[81] "Singing Circle Soloist." *Buffalo Courier*-Express, 4 Apr. 1928, p. 5.

[82] "Chopin Society to Meet." *Buffalo Evening News*, 21 Apr. 1928, p. 4.

directors, founding members and a past president. At the conclusion of the event, 52 new members were inducted into the Society and the choir sang a few numbers for those gathered.[83]

The public opening of the clubrooms on May 6 was an equally grand affair.[84] Seth Clark arranged 40 members of his Guido Chorus to serenade the members and guests of the Sunday evening housewarming party. The Fredro Singing Society, the St. Stanislaus Athletic Club, and the Dom Polski Association sent representatives to take part in the festivities. The 300 guests danced and celebrated well into the wee hours of Monday morning.[85]

As the club was heading into summer, they decided to make their annual picnic a community wide event. They rented Anthony Olesky's grove on Bowen Road in Lancaster for the July 15 party.[86] For entertainment, courses were laid out for men and women to race, areas for games to be played were arranged, part of a field was made into a baseball diamond where the married men played the bachelors, and a stage was set up for the choir to sing a few songs. With 200 members from Chopin alone attending, cars were arranged to ferry people from the clubrooms to the event.[87] Beginning at 11 in the morning the drivers started on the 20-mile round trip to the grounds. Despite St. Peter's Society 65 of the Polish Union of American holding an event at Wahl's Grove in Ebenezer, and St. Hyacinth's Society 868 of the Polish Roman Catholic Union having an outing at Liberty Park in Cheektowaga, 2,000 people attended the party in the grove.[88] Louis L. Fereil, Fred Pinker, Adam Dyzmika and Stanley Domulski were roundly applauded for their effort in arranging the day.[89]

In late summer a rumor began being whispered around East Buffalo that Chopin and the Polish Singing Circle were going to merge. Whispers turned to murmurs, and murmurs became open talk. In early October President Widzinski had had enough and issued a statement fully denying the possibility of a merger. Widzinski reiterated that the Society just spent thousands of dollars in remodeling the

---

83 "Chopin Society's Hall Opened with Ceremony." *Buffalo Evening News*, 23 Apr. 1928.
84 ibid
85 "Guido Chorus Serenades Chopin Singing Society." *Buffalo Evening News*, 8 May 1928.
86 "Singing Society Plans Picnic." *Buffalo Evening News*, 14 June 1928, p. 20.
87 "Chopin Singing Society to Attend Picnic Sunday." *Buffalo Evening News*, 14 July 1928, p. 18.
88 "Poles Hold Outings." *Buffalo Evening News*, 16 July 1928, p. 11.
89 "More Than 2000 Attend Singing Society Outing." *Buffalo Evening News*, 16 July 1928, p. 22.

clubrooms and that the membership disfavored the idea of consolidating with the Circle or any other group. The two groups were exchanging conductors, with Clark going to the Circle for a time and Nadolny performing with Chopins for a spell, but it was no more an indication of them merging than when Olszewski was simultaneously directing both groups a decade earlier.[90]

To celebrate All Hallows' Eve, Sylvester Dzimian was selected to organize a masquerade party and dance for the Monday before the holiday.[91] While preparations for that event were underway, many of the members of Chopin were practicing with a community chorus organized to celebrate the 10th anniversary of Polish independence. Held the day before the party, Chicago newspaperman and prominent Republican Anthony Czarnecki was the keynote speaker while Scoutmaster Leonard F. Gabrylewicz (Gabryelewicz) led a parade of 5,000 from the Broadway Market to the Broadway Auditorium where speakers and singers engaged with the crowd.[92] The next day at 9 in the evening, fools and kings, ghouls and geese, queens and priests, packed the clubrooms at 1212 Broadway and enjoyed themselves well into the night.

As 1928 ended, elections for the next year's board were held. The results saw Albert L. Widzinski return for a third term, with Felix Kulwicki, Leonard Knast, Edward Czuprynski, Walter Skierczynski and Joseph Poczekaj coming on to the board.[93] Members also made a rare move by wading into the world of politics when they, along with 20 other Polish organizations, endorsed Assemblyman Ansley B. Borkowski for the position of City Court Judge, opened up by the unexpected passing of Judge Albert A Hartzell.[94] While Borkowski would be passed over for this position when Mayor Schwab named Samuel J. Dickey judge,[95] Ansley would go on to have a successful career as the Clerk of the New York State Assembly.[96]

To close out the year, Stanley Domalski and Louis Finzel were

---

[90] "Merger Reports Denied by Two Singing Clubs." *Buffalo Evening News*, 5 Oct. 1928, p. 38.
[91] "Special Features Are Being Planned..." *Buffalo Evening News*, 17 Oct. 1928, p. 16.; "Masque Dance." *Buffalo Evening News*, 27 Oct. 1928, p. 16.
[92] "5000 To Celebrate Polish Freedom Day." *Buffalo Evening News*, 30 Oct. 1928, p. 23.
[93] "Albert Widzinski Elected Head of Singing Society." *Buffalo Evening News*, 11 Dec. 1928.
[94] "Poles Backing Borkowski." *Buffalo Evening News*, 11 Dec. 1928.
[95] "Nuese Withdraws in Judgeship Race." *Buffalo Evening News*, 11 July 1929, p. 18.
[96] "Borkowski's Humor Relaxes Legislators." *Buffalo Courier*-Express, 8 Jan. 1965, p. 3.

placed in charge of the New Year's Eve dance.[97] For the evening, the hall was decorated, refreshments were arranged for,[98] and by all accounts the evening was a success,[99] but it is unknown if it would have been more jubilant had George Howard's rum boat not been intercepted by the Coast Guard.[100]

The members of Chopin kicked off the year 1929 with a grand banquet and installation celebration of their board and president. The evening also saw the election of the Ladies Auxiliary president, Mrs. Thaddeus Puchalski, who had been informally leading the group up to that point.[101]

The good times continued to roll that summer. Not wanting to drive all the way out to Lancaster to picnic, Chopins held their summer festival closer to home at Genesee Park. Over 2,500 people came out to enjoy the outdoor card tournament, walking and running races, and other athletic events. A "near beer" drinking contest followed by impromptu songs by the members enthralled those gathered. In the center of it all was a 12-piece orchestra playing as couples danced the afternoon and evening away.[102] The singing society, if not all of Polonia, was on top of the world.

On September 16, the chorus opened their fall concert season with 200 guests in their clubrooms.[103] Half a world away Clarence Hatry was trying to finance the purchase of United Steel Companies, overextending his own company, and forged some bonds to make up the cash. Four days later his fraud had become known, and the Hatry Group collapsed. While having little impact on the U.S. financial markets, it reminded investors that "all that glitters is not gold."[104]

While the sun was still shining brightly in the land of Washington, the Poles of Buffalo celebrated the sesquicentennial of the death

---

97 "Chopin Singing Society Dance New Year's Eve." *Buffalo Evening News*, 27 Dec. 1928, p. 3.

98 "Chopin Singing Society Dance." *Buffalo Evening News*, 20 Dec. 1928, p. 34.

99 "Whoopee Reigns as Little Makes His Bow." *Buffalo Courier*-Express, 1 June 1929, p. 39.

100 "Shot Across Bow Stops Rumboat with Good Cargo." *Buffalo Evening News*, 31 Dec. 1928, p. 30.

101 "Chopin Society Meeting." *Buffalo Evening News*, 9 Jan. 1929, p. 12.

102 "Weather Fails to Stop Chopin Society Outing." *Buffalo Courier*-Express, 8 July 1929, p. 4.

103 "Chopin Singing Society Opens Year with Dance." *Buffalo Evening News*, 17 Sept. 1929, p. 11.

104 Roberts, Richard. "The Financial Times: A Financial History of the Last 120 Years." Financial Times Historical Archive, Cengage Learning, 2010, www.gale.com/intl/essays/richard-roberts-financial-times-financial-history.

of their own Revolutionary war hero, Casimir Pulaski. Held at the Broadway Auditorium and headed by Stanley E. Czaster, the October 13 event was highlighted by a Mass, speakers, and a parade. Following a morning service at Transfiguration, eleven divisions of paraders filled the side streets of Broadway from Gibson to Loepere. As part of the fourth division, the members of Chopin marched and sang along with the members of Lirnik, Kalina, Fredro, Moniuszko, and the Polish Singing Circle under the direction of Joseph Kaminski of Moniuszko and Vincent Zawadski of the Circle. At the auditorium, Mayor Schwab, Polish Consul of Buffalo Dr. Rocicki, and Dr. Fronczak spoke to the masses gathered. They were followed by the main speakers, Buffalo native and First World War hero William J. Donovan and Polish author and politician Waclaw Sieroszewski, who traveled to the U.S. exclusively for this event.[105]

By the time Pulaski Day ended, the Dow Jones Industrial Average had fallen 6% from the 372 points it sat at when Chopins opened their season. In the weeks following the event, equity markets would see Black Thursday, Black Monday, and Black Tuesday. At the close of the markets on November 13, 1929, the Average had lost 46% of its value and America began facing an economic Ice Age.[106]

With a depression looming and fear stalking the land, it became difficult to find someone to captain the Chopin ship. Widzinski stepped down as president but agreed to stay on as an advisor. Former president and newly elected 9th Ward Supervisor John A. Mikolajczak was the first nominee, but he promptly refused to stand for the election and his name was withdrawn. Having overseen the choir for six years Krysztafkiewicz's name was put up, but like Mikolajczak he requested his name be withdrawn. Finally, Vice President Stanislaus Jendrasiak was put forward. With all eyes on him, Stanley agreed to lead the organization through what he hoped would be a short time of uncertainty.[107]

---

[105] "Buffalo Poles to Honor Pulaski." *Buffalo Courier*-Express, 13 Oct. 1929, p. 1.

[106] "Dow Jones - 1929 Crash and Bear Market." MacroTrends, Macrotrends LLC, www.macrotrends.net/2484/dow-jones-crash-1929-bear-market.

[107] "Jendrasiak President." *Buffalo Evening News*, 6 Dec. 1929, p. 12.

Chapter 4

Depression

At the New Year's Eve dance for 1930 Stanislaus Jendrasiak was installed as president. Rounding out the leadership of the choir were John Noryskiewicz, Felix Kulwicki, Stephen Skierczynski, and Thaddeus Puchalski.[1] The immediate task at hand for the group was finding a musical director to lead them as Nadolny had departed. Word had come through that former general director of the Polish Singers Alliance of America, Jan Karol Kapalka had secured the position of orchestra leader for the Fillmore Theater and would be open to other work in the community as well. A meeting was arranged, terms agreed to, and on January 22 Kapalka held his first practice session with the Society in their clubrooms.[2]

With Kapalka's musical guidance the Society could focus on holding concerts to raise money and host their much-needed parties. They opened their festive season with a spring dance held on Dyngus Day evening at the Dom Polski.[3] The Easter Monday party, as well as an early May card party fundraiser were a nice reprieve for the members as the economy was rallying and the worst of the economic crisis looked to be over. [4]

The choir followed up the Dyngus Day party with a wreath laying ceremony in early June at the Chopin monument in honor of the fifth anniversary of its dedication. While Jan arranged a short program, and Paul P. Myszka of the *Dziennik Dla Wszystkich,*[5] Councilman John A. Ulinski,[6] and Chauncey J. Hamlin president of the Buffalo Society of Natural Sciences spoke, the real highlight of the day was the concert held that evening at the Polish Union Hall.[7]

---

1 "New Year Greeted by Polish Societies." *Buffalo Evening News*, 2 Jan. 1930, p. 14.
2 "Chor Chopina Zyskal Nowego Dyrygenta." *Dziennik Dla Wszystkich*, 21 Jan. 1930, p. 9.
3 "East Side Briefs." *Buffalo Evening News*, 16 Apr. 1930, p. 38.
4 "East Side Briefs." *Buffalo Evening News*, 13 May 1930, p. 18.; "1929-1930 Stock Charts of the Great Depression Era." Online Stock Trading Guide, Online Stock Trading Guide, www.online-stock-trading-guide.com/1929-1930-stock-charts.html.
5 "Chopin Anniversary." Lockport Union-Sun and Journal, 4 June 1930, p. 5.;
6 "Place Wreath on Monument of Composer." *Buffalo Courier-Express*, 9 June 1930, p. 5.
7 "Society to Place Wreath on Chopin Monument." *Buffalo Courier-Express*, 27 May 1930, p. 8.

That July the members of Chopin held their summer outing at Genesee Park,[8] while in August President Jendrasiak represented the Society at the 10th Anniversary of the Battle of Warsaw celebration at the Broadway Market.[9] Both the outing and anniversary would serve as a warm-up for the biggest event of the year, the golden jubilee of the Polish National Alliance.

The Society began practicing for the mid-August celebration earlier in the summer, even before their outing. By August 15, Kapalka had the voices of the men exactly where he wanted them to be for the region wide event.[10] As the singers finished up practice, delegates from Niagara Falls, Batavia, Perry, Dunkirk, Rochester, Olean, Elmira, Auburn, Syracuse, Pittsburgh, and Chicago, began arriving in Buffalo for the celebration on Sunday, August 17. After a weekend of enjoying the delicacies and delights of Broadway-Fillmore, the 2,000 representatives of the PNA gathered at St. Adalbert Basilica for a special Sunday service. Following the Mass, the members of Chopin acted as escorts for the Alliance as they first laid a wreath at the monument of Chopin, then another at the grave of their founding father, Julian Lipinski, at the Holy Mother of the Rosary Polish National Catholic Cemetery.[11] The last engagement of Chopins with the PNA celebration would be at the closing afternoon concert where they were led by Kapalka.[12]

Almost as soon as they were done with the Polish National Alliance celebration, the members of Chopin were off to the studios of WKBW for another special event, the docking of the S.S. Kosciuszko at New York Harbor. The celebration was two-fold, it was the first steamer to sail under the Polish flag and it was the conclusion of its maiden voyage. The star of the August 26 broadcast was Polish tenor, August Jan Suzin, under his stage name Gustaw Chorjan. But Chopins, violinist Jan Wollanek, and Kapalka's Orchestra were also featured performers. Polish Consul Tadeusz Marynowski closed the show speaking about how the docking of the Kosciuszko heralded a new epoch in maritime activities of Poland.[13]

In October, the Society was invited to participate in one of the

---

[8] "East Side Briefs." *Buffalo Evening News*, 2 July 1930, p. 40.
[9] "5000 Will Attend Battle Anniversary." *Buffalo Evening News*, 9 Aug. 1930, p. 7.
[10] "East Side Briefs." *Buffalo Evening News*, 14 Aug. 1930, p. 20.
[11] "Jubilee Observed by Polish Alliance." *Buffalo Evening News*, 18 Aug. 1930, p. 11.
[12] "Polish Order to Celebrate Golden Jubilee." *Buffalo Courier-Express*, 17 Aug. 1930, p. 1.
[13] "Polish Tenor's Solo to Salute S.S. Kosciuszko." *Buffalo Courier-Express*, 26 Aug. 1930, p. 8.

most important events of the year, the silver jubilee of the founding of the Dom Polski Association. Formed to open a YMCA-type building in East Buffalo, the association succeeded in their effort with a groundbreaking ceremony on May 8, 1905. For the silver celebration a special Mass was held on the morning of October 19 at St. Stanislaus Church with a dinner that evening. The Chopin Singing Society, the Polish Singing Circle, and the Kalina Singing Society each performed while Dr. Francis Fronczak, Msgr. Alexander Pitass, brewer Anthony Schreiber, Deputy Attorney General Leonard Lipowicz, and Dom Polski President Stanley Jakubowski each gave a speech.[14]

The singers closed out 1930 with two special concerts. The first was a recital by Edwin Arthur Kraft of St. Paul's Episcopal Church in Cleveland on the new organ at Queen of Peace parish. The recently completed church hosted the recital headed by Mr. Kraft and featured the members of Chopin, the choir of Queen of Peace Church, the Orpheus, the Maennerchor Bavaria, the Polish Singing Circle, members of the Moniuszko Singing Society, and the Lirnik Singing Society. The second was a November 24 farewell concert by Jan Karol Kapalka and his orchestra as he prepared to move to Ohio.[15]

As the severity of the Depression made itself evident, Chopins began to focus on fundraisers to stay afloat. To that end, Frank J. Mikolajczak with the guidance of the board, organized a card party and reception at the start of 1931.[16] The club would follow this up with almost monthly dances,[17] card parties,[18] and concerts put on by the Women's Auxiliary. [19] To further supplement their income, the club let out their rooms for other organizations for a small fee. This saw the Polish Literary Circle,[20] the Ladies Auxiliary of Polish Physicians and Dentists Association,[21] the Polish Nationals basketball team,[22] and Alpha Delta Tau sorority utilize 1212 Broadway.[23]

While Mikolajczak was occupied with raising funds, President Zdzislaw Krysztafkiewicz was working on a replacement for Kapalka.

---

14 "Dom Polski Silver Jubilee Celebration Opens Sunday." *Buffalo Evening News*, 17 Oct. 1930, p. 34.

15 "Kapalka i Jego Zespol..." *Dziennik Dla Wszystkich*, 22 Nov. 1930, p. 8.

16 "Chopin Society Party Today." *Buffalo Courier-Express*, 18 Jan. 1931, p. 3.

17 "The Daily Calendar." *Buffalo Evening News*, 4 Apr. 1931, p. 18.

18 "The Daily Calendar." *Buffalo Evening News*, 15 Jan. 1931, p. 38.

19 "The Daily Calendar." *Buffalo Evening News*, 25 May 1931, p. 28.

20 "East Side Briefs." *Buffalo Evening News*, 28 Dec. 1931.

21 "The Daily Calendar." *Buffalo Evening News*, 19 May 1931, p. 31.

22 "Polish Nationals' Dance." *Buffalo Courier-Express*, 21 Apr. 1931, p. 15.

23 "Alpha Delta Tau." *Buffalo Courier-Express*, 15 Oct. 1931, p. 10.

Having already been acquainted with Arnold Cornelissen from the Buffalo Symphony Orchestra, Krysztafkiewicz invited him to try out for the position of musical director. On April 6, 1931, Cornelissen arranged a choral selection for the Society's spring dance and fashion show. Closed to the public, the members of Chopin and their friends with Kalina, the Circle, Moniuszko, Fredro, and Lirnik heard Arnold's score.[24] Following the performance, all agreed that Cornelissen was the man for the job, and on May 25, Arnold directed his first public concert for Chopin at the Polish Union Hall.[25]

For his debut Arnold chose a selection from *Halka*, "Going Home" by Dvorak, and "Winter Song" by Bullard. He also arranged for Stanley Zakrzewski, accompanist for the Society, to perform a couple of his own original works "Polonaise Militaire in D Minor" and "Etude in D Flat" and had Walter Bakos sing "Serenada" and "The Old Refrain."[26]

Cornelissen's second major public engagement with Chopin was that summer as part of the anniversary of Poland's victory in the Polish–Soviet War. With a parade from Ss. Peter & Paul Parish on Clinton to the Broadway Market and concluding at Humboldt Park the afternoon was marked with speakers, presenters, and drills.[27] Arnold conducted the members of Chopin in the evening for a near capacity crowd at Bison Stadium as part of a full Polish program.[28]

While the members of Chopin were proudly showing off their new music director to Polonia, their new music director was proudly showing them off to greater Buffalo. In November Arnold arranged for the men of Chopin to sing at a special service at St. Mary's-On-The-Hill Episcopal Church on Buffalo's West Side. The congregation of Cornelissen's home church embraced the members of Chopin with the same love that Polonia felt for Arnold.[29]

As the year was coming to an end the members of Chopin began to prepare for the annual benefit show for the Polish-American

---

24 "Chopin Society Dance." *Buffalo Courier-Express*, 5 Apr. 1931, p. 9.

25 "Koncert Choru Chopina Bedzie Wielka Uczta Dla Milosnikow Muzyki i Spiewu." *Dziennik Dla Wszystkich*, 23 May 1931, p. 5.

26 "Chopin Society Choir to Present Concert." *Buffalo Evening News*, 22 May 1931, p. 38.

27 "Polish Residents Celebrate Independence Today." *Buffalo Courier-Express*, 9 Aug. 1931, p. 2.

28 "Rejoice In Ties Binding Nations in One Accord." *Buffalo Courier-Express*, 10 Aug. 1931, pp. 11–17.

29 "Chopin Singing Society to Entertain in Church." *Buffalo Courier-Express*, 7 Nov. 1931, p. 6.

Welfare League. The December 15 program would feature a movie, vaudeville acts, and singers. As practice was underway Chopins received an invitation to sing a couple of songs for a new radio show Father Figas was trying out at Corpus Christi Church called the *Rosary Hour*.

Father Justin Figas, OFM Conv. was already a bit of a radio star before launching his own show in late 1931. As early as 1926 he was a featured guest on the WEBR comedy *Podeszwa and Kordula* giving talks and advice on religious and personal matters. Seeing the value of mass communication, Figas organized the Great Lakes Network with stations in Buffalo, Chicago, Cleveland, Detroit, Milwaukee, Pittsburgh, and Scranton, that he would use to launch his own program, the *Father Justin Rosary Hour*. At 6 pm on December 6, 1931, Joseph Dombrowski welcomed listeners from across the northeast while Ethelbert Nevin's "The Rosary" was played as the theme song. Father Figas began the program tracing the history of Poles in America, giving a lesson on obedience, and answered questions on religion from a "Question Box." For the second hour of the show Justin welcomed on air thirty-five members of the Chopin Singing Society. Under Cornelissen the men sang an entire segment of music before giving up the stage to the Corpus Christi Choir who finished the program.[30] It is unknown how many heard Chopins that first night, but over the next 20 years, Figas would expand his network, and the *Rosary Hour* eventually reached 6.5 million homes across the U.S. and Canada.[31]

A little over a week later, the men of Chopin took the stage at Shea's Roosevelt at the corner of Detroit and Broadway for the benefit of the Polish-American Welfare League. The heart of the fundraiser was the midnight debut of the Elissa Landi and Lionel Barrymore film *The Yellow Ticket*, but the men of Chopin and the women of newly organized Samarytanek Society sang a few songs as the crowd filed in to the sold out 1,774 seat theater. Following the performances, Stanley M. Puchalski, president of the League thanked the groups, welcomed the film enthusiasts, and thanked them all for their support as the lights dimmed and the movie began.[32] The members of Chopin would meet at the end of the month and choose a board of directors led by

---

[30] "Rosary Hour Inaugurated." *Buffalo Evening News*, 7 Dec. 1931, p. 14.

[31] "Father Justin to Observe 50 Years of Service to God." *Buffalo Evening News*, 7 Sept. 1954, p. 23.

[32] "Benefit Show Held." *Buffalo Courier-Express*, 13 Dec. 1931, p. 10.

Stanislaus Jendrasiak for 1932.

The beginning of Stanislaus's second term was a light one. In February Jendrasiak, Krysztafkiewicz, and Puchalski began planning for Chopin's Spring Concert at the new St. John Kanty's Lyceum.[33] While the three concert committee members were working on the logistics of the show, Cornelissen was occupied with the program for the evening. By mid-month, the group announced that Constance Nowakowski-Hejda, the contralto opera singer from Baltimore who made a name for herself with the touring performance of the *King's Henchmen*, would be the featured artist of the evening.[34] As work continued on the concert, Zdzislaw Krysztafkiewicz was selected to represent Chopin on the Polish Centennial Committee, the group chosen to represent Polonia as part of Buffalo's Centennial celebration.[35]

After a month of practicing, the members of Chopin and special guest Constance Nowakowski-Hejda were ready to take the Lyceum stage. The men opened the evening with Willis Clark's "Wedrowni Spiewacy" and Lachman's "Klechda." They then gave way to Ms. Hejda who performed a triptych of songs including an entertaining rendition of Kotarbinski's "Zaby." Messrs Bakos, Gurbacki, and Zgoda each gave a solo performance, and the evening concluded with S. Ogurkowski's "Good Night."[36]

Reviews for both of Buffalo's daily English language newspapers raved about the pieces. Mary Swan from the *Courier-Express* said:

> Both in accompanied and unaccompanied work, disclosed musical intelligence and a regard for shading and rhythm. There is a fine balance of voices in this chorus, and some beautiful tonal effects were obtained. Mr. Cornelissen conducted with such admirable musicianship as to receive enthusiastic support from his choristers. Mr. Zakrzewski as official accompanist for the chorus added to the value of the program.[37]

While the *Buffalo News* said, "[t]his chorus which contains a goodly

---

[33] "Chopin Singing Society to Give Concert in April." *Buffalo Evening News*, 17 Feb. 1932, p. 23.

[34] "Chopin Society Engages Contralto for Concert." *Buffalo Evening News*, 19 Feb. 1932, p. 29.

[35] "Polish Centennial Committee Named." *Buffalo Evening News*, 5 Mar. 1932.

[36] Swan, Mary B. "Music." *Buffalo Courier-Express*, 27 Mar. 1932, p. 6.

[37] Swan, Mary B. "Music Review." *Buffalo Courier-Express*, 31 Mar. 1931, p. 12.

amount of young blood responds readily to the beat of its conductor, Arnold Cornelissen. The singing of an interesting and varied program was marked throughout by spirit and precision as well as sincere regard for essentials of interpretation."[38]

Although the show was a great success, the economic depression was still spiraling downward. To help shore up the Society's finances the Woman's Auxiliary led by Jadwiga Urbanczyk, Jean Podlecki, and Mary Jendrasiak,[39] held regular card parties and the occasional dance.[40]

Between their own performances, Chopins lent their voices out as a community service. During a May 1 event that recognized Polish Constitution Day and Polish National Alliance Day, the male choir sang at a special presentation as part of the celebration.[41] At two in the afternoon, Polish Consul General Mieczyslaw Marchlewski, along with a detachment from the Adam Plewacki Post laid a wreath at the foot of the Monument to Chopin followed by a brief address from Krysztafkiewicz. The ceremony concluded with a choral selection by the singers.[42]

The Society also sang at three services honoring the fallen Polish and Polish Americans of the Great War, in cooperation with the Adam Plewacki Post that Memorial Day· The two groups held ceremonies at St. Stanislaus and St. Adalbert Cemeteries. Reverend Michael Biniszkiewicz of St. Stanislaus delivered a memorial address while the Post held bugle salutes to the colors, a three-shot salute, and the placing of flowers on their comrades' graves. For their part, the Society sang Chopin's "Funeral March," "W Mogile Ciemnej," and "Juz Opuscili" at each location.[43]

For their 1932 summer outing, a committee chaired by Krysztafkiewicz, and including President Jendrasiak, Thaddeus J. Puchalski, Henry Zabrocki, Leonard Knast, and Felix Kulwicki decided that Liberty Park at Union and William Street in Cheektowaga would be the best spot for their annual event. The plans called for sporting events, an orchestra,[44] and a Polish folk dance presentation by the members of

38 "Polish Singers Give Successful Concert." *Buffalo Evening News*, 31 Mar. 1932, p. 15.
39 "Brief Items and Personals." *Buffalo Evening News*, 4 Nov. 1932, p. 33.
40 "Brief Items and Personals." *Buffalo Evening News*, 11 Apr. 1932, p. 25.
41 "America Is Praised as Friend of Poland." *Buffalo Evening News*, 2 May 1932, p. 15.
42 "Polish Consul General Feted at Dom Polski." *Buffalo Courier-Express*, 2 May 1932, p. 8.
43 "Entreats Preparedness as Safeguard of Peace." *Buffalo Courier-Express*, 30 May 1932, pp. 1–2.
44 "Male Chorus to Sing." *Buffalo Evening News*, 2 Aug. 1932, p. 24.

the Wiedza Society Branch 345 of the Polish Union of America. At the end of the day, 40 members would sing for their guests in Polish peasant costumes. When August 7 finally arrived, over 400 guests boarded buses at the clubrooms and headed out to Cheektowaga to a day of fun.[45]

Two weeks later, the members of Chopin as well as the Polish Singing Circle took the stage at St. John Kanty Lyceum at a reception for amateur airman Stanislaus Hausner. Hausner was on tour after his second attempted solo flight from New York to Warsaw. During the voyage he vanished over the Atlantic, only to be plucked from the sea after 8 days of being adrift.[46] The hero aviator who was still in the ocean 72 days earlier, was on a combination victory and fundraising tour with Stanislaus and his wife visiting cities with large Polish populations. Hosted by Dr. Fronczak and Harry Posmantur, Stanislaus spent two days in the city gaining support for a third flight to Poland.[47] Hausner would continue to successfully drum up support for a third flight over the next three years. Tragically, his new plane, the Marshal Jozef Pilsudski, lost a wing and fell from the sky at an event in Detroit, killing the Polish American pilot.[48]

In the fall, the members of Chopin sang at an event hosted by the Buffalo Central Council of Polish Organizations marking the 153rd anniversary of the death of General Pulaski. Held at the Polish Union Hall, the day also saw Dr. Francis E. Fronczak behind the podium speaking about the decline of politics as he ran for the Democratic nomination for Congressman in the 41st District.[49]

The Society wrapped up its year with a radio performance, its annual New Year's Eve party, elections, and planning for next year's concerts. Wanting to return to the Kanty Lyceum in that next spring, Chopins already began working with the parish to host the first post-Lenten event at the location with a special Easter Monday concert.[50]

On Christmas Day 1932, Cornelissen arranged for the full choir of 40 voices to follow under his baton on a performance broadcast on WKBW. The group sang Polish Christmas carols for the program that was sponsored by Father Joseph J. Winnicki of Precious Blood

---

[45] "400 Going to Outing." *Buffalo Evening News*, 6 Aug. 1932, p. 14.
[46] "Group Will Greet Hausner on Sunday." *Buffalo Evening News*, 18 Aug. 1932, p. 24.
[47] "Hundreds Cheer as Hausner and Wife Land in Buffalo." *Buffalo Evening News*, 20 Aug. 1932, pp. 1–4.
[48] "Hausner, Polish Flier, Dies in Crash." *Buffalo Evening News*, 18 May 1935, pp. 1–2.
[49] "Fronczak Has Some Comment on Veracity." *Buffalo Courier-Express*, 10 Oct. 1932, p. 20.
[50] "Lyceum to Show Talking Pictures." *Buffalo Evening News*, 29 Nov. 1932, p. 6.

Church. A few days prior to the program, the group elected Boleslaus Lemanski to be the president for 1933. Soon after, the New Year's Eve party held in the clubrooms went off with great success. [51]

While Chopin and the Auxiliary were starting off the year with card parties, Cornelissen made a trip up to North Tonawanda to meet and greet the newly formed Arion Singing Circle.[52] Under the direction of Joseph Plewinski, the Arions also known as the Arjons were making a name for themselves not just in the Lumber City but across all of Western New York.[53]

After four months of preparation, the choir was ready for their Dyngus Day evening concert at St. John Kanty Lyceum. Performing with soloists Mary Konikoff and Florence Ann Reid, as well as the Buffalo Ensemble, the members of Chopin sang the sea shanty "A roving," the spiritual "Go Down Moses," and the English folk song "O No, John."[54] The choir followed up this spring concert with a performance at the Buffalo Science Museum's auditorium. Chopins opened the Sunday afternoon show with "Marsz Z Roku 1920" and "Pozegnanie Zolnierza" by Maszynski and "Wisla" by Nowakowski. The audience also heard solo recitals by tenor Walter Bakos and bass Frank Zgoda.[55]

As they had in the past, the members of Chopin worked with the Adam Plewacki Post to honor the fallen dead at St. Stanislaus, St. Adalbert and the Holy Mother of the Rosary Cemeteries as part of Memorial Day services.[56] Something new for the organization that summer was taking part in the memorial services honoring the members of Haller's Army buried at the Polish Cemetery at Niagara-On-The-Lake, Ontario. Hosted by the Plewacki Post, the day saw a Mass by Father Ladislaus Brejski of Assumption Church in Black Rock in which the members of Chopin sang. The Mass was followed by speeches from Dr. John Adamkiewicz, the Polish Consul General of Ottawa, Chester Mrozowski, National Secretary of the Polish Army Veterans Association, and Elizabeth Asher. During the war, Asher became known as the "mother of the Polish Army" since she cared for the ill soldiers at the camp and retained the title after becoming the caretaker of the

---

51 "Singers Plan Dance." *Buffalo Evening News*, 23 Dec. 1932, p. 15.
52 "Arion Singing Circle Holds Card Party, Entertainment." Evening News, 16 Apr. 1933.
53 "Tribute Director." Evening News, 28 Mar. 1933, p. 3.
54 Swan, Mary B. "Music." *Buffalo Courier-Express*, 16 Apr. 1933, p. 8.
55 Swan, Mary B. "Music." *Buffalo Courier-Express*, 21 May 1933, p. 8.
56 "Plewacki Post Plans Services to Honor Dead." *Buffalo Courier-Express*, 26 May 1933, p. 5.

cemetery. Dr. Fronczak, Buffalo's Health Commissioner and a friend of General Haller who worked closely with him during the Great War also spoke.[57]

The back half of the year saw Chopins in two major performances, one as part of the silver jubilee of the Polish Literary Circle[58] and the second in a dual concert with the Polish Singing Circle at the Albright Art Gallery.[59] The concert for the Literary Circle was part of a day that included the retelling of how the circle was formed at Fosdick-Masten Park High School. Addresses by Dr. Mieczyslaw Marchlewski, the Polish Consul General in New York, and Prof. Stanislaus Galazka of the Polish Ministry of Education were also given, and a formal ball held at the Polish Union Hall ended the day. The concert with the Singing Circle was part of the opening of the Polish exhibition at the Art Gallery on December 8. The members of Chopin ended their year with a Christmas party in their clubrooms, hosted by the Ladies Auxiliary.[60]

As the Depression dragged on, the next few years would be light in programming for the Society. Still, the year 1934 would be a banner one for Chopins. Locally it was their 35th anniversary celebration while nationally the Society made a major move as they decided to rejoin the Polish Singers Alliance after an absence.

One of the few shows the group did put on that year was a late winter concert with the Buffalo Community Orchestra at the Elmwood Music Hall. As part the February evening's *Polish Night,* Chopins sang, as violinist Jan Pawel Wolanek serenaded the audience with an instrument crafted by Giuseppe Guarneri.[61] In the same month the Society was feted at a 35th birthday party held for them at St. John Kanty Lyceum. Father Kasprzak and Dr. Fronczak were the principal speakers and the thousands in attendance were entertained by choirs including Moniuszko, Kalina, Fredro, Lutnia Singing Society of Lackawanna, Echo of Niagara Falls, Arion of North Tonawanda.

Two weeks after their Easter Monday party the members of Chopin hosted their own 35th anniversary celebration.[62] Held at

---

[57] "Poles Who Fought for Haller Lauded." *Buffalo Evening News*, 26 June 1933, p. 5.

[58] "Polish Literary Unit Here Lauded by Consul General." *Buffalo Evening News*, 23 Oct. 1933, p. 26.

[59] "Exhibition of Polish Art Draws Throngs to Gallery." *Buffalo Courier-Express*, 9 Dec. 1933, p. 20.

[60] "The Daily Calendar." *Buffalo Evening News*, 26 Dec. 1933, p. 25.

[61] "Chopin Singing Society to Appear in Concert." *Buffalo Evening News*, 14 Feb. 1934, p. 25.

[62] "Events Monday." *Buffalo Evening News*, 2 Apr. 1934, p. 29.

Kanty's Lyceum the April 15 program listed songs by Katski, Zelenski, Gluzinski, and Paderewski in the program for the now 80 voice choir to sing.[63] The soloists for the evening were Anthony Witkowski and Mieczyslaw Seidel. Soprano Marja Bogucka and pianist Zygmunt Stojowski were the special guests.[64] All the performers won praise for the concert with Bogucka and Stojowski receiving particular recognition.[65] Chopin would return to the Lyceum for a third time a month later as part of General Jozef Haller's 1934 American tour.[66]

The 35th season of Chopin would come to an end on November 4 with a final appearance at the Lyceum. The special guest for the night was Andrew Waclawski, a violinist and faculty member of the Toronto Conservatory of Music.[67] Performing a mix of Polish folk songs, some of Chopin's works, and a couple of English songs, the choir ended the year on a high note and much acclaim.[68]

With Krysztafkiewicz returning as president, the Society maintained their low-key singing schedule while still engaging in social and civic activities. They started their year with an early February fish fry for the public in their Broadway clubroom with plenty of entertainment.[69] One of the hot topics of discussion that evening was the community's effort to have the proposed Kleinhans Music Hall built in Humboldt Park. The Board of Chopin sent a petition along with the German Broadcasting Club, the Rainbow Dramatic and Singing Society, Maennerchor Bavaria, the Buffalo German Athletic Club, and the Polish Singing Circle to the Buffalo Common Council in favor of the site. In time the park would be passed over for a lower West Side location[70].

As they had been trending in years past, Chopins' biggest show of 1935 was their annual concert. Held again at the Kanty Lyceum, Choir Master Cornelissen guided the singers through several works including those of Pierre Luboshutz, Leo Delibes, and Teresa del

---

63 "Chopin Chorus to Sing." *Buffalo Evening News*, 7 Apr. 1934, p. 4.
64 Swan, Mary B. "Music." Buffalo Courier Express, 8 Apr. 1934, p. 7.
65 "Polish Singing Society Notes 35th Birthday." *Buffalo Courier-Express*, 16 Apr. 1934, p. 16.
66 "Buffalo Welcomes General Haller, Polish Hero of World War." *Buffalo Evening News*, 4 May 1934, p. 9.
67 "Jagel Is Monday's Soloist." *Buffalo Evening News*, 3 Nov. 1934, p. 3.
68 Durney, Edward. "Chopin Society Gives Concert." *Buffalo Evening News*, 5 Nov. 1934, p. 6.
69 "Chopin Singing Society to Hold Fish Fry Tonight." *Buffalo Evening News*, 2 Feb. 1935, p. [illegible].
70 "To Receive Petitions." *Buffalo Courier-Express*, 19 Mar. 1935, p. 22.

Riego.[71] The special guests of the evening were the Buffalo Mixed Quartet who gave renditions of the old English poems, "Good Ale" and "Phyllida and Corydon." M. Gurbacki, A Witkowski, E. Gertz and D. Crosson each gave solo performances all of which earned rave reviews.[72]

As plans for the Music Hall were being finished up, an effort to permanently establish the Buffalo Philharmonic Orchestra was being undertaken by Mrs. Florence B. Wendt. Many in Western New York's Polonia served on the 1936 fundraising committee, including president Krysztafkiewicz on behalf of the Chopin Singing Society.[73]

For the annual concert that year soprano Marie Obarska Wright of Chicago and baritone Edward M. Gertz served as soloists, while the 60 voices of the choir sang works from Kotarbinski, Chopin, and Niewiadomski. Cornelissen also used the occasion to premiere one of his own works, "Sea Fever,"[74] to the audience of 2,000.[75] The last public appearance of the year for the members of Chopin was as part of a special presentation on Henry Sienkiewicz. Hosted by the Federation of Polish-American Youth Clubs, the evening also saw the club's president Joseph Janaczek and Dr. Arthur Prudden Coleman professor of Slavonic languages at Columbia University take to the podium and the St. Stanislaus parish choir take to the stage. The Perla Dramatic Circle also presented a tableau in honor of the great author.[76]

For their final private event of the year, the members held a testimonial dinner for Zdzislaw Krysztafkiewicz on his twelfth election to the post of president. Krysztafkiewicz was celebrated not just for his leadership of the Society but for his role as chairman of the Polish Singers Alliance, Western New York Circuit, and his work for Polish music across the nation.[77] The Allied Musical and Singing Organizations of Warsaw also entrusted Dr. Fronczak to present Zdzislaw a medal and diploma on their behalf.[78]

---

[71] Swan, Mary B. "Music." *Buffalo Courier-Express*, 28 Apr. 1935, p. 4.

[72] Durney, Edward. "Chopin Society Offers Program." *Buffalo Evening News*, 29 Apr. 1935, p. 6.

[73] "Campaign For Orchestra to Be Citywide." *Buffalo Courier-Express*, 21 Feb. 1936, p. 13.

[74] Swan, Mary B. "Music." *Buffalo Courier-Express*, 12 Apr. 1936, pp. 9–11.

[75] "Chopin Singing Society Gives Pleasing Concert." *Buffalo Evening News*, 20 Apr. 1936, p. 23.

[76] Pawelek, Anne. "Visit To U.S. Inspiration to Polish Author." *Buffalo Courier-Express*, 14 Dec. 1936, p. 6.

[77] "Head of Chopin Singing Society to be Honored." *Buffalo Courier-Express*, 22 Nov. 1936, pp. W-5.

[78] "Chopin Society Pays Tribute to President." *Buffalo Courier-Express*, 21 Dec. 1936, p. 9.

Chopins had a slightly more robust year in 1937, taking part in the Centennial Celebration of Music in Buffalo Public Schools, their own annual concert, an outing to Liberty Park, and the Polish Singers Alliance of America competition in Chicago. The annual concert was again held at St. John Kanty that spring. Described as a well-balanced performance of both Polish and English music, Cornelissen won praise for his careful guidance of the singers.[79] The show opened with "Polonaise Militaire" by Chopin and included "Walery Stys Wez Konia Do Stajni" by Jotejko, while closing the show with Yourman's "Without a Song" and Mattei's "Non E Ver" in Italian. The special guests of the evening were Lydja Korecka, a mezzo-soprano who rose to fame at the Chicago Opera and New York City tenor Sigmund B. Swierzynski with the entire affair concluding with a dance in the parish lyceum.[80]

For the centennial celebration, the choir participated in the Male Chorus Festival on the second night of the event at the Elmwood Music Hall. Besides the Chopin singers, the dozen choir lineup included the Hornell Male Chorus, the Rochester Orpheus, and Guido Chorus. For their set the Polish singers reprised their performance of "Walery Stys Wez Konia Do Stajni" from their annual concert and followed it up with "Chlop Se Jestem Z Ojca Dziada" to an enthusiastic and packed house. [81] To close out the first half of the year, the men traveled to Chicago to take part in the 25th national convention of the Polish Singers Alliance of America. Over three days of fierce competition, the members of Chopin took home second prize with a rendition of Waclaw Lachman's "Klechda."[82]

The Society opened the second half of the year with their annual picnic and music festival at Liberty Park.[83] They followed their outing by hosting the summer meeting of Circuit 9 of the Polish National Singers Alliance in the clubrooms.[84] The latter part of the year also saw them playing an important role in that year's local elections. In June, Mayor Zimmermann appointed member Michael E. Zimmer to the city court bench, making Zimmer the first Polish American

79 Boris, Theodolinda C. "Chopin Singers Score in Convert Program." *Buffalo Evening News*, 5 Apr. 1937, p. 6.
80 "Swieto Piesni Polskiej Choru Chopina." *Dziennik Dla Wszystkich*, 3 Apr. 1937, p. 12.
81 "Centennial Festival Concerts." *Buffalo Courier-Express*, 11 Apr. 1937, pp. 9–11.; "Three Groups Of 1,000 Each Engage in Song." *Buffalo Courier-Express*, 13 Apr. 1937, p. 7.
82 "Music." *Buffalo Courier-Express*, 24 Apr. 1938, p. 11.
83 "Events Sunday." *Buffalo Evening News*, 17 July 1937.
84 "Arion Singing Soc. Not to Meet Tonight." The Evening News, 24 Aug. 1937, p. 9.

judge of the Queen City.[85] In October, mayoral candidate Thomas L. Holling stopped by the clubrooms to drum up much needed support from the Polish community.[86] Members Joseph Pesta and Joseph Mruk also looked to their fellow members to ensure their successes in running for the Supervisor in the 9th Ward and Walden District councilman respectively.[87] When all the votes were counted that November, the members delivered a victory to Holling and Mruk, while Pesta fell short.[88]

With a trophy in hand from the previous year's national competition, the men of Chopin knew what Arnold would choose as the highlight for the April 1938 annual concert, none other than their award winning rendition of Lachman's '"Klechda."[89] Cornelissen filled out the rest of the program with "Piosnka o Belinie" by Zyczkowski, "The Hills of Home" by Fox, and Handel's "Hallelujah."[90] The special guests that evening were local sopranos Helena Januszcak and Regina Cieslinska-Wieklinski while Frances Engel Messersmith served as the accompanist.[91]

On June 5 the Junior Chamber of Commerce sponsored a civic concert at the still new Roesch Memorial Stadium on Dodge Street. Of the 500 voices participating in the event, 70 of them were from the members of Chopin.[92] Joining the Bavarian Singers, the Guido Chorus, the Jackson Glee Club, the Moniuszko Singing Society, the Operetta Group, the Orpheus Club, the Polish Singing Circle, the Shrine Chanters, and United German Singing Society, the combined choir entertained an estimated crowd of 25,000 that day.[93] The Society would close out the year with their elections which would see Zdzislaw F. Krysztafkiewicz run for and win the presidency one final time.

Nineteen thirty-nine would be a year seared onto the heart of

---

85 "Mayor Appoints Zimmer Judge of City Court to Fill Vacancy." *Buffalo Courier-Express*, 14 June 1937, p. 13.
86 "Holling Lays Stress on His Independence." *Buffalo Courier-Express*, 25 Oct. 1937, p. 22.
87 "Candidates on Parade." *Buffalo Evening News*, 15 Oct. 1937, p. 21.; "Candidates on Parade." *Buffalo Evening News*, 23 Oct. 1937, p. 18.
88 "Tabulation Shows Results for Supervisors by Wards and Towns." *Buffalo Evening News*, 3 Nov. 1937, p. 17.
89 Boris, Theodolinda C. "Lachman Number Features Concert." *Buffalo Evening News*, 25 Apr. 1938, p. 22.
90 "Music." *Buffalo Courier-Express*, 24 Apr. 1928, p. 11.
91 Evans, Isabelle Workman. "Music Review." *Buffalo Courier-Express*, 25 Apr. 1938, p. 4.
92 "Chorus Of 500 To Be Heard at Civic Festival." *Buffalo Courier-Express*, 3 May 1938, p. 7.
93 "Music Festival Likely to Draw 25,000 Persons." *Buffalo Courier-Express*, 15 May 1938, p. 3.

not only Chopins, but Poland and Polonia as a whole. It would have its triumphs and sorrows and be the prelude to a decade of struggle for Buffalo and the nation. The year started out simply enough for the members of the Society with the planning of their 40th anniversary concert, member Stanley Zacharyasz being installed as the new president of the Ninth Circuit of the Polish Singers' Alliance,[94] and a cohort of singers traveling down to Lackawanna to fete retiring Lutnia president, Ira Sobczak.[95] After months of practicing, the singers were ready for their mid-April annual concert at Kanty's Lyceum. With a selection that consisted of Lorenz's "Hej Dalej na Wode," Prosnak's "Niewierny," Bartholomew's "Black Eyed Susie," and their conductors' own musical work "Drinking Song," the men were sure it would be a night to remember. [96] The highlight for all present that evening was the return of former member Edward Gertz from New York City with three years of training as a baritone under his belt,[97] but it would be the solo debut of little Genia Jakubczak that would make history that night,[98]

Genia Jakubczak (Las) was just turning 13 when she took the stage at St John Kanty as soloist at the Chopin Concert, but she already had a lifetime of experience as an entertainer and singer.[99] The daughter of John and Julia Jakubczak, Genia grew up in the family bakery at 1266 Sycamore and their stand in the Broadway Market.[100] As a student at Villa Maria Academy, the professional ear of her music teacher could hear the potential of the young Jakubczak. With her teacher's encouragement Genia came under the tutelage of Charles Morati. Before her formal voice lessons started, Jakubczak had a small role in American film history. In 1938, director Alvin Wyckoff traveled to Buffalo to film *The Peasant's Wedding* or *Wiejskie Wesele*. In this first color, Polish language film in America, Miss Jakubczak earned a screen credit as "girl soloist."[101] While never seeing wide distribution,

---

94 "Singers' Alliance Installs Officers." *The North Tonawanda Evening News*, 10 Mar. 1939, p. 6.

95 "Lutnia Honors Retiring President with Banquet." *The Lackawanna Herald*, 23 Mar. 1939, p. 1.

96 Boris, Theodolinda C. "Song Programs Offer a Music-Filled Week." *Buffalo Evening News*, 15 Apr. 1939, p. 3.

97 "Music." *Buffalo Courier-Express*, 9 Apr. 1939, p. 4.

98 "Music." *Buffalo Courier-Express*, 9 Apr. 1939, p. 4.

99 Oron, Aryeh. "Genia Las (Soprano, Mezzo-Soprano)." *Genia Las (Soprano, Mezzo-Soprano) - Short Biography*, Bach Cantatas Website, Sept. 2019, www.bach-cantatas.com/Bio/Las-Genia.htm.

100 "Mrs. John Jakubczak." *Buffalo Courier-Express*, 8 June 1957, p. 9.

101 "Film Produced on East Side Given Preview." *Buffalo Courier-Express*, 19 Feb. 1939, p. 2.

the *New York Times* was able to see a screening of the Polish Pictures Company production at St. Mark's Theatre saying, the film "while not outstanding from the technical side, is pleasant and interesting for students of foreign customs."[102]

Shortly before the release of the film Genia would make her first public performance as part of a quartet with Morati, Evelyn Muszynski, and Charles Napper at a March 1939 concert sponsored by the Buffalo Orpheus.[103] On April 16, the future Ms. Las made her solo debut as a coloratura soprano at the 40th Anniversary concert of the Chopin Singing Society where she sang "Una Voce Poco Fa" from Rossini's *The Barber of Seville* and Moniuszko's "Dumka Zosi" from *Flis.*[104] This would be the start of a long and illustrious career seeing Las sing with the Toronto Symphony Orchestra, Detroit Symphony Orchestra, and the Chicago Symphony Orchestra. She would go on to make her operatic debut in Georges Bizet's *Carmen* with the New York City Opera and in Europe she rehearsed with Maria Callas who called her "very good," an exceedingly high compliment from the notorious diva. By the time of her death in 2018, Las had performed in 87 operas, including 18 premieres, and recorded for RCA Victor and NBC.[105]

Not to be completely overshadowed by Las, Gertz would also go on to have a successful musical career. Using the stage name Eddie Michaels, Gertz would perform on Broadway, sing for the Army during the Second World War, play the Florida nightclub circuit, and in the 1960s be the resident singer on several Caribbean cruises.[106]

In her review of the Chopins' 40th anniversary concert, Ms. Workman-Evans of the *Courier-Express* praised Cornelissen and the 63 singers of Chopin, but she simply glowed about the young Genia saying:

> One of the highlights of the evening was the appearance of the thirteen-year-old soprano. Genia Jakubczak. This talented young singer has been endowed with a lovely voice which if nurtured carefully and trained properly should carry her to a

---

[102] "The Screen; At the St. Mark's Theatre." *New York Times*, 19 Apr. 1939.
[103] "Music." *Buffalo Courier-Express*, 19 Mar. 1939, p. 7.
[104] "Music." *Buffalo Courier-Express*, 9 Apr. 1939, p. 4.
[105] Oron, Aryeh. "Genia Las (Soprano, Mezzo-Soprano)." *Genia Las (Soprano, Mezzo-Soprano) - Short Biography*, Bach Cantatas Website, Sept. 2019, www.bach-cantatas.com/Bio/Las-Genia.htm.
[106] Staff. "Edward Gertz, Singer in New York, Florida." *Buffalo News*, 23 Feb. 1989,

> brilliant career. It was gratifying to hear that this charming girl is not forcing her voice, which although still immature is of lovely quality. Her natural musicianship and temperament made her offerings...extremely enjoyable. Miss. Jakubczak responded generously to the enthusiastic applause.[107]

In the month following their show, the men of Chopin joined with the women of Kalina to take part in a celebration marking both the 148th anniversary of Poland's first constitution and the fourth anniversary of the death of Marshal Pilsudski. Held under the auspices Council 19 of the Polish National Alliance, the day saw a special Mass at St. Luke Church, a service that also marked the 35th anniversary of Father Fimowicz as head of the Sycamore Street parish. The Mass was followed by a parade, and an afternoon full of speakers and presenters at the Dom Polski.[108] The singers listened intently as Dr. Louis Krzyzanowski the Polish Consulate General in New York, spoke of the imposing threat of Hitler saying, "Col. Jozef Beck told the entire world how Poland feels about Hitler's threats, which are a menace to peace. Poland cannot be compared to Czechoslovakia, because Poland, not an aggressor, will not surrender an inch of her territory. Poland has revealed to the world she is ready to carry on the campaign to 'Stop Hitler.'"[109] Krzyzanowski then went on to say how the departed marshal foresaw Hitler's rise and tried to preserve Poland when he, "called upon England and France to weigh the coming Hitler menace, but as neither of the two countries failed to recognize Pilsudski's warnings, Poland signed a non-aggression pact with Germany in 1934. Pilsudski's foresight of Hitler's policies in an attempt to absorb one country after another was not recognized by other European' powers." He closed his comments saying, "Poland will take up arms only as the last resort."[110]

With civic zeal, the members of Chopin's joined in the Plewacki Post's Flag Day celebration at the Civic Stadium as one of their musical guests.[111] Their day started with an enjoyable parade down Best Street from Humboldt Park to the stadium with 110 other

---

[107] Evans, Isabelle Workman. "Music Review." *Buffalo Courier-Express*, 17 Apr. 1939, p. 16.
[108] "Buffalo Poles Will Observe Historic Dates." *Buffalo Courier-Express*, 7 May 1939, p. 5.
[109] "Poland Won't Give Inch, Consular Official Says." *Buffalo Evening News*, 8 May 1939, p. 27.
[110] ibid
[111] "41 Groups to Take Part in Flag Day Exercises." *Buffalo Evening News*, 19 May 1939, p. 33.

military and civic organizations and concluded with their performances in front of a packed audience.[112] The choir would have one last fine time that summer as they held their annual picnic with hundreds of their closest friends at Genesee Park.[113] As the sun was setting that July evening the throngs of members enjoying ice cream, playing games, and singing a few songs, had little idea what was in store for them and their homeland.

Gdansk was fast asleep in the newborn hours of the first day of September. The weather was warm, and the weekend was only one day away. While the Nazis had been posturing for months, no one gave the ceremonial *SMS Schleswig-Holstein* anchored in Gdansk's harbor much thought. The relic of the Great War could never pose any real threat to the Free City and wasn't worth noticing. So, no one noticed the guns turning at 4:44 AM, training its sights on the depot at Westerplatte. But a minute later the entire world heard as the cannons ripped and the first blood of Poland was drawn. In a few hours German and Slovak ground troops would cross the border, followed by their Russian counterparts 16 days later.

Within a week of the opening salvo, Chopins, along with Lackawanna Mayor John A. Aszkler, Father Alexander Pitass, the Polish Women's Alliance, and other organizations of Polonia called upon President Roosevelt and Congress to rescind the Neutrality Acts that prevented America from coming to Poland's aid. While pledging their loyalty to the U.S., the group began fundraising for the Red Cross for the relief of Polish noncombatants.[114]

As Warsaw surrendered and the idea of Poland being an occupied nation again seeped into the nation's consciousness, Polonia began holding events again in hopes of cheering themselves up. The Lirnik Singing Society of Black Rock held their annual concert that October and invited Chopin as their guest choir. Under the baton of Lirnik music director Joseph A. Raszeja, the men sang a few traditional Polish folk songs but closed their set with an energetic version of Will Glahe's "Beer Barrel Polka."[115]

The men of Chopin would have their own celebration in recognition of their 40th birthday shortly thereafter. The affair with 1,500 in attendance didn't see the entire singing body take the stage of the

---

[112] "Parade to Climax Flag Day Celebration." *Buffalo Evening News*, 9 June 1939, p. 33.
[113] "Singing Society Attends Picnic." *Buffalo Courier-Express*, 3 July 1939, p. 9.
[114] "Local Poles Pledge Loyalty to America." *Buffalo Evening News*, 8 Sept. 1939, p. 43.
[115] "Concert to Feature Polish Folk Songs." *Buffalo Evening News*, 7 Oct. 1939, p. 12.

Lyceum, but did have a few quartets entertain, Miss Jean Radde as the headline, and Mr. Stephen Mikolajczak acting as the master of ceremonies to keep the evening moving along.[116]

On New Year's Eve the members and friends of Chopin packed into their hall to cheer out their 40th anniversary year and rang in 1940. The group hoped that the next decade would be better than the last.[117] They prayed that President Boleslaus Lemanski would guide them well and that there would be peace in Europe, even if it meant American intervention.[118]

---

116 "Anniversary Noted." *Buffalo Evening News*, 23 Oct. 1939, p. 22.

117 "Noisy Welcome Given 1940 At East Buffalo Parties." *Buffalo Evening News*, 2 Jan. 1940, p. 24.

118 "Society to Have Ball." *Buffalo Courier-Express*, 17 Nov. 1939, p. 9.

Chapter 5

War and Peace

With Poland occupied, war fever rising, and the lingering effect of the Great Depression still hanging in the air, the singers of Chopin prayed that Boleslaus Lemanski returning to the presidency would be the rudder they needed to guide them through the uncertain times.

The year of 1940 opened with the election of the Ladies Auxiliary, which saw Mrs. Mae Mazikowski as president and Anna Borkowski, Helen Urbanski, and Josephine Kujawa ascend to other leadership positions.[1] As relief for Poland continued into the New Year, President Lemanski joined the benefit committee sponsoring a performance of *Our Town* at the Erlanger Theater. The money raised at the January 25 show went to support the American Red Cross Polish and Finnish Relief Fund.[2] For their part, the Ladies Auxiliary held a fundraiser and card party in preparation for Lent with hundreds of members and their friends attending.[3]

The dominating event of the year was the Polish Singers Alliance of America District Nine January concert. Planning began in earnest in October of 1939 after the singers of Kalina, Chopin, Fredro, Lirnik, Echo, Lutnia, and Arion announced that the convention and mass concert would be held at the Broadway Auditorium in the upcoming year.[4] The groups also agreed that the money from the show would also go towards the Polish relief fund.[5] As representatives to the convention, the members of Chopin chose, Zdzislaw Krysztafkiewicz, Victor B. Jakubowski, Julian Kowalewski, Bernard Drews, Bronislaus Cholewka, Sigmund Ploch, Henry Kolber, and President Lemanski.[6] On the day of the event, 350 singers arrived at the auditorium ready to sing. The men of Chopin gave a rendition of L. Lewandowski's

---

[1] "Chopin Society Auxiliary Installs Officers." *Buffalo Evening News*, 4 Jan. 1940.
[2] "Benefit Show Aides Chosen." *Buffalo Courier-Express*, 11 Jan. 1940, p. 8.
[3] "Chopin Singers to Hold Card Party Feb. 4." *Buffalo Evening News*, 19 Jan. 1940, p. 33.
[4] "Circuit Concert." *Buffalo Evening News*, 13 Oct. 1939, p. 34.
[5] "Benefit Concert." *Buffalo Evening News*, 26 Jan. 1940, p. 31.
[6] "Convention Delegates Names by Chopin Society." *Buffalo Evening News*, 22 Jan. 1940, p. 21.

"Mazur," before joining the other groups to sing Paderewski's "Minuet" and "Sztandary Polskle W Kremlu" under the direction of Matthew Zydowicz.[7] Many at that concert would travel east in May to the Ninth National Convention of the Polish Singers Alliance of America held in Utica, NY. After a fierce weekend of competition, the 200 voices of Chopins brought home the silver cup in the male choir category.[8]

Before their annual concert in March, the members of Chopin took part in a lecture to raise awareness of what was happening in Poland. Held under the auspices of the Buffalo Council of the Knights of Columbus, Reverend Timothy J. Coughlin, S. J., president of Canisius High School and rector of St. Michael Church gave a presentation on the history and state of Poland as of early February. As part of his talk, Father Coughlin invited the Society to sing a few traditional Polish songs.[9]

Planning for the March 31 annual concert began in the winter with auditions for soloists underway by the start of Lent. [10] Of the dozens that applied, soprano Dorothy Lachajczyk and pianist Jeno Swislowski were the two selected for the evening show. At the Kanty Lyceum show the 200 voices of Chopin performed works by M. Kotarbinski, Lewandowski, and F. Rylinga which "won prolonged applause from the listeners."[11] A week after the annual concert, the men of Chopin were onstage again, this time at the Polish Union Hall to perform for General Jozef Haller and 500 guests. The former leader of the Polish Blue Army was touring the States on behalf of Polish interests, while looking for the moral and spiritual support of the American people.[12]

The members of Chopin would be guests again of the Polish Union of America, this time as celebrants of the Union's 50th anniversary. Many of the members attended the birthday party held at Liberty Park that August, while others marched in a parade around Polonia as

---

7 "Six Choirs Heard in Benefit Concert." *Buffalo Evening News*, 26 Jan. 1940, p. 6.
8 "Buffalo Choirs Win Prizes." *Buffalo Courier-Express*, 28 May 1940, p. 28.
9 "K. of C. to Hear Lecture Series." *Buffalo Courier-Express*, 8 Feb. 1940, p. 19.
10 "Chopin Society Directors Make Plans for Concert." *Buffalo Evening News*, 16 Jan. 1940, p. 23.; "Local Talent to Perform at Chopin Society Concert." *Buffalo Evening News*, 30 Jan. 1940, p. 19.
11 Boris, Theodolinda C. "Chopin Singers Excel in Descriptive Songs." *Buffalo Evening News*, 1 Apr. 1940, p. 4.
12 "Gen. Haller Says Nazis Plan to Wipe Out Poles as a Race." *Buffalo Courier-Express*, 8 Apr. 1940, p. 24.

part of the celebration.[13]

As the year ended more men were looking at ways to join the international military services to fight for the freedom of Poland. In support of their efforts, the members of Chopin passed a resolution exempting those in military services from paying their membership dues.[14]

January of 1941 saw Stanislaus Jendrasiak return to the role of president at Chopin. As the choir settled into the New Year, auditions for the annual concert's special guest performers were soon underway. For three hours Dr. Royal Paxton, Dr. Jules Nowotny, Mrs. Marie Wright, Mrs. Bruno S. Linetty, Arnold Cornelissen and E. Krystaf listened to over a dozen performers from across Western New York show off their talents.[15] After much deliberation the committee finally chose Elaine Majchrzak, soprano, of Stewart Avenue; violinist Carl P. Barabaas of Liddell Street; and pianist Eugenia Plewinska of North Tonawanda as the guest performers for their 42nd annual concert.[16] At the April 30 show at the St. John Kanty Lyceum, under the direction of Arnold Cornelissen, the 74 singers went through works by Bursa, Lachman, and Jan Gall.[17] The review from the *Buffalo Evening News* stated "Characteristic of the chorus' singing were the sharp and sudden contrasts between loud and soft, thus making the interpretations very dramatic. There was good tonal quality with little forcing of the tone, however, even in the most vigorous passages."[18]

But before the members of Chopin could stage their annual show, they had two other noteworthy performances and were visited by a special guest. The first show was a February concert of District 9, Polish Singers Alliance of America in which they sang a couple of songs and the second was a short musical program for the Most Reverend Francis C. Kelley, bishop of the Diocese of Tulsa and Oklahoma City.[19] In March the Society hosted the colorful, Captain Eustazy

---

[13] "4,000 Attend Polish Union's Outing in Park." *Buffalo Courier-Express*, 5 Apr. 1940, p. 22.
[14] *Towarzystwo Śpiewu Fryderyka Chopina 1899-1949*. Tow. Śpiewu Fryderyka Chopina, 1949.
[15] "Chopin Society Holds Audition for Aspirants." *Buffalo Courier-Express*, 29 Jan. 1941, p. 6.
[16] Evans, Isabelle Workman. "Music." *Buffalo Courier-Express*, 20 Apr. 1941, p. 12.
[17] Evans, Isabelle Workman. "Music Review." *Buffalo Courier-Express*, p. 5.; Boris, Theodolinda C. "Choir Festivals Are Lauded." *Buffalo Evening News*, 19 Apr. 1941, p. 9.
[18] "Chopin Singers Give 42d Annual Concert." *Buffalo Evening News*, 21 Apr. 1941, p. 15.
[19] "Choirs' Concert Gives Example of Polish Unity." *Buffalo Evening News*, 3 Feb. 1941, p. 20.; "Bishop Urges Use of Charity to Balk Chaos." *Buffalo Courier-Express*, 11 Mar. 1941, p. 7.

Borkowski of MS *Batory* fame. The self-created legend was touring and lecturing across the U.S. in support of Polish relief, landing in the Queen City where Chopins hosted his arrival ceremony in their clubrooms.[20]

The Society kept the rest of their year relatively light. They sang the national anthems at the annual memorial service to the Blue Army soldiers buried at Niagara-On-The-Lake while also taking part in the Good-Neighbor Festival at Buffalo's Civic Stadium.[21] One of their last performances of the year was an impromptu concert held for mayoral hopeful William P. Fisher. Taking to the streets of the East Side the men belted out the campaign song "Fisher Will Shine To-night" as the candidate arrived to address the choir that October.[22]

Despite the support of Chopins, Fisher did not become mayor. The election instead went to Democrat Joseph J. Kelly. But before Kelly could even warm the seat in his office, Japanese submarines and planes attacked Pearl Harbor, thrusting America into the global conflict. As the U.S. formally entered the Second World War, Jendrasiak was once again elected to the presidency of Chopin.

With the New Year dawning, the members of Chopin said goodbye to an old friend with a memorial service for their former music director Seth Clark. Succumbing to a long illness in June of 1941, the family decided to have Clark's celebration of life at the end of winter. Joining the Guido Chorus at Trinity Episcopal, the members of Chopin sang a special remembrance to their former director under the hand of Cornelissen.

With America's entrance into World War II, Chopins and other Polish choirs greatly curtailed their schedules. The choir took much of the year off, except for participating in the Singers Alliance concert, a Polish Constitution Day celebration, and their own annual concert on April 12.[23] For the year's set, Cornelissen mixed Polish folk songs with Gregorian melodies, Dutch hymns, and some English selections for rousing performances. Opening with the national anthems of both Poland and America, the show was described as "...excellent in contrast and communicativeness. The spirited, humorous Krakowiak, for

---

20 "$2000 Donation Swells Area's Polish Relief Fund to $61,936.48." *Buffalo Evening News*, 22 Mar. 1941, p. 16.

21 "Field Mass Honors Patriots Who Died in Flu Epidemic." *Buffalo Evening News*, 16 June 1941, p. 15.; "Choruses to Unite at Stadium Party." *Buffalo Evening News*, 3 Jan. 1941, p. 4.

22 "Defense Program His First Concern, Fisher Points Out." *Buffalo Evening News*, 25 Oct. 1941, p. 3.

23 "Polish Singers Win Praise." *Buffalo Evening News*, 26 Jan. 1942, p. 19.

which Max Gurbacki sang the incidental solo, roused the audience to such a pitch of enthusiasm that even when it was sung for a second time the applause broke out before the final chord." The special guest performers that year were the youthful Adele Jarembek, mezzo-soprano, and 18-year-old Raymond Fabiniak, tenor.[24]

Under the guidance of newly elected president Reverend Joseph Winnicki, the choirs truncated their shows again in 1943 to a mere handful. The first was the annual concert held on May 2 while the second was held in the fall. In lieu of having guest soloists that year, the Chopinites felt it better to bring in two other choirs as special performers. The Canisius College Glee Club and the Guido Chorus joined Chopins at St. John Kanty Lyceum and gave a rousing performance. The boys of the Glee Club sang "Gospodi Pomiluj" and service songs while Chopins focused on Polish folk songs and the Guidos sang a medley of works.[25] The big surprise of the night was when Bulgarian baritone Ivan Petroff took the stage and sang a selection of operatic works ranging from Rossini to Martini.[26]

The second appearance of the singers that year would be at the Polish Union Hall as part of a mass rally recognizing the fourth anniversary of the Nazi invasion of Poland. Chopins provided musical entertainment between speakers praising American involvement in the war and others calling for a post conflict peace-enforcing agency.[27] As the year closed out, the members of the Society held a grand celebration as one of their own, Joseph Mruk, was sent to Congress representing the 41st District of New York.

In his second year as president, Father Winnicki began scouting out possible locations and holding light negotiations with the hopes of purchasing a new clubhouse for the Society, rather than renting. The old Postal Station F at 681 Fillmore Avenue was proposed as the new location, but the members decided that the cost of the old station was too great and would leave their coffers bare. This would be an unenviable position to be in, considering that their ranks were diminishing as many young men were entering military service. Since they chose not

---

[24] Boris, Theodolinda C. "Folk Songs Delight Audience." *Buffalo Evening News*, 13 Apr. 1942, p. 4.

[25] "Glee Clubbers Add Voices to Joint Concert." *The Griffin*, 14 May 1943, p. 1.; Evans, Isabelle Workman. "Music World." *Buffalo Courier-Express*, 25 Apr. 1943, p. 10.

[26] Boris, Theodolinda C. "Two Guest Choruses Appear at Chopin Society's Concert." *Buffalo Evening News*, 3 May 1943, p. 10.

[27] "Poles Here Demand Axis be Punished for Crimes." *Buffalo Courier-Express*, 4 Oct. 1943, p. 20.

to invest in real estate, the Society instead purchased a new $500 war bond, bringing their total holdings to $1,800.[28]

The singers of Chopin held a light schedule as the war raged. The 1944 annual concert was held at St. John Kanty with special performances by Canadian piano prodigy Marian Grudeff and Buffalo soprano Helen Wieczorek. In her review of the 45th annual concert Ms. Boris of the *Buffalo Evening News* was both praiseful and understandably forgiving when saying, "[t]he chorus, like all male choruses these days, sang with thinned ranks but, under Arnold Cornelissen's discipline and forceful directing, sang proficiently and with considerable finesse in matters of phrasing and dynamics."[29] The other noteworthy performance given that year marked another anniversary of the Nazi invasion of Poland. With a dwindling performance staff, almost 50 singers were serving in the Armed Forces,[30] the Society could only send a quartet to the Polish Central Council sponsored event.[31] The Society did send delegates to the Polish Singers Alliance of America 27th National Convention in Cleveland in May.

Returning to the presidency of Chopin in 1945, Boleslaus Lemanski and other prominent members of the Society laid a wreath at the Chopin monument in celebration of the composer's 135th birthday. The deep snow and frigid temperatures kept all but the most dedicated members of Polonia away from the brief ceremony led by Director Cornelissen.[32]

The weather was a little better that March as a handful of members from the choir performed in the Polonia Opera Company of New York's production of *Halka* at Kleinhans Music Hall.[33] Starring Ladis Kiepura and Barbara Darlys, the show was warmly received by both Polish and American audience members.[34]

As the war was entering its closing stage, the number of men available to sing was low, so the Society chose to again put all their

---

28 "Chopin Society Buys $500 Bond." *Buffalo Courier-Express*, 24 Jan. 1944, p. 7.
29 Boris, Theodolinda C. "Two Talented Soloists Presented by Society." *Buffalo Evening News*, 17 Apr. 1944, p. 16.
30 The Chopin Singing Society. *46th Annual Concert*. Chopin Singing Society, 1946.
31 "Strong Poland Seen Bulwark Against Wars." *Buffalo Courier-Express*, 18 Sept. 1944, p. 10.
32 "Tribute is Paid Polish Composer." *Buffalo Courier-Express*, 5 Feb. 1945, p. 17.
33 Boris, Theodolinda C. "Dorothy Maynor Will Include Four Favorite Spirituals." *Buffalo Evening News*, 27 Jan. 1945, p. 3.
34 Boris, Theodolinda C. "Polonia Opera's Melodious 'Halka' Applauded By 3000." *Buffalo Evening News*, 19 Mar. 1945, p. 4.

focus on the annual concert and ball, that year held on April 8.[35] Only nine works were performed by the choir and special guests Alma Kedzierska and Dorothy Nawrocka each sang a single song.[36]

Like the rest of the nation, members took to the streets to celebrate both Victory in Europe Day in the spring and the end of the war that summer. In autumn they took part in another celebration, the golden jubilee of the Adam Mickiewicz Library & Dramatic Circle by sending a delegation to the event. The group closed out the year by donating funds to several emerging organizations that helped the wounded returning from the war.[37] These vets began to sign up to singing societies across the city and country, adding 30 new names to Chopin's membership roster.

While the ranks filled, much of the previous leadership stayed the same in 1946. Lemanski was again chosen as president with Edward Kolber as vice president, Joseph Dulski as secretary, Vincent F. Widzinski treasurer, Felix F. Kulwicki as financial secretary, Stanley Zajac as librarian, Julian Kowalewski as marshal, and for choir chairman, Edward Halicki.[38] The increasing membership did cause some growing pains and the club brought in a few slot machines for the backroom as another revenue stream.[39]

As chair of the concert committee Joseph C. Nowak began planning for the annual show in late 1945. By March of 1946 he announced that the concert would be April 28 at St. John Kanty Lyceum with over 60 singers taking the stage.[40] Following the proclamation a handful of members traveled to North Tonawanda for the annual convention of the Polish Singers Alliance District 9.[41]

At the spring concert, the full chorus sang works by Kjerulf, Lachman, and Cornelissen. Both Raymond Fabiniak and Joseph Grabowski served as soloists while Austrian born operatic bass-

---

[35] Evans, Isabelle. "Thoughts About Music." *Buffalo Courier-Express*, 8 Apr. 1945, p. 4-D.

[36] Boris, Theodolinda C. "Draper, Adler Perform Tonight; Albeneri Trio on Monday." *Buffalo Evening News*, 7 Apr. 1945, p. 3.

[37] "Gift to Smokes Fund Tells Wounded Men You Remember." *Buffalo Evening News*, 27 Dec. 1945.

[38] Boris, Theodolinda C. "Francescatti, Solomon to Be Philharmonic Guests." *Buffalo Evening News*, 5 Jan. 1946, p. 3.

[39] "Witness Says Levitt Admitted Income From 16 Slot Machines." *Buffalo Evening News*, 21 Apr. 1954, p. 61.

[40] "Kantowski Joins Chopin Singing Society." *Buffalo Courier-Express*, 18 Mar. 1948, p. 11.

[41] "Polish Singers to be Guests of Arion Society March 31." *Tonawanda News*, 25 Mar. 1946, p. 4.

baritone, Rolf Telasko was the evening's special guest.[42] Theodolinda Boris, the reviewer for the *Buffalo Evening News* praised Telasko saying that his "rich dark-hued tones and his ability to project a song betokened an excellent musical background and a good understanding of the stylistic requirements of his solos." Miss Boris was so enamored by Telasko she even chided the Society for not doing more to promote him saying the "Society had made little advance fanfare about the guest soloist... it could very well have done a bit of boasting in anticipation of the appearance."[43]

Chopins followed up their 47th annual concert with a Memorial Day service in conjunction with the Adam Plewacki Post at St. Stanislaus Cemetery.[44] As part of the day, a quartet of members also performed at the unveiling of a portrait of Raymond P. Pawlowski, the first Buffalo service man killed in World War II at Pearl Harbor, at the Pawlowski Post Hall at 1015 Fillmore Ave.[45]

In October, President Lemanski made a declaration not heard in nearly a decade, the Chopin Singing Society would hold a fall concert. With 70 singers and Edward Gertz as the guest soloist, the announcement spread through Polonia like an electric current. The Society needed to fill Kanty's hall for the event as they were using it as a fundraiser for their 1947 trip to the Polish Singers Alliance national convention in New York City.[46] In a show that was a mix of Polish and English songs, the choir gave a zesty performance that energized the audience.[47] Gertz was noted for his warm and substantial textured voice.[48]

On February 22, 1947, the Chopin Singing Society suffered both a great spiritual and emotional loss with the passing of its founder Boleslaus Michalski.[49] While not an overly active member, and almost a half century since he led the organization, the death of Michalski meant the organization was ever creeping towards its second saeculum. As a tribute to their founder, the Society placed a wreath on

42 Boris, Theodolinda C. "Jazz, Chopin Society Concerts Head Week's Activities." *Buffalo Evening News*, 27 Apr. 1946, p. 3.
43 Boris, Theodolinda C. "Telasko's Singing Features Conceert of Chopin Society." *Buffalo Evening News*, 29 Apr. 1946, p. 12.
44 "Erie County Legionnaire." *Buffalo Evening News*, 22 May 1946, p. 18.
45 "Post Honors Pearl Harbor Attack Victim." *Buffalo Courier-Express*, 8 July 1946, p. 16.
46 "Singing Society to Give Concert." *Buffalo Courier-Express*, 31 Oct. 1946, p. 20.
47 Evans, Isabelle W. "Music Review." *Buffalo Courier-Express*, 21 Nov. 1946, p. 12.
48 Boris, Theodolinda C. "Gertz Is Acclaimed as Chopin Soloist." *Buffalo Evening News*, 21 Nov. 1946, p. 27.
49 "Boleslaus Michalski." *Buffalo Courier-Express*, 24 Feb. 1947, p. 18.

Michalski's coffin and served as an honor guard, escorting his remains during the funeral.

The Sunday following Easter saw the Society's annual concert held in front of an audience of 1,500.[50] In addition to the 64 singers on stage, Thaddeus Sztuka of Chicago served as guest vocalist for the night. The reviews of the show complimented Chopins for a particularly strong performance, a product of the group preparing for the annual concert as well as the Singers Alliance competition scheduled for the end of May.[51]

Just before June, a delegation of singers traveled east to New York for the 28th Convention of the Polish Singers Alliance. In the competition Chopins gave a command performance but fell short to Kolko Filaretro.[52] In the meeting portion of the convention the delegates signed on to a letter sent to Congress in support of helping 400,000 displaced persons from Poland move to America.[53]

As the members returned from Manhattan, the idea of owning their own building began to stir again. They realized that if they could find a building big enough, they could put their money where their mouth was and house a few displaced Poles themselves. Working with attorney Louis Pelowski the board of Chopin opened talks with the Methodist Deaconess Settlement House at 18 Kosciuszko about buying their building. The kindergarten with classrooms, meeting lounges, and a hall were perfect for the Society and what they had planned for the space.[54] After some intense negotiations the two organizations agreed on a price of $9,000. With the property secured, the members of Chopin began remodeling the premises. They added a bar, a library, practice areas, and unconventionally, apartments. These suites would become the most precious spaces in the building as they became filled with war ravaged Polish families settling in America.[55]

In early 1947 the Society took part in one of the biggest liturgical music events of the year, the dedication of a new organ at

---

[50] "Chopin Concert Attracts 1,500." *Buffalo Courier-Express*, 14 Apr. 1947, p. 4.

[51] Boris, Theodolinda C. "Polish and English Songs on Program of Chopin Singers." *Buffalo Evening News*, 14 Apr. 1947, p. 14.

[52] Blejwas, Stanislaus A. *The Polish Singers Alliance, 1888-1998: Choral Patriotism*. University of Rochester Press, 2005.

[53] *Towarzystwo Spiewu Fryderyka Chopina 1899-1949*. Tow. Spiewu Fryderyka Chopina, 1949.

[54] "Methodist Deaconess Home Mortgage to be Burned." *Buffalo Courier-Express*, 3 Dec. 1927, p. 8.

[55] *Towarzystwo Spiewu Fryderyka Chopina 1899-1949*. Tow. Spiewu Fryderyka Chopina, 1949.

Transfiguration. Led by parish organist John D. Raszeja, the Kalina and Chopin Singing Societies and the Raszeja Trio each sang a number accompanied by the new organ.[56] The dedication was quickly followed with the Polish Singers Alliance of America Circuit 9's first post-war concert. Under the direction of Cornelissen, the group chose the anthem "Chorale" by Ujejski and Nikorowicz and Chopin's "Prelude, Op. 7, No. 28" for their two-song selection.[57] They were then joined by the Lirnik, Lutnia, Arion, Echo, Aurora, and Paderewski Societies to sing Moniuszko's "After Vespers," under the direction of John J. Lezon of Kalina.[58]

That spring Chopins held their annual concert with special guest soprano Patricia Czarnecki from Chicago. Miss Czarnecki chose several arias from *Madame Butterfly*, *Pagliacci*, and *La Traviata* to demonstrate the full range of her voice, while the choir chose works by Beethoven, Veit, Jan Gall, Zelenski, Haydn, and Moniuszko.[59] For their performances the audience answered each song with enthusiastic applause.[60]

Arnold Cornelissen would put the choir's next project together, a Spring Festival of Joint Choruses set for May 24 at Kleinhans Music Hall.[61] Under the direction of Cornelissen, Chopin Singing Society, Canisius College Glee Club, Guido Chorus, and Niagara Frontier Male Chorus each performed five songs, while the united choruses of 275 voices opened and closed the evening.[62] Chopin's set landed well "with their enthusiastic Polish folk tunes."[63]

As the year rounded itself out, a delegation of members was sent to a banquet held in honor of the visit of Stanislaw Mikolajczyk, the former Prime Minster of Poland. Then planning soon began for the biggest celebration in Chopin's history, their golden jubilee.

The 50th anniversary year, 1949, started out with a joint concert of the local Polish Singers Alliance of America District members

---

56 "Organ Dedicated Prior to Recital." *Buffalo Evening News*, 19 Jan. 1948, p. 23.
57 Boris, Theodolinda C. "Eleanor Steber Sings Tuesday; Chamber Concert Monday." *Buffalo Evening News*, 24 Jan. 1948, p. 6.
58 "9 Polish Choruses Join in Concert." *Buffalo Evening News*, 26 Jan. 1948, p. 20.
59 "In the Realm of Music." *Buffalo Courier-Express*, 4 Apr. 1948, pp. 5-C.
60 "Big Audience Hears Chopin Society." *Buffalo Evening News*, 5 Apr. 1948, p. 12.
61 "Spring Festival of Joint Choruses." *Buffalo Evening News* [Buffalo, NY], 22 May 1948, p. 4.
62 Boris, Theodolinda C. "Chorals, by Brass Quartet, to Precede Bach Festival." *Buffalo Evening News*, 22 May 1948.
63 "Music Review." *Buffalo Courier-Express*, 25 May 1948, p. 26.

at Buffalo's Dom Polski Hall.[64] This was soon followed by a second Spring Festival of Joint Choruses put together by Cornelissen.[65] As part of the celebration of their golden jubilee, Chopins hosted a series of open houses that brought the public into the club's sanctum sanctorum. Chaired by Henry A. Marcinkiewicz the series was kicked off by the Buffalo Wholesale Food Distributors, 15 of whom displayed their offerings to over 4,000 attendees.[66]

On April 24, the choir held their Golden Jubilee Spring Concert at St. John Kanty Lyceum. With baritone Alfred Orda as their guest singer, the group also used the concert as an opportunity to recognize the centennial of Chopin's passing. With the largest audience in years, the men sang from their expansive repertoire of Polish folk songs as well as English works by Reichhardt and Director Cornelissen.[67] Especially for the concert, the group also performed Gearhart's arrangement of "Dry Bones" that included bass effects by Nelson Muszynski and George D'Anna on xylophone.[68]

As part of the golden jubilee the Society's new clubhouse was officially opened on February 27 and quickly proved to be a popular destination for not just locals, but politicians and journalists as well. Over the years the *Courier-Express*'s "Enquiring Reporter" would stop in and ask "man on the street" questions of patrons such as, "Do you have a nickname or pet name?" and "What Traits Do You Like in Friends?"[69] Of the former question, meat magnate Edmund J. Cichocki, Sr. replied with "Cy," a play on his surname, while future ceramics industrialist Eleanor Szymborski responded with "Honey" and club steward Stan Jendrasiak stated "Skipper," a title he earned while president of Chopins.[70]

The clubhouse soon had some unexpected guests as the Gieracz, Michelewicz, and Swacha families had to move in. Originally destined for the Midwest, these Polish refugee families were left stranded as the farms they were headed to for work rescinded the

---

64 "Polish Choruses Join in Concert." *Buffalo Evening News*, 31 Jan. 1949, p. 11.

65 "Buffalo Concert Planned by Joint Choruses of Area." *Niagara Falls Gazette*, 11 May 1949, p. 11.

66 "Food Distributors Show Wares at Open House." *Buffalo Courier-Express*, 28 Mar. 1949, p. 8.

67 Gill, Kenneth C. "In the Realm of Music." *Buffalo Courier-Express*, 24 Apr. 1949, pp. 12-B.

68 "Music Review…" *Buffalo Courier-Express*, 25 Apr. 1949, p. 7.; "Chopin Unit Marks 50th Anniversary." *Buffalo Evening News*, 25 Apr. 1949, p. 17.

69 "Enquiring Reporter." *Buffalo Courier-Express*, 12 Oct. 1955, p. 16.

70 "Enquiring Reporter." *Buffalo Courier-Express*, 4 Apr. 1949, p. 10.

offers. The club not only took them in and provided food and shelter, but members were also even able to find them jobs on local farms, giving the families the opportunity to start making a life in Western New York.[71]

The members ended their celebratory year in a spectacular way. They first held a wreath laying ceremony at Chopin's monument with a concert by the entire Polish Singers Alliance of America District 9 under the direction of Matthew Zydowitcz. This was followed by speeches given by Robert E. Maclntyre, the manager of the Buffalo Philharmonic Orchestra, Stanley Jasinski, and Father Winnicki. The crowd, led by Grand Marshal Mruk and a color guard provided by the Plewacki Post, paraded from Humboldt Park to the Chopin clubrooms on Kosciuszko Street.[72] Later that October the members held an intimate anniversary banquet at the Dom Polski. With a guest list limited to 300, the friends of the Society heard presentations by the leadership of the club with Stefan Minkowski, the president of the Polish Singers Alliance, giving the keynote address. The members' merry making made its way into the wee hours of the next morning.[73]

The members of Chopin closed out 1949 by campaigning hard for their fellow Chopin member, friend, and Republican mayoral candidate for Buffalo, Joseph Mruk. They took part in car parades around the East Side, opened their clubrooms as a campaign location, and made sure all of Polonia made it to the polls, be they Democrat, Independent, or Republican, knowing that every Pole would vote for Mruk. When the votes were finally tallied, Joseph Mruk was elected the first Polish American mayor of Buffalo.[74]

Exhausted from the golden jubilee, the Chopinites kept 1950 a relatively relaxed year. Longtime member Raymond Fabiniak was elected president, which brought on some youthful energy the organization greatly needed. The front half of the year was focused on the 51st annual concert which saw Edward Gertz return to Chopin's

---

[71] "Refugees, Without Jobs Temporarily, Find Work in WNY." *Buffalo Evening News*, 21 July 1949.

[72] "Tribute Paid to Chopin, Polish Composer, Patriot." *Buffalo Courier-Express*, 17 Oct. 1949, p. 6.

[73] "Anniversary Noted by Chopin Singing Society." *Buffalo Courier-Express*, 31 Oct. 1949, p. 20.

[74] McCarthy, Ed. "Mruk Invades Hillery Territory in South Side." *Buffalo Courier-Express*, 3 Nov. 1949, p. 28.

stage.[75] Mr. Gertz sang in both Polish and Italian while the choir performed the works of Listowski, Lewandowski, and Orlowski.[76] In the summer the clubhouse hosted some light entertainment with suppers, socials, and garden parties.[77] That fall the Society did some campaigning that helped send Edmund P. Radwan to the 82nd United States Congress.[78]

To set off his second year as president, Fabiniak decided to take on the task of keeping the Buffalo Philharmonic Orchestra solvent. Organizing the Paderewski Singers, the Polish Singing Circle, Kalina, and Aurora, Ray pledged to Charles H. Augspurger, General Chairman of the Maintenance Fund Campaign, that the Poles would do their part to raise the $131,000 needed to keep the orchestra going.[79]

While the club worked to raise the funds, Cornelissen began preparing for the annual concert. For the special guest, Detroit native and coloratura soprano Nadja Witkowska was invited to perform. Fresh off her tour of the *Barber of Seville* and still glowing from her recent win of the Grinnell Foundation Scholarship, Witkowska sang Italian and Polish arias.[80] The men sang a variety of Polish and English songs which were "directed vigorously by Arnold Cornelissen, who puts young men to shame with his vitality and bounce."[81]

As they had with Mruk in '49, the members of Chopin threw their weight behind fellow Pole Chester A. Kowal in his fight for city comptroller. They once again paraded around the East Side, opened their clubrooms as a campaign location, and made sure all of Polonia made it to the polls knowing that a Pole in the booth was a vote for Kowal. Once again, when the ballots were counted it was revealed that Chopins helped another Pole get into office as Chet Kowal became the new Buffalo comptroller.[82]

The year 1952 would be the last of an era of stability and predictability for the Chopin Singing Society. As they had for most of the

---

[75] Boris, Theodolinda C. "Choice of Piano, Organ, Vocal Music Scheduled for Coming Week." *Buffalo Evening News*, 15 Apr. 1950, p. 5.

[76] Gill, Kenneth C. "In The Realm of Music." *Buffalo Courier-Express*, 16 Apr. 1950, p. 13.

[77] "Where to Go Tomorrow." *Buffalo Evening News*, 9 June 1950.

[78] "Rally for Radwan." *Buffalo Evening News*, 2 Nov. 1950, p. 56.

[79] "Singing Groups Back Drive by Philharmonic." *Buffalo Courier-Express*, 27 Jan. 1951, p. 19.

[80] Boris, Theodolinda C. "Jan Peerce Recital Tuesday; Two Chamber Music Programs Scheduled." *Buffalo Evening News*, 31 Mar. 1951, p. 5.

[81] Boris, Theodolinda C. "Detroit Soloist is Charming with Chopin Singers." *Buffalo Evening News*, 2 Apr. 1951, p. 13.

[82] "Campaign Begun for Chet Kowal by Nonpartisans." *Buffalo Evening News*, 12 Sept. 1951.

last decade the choir did the three-step dance of public event, annual concert, and political support. They once again signed up with the Buffalo Philharmonic Orchestra's drive to raise $131,000 for the organization.[83] They returned to St. John Kanty Lyceum in April for their annual concert with contralto Justine Gladkowska as the special guest, both winning praise by local reviewers for their range and entertaining performances.[84] Again the members would dip their toes into the political waters, this time supporting members Philip V. Baczkowski and Stanley J. Bauer.[85]

The first inkling of the change ahead for the Society came at the board elections in December of 1952. While Fabiniak was once again elected president, the members elected a new board member, John Kedzierski, who in a few short years would revolutionize what Chopins was and light a path for what they could be.[86]

---

83 "Orchestra Fund Drive Reaches 20.1% of Goal." *Buffalo Courier-Express*, 31 Jan. 1952.
84 Boris, Theodolinda C. "Albeneri Concert on Monday to Be Last in Chamber Society Series." *Buffalo Evening News*, 19 Apr. 1952, p. 5.; "Polish Folk Songs Stir Enthusiam at Chopin Concert." *Buffalo Evening News*, 21 Apr. 1952.
85 "Sketches of Candidates - Philip V. Baczkowski." *Buffalo Evening News*, 24 Oct. 1952, p. 55.; "Sketches of Candidates - Stanley J. Bauer." *Buffalo Evening News*, 17 Oct. 1952, p. 52.
86 "Singing Society Head Re-Elected." *Buffalo Courier-Express*, 22 Dec. 1952, p. 26.

Chapter 6

The Second Saeculum

The year 1953 marked the start of a triennium that would lead the Chopin Singing Society into a new era. It was the birth of a second saeculum with new members, new music, new events, and would impact not only Buffalo's Polonia but the world's. The members of Chopin would tour in places Michalski and Olszewski could never have dreamt of and meet luminaries that would leave even Presidents Mrugowski and Jendrasiak wonderstruck. But first, the choir had to get through some very difficult times.

While Arnold Cornelissen was preparing to donate his body of work to the Music Library of the Buffalo Museum of Science, he was also planning for the Chopin's 54th annual concert.[1] On April 12, at St. John Kanty's large Lyceum, North Tonawanda native Dorothy Budnik graced the stage with her soprano voice, joined by guest violinist Karol Barabasz.[2] Each performed three numbers while the choir had a set of 14 songs that included works by Chlondowski, Purcell, Kremser, as well as a number of folk songs.[3] In her review, critic Theodolinda Boris was harsh but truthful of the aging group when she said, "the tone had not the musical sound we would have liked to hear from this male chorus, the choral work had plenty of zest and good spirit." Her praise of Arnold Cornelissen and his "always... youthful ebullience" was affectionate but would soon be proven to be woefully inaccurate.[4]

As the spring of 1953 closed out, Cornelissen began to feel unwell. He first went to see his local doctor before being transferred to the Soldiers and Sailors Memorial Hospital is Wellsboro, PA, until he was finally sent to New York City. While several treatment plans were tried, they all failed to cure the maestro and on August 1 Arnold

---

[1] "Composer Gives Life's Work to Library." *Buffalo Courier-Express*, 22 Feb. 1953, pp. 25-A.
[2] "Soloist With Male Chorus." Evening News, 8 Apr. 1953, p. 9.
[3] Boris, Theodolinda C. "Concert Satirist Will Be Heard Tuesday; Chopin Program Tomorrow." *Buffalo Evening News*, 11 Apr. 1953, p. 4.
[4] Boris, Theodolinda C. "2 Soloists Grace Chopin Society's Annual Concert." *Buffalo Evening News*, 13 Apr. 1953, p. 26.

passed away.[5] With Cornelissen gone the search for a new conductor began, but even with the hiring of Peter J. Gorecki that fall, Chopin's musical season was over.[6]

While they were no longer performing for the rest of the year, the members of Chopin were still active in other aspects of public life. That political season, they sponsored events, organized, and campaigned for Steven Pankow to be the 55th and second Slavic, Mayor of Buffalo.[7] The group's work was fruitful and on January 1, 1954 Pankow became the first Democrat to hold the title of mayor in 12 years.[8]

Renting out the hall and having a few slot machines in the backroom provided a nice supplemental income for the singers.[9] This helped them support other organizations in the community such as the Buffalo Philharmonic.[10] It also helped pay for the bright young Gorecki, who had the choir of just over 30 holding more concerts than ever. For 1954 Chopins opened the year with the Polish Singers of America Circuit 9 annual concert.[11] They were also soon singing at St. Stanislaus Church on Peckham again, now with the parish choir and Kalina for a special evening of sacred music. This event also heard the premiere of the "Cantata to St. Stanislaus," composed by choirmaster Gorecki in gratitude to the saint for helping to cure his dying son.[12]

Peter put his stamp on the annual concert as well by changing the venue from the large St. John Kanty Lyceum to the comparatively intimate Dom Polski Hall. Dedicating the concert to Cornelissen, the men sang works by Rogers and Hammerstein, Luvaas, and Lachman. The special guest for the night was Chopin's Octet.[13] The reviews of the program came in fast and heaped praise on the new conductor. The *Buffalo Evening News* said, "[t]he disciplined singing of the Chopin

---

5 "Arnold Cornelissen, Conductor, Pianist, Composer, Dies at 63." *Buffalo Evening News*, 1 Aug. 1953, p. 9.

6 "From Pole to Pole." *Dziennik Dla Wszystkich*, 6 Oct. 1953, p. 9.

7 "Pankow Sick, Wife Speaks in His Behalf." *Buffalo Courier-Express*, 28 Oct. 1953, p. 15.

8 "Pankow Sworn In; First Democrat in 12 Years." *Jamestown Post-Journal*, 2 Jan. 1954, p. 2.

9 "Ad Man to Speak." *Buffalo Courier-Express*, 19 Jan. 1954, p. 7.; "Witness Says Levitt Admitted Income From 16 Slot Machines." *Buffalo Evening News*, 21 Apr. 1954, p. 61.

10 "Polish Groups Pledge Aid to Philharmonic." *Buffalo Courier-Express*, 28 Jan. 1954, p. 11.

11 "Polish Singers Hold Annual Concert Here." *Buffalo Courier-Express*, 8 Feb. 1954, p. 18.

12 Gill, Kenneth C. "Ensembles Outdraw Individuals, So Coming Concerts Stress Groups." *Buffalo Courier-Express*, 14 Mar. 1954, p. 10C., Schlaerth, J. Don. "It's Holiday Mood for Chopin Singers." *Buffalo Evening News*, 5 Dec. 1962, p. 57.

13 Boris, Theodolinda C. "Community School Recital Monday: Mothersingers Concert Tuesday." *Buffalo Evening News*, 22 Mar. 1954, p. 4.

Singing Society... reflected the solid musicianship of its new director, Peter Gorecki," and Gorecki's "'Piosnka Szopenistow' (Chopin Song), especially composed for this concert as a sort of theme song for the society," had "a light-hearted swing to it that caught the fancy of the listeners immediately and had to be repeated."[14] While the *Courier-Express* stated, "[c]onductor Peter Gorecki worked impressive vocal effects from his 31 male voices forming a program both artistic and entertaining."[15]

Following the election of Fred Netzel as president, Gorecki once again led Chopins at the 1955 District 9 concert and was soon preparing them for their own annual show.[16] But while the maestro was making song selections, a turning point in the history of Chopins was occurring a few miles north.

In his home on Jackson Avenue in North Tonawanda, former president and last surviving founding member of the Chopin Singing Society, Michael J. Stefanski died suddenly. Having left the East Side and the choir almost 40 years earlier, his passing was only noted with an obituary in the *Tonawanda News* and was completely missed by Polonia beyond the Niagara County border. But his loss marked the end of the first saeculum of the Society and the last vestige of its humble origin.[17]

While the year would see the end of the founding generation, it would also see the seed of the next generation being planted. Through the recruiting efforts of former President Fabiniak, Jim Mikoll a familiar face around the club in his childhood, joined the Society.[18] In short order his brother Ted signed up and he brought his wife Ann to Chopins as well. Soon the Mikolls were fixtures at the club and would begin their meteoric rise in the Society. They would usher in a new epoch for not just the singers, but Polonia as a whole.[19]

By the first of April, Gorecki had his songs selected for the annual show, secured local soprano Theresa Skotnicka as the evening's guest, and began warming up his singers for the new venue chosen for

---

[14] Boris, Theodolinda C. "Chopin Singers Show Discipline and Musicianship." *Buffalo Evening News*, 24 May 1954, p. 14.
[15] Gill, Kenneth C. "Chopin Society Concert Gets Big Ovation." *Buffalo Courier-Express*, 24 May 1954, p. 7.
[16] "Polish Units Offer Varied Songfest." *Buffalo Courier-Express*, 23 Jan. 1955, pp. 15-B.
[17] "Stefanski." *Tonawanda News*, 10 Mar. 1955, p. 15.
[18] *Chopin Singing Society 75th Anniversary, 1899-1974*. The Society, 1974.
[19] "Enquiring Reporter." *Buffalo Courier-Express*, 12 Oct. 1955, p. 16.

the 56th annual concert, the Statler Ballroom.[20] To further appeal to the great Buffalo audiences, Gorecki held open practices in the hotel leading up to the April 16 event.[21] With works by Moniuszko, Kazuro, Romberg, and a piece by Wieniawski arranged by Matthew Zydowicz, the choir of three dozen earned high praise from the larger than expected audience.[22]

In the back half of the year, the Chopin Singing Society's Octet was the guest group for the golden jubilee concert of the Lirnik Singing Society held at the Polish Cadets Hall.[23] While in politics the membership campaigned for Anthony R. Lombardo in his failed attempt to secure the Buffalo City Council presidency.[24]

For their only solo performance of 1956, Chopins returned to the Statler to host their 57th annual concert. That year Gloria Gerula, the coloratura from Hamilton, Ontario was tapped to serve as the special guest.[25] For the crowd of 400, the singers performed works by Alabeiff, Chopin, folksongs, and their contest song for the 1956 Polish Singers Alliance convention "Hejnal" by Garbusinski.[26] While their program was lauded in Buffalo, "Hejnal" was less warmly received by the judges at the New York competition. There, the Chopin Singing Society of Buffalo fell to the Chopin Singing Society of Passaic, New Jersey who scored 97.4 points with the same song in the male chorus division.[27]

The 1957 annual concert would also be the only solo show for the Society that year. The 30 men sang works by Orlowski, Schumann, Gall, and Poland's oldest known hymn "Bogurodzica" in memory of longtime board member Felix Kulwicki. At the Hotel Statler Ballroom two guests took the stage for the 58th annual concert, the Schwabischer Maennerchor who were also being directed by Gorecki, and

---

20 The Chopin Singing Society. *56th Annual Concert*. Chopin Singing Society, 1955.
21 "What's Doing?" *Buffalo Courier-Express*, 12 Apr. 1956, p. 19.
22 Boris, Theodolinda C. "Large Audience Hails Chopin Singers." *Buffalo Evening News*, 18 Apr. 1956, p. 20.
23 Boris, Theodolinda C. "Concert Tomorrow Evening for Villa Maria Alumnae." *Buffalo Evening News*, 1 Oct. 1955, p. 6.
24 "Lombardo Assails Spending; Lawless Raps 'Power Grab'." *Buffalo Evening News*, 25 Oct. 1955, p. 41.
25 Gill, Kenneth C. "Ismailia Temple's Chanters Will Present Concert at Chautauqua on June 30." *Buffalo Courier-Express*, 6 May 1956, pp. 9-D.
26 "Chopin Singing Society Entertain 400 at Statler." *Buffalo Courier-Express*, 13 May 1956, pp. 2-B.; The Chopin Singing Society. *57th Annual Concert*. Chopin Singing Society, 1956.
27 Blejwas, Stanislaus A. *The Polish Singers Alliance, 1888-1998: Choral Patriotism*. University of Rochester Press, 2005, p. 265.

Panna Genia Las. For their selection, the Maennerchor sang works by Sendt and Chopin, as well as Brue's "Ewig liebe Heimat" which won them first prize at the 17th Annual Saengerfest the previous year. They concluded their set with "Mit dem Schwabischer Maennerchor" a work Gorecki composed especially for them. When Panna Las took the stage that night, the little girl that was a guest soloist at the 1939 Chopin concert 18 years earlier had grown into a diva touring over 25 cities in the U.S. and Canada and had already worked with the New York, Newark, and Hartford Opera Companies. For her first set Genia sang two arias from *Carmen* before returning to the stage to sing works by Paderewski, Chopin, and Niewiadomski. In her third appearance, Panna Las joined the united Chopin and Schwabischer Maennerchor Choir to sing the solo part from "The Lost Chord."[28] In his review of the show, the *Buffalo Evening News* music columnist said, "[t]he Chopin ensemble was very well received in a selection of both spirited and tender Polish songs, including an arrangement and composition of Mr. Gorecki."[29]

Chopins returned the favor of the Maennerchor later in the year when the Polish choir joined them at the Harugari Temple on Genesee Street for the German singers' annual show. Chopins sang selections by Lachman and Moniuszko and the Schwabischers sang Hansen, Abt, Renner, and Brenner. Together the two groups performed pieces by Bohm, Schubert, Ronald, and Brown, all under the direction of Gorecki.[30]

That summer the Society held their annual elections which saw John Kedzierski, Joseph Dulski, Louis Piotrowicz, Raymond Butzek, Lawrence Nagowski, Daniel Tryjanowski, Julian Kowalewski and President Frederick Netzel all re-elected, with up-and-coming member Matthew Peters added to the board.[31] Re-electing familiar faces year after year ensured continuity within the organization, even if it also allowed for some complacency to set in. That continuity, and in turn complacency, would be rocked in October with the unexpected passing of Joseph S. Dulski. With the loss of the man who chartered Chopin in 1914 and served as secretary for four decades, the Society saw that to

---

[28] The Chopin Singing Society. *58th Annual Concert*. Chopin Singing Society, 1957.
[29] "2 Singing Groups Join in Concert." *Buffalo Evening News*, 6 May 1957, p. 18.
[30] "Marie Werzinger to Sing in Maennerchor Concert." *Buffalo Evening News*, 15 Oct. 1957, p. 22.
[31] "Netzel Elected Board President by Chopin Singers." *Buffalo Evening News*, 26 June 1957, p. 63.

survive into the future new members and fresh leadership would be needed sooner rather than later.[32]

As the local election season rolled in, the members of Chopin once again threw their support behind Chester Kowal, this time for his run for Buffalo mayor. At a late September rally at the clubhouse the Society unanimously endorsed Kowal saying he was the candidate "best qualified to cope with municipal problems."[33] While the support of Chopin wasn't enough to get Kowal over the top this time, East Buffalo did elect two politicians closely associated with them. Both member Michael E. Zimmer and friend Ann T. Mikoll won their re-elections as Associate City Court Judges.[34]

By 1958 the aging population of Chopin membership caught up with the Society. For the first time in nearly a half century the choir gave their annual performance with less than 30 singers, despite adding brothers Thaddeus and James Mikoll to their ranks. The late May program was moved from the Statler Ballroom to the Polish Union Hall, and the once illustrious guest singers from Poland, New York, and Chicago were replaced by the St. Stanislaus Boys Choir.[35] For Chopins, the songs focused more on works in the English language than in Polish, despite Gorecki's push for more folk music. Even the once voluminous reviews found in the local newspapers had been reduced to a couple of paragraphs saying the group and its singers were "well voiced."[36]

While the members looked backwards to Father Winnicki as their president for the year, a man first elected 15 years earlier, they did have a bit of an eye to the future. After his successful completion of the bar examination and her election to a judgeship, Chopins planned a testimonial dinner in honor of Ted and Ann Mikoll. Former Mayor Steven Pankow would have been chairman, and Port Director John A. Ulinski was planned as the keynote speaker, with Msgr. Adamski of St. Stanislaus scheduled to give the invocation for the event. Almost are soon as the press release was issued, the Mikolls knowing the fragile economic state of the club politely declined the honor saying, "[w]e are both honored that they should value our association with

---

[32] "Joseph S. Dulski." *Buffalo Evening News*, 17 Oct. 1957, p. 67.

[33] "Chopin Society Supports Kowal." *Buffalo Evening News*, 25 Sept. 1957, p. 79.

[34] "East Side Help Counts in Zimmer, Mikoll Victories." *Buffalo Evening News*, 6 Nov. 1957, p. 89.

[35] The Chopin Singing Society. *59th Annual Concert*. Chopin Singing Society, 1958.

[35] Gill, Kenneth C. "Singers Present Sacred Music in Fine Concert." *Buffalo Courier-Express*, 26 May 1958, p. 16.

the club so highly. However, under the circumstances, we have declined the honor and have offered our aid to the cultural aims of the Society in any program it might plan for the future."[37]

To firm up their weakened treasury the club held a sports night fundraiser, an evening of fun, food, and chitchat, with local professional athletes.[38] The extra cash from the event would be needed as burglars broke into the club that November, raiding the cigarette machine and all its cash. While the haul was not huge, it did hurt the struggling club.[39] As the singers began preparing for their 60th annual concert,[40] many inside and out of Chopin were worried that the Society's obituary was already written.[41]

In early February of 1959 the Chopin Singing Society announced plans for their 60th anniversary celebration. They would start the year off with a special High Mass at St. Stanislaus Church in their founding month of March, then return to their longtime venue of St. John Kanty Lyceum for their April 4 annual concert.[42] The only problem the group faced was that they were down to 15 singers.[43] The entire Society went into recruitment mode to build up their numbers for the important anniversary. Daniel Kij of the Paderewski Singing Society agreed to join them for the event and Max Gurbacki, Thaddeus Kowalski, Walter Przybysz and Wallace Gardon decided to join the group as members.[44] After becoming the musical director of the Polish Singing Circle,[45] Gorecki was able to convince a dozen singers and President Marion Kwiatkowski to join Chopins on stage for the concert as well. [46]

The special guest singers for the evening were the Senior Chorus of the Immaculate Heart of Mary Academy—later renamed Villa Maria--under the direction of S.M Celina and S.M Felicitas. To serve

---

[37] "Mikolls Decline Dinner Planned in Their Honor." *Buffalo Evening News*, 5 Sept. 1958, p. 36.
[38] "Sports Night." *Buffalo Courier-Express*, 9 Sept. 1958, p. 10.
[39] "Burglars Invade Club." *Buffalo Evening News*, 3 Nov. 1958, p. 25.
[40] "Meeting." *Buffalo Courier-Express*, 13 Oct. 1958, p. 7.
[41] Williams, Bob. "Chopin Society—Their Songs Come from the Heart." *Buffalo Evening News Magazine*, 28 Apr. 1962, p. 1.
[42] "Chopin Society Concert April 4." *Buffalo Courier-Express*, 9 Feb. 1959, p. 18.
[43] Williams, Bob. "Chopin Society—Their Songs Come from the Heart." *Buffalo Evening News Magazine*, 28 Apr. 1962, p. 1.
[44] Kowalewski, Ed. "Paderewski Society Cherishes Name Group Has Signed Picture of Pianist." *Buffalo Evening News*, 21 Dec. 1954, p. 33.
[45] "New Director of the Polish Singing Circle." *Buffalo Evening News*, 28 Feb. 1959, pp. B-5.
[46] "Polish Singing Circle Votes Support of Chair." *Buffalo Evening News*, 25 May 1959, p. 23.; The Chopin Singing Society. *60th Annual Concert*. Chopin Singing Society, 1959.

as accompanists to the choirs, the husband-and-wife team of Dorothy and Thaddeus Biernat were secured.[47] Thaddeus, the musical director of the Lirnik and Arion Singing Societies accompanied Chopin and the Polish Singing Circle through their performances of Romberg's "Drinking Song," Gorecki's "Piosnka Szopenistow," and Chopin's selection for the 1959 Polish Singers Alliance of America competition, "Przez łąki." Combined, the Biernats played three works by Chopin and a piece by Clementi on their Wurlitzer pianos before Dorothy took over to serve as accompanist for the Senior Chorus.[48] The evening concluded with all three choruses and both accompanists performing all five movements of Gorecki's "Cantata of Saint Stanislaus B.M."[49]

Back down to less than 20 singers, the chorus only had one other performance in 1959, providing music at a Memorial Day service at St. Stanislaus Cemetery.[50] With little left to go on, the surviving members of Chopin elected John A. Kedzierski as president. The old singers of the group hoped that the young man and his friends would be able to breathe new life into the Society and head it down a brighter path.

---

47 "Pianists to Demonstrate Skills at Area Concert." *Tonawanda News*, 1 Apr. 1959, p. 6.
48 The Chopin Singing Society. *60th Annual Concert*. Chopin Singing Society, 1959.
49 "All Brahm's Concert Will Feature Elman." *Buffalo Evening News*, 4 Apr. 1959, pp. B-5.
50 "Homage to War Dead is Paid by Thousands." *Buffalo Courier-Express*, 25 May 1959, p. 30.

Chapter 7

A New Golden Age

With John Kedzierski as president, and James, Ann, and Ted Mikoll among the club's leaders, the Chopin Singing Society underwent a radical transformation in the early months of 1960. These young leaders would reimagine the men's singing group into a powerhouse of Polish American culture, entertainment, and influence. Although they would do away with some of the old traditions of the choir, others they recommitted to, with a new zest and fervor.

One tradition Chopins stayed with was their participation in the Polish Singers Alliance. As Chopin #219 the group performed at the Polish Union Hall with the Echo Singing Society, Arion Singing Society, and the newest member, the Symfonia Singing Society of Hamilton, Ontario at the annual District 9 concert in late January.[1]

The new crew also kept alive the ailing annual concert of early spring. Announcing that they would be holding a concert in the autumn in celebration of Frederic Chopin's one hundred and fiftieth birthday, there was no big push or pomp and circumstance for the program. Only the *Courier-Express* ran a small announcement for the show.[2] With fewer than 30 performers, the Villa Maria Choir, and the Tatra Dancers far outnumbered the Chopin singers.[3] Despite their small number, the event was well received by Polonia. They performed one more concert that spring, at the golden jubilee banquet for Reverend Mother Mary Annette at Villa Maria.[4]

After months of recruiting, coordinating, scheduling, and practicing, Chopins began the media blitz for their *Festival of Folk Songs and Dances* in early September.[5] Following the press release that formally announced their unofficial 61st annual concert, 70 women from the Villa Maria Alumnae Choir, 40 men from Chopin, and the Merry

---

[1] "Polish Concert Set." *Buffalo Courier-Express*, 27 Jan. 1960, p. 17.
[2] Gill, Kenneth C. "Rene Wiegert Will Lead Melody Fair Orchestra." *Buffalo Courier-Express*, 24 Apr. 1960, pp. 37-A.
[3] The Chopin Singing Society. *61st Annual Concert*. Chopin Singing Society, 1960.
[4] "Mrs. Podd Is Chairman for Villa Maria." *Buffalo Evening News*, 17 May 1960, p. 17.
[5] "Singing Society to Pay Tribute to Chopin's Memory." *Buffalo Evening News*, 3 Sept. 1960, pp. A-3.

Tatra Dancing Troupe put on a 9:30 AM mini performance leading up to the big event. Three days before the show, on a stage built between the Broadway Market and Sattler's and at the behest of the Broadway-Fillmore Merchants Association, the groups previewed their upcoming show.[6] Inside the 998 Broadway location, Sattler's sold tickets for the festival and donated display space to the Society for an exhibit on Chopin.[7] Curated by member Stanley T. Zakrzewski the exhibition included a copy of Chopin's birth certificate, letters to George Sand and Franz Liszt, and a number of art pieces depicting the composer.[8]

As the enormity of the forthcoming production became obvious, every sitting politician and candidate running wanted an ad in the program and a table at the show. Over 50 politicians ranging from Buffalo's 6th Ward Supervisor to the president of the United States had their name in the program. Every elected official wanted to make sure that Polonia knew who was and wasn't supporting the Chopin Singing Society and its Polish American heritage.[9] In preparation for the deluge of candidates arriving the night of the show, each political party was given its own cluster of tables, to avoid any awkward seating arraignments.[10]

As the day turned to evening on October 15 the ticket holders began to arrive at the doors of St. Stanislaus's new Social Center on the corner of Fillmore Avenue. The light drizzle didn't deter the crowds of prospective attendees from waiting in line to purchase tickets.[11] In short order, the line snaked out the doors, and slowed traffic on Peckham Street. Just before 8:30, the entire hall of 1,300 seats were sold out and the unprepared multitudes were sent home empty handed.[12]

The night's entertainment opened with a processional composed by Peter Gorecki as a tribute to both America and Poland. The 18 Merry Tatra Dancers set the pace of the show, opening with the

---

6 "Singers, Dancers Will Take Part in Folk Festival." *Buffalo Evening News*, 8 Oct. 1960, pp. A-14.
7 Sattler's. "You Are Invited..." *Buffalo Evening News* [Buffalo, NY], 11 Oct. 1960, p. 36.; "Chopin Mementos Placed on Display." *Buffalo Evening News*, 13 Oct. 1960, p. 65.
8 "Chopin Society to Honor Composer." *Buffalo Courier-Express*, 9 Oct. 1960, pp. D-1-D-6.
9 *A Festival of Folk Songs and Dance - Oct. 15, 1960*. Frederick Chopin Singing Society, 1960.
10 "Political Notes." *Buffalo Evening News*, 14 Oct. 1960, p. 22.
11 "October 15, 1960 Weather History in Buffalo New York, United States." *Buffalo October 15, 1960 Historical Weather (New York, United States) - Weather Spark*
12 "Bright Color, Verve Mark Polish Festival by Chopin Society." *Buffalo Evening News*, 28 Nov. 1960, p. 31.

dance Polonez Warszawski. The 41 singing members of Chopin along with the Villa Maria Choir then took the stage to give renditions of works by Stanislaus Hadyna, Tadeusz Sygietynski, and Jan Maklakiewicz, with the dancers giving the singers a rest after every few songs. Theresa Skotnicka, a Voices of Tomorrow winner and performer with the Buffalo Philharmonic Orchestra, was the soloist on "Hej, Tam W Dolinie," and both Ms. Skotnicka and Louis Distel sang a duet from the operetta *Sluby Debnickie*.[13] Miss John Kopciuch and Paul Chodkowski performed solos in the Gorecki arranged "Szla Dzieweczka Do Laseczka." With the vivid color and coordinated dance of Dan Chojnacki's troop, the new depth of sound from the expanded Chopin choir, and the beautiful voices of the Villa Maria singers, the crowds went wild with applause and cheers. After multiple bows, the Chick Cyran Orchestra struck up for the dance that followed the show. But to the dismay of Cyran and his crew, the music was almost completely drowned out by everyone raving about the evening's show.[14] Seeing the success they had, and the great throngs of people who wanted to see the show but couldn't, it was soon decided to expand the program and restage the show at Kleinhans Music Hall the next month.

With a 40% larger show and hundreds more seats to fill, Chopins made sure tickets were available in every corner of Polonia and accessible to the general public. From Gawel Jewelers on Broadway to Frontier Radio in Black Rock, Szklarz Pharmacy in Kaisertown to Ruda's Records in Lackawanna, just about every Pole in Buffalo was only a 10-minute drive from a ticket outlet.[15]

Not only did the singers add more songs and dances, they also brought on 28 members of the Buffalo Philharmonic Orchestra to form a small symphonette for the evening. In only a few weeks, between practices for the show and his other rehearsals, Gorecki arranged all the music for the orchestra, an accomplishment even the most seasoned musical professionals were impressed by.[16]

After only six weeks of preparation the Society launched into their repeat performance of *Festival of Folk Songs and Dances* at 8:15

---

[13] "New, Larger Polish Festival Planned by Chopin Society." *Buffalo Evening News*, 23 Nov. 1960, p. 8.

[14] "Philharmonic From Israel to Play in Kleinhans Hall Tomorrow." *Buffalo Evening News*, 12 Nov. 1960, pp. B-5.

[15] Chopin Singing Society. "A Festival of Polish Folk Songs and Dances." *Buffalo Evening News* [Buffalo, NY], 19 Nov. 1960, pp. A-13.

[16] Gill, Kenneth C. "Piatigorsky to Be Soloist with Philharmonic." *Buffalo Courier-Express*, 20 Nov. 1960, pp. 11-D.

sharp. The show was everything they demonstrated at St. Stanislaus and more. The Tatras added two dances, with the singers adding eight songs and an intermission.[17] Over the next few days, it was declared a smashing success by both major newspapers and the 4,500 attendees of both shows. The *Buffalo Evening News* raved about the evening of song and dance by saying, "[i]t was all on a happy, life-loving note, with the natural and immediate appeal of the old traditional folklore leading the way."[18] At the *Courier-Express* Ken Gill wrote, "[a]n abundant variety of well-prepared Polish folk songs and dances kept a large audience applauding last night in Kleinhans Music Hall Auditorium...Polish folk songs of ballad, novelty and classic types were sung with spirit and vitality by the well-trained units, while colorful costumes lent additional flavor to the schedule. As well received by the audience was the work of the Merry Tatra Dancers, directed by Daniel Chojnacki. Mountain dances, Masovian rhythms and formal patterns were performed in graceful formation with the dancers attired in native garb."[19] In just under a year it became clear to both Polonia and the entire Niagara Frontier that Chopin was no longer just a singing group, but a powerful force in spreading Polish culture across the region.

With the Society garnering so much attention, the Buffalo Common Council discussed moving the statue of Chopin from Humboldt Park to Kleinhans Music Hall. The convivial discussion of the possible action revealed that Chopin was the favorite composer of North Councilman Victor E. Manz as well as Councilman-at-Large Stanley M. Makowski. Delaware Councilman Benzow was on board even going so far as to propose that the bust of Mozart join Chopin. When it was suggested that Verdi could also be moved to Kleinhans, Councilman John Ramunno Sr. was less than enthused and focused on keeping Dante Place downtown from being renamed Marine Drive.[20] The entire conversation would become moot four days later when Public Works reported it would cost $1,000 to move just the Chopin statue, an amount higher than any of the council members were ready

---

[17] *A Festival of Folk Songs and Dance - Nov 26, 1960. (Repeat Performance).* Frederick Chopin Singing Society, 1960.

[18] "Bright Color, Verve Mark Polish Festival by Chopin Society." *Buffalo Evening News*, 28 Nov. 1960, p. 31.

[19] Gill, Kenneth C. "Polish Songs, Dances Applauded at Kleinhans." *Buffalo Courier-Express*, 27 Nov. 1960, pp. 9-A.

[20] "Artistic Feelings Aroused as Council Discusses Statues." *Buffalo Evening News*, 16 Oct. 1960, p. 39.

to attach their name to.[21]

As the success of the festival was still being talked about well into the winter and the New Year,[22] it was decided to capture some of that lightning in a bottle by expanding the Society and creating a Chopin Women's Choir in 1961. With several singers from the Villa Maria Alumnae Choir forming the core of the new group, ladies from across Polonia joined up. By the time practice began in early 1961, their ranks swelled to 76 voices, 17 more than the men.[23] With so many ladies now part of the club, Chopins began holding more events geared toward women. In partnership with Sattler's, the women's choir held the *High Notes of Fashion* show at the Adam Plewacki Post. Highlighting the latest trends on sale at the retail super center, the proceeds from the ticketed event would go towards Chopin's grand project for 1961, *The Many Faces of Poland.*[24]

Having made it clear that the Singing Society was a fresh, young, and inclusive organization the group felt secure in renaming the 62nd annual concert *The Many Faces of Poland.* Promotions for the show started a month out from the April 15 performance and were seen around Western New York. Returning to Kleinhans, Chopins again had tickets available across the region and met with media members in every major market.[25] As the concert inched ever closer, they doubled down on their practice sessions.[26] But the combination of extra time with Chopin, and the marathon of parish Easter programs, the members began to run a little ragged and needed a release. With just about everything closed for Easter Monday several of the Chopinites gathered at the clubhouse to have a little party in celebration of Dyngus Day.[27]

Returning to Kleinhans for the April 15 program, the choir was once again accompanied by members of the Buffalo Philharmonic Orchestra. The Merry Tatra Dance Troup also returned to provide an

---

[21] "Moving of Statue to Cost $1,000." *Buffalo Courier-Express*, 23 Nov. 1960, p. 13.

[22] "Two Judges Brushing Up for Song Festival Next Mon." *Buffalo Evening News*, 9 Mar. 1961, p. 40.

[23] Chopin Singing Society. *The Many Faces of Poland - April 15, 1961*. 1961.

[24] "Benefit Arranged by Chopin Choir." *Buffalo Evening News*, 10 Feb. 1961, p. 10.

[25] "Chopin Choir Concert Set for April 15." *Lackawanna Leader*, 16 Mar. 1961, p. 6.

[26] Rehearsals At Chopin's Weekly for April Show Article. *Chopin Singing Society Scrapbook, 1960-1963*. Archives, Chopin Singing Society, Buffalo, NY

[27] Chopin Singing Society. "Dyngus Day - Hearthstone Manor." *The Am-Pol Eagle's Dyngus Day Guide 2013*, 2013, p. 7.

additional layer to the evening's entertainment.[28] Under the guidance of Show Chairman Ted Mikoll, the Music Committee of John Zabinski, Floyd Mazikowski, and Ludwig Distel divided the program into four parts. The night opened with an overview of Classical Poland, moved into Contemporary Poland, then revived Gorecki's "Cantata of Saint Stanislaus B.M." to cover Religious Poland. In their last set, Folk and Patriotic Poland, the choir changed out of the formal dress wear and into Polish folkwear for a set of 18 works, highlighted by solo performances by Maria Gorecka and Louis Distel.[29]

Kenneth Gill's *Courier-Express* review of the evening stated, "[e]very chair filled and a generous amount of standees attested to the popularity of the Chopin Singing Society at its annual concert in Kleinhans Music Hall, last night.... Anthems, operatic airs, dance rhythms and folk songs had special Gorecki settings and each had enjoyable flavor" and "[l]engthy applause greeted each segment of choral, solo and choreographed selections."[30]

The choir was back on stage in less than a month, this time at Black Rock's Polish Cadets, sharing the spotlight with the dancers of the Wieniec Polek Society 1591 of the Polish National Alliance. Taking part in a 170th anniversary observance of the May 3 Constitution, Chopins and 500 audience members heard John F. Aszkler, president of the Catholic League for Religious Assistance to Poland, speak. The former mayor of Lackawanna discussed how the Church was the last bastion of hope from the complete Communization of Poland.[31] The singers repeated their performance three days later in observance of Polish-American Day at the St. Stanislaus Social Center. This time they heard Dr. Tadeusz Romer, a former Polish diplomat and faculty member at McGill University, speak on Communism in the Slavic nations saying, "[w]hile Poland and Eastern European nations are now Soviet satellites, the U.S. should not give them up for lost, the peoples of Eastern Europe are freedom-loving people who are resisting communistic ideology by maintaining their religion and traditions."[32]

---

28 "Orchard Park, UB Concerts, Krips Program Next Week." *Buffalo Evening News*, 26 Mar. 1961, pp. B-3.

29 "A Musical Evening in Poland." *Buffalo Courier-Express Pictorial*, 9 Apr. 1961, p. 24.; Chopin Singing Society. *The Many Faces of Poland - April 15, 1961.* 1961.

30 Gill, Kenneth C. "Chopin Singing Society Gives SRO Performance." *Buffalo Courier-Express*, 16 Apr. 1961, p. 20.

31 "Anniversary of Polish Constitution Observed." *Buffalo Courier-Express*, 4 Mar. 1961, p. 40.

32 "Speaker Belittles Russian Strength." *Buffalo Courier-Express*, 8 May 1961, p. 8.

Wanting to continue an already popular cultural program, the Buffalo Park's Department brought back their summer Pop Concert series. To lead the Buffalo Community Orchestra for the July half of the program the city engaged the services of Peter Gorecki as conductor.[33] Given a great degree of freedom, Gorecki decided to utilize the voices of Chopins for his early July concert in Delaware Park.[34] The audience of 5,000 at the evening's program warmly received the Buffalo Community Orchestra's renditions of Romberg's "Desert Song" and Loew's "My Fair Lady," and raucously applauded the highlight from Chopin's set, "Polonaise Militaire."[35]

Closing in on their twentieth month of success since the new regime took over, Chopins ran into their second major hurdle of the year. Earlier in February the club was hit with a $2,000 bill when the boiler blew the night before a fundraiser. The still depleted coffers were insufficient to cover the cost and the club had to borrow money to pay for the repairs.[36] Just as things were starting to look up, burglars broke into the Kosciuszko Street home in September and stole over $500, five cases of liquor, and cleaned up by taking the vacuum.[37] After word got around about the huge haul, thieves hit again in October absconding with the substantial sum of $3.00.[38]

The lows of the burglary were offset by the highs of the 1961 Annual Pulaski Day Parade. Commemorating the 182nd anniversary of the death of Gen. Casimir Pulaski, Chopins participated in style. Led by Miss Polonia, Therese Marie Zabielski of Lackawanna, the singers were decked out with colorful costumes with a sleek car that left the attendees and judges in awe. When the Central Council of American Polish Organizations of Buffalo and Erie County handed out the trophies for the year's best floats, the Singing Society placed third, after the diamond jubilee float of St. Adalbert Basilica and the Great Lakes Drum and Bugle Corps of Buffalo.[39]

To close out the year the singers put on two distinct

---

[33] Gill, Kenneth C. "Parks Departments Concert Series Will Open This Evening." *Buffalo Courier-Express*, 2 July 1961, p. 12.
[34] Gill, Kenneth C. "Clarence Orchestra Opens Summer Series Today." *Buffalo Courier-Express*, 9 July 1961, p. 12.
[35] "Singing Unit Is Applauded." *Buffalo Courier-Express*, 13 July 1961, p. 5.
[36] "Chopin Singers Back to the Blues After $800 Loss." *Buffalo Evening News*, 16 Sept. 1961, pp. A-3.
[37] "Singing Club Looted." *Buffalo Courier-Express*, 16 Sept. 1961, p. 4.
[38] "Singing Society Is Victim Again." *Buffalo Courier-Express*, 8 Oct. 1961, p. 31.
[39] "Pulaski Day Parade Attracts Throng." *Buffalo Courier-Express*, 9 Oct. 1961, p. 17.

performances. The first was part of Sattler's 14th Annual Santa Claus Parade in late November. They shared the stage with Ann Hudson (Dupee) of the Ice Capades, Sattler's mascot Sandy B. Thrifty, and Parade Marshal Art James of NBC's *Say When* fame.[40] For the final appearance of the year the group was invited to take part in the Buffalo Philharmonic Orchestra's Winter Pops program. Billed as *Polish Nite at the Pop's,* Chopins sang popular American and Polish songs.[41] As part of the show the Merry Tatras danced a few steps with Judith Wnek and Paul Chodkowski serving as soloists.[42]

In early 1962 the sea change from the old Chopins to the new was complete with the election of Theodore V. Mikoll as president. While the occasion marked a new generation taking over the organization, keynote speaker Judge Michael E. Zimmer's remarks harkened back to Leon Olszewski's ideals about the importance of the Singing Society with his statement, "[i]t was the song that kept the spirit of Poland alive for nearly 100 years, and that even today while that country is in bondage her singing cultural emissaries are sent abroad to delight the world." Zimmer further urged the members to maintain their cultural traditions and keep the spirit of a free Poland alive.[43]

The changes led by Mikoll saw the choir grow from 27 singers to 150. The desire to join was so great amongst the populace that a membership cap was instituted by the Society and soon even the wait list had scores of names on it. A new diversification could also be seen in the occupations of the singers. What were once retirees and near-retirees now included two physicians, a grocer, a milkman, two contractors, a plant executive, shop workers, nurses, secretaries, file clerks, lawyers, actors, a barber, high school students, interpreter, engineer, caterer, painter, sweater weaver, health inspector and handyman. The oldest member was 84 and the youngest wasn't even old enough to vote or drink at the bar, at the age 16.[44]

Launching into the marketing campaign for their 63rd annual concert in early April, the singers were proud to announce that the title for May 5 show would be *Spring Time in Poland*. With costumes inspired by the Lowicz region, and local singer, actor, and radio

---

40 Sattler's Department Store. "Sattler's 14th Annual Santa Claus Parade." *Buffalo Courier-Express* [Buffalo, NY], 10 Nov. 1961, p. 11.
41 Holynski, Tony. "The Chit-Chat Corner." *Lackawanna Leader*, 30 Nov. 1961.
42 *Fourth Concert Winter Pops*. Buffalo Philharmonic Orchestra, 1961.
43 "New Officers Are Installed by Singers." *Buffalo Courier-Express*, 12 Feb. 1962, p. 8.
44 Williams, Bob. "Chopin Society—Their Songs Come from the Heart." *Buffalo Evening News Magazine*, 28 Apr. 1962, p. 1.

personality Raymond Fleszar as the stage producer, they were confident that the 1962 show would be one of their best.[45] To head up planning for the event the committee chose Councilman At-Large Stanley Makowski while Dr. Eugenia Fronczak-Bukowski and industrialist Frank X. Wardynski served as honorary chairpersons.[46]

For the show, Gorecki directed the male and female choruses in a selection of Polish folk songs, works by Chopin, Sygietynski, Kowalski, and an arrangement by Dr. Frederick J. Fleszar. To achieve the full sound that worked best at Kleinhans, musicians from the Buffalo Community Orchestra were brought on to fill the pit. Rounding out the event, the Tatra Dances once again joined Chopins onstage, while Ray Fleszar, Marcia Karaszewski, Theresa Skotnicki-Dybas, and Max Gurbacki each had solos.[47]

As he had in previous years, the *Courier-Express* reviewer lauded the annual concert, but this year admiration even came from everyday Buffalonians.[48] In a Letter to the Editor, A. Brown of Buffalo praised the Society by saying, "Buffalo can well be proud of its Polish citizens! What they are contributing to the culture and art of our great city was vividly revealed at last Saturday's evening of song and dance... The program was the outstanding work of a large group of members dedicated to paying tribute to this great pianist," and to the challenge "[m]ay we strive to have a better understanding of the creative contributions of all races that unite with us native-born Americans to make the beautiful city of Buffalo the happy place we call home."[49]

With the concert over, Chopins focused on raising funds and having a good time over the summer. Opening with a Hawaiian luau in May, then moving into a space-themed party for June, they closed the season with a Roaring Twenties evening of drink and dance.[50] In the

---

[45] Williams, Bob. "Chopin Society—Their Songs Come from the Heart." *Buffalo Evening News Magazine*, 28 Apr. 1962, p. 1.

[46] "Polish Song Festival Scheduled for May 5." *Buffalo Courier-Express*, 1 Apr. 1962, pp. 30-D.

[47] The Chopin Singing Society. *63rd Annual Concert - Springtime in Poland.* Chopin Singing Society, 1962.

[48] Gill, Kenneth C. "Concert Is Applauded." *Buffalo Courier-Express*, 6 May 1962, pp. 5-A.

[49] Brown, A. "Hails Polish Contribution to Buffalo's Culture." *Buffalo Courier-Express*, 10 May 1962, p. 22.

[50] Hawaiian Luau at Chopin's Invitation, June 3, 1962. *Chopin Singing Society Scrapbook, 1960-1963.* Archives, Chopin Singing Society, Buffalo, NY; Chopin Presents the Big Blast Off Invitation, June 3, 1962. *Chopin Singing Society Scrapbook, 1960-1963.* Archives, Chopin Singing Society, Buffalo, NY; Chopin Roaring 20's Party Invitation, September 29, 1962. *Chopin Singing Society Scrapbook, 1960-1963.* Archives, Chopin Singing Society, Buffalo, NY

midst of all these parties, the singers performed a single show as part of the City of Buffalo Summer Concert at Delaware Park. Directed by Gorecki and music by the Buffalo Community Orchestra, the choir gave a concert of Polish folksongs, show tunes, and classic standards to the North Buffalo crowd.[51]

As summer gave way to autumn, Chopins prepared for two of the biggest events in the history of the choir. The first was a six-month contract to perform a monthly concert for WBEN-TV Channel 4, and the second was President Kennedy's visit and attendance at the Pulaski Day parade.[52] Sponsored by the Erie County Savings Bank, the concert series was the largest local musical production any Western New York television station had undertaken at that point.[53] As Gorecki mapped out the 77 songs that would make up the six performances, the 150 singers of the group began to vigorously practice for the October 9 recording date at Kleinhans Music Hall.[54] Leading up to the night, the station tapped newscaster Steve Geer as host and began a full marketing blitz, with lead Tatra dancer Carol Chojnacki becoming the media face of the event.[55]

With a packed house, the recording went off without a hitch, and the October 10 telecast was adored by audiences. Writing to her local newspaper editor, Ms. Joseph Varge said:

> What a boost (Buffalo) received last Wednesday evening with the first concert of the Chopin Singing Society of Buffalo. Here surely is a vocal group that ranks with the best. A delight to hear, even though one understands no word of the language, a charming sight to see in colorful folk costumes, this is a group to enhance the musical and cultural life of Buffalo... Was there a toe of anyone in the TV audience that did not tap in tempo when the Merry Tatra Dancers whirled on stage? The nimble footwork and sparkling costuming brought to life for young and old the traditional folk stories in dance. Over-all

---

51 1962 Summer Concert, September 5, 1962. *Chopin Singing Society Scrapbook, 1960-1963*. Archives, Chopin Singing Society, Buffalo, NY

52 "Television Highlights." *Union Sun & Journal*, 10 Oct. 1962, p. 15.

53 Noted Chopin Singing Society Starts Monthly Concerts on WBEN-TV Oct. 10. *Chopin Singing Society Scrapbook, 1960-1963*. Archives, Chopin Singing Society, Buffalo, NY

54 Schlaerth, J. D. "TV Has a Niche for Chopin Singers." *Buffalo Evening News*, 18 Sept. 1962, p. 28.

55 "Introduces Chopin Singers:" *Tonawanda News,* 12 Nov. 1962, p. 9.; "Chopin Dancer." *Tonawanda News*, 10 Oct. 1962, p. 11.

> production was excellent—fine sound, brisk pace, imaginative camera work.[56]

Alas, Chopins didn't have the time to bask in the praises of their TV audience, because in four days they would be parading down Broadway with the president of the United States.

With President Kennedy in town stumping for Democratic Congress members, the 1962 Pulaski Day Parade was a highly organized and choreographed affair. With an estimated 10,000 marchers and 21 divisions, headquarters were set up along Broadway from Fillmore to Memorial Drive. Chopins oversaw Division 17, organizing the few hundred marchers from their Kosciuszko Street clubrooms. At 1:30 p.m. the marchers began parading down Broadway along the two and a quarter mile route to Buffalo's City Hall. Touching down in Niagara Falls at 2:10 p.m. after the parade started, President Kennedy was greeted by a delegation of Niagara Falls politicians and his two escorts for the day, Henry J. Osinski, president of the Central Council of Polish Organizations and Representative Thaddeus J. Dulski. Leaving Niagara County by way of Grand Island, Kennedy joined up with the parade at Fillmore by 3:10 p.m. Entering near the Chopin float, the president and his motorcade would make their way down Broadway for a mile and a half, turning off at Elm, so that by the time he made it to the dais at City Hall, the final units would be at Niagara Square.[57] In their coverage of Kennedy's speech on Pulaski, defending against communism, and drumming up support for Democrats, even the national news agencies took note of Chopin's folk-themed float and automobiles,[58] giving the Society some name recognition up and down the Eastern Seaboard.[59]

Between the WBEN performances both Chopins and Tatras stayed busy with other events. The Tatras took part in the Prespa Society-sponsored Fifth Annual Folk Dance Festival at St. Stephen Serbian Church in Lackawanna while Chopins sponsored a "His and Hers" card party in their clubrooms.[60]

---

[56] Chopin Singing Society Article. *Chopin Singing Society Scrapbook, 1960-1963*. Archives, Chopin Singing Society, Buffalo, NY

[57] "J.F.K. Schedule Is Closely Timed." *Buffalo Courier-Express*, 12 Oct. 1962, p. 8.

[58] "Music and Politics." *Buffalo Courier-Express*, 15 Oct. 1962, p. 16.

[59] "Kennedy Gets Big Welcome from Pulaski Day Throng." *Philadelphia Inquirer*, 15 Oct. 1962, p. 6.

[60] "Prespa Society Plans Folk Dance Festival." *Lackawanna Leader*, 1 Nov. 1962, p. 12.; "Variety Party Planned by Chopin Singing Unit." *Lackawanna Leader*, 22 Nov. 1962, p. 8.

The singers returned to the Kleinhans stage and television screens in November with a folk-focused program while their December program had a Christmas flavor to it.[61] As the performances continued, attendance at the live recordings and at-home viewership grew.[62] In the New Year, dances took center stage as tangos, waltzes, and polonaises were highlighted.[63] In their penultimate February broadcast the Chopinites highlighted the Polish folk songs that were near and dear to their heart.[64] To close out their WBEN contract and Symphony Circle residency, the singers touched on all of Poland with a focus on regional melodies.[65]

As the airwaves were abuzz with the voices of Chopin, so too were the hallowed halls of the State Department Building as the Society received an invitation from the Polish Government to tour Poland. Approaching them earlier in the year and offering to pay for the entire trip, the Government of Poland hoped that a three-week, multi-city tour would be a good cultural exchange.[66] Even with member Congressman Thaddeus Dulski taking the lead, the slow gears of politics in the State Department dragged on over the details about the exchange for the better part of the year. The tragedy in Dallas brought all talks to a halt and the prospects of the Chopin Singing Society singing in Poland slowly slipped away.[67]

On February 9, 1963, Ted Mikoll took his second oath of office as president. To mark the occasion the Society surprised Mikoll with a portrait of him by artist Jerome T. Cieslikowski and presented former president, Boleslaus Lemanski, a plaque for his decades of loyal service. [68] Upon receiving the gift, President Mikoll thanked Mr.

---

61 WBEN-TV. *The Chopin Singing Society in A Special TV Concert - November 12, 1962*. Erie County Savings Bank, 1962.; WBEN-TV. *The Chopin Singing Society in A Special TV Concert - December 3, 1962*. Erie County Savings Bank, 1962.

62 Schlaerth, J. Don. "It's Variety Night for Chopin Singers." *Buffalo Evening News*, 14 Nov. 1962, p. 51.

63 WBEN-TV. *The Chopin Singing Society in A Special TV Concert - January 28, 1963*. Erie County Savings Bank, 1963.

64 WBEN-TV. *The Chopin Singing Society in A Special TV Concert - February 20, 1963*. Erie County Savings Bank, 1963.

65 WBEN-TV. *The Chopin Singing Society in A Special TV Concert - March 25, 1963*. Erie County Savings Bank, 1963.

66 Chopin Singing Society Gets Invitation from Poland. *Chopin Singing Society Scrapbook, 1960-1963*. Archives, Chopin Singing Society, Buffalo, NY

67 "U.S. Shift Will Delay Decision on Chopin Tour." *Buffalo Evening News*, 16 Jan. 1963, p. 35.

68 "Chopin Singing Society." *Buffalo Courier-Express*, 10 Feb. 1963, pp. 9-A.; "Singing Society Dinner Saturday." *Buffalo Evening News*, 6 Feb. 1963, p. 44.

Cieslikowski quipping "He did so well, with a poor subject."[69]

Before the Society launched its Summer Fashion Show on May 15,[70] they had already held several fundraisers and parties. From a Miami Beach themed event to a St. Patrick's Day gala, their Dyngus Day party, and an event honoring Ms. Genia Las, Chopins had a full calendar for the first half of the year.[71]

The singers opened their 1963-64 concert season with a grand celebration at the end of August and were soon practicing for their upcoming shows.[72] This practice would be put to good use as they returned to Kleinhans for a second WBEN concert series sponsored by the Erie County Savings Bank. The three-concert program scheduled for December 2, January 29, and March 26 would once again feature Chopins, the Tatra Dancers, and a 21-piece orchestra of Buffalo Philharmonic members.[73] For a special opening presentation, the singers focused on the music of Stanislaw Moniuszko, performing a mix of seven songs from *Halka* and *The Haunted Manor.*[74] The January 29 show was dedicated to the music of Chopin while the final broadcast featured Polish Folk songs.[75]

Between their televised performances Chopins continued to hold fundraisers and dances in their clubrooms. With music provided by the Original Polkateers and Joy Jay & the 4 Spacemen, their January Miami Beach Party was a hit; and their Lincoln's Day Double Header featuring the New Yorkers and Eli Konikoff, and the Yankee 6 brought in a fair crowd. They later held a Mardi Gras Party, a March Polka Festival, and a Dyngus Day party, that was growing in popularity.[76] The major club event of the winter was the installation banquet on February 15. While the members and guests dined on turkey breast

---

[69] "Mikoll Receives Self-Portrait at Chopin Singing Society's Installation." Am-Pol Eagle, 14 Feb. 1963, p. 1.

[70] "Singing Society Presents Fashion Show." *The Lackawanna Leader*, 9 May 1963, p. 1.

[71] *Chopin Singing Society Scrapbook, 1960-1963*. Archives, Chopin Singing Society, Buffalo, NY

[72] "300 Attend Party of Chopin Singers." *Buffalo Courier-Express*, 5 June 1963, p. 2.

[73] "Chopin Singers Will Give Three Concerts on Channel 4." *Buffalo Evening News*, 7 Aug. 1963, p. 62.; Allen, Jack. "Networks Reappraising Shows for Good Taste." *Buffalo Courier-Express*, 4 Dec. 1963, p. 12.

[74] WBEN-TV. *The Chopin Singing Society in a Special TV Concert - December 2, 1963*. Erie County Savings Bank, 1963.

[75] *Chopin Singing Society Scrapbook, 1964-1966*. Archives, Chopin Singing Society, Buffalo, NY

[76] *Chopin Singing Society Scrapbook, 1964-1966*. Archives, Chopin Singing Society, Buffalo, NY; The Chopin Singing Society. *Lincoln's Day Double Header*, The Chopin Singing Society, 1964.

and pork chops, they heard U.S. Senator Kenneth B. Keating discuss aid to Poland as well as the current issues in Panama, Cyprus, Vietnam, and Cuba. [77]

To officially mark the organization's 65th birthday Chopins held their annual Mass and Breakfast at St. Stanislaus Church. The Very Rev. Msgr. Chester A. Meloch of the Diocesan Tribunal served as the guest speaker at the meal served at the clubhouse.[78] Managing all the breakfasts, dinners, parties, weddings, meetings, and rentals happening at the Kosciuszko Street building was becoming more than the small house committee could handle, so in the summer of 1964 John A. Zabinski became the permanent house manager of the organization.[79]

October of 1964 would be a significant month for the choir. They would place second in the annual Pulaski Day Parade in which both New York Senatorial candidates Kenneth B. Keating and Robert F. Kennedy took part,[80] they launched the club newsletter, *The Chopin Staff* with Joan B. Kopciuch serving as editor, and the Society was able to present a portrait of Chopin to President Lyndon B. Johnson during his visit to Buffalo.[81] The president along with Robert and Ethel Kennedy, Congressman Thaddeus J. Dulski, and a small entourage were visiting the Queen City to secure the votes of Buffalonians for their upcoming elections. While still on the tarmac at the Buffalo-Niagara Airport, Danielle Megger, Patricia Burzynski and Patricia Panek, dressed in Polish folk costumes, presented a portrait of Chopin to the president on behalf of the Society. Not forgetting Mrs. Kennedy, Isabella Salczyski and Anthony Markut presented the future senator's wife a bouquet of roses.[82]

For the third year in a row the Erie County Savings Bank sponsored a televised concert series featuring Chopin singers and premiering the organization's dance troupe. Airing October 28, December 23,

---

[77] The Chopin Singing Society. *Frederick Chopin Singing Society 65th Annual Installation Banquet*. The Chopin Singing Society, 1964.; "Keating Will Speak to Chopin Society." *Buffalo Courier-Express*, 14 Feb. 1964, p. 17.

[78] "Chopin Singing Unit to Attend Services." *Buffalo Courier-Express*, 14 May 1964, p. 8.

[79] "Zabinski Named." *Buffalo Courier-Express*, 29 July 1964, p. 28.

[80] Engelman, Esther. "Sen. Keating, Kennedy Join Pulaski Parade Marchers." *Buffalo Courier-Express*, 12 Oct. 1964, pp. 1–3.

[81] "Chopin Staff." Oct. 1964.

[82] Higgens, Joe. "Cheers for Johnson Follow Him All the Way." *Buffalo Courier-Express*, 16 Oct. 1964, p. 6.

and March 17, the concerts focused on the music of Dozynki,[83] Christmastime in Poland,[84] and a Polish Wedding, respectively.[85] An additional event closing out the year was a November sports night fêting members of the Buffalo Bills. The guests that evening were the "Voice of the Bills" Van Miller, halfback and future Erie County Executive, Ed Rutkowski, defensive tackle Tom Sestak, and tight end Ernie Warlick.[86]

In addition to their usual bevy of parties, fundraisers, weekend outings, and gatherings, 1965 was notable for two major events. The first was the April 4 Grand Spring Music Festival. Held at Kleinhans Music Hall and sponsored by the United German-American Singing Societies, the festival presented 10 German singing societies, with Chopins serving as special guests, all under the baton of Peter Gorecki.[87] The second was the institution of the Chopin Young Pianists Competition. Conceived by President Ted Mikoll and guided by Mr. Alan Giles and Sister Mary Evangeline of the Villa Maria Musical Institute, Chopins organized, promoted, scheduled, and executed the new international competition with the goal to "assist talented young artists of piano."[88] In the first year, eight finalists competed at Villa Maria College for a $500 scholarship, with four participants coming from Western New York and others traveling from New York City, Washington, D.C. and Pennsylvania.[89] After a day of grueling competition, judges Ruth Slenczynska, Eugene List, and assistant conductor of the Buffalo Philharmonic Orchestra, Richard Dufallo, chose 15-year-old Diane Walsh, a student of Irwin Freundlich at the Juilliard School of Music, as the inaugural winner.[90]

As much joy the Society created that year, there was a great mark of sadness. While driving home from singing practice at the clubhouse, Ms. Joan B. Kopciuch was fatally injured when a car she was riding in was struck, resulting in a fiery collision on Broadway

---

[83] WBEN-TV. *The Chopin Singing Society in A Special TV Concert - October 26, 1964*. Erie County Savings Bank, 1964.
[84] WBEN-TV. *The Chopin Singing Society in A Special TV Concert - December 21, 1964*. Erie County Savings Bank, 1964.
[85] WBEN-TV. *The Chopin Singing Society in A Special TV Concert - March 15, 1965*. Erie County Savings Bank, 1965.
[86] "Chopin Staff." Oct. 1964.
[87] "Music Festival to Be Held Sunday." *Frontier Herald*, 1 Apr. 1965, p. 22.
[88] *Chopin Singing Society 75th Anniversary, 1899-1974*. The Society, 1974.
[89] "Berio to Conduct Premiere Today." *Buffalo Courier-Express*, 21 Nov. 1965, p. 22.
[90] "Piano Contest at Villa Maria." *Tonawanda News*, 9 Dec. 1965, p. 9.; *Chopin Singing Society 75th Anniversary, 1899-1974*. The Society, 1974.

near Lathrop. The loss of the 23-year-old who served not only as editor of the club newsletter, but also as a key member of the Ladies' Choir Committee and Social Committee would be felt by the organization for years to come.[91]

Becoming an annual tradition, Chopins was again engaged to put on three winter performances for Channel 4. The three shows aired between November and February and featured an evening in Warsaw, Christmas music,[92] and in the New Year, the songs of Poland.[93]

The year 1966 was a monumental one for both Poland and Polonia as both celebrated a Millennium of Christianity in their Slavic homeland. With over a year of planning the Millennium would be celebrated over 18 months with shows, speakers, rallies, a fair exhibit, a lecture series, a Polish art exhibition, a banquet hosting Vice President Hubert H. Humphrey, and a special Mass, to name but a few of the events. Although officially opened on January 8, 1966, the Polish Millennium had several events held in 1965, including an October fashion show where the members of Chopins gave a Dozynki-themed performance.[94] Other members of Chopin would play key roles in the celebration over the course of the next year. Both Peter Gorecki and Judge Ann Mikoll would sit on the General Committee with Gorecki helping to oversee the music. Ann later took part in the lecture series with her presentation titled, "Development of Social and Political Thought in Poland."[95]

With so much focus on Polonia and the Polish American community, outside organizations also held Polish and Poland-themed events. The Buffalo and Erie County Historical Society hosted *Polkas and Polish Dances* where both Polish experts, Daniel Kij and director of the Pic-a-Polka Orchestra, Joseph Macielag, explained that Polkas were of Bohemian origin due to their 2/4 time signature, while most Polish folk songs were in 3/4. To demonstrate some Polish folk dances, the Chopin Singing Society Dance Group gave a few examples

---

91 "Fiery Crash Fatal to One, Injures Four." *Buffalo Courier-Express*, 29 Apr. 1965, p. 5.
92 *Chopin Singing Society Scrapbook, 1964-1966*. Archives, Chopin Singing Society, Buffalo, NY
93 WBEN-TV. *The Chopin Singing Society in A Special TV Concert - January 24, 1966*. Erie County Savings Bank, 1966.
94 "Lead Roles Assigned in Skits." *Buffalo Courier-Express*, 11 Oct. 1965, p. 13.; Kobielski, Milton J. *Millennium of Christianity of the Polish People, 966-1966: Buffalo Diocesan Observance*. Millennium Committee of the Diocese of Buffalo, 1966.
95 Kobielski, Milton J. *Millennium of Christianity of the Polish People, 966-1966: Buffalo Diocesan Observance*. Millennium Committee of the Diocese of Buffalo, 1966.

under the direction of Ann Mikoll.[96]

While they had been holding a Dyngus Day celebration for years, the Millennium celebration brought about a new interest in the celebration from the greater Western New York community. H. Katherine Smith of the *Courier-Express* did a deep dive into the religious, cultural, culinary, and artistic traditions of "Dyngus Day," highlighting the hundreds of participants that packed the Chopin clubrooms every year.[97]

Wanting to capitalize on the great interest in Polish culture the Millennium had spurred, Erie County Savings Bank and WBEN-TV sponsored a televised Polish Millennium concert. Held three days after Dyngus Day, Chopins demonstrated a mix of Polish religious and secular music while the Chopin dancers provided some visual entertainment. The St. Stanislaus Boys Choir was selected as the special guests of the evening concert, delighting mothers across East Buffalo.[98]

In addition to their own shows, Chopins sponsored other performers across Polonia. In May they presented the Theresa Skotnicka Dybas recital at Villa Maria College and at the end of the year held the second Young Pianists Competition.[99] The stiff competition featured 11 contestants from as far away as Arizona and Venezuela,[100] but in the end Austrian born but living in Kenmore, Claudia Maria Hoca was chosen as the 1966 winner.[101]

For their winter concert series that year, both The Big E Saving Bank and Adam, Meldrum & Anderson Co. sponsored the Society for three televised shows. The themes featured were Christmas music and *100 Years of Polish Song* under the hand of Peter Gorecki.[102] The *100 Years of Polish Song* program aired on March 21 and had a special guest dance troupe, the Matusz Polish Dance Circle of New York City. It was the first time the dancers performed on Western New York

---

96 "Bohemia Given Credit for Polka." *Buffalo Courier-Express*, 7 Mar. 1966, p. 7.

97 Smith, H. Katherine. "Easter Monday of Revelry for Area Poles." *Buffalo Courier-Express*, 10 Apr. 1966, pp. 1-D-3-D.

98 WBEN-TV. *The Chopin Singing Society in A Special TV Concert Celebrating the Polish Millennium - April 13, 1966.* Erie County Savings Bank, 1966.

99 "Chopin Unit Will Sponsor Recital Here." *Buffalo Courier-Express*, 8 May 1966, p. 44D.

100 "Piano Competition Has Area Finalists." *Tonawanda News*, 23 Nov. 1966, p. 8.

101 "Kenmore Girl Wins Chopin Competition." *Buffalo Courier-Express*, 27 Nov. 1966, p. 12B.

102 WBEN-TV. *The Chopin Singing Society in A Special TV Concert - December 19, 1966.* Erie County Savings Bank, 1966.; WBEN-TV. *The Chopin Singing Society and The Matusz Polish Dance Circle in 100 Years of Polish Songs - March 21, 1967.* Adam, Meldrum & Anderson Co., 1967.

television, but was the last year for this televised winter concert series.[103]

Chopins opened 1967 by participating in February's *Polish American Cultural Night* sponsored by the Polish Union of America. Held at the Buffalo and Erie County Historical Society, the program included the St. Stanislaus Boys Choir, a drill team from the Adam Plewacki Post and pianist Thomas Kaminski.[104] The Society would take the stage again in May, this time at the Villa Maria College Auditorium. Billed as *The Melody Lingers On*, the performance was sponsored by the Villa Maria Academy Parent's Guild as a fundraiser for the girl's high school, Immaculate Heart of Mary Academy.[105] Between the two shows the Society enjoyed an evening with the Very Rev. Cornelian Dende, OFM. Conv., director of the *Rosary Hour* radio program.[106]

The finals for the third Young Pianists Competition were held in November with Melvin Strauss, associate conductor of the Buffalo Philharmonic Orchestra; William Masselos, pianist in residence at Catholic University, Washington; and Robert Dumm, head of the piano pedagogy department at Catholic University, judging.[107] Of the finalists, Philip Highfill III of Bethesda, Maryland, a student of Ylda Novik was chosen as the winner.[108]

January of 1968 proved once again that the Chopin Singing Society was a major political destination when Robert F. Kennedy visited for a luncheon in his honor as he was touring the state.[109] The tour was only two months prior to the senator's entering the 1968 Democratic presidential primary. He spoke about how America could use its wealth and power to make it an envoy of peace across the world.[110]

At the January 16 luncheon the Kennedys enjoyed a Polish American menu while the senator talked about how his brother garnered 91% of the Polish vote when he ran for president. On policy, Kennedy addressed the need to modernize police forces, and to

---

[103] "Dance Circle Appeared on Buffalo TV." *Greenpoint Weekly Star*, 31 Mar. 1967, p. 4.

[104] "Music to Mark Polish Night." *Buffalo Courier-Express*, 22 Feb. 1967, p. 24.

[105] Villa Maria Academy Parent's Guild. *"The Melody Lingers On" with the Chopin Singing Society for Immaculate Heart of Mary Academy*. Am-Pol Eagle, 1967.; "Villa Maria Guild to Sponsor Concert." Buffalo Courier Express, 5 Mar. 1967, p. 5A.

[106] "Chopin Unit Hears Talk by Fr. Dende." *Buffalo Courier-Express*, 5 Mar. 1967, p. 5A.

[107] "Music Notes." *Buffalo Courier-Express*, 25 Mar. 1967, p. 8.

[108] *Chopin Singing Society 75th Anniversary, 1899-1974*. The Society, 1974.

[109] "R.F.K. to Be Guest." *Buffalo Courier-Express*, 13 Jan. 1968, p. 19.

[110] Warren, Lucian C. "Kennedy's, Aides Get Chilly Greeting from WNY Winter." *Buffalo Courier-Express*, 16 Jan. 1968, p. 13.

institute gun control. As a special gift to both Ethel and Robert, the men of Chopin sang "Sto Lat" to them, wishing them a long and happy life.[111] One hundred forty-two days later Robert F. Kennedy was assassinated by Sirhan Sirhan with an Iver Johnson Cadet 55-A revolver in the kitchen of the Ambassador Hotel, Los Angeles, California.

In October, Chopins hosted another political luncheon, this time for former Ambassador to Poland John A. Gronouski. Gronouski was in Buffalo campaigning for Democratic presidential nominee Hubert Humphrey and his running mate Edmund Muskie, a Polish American with roots in Buffalo's East Side.[112]

Though not starring in a series of television performances in 1967-68, Chopins did have a single WBEN-TV show in May of 1968. Hosted by Dick Rifenburg and aired in full color, they presented a spring concert with the Matusz Dance Circle of New York and Barbara Weintraub, a finalist in the 1967 Young Pianists Competition.[113] At home, the members undertook a major effort to refurbish and remodel their Kosciuszko Street clubrooms. The dining room, practice hall, and several meeting rooms were all touched up, while a sgraffito of Chopin by Jozef Slawinski was given pride of place in the lounge. Chopins would engage Slawinski again in 1968 to produce a copper bas relief of Van Cliburn which was presented to the pianist at a reception following his March concert at Kleinhans.[114]

Of the three finalists from Bronx, NY, Rochester, NY and Sappington, MO, Ms. Kristin Prior of the Flower City was the 1968 winner of the Young Pianists Competition. Besides taking home the $500 scholarship, Ms. Prior was invited to perform with the Society and the Buffalo Philharmonic Orchestra at the *Chopin Pops* concert.[115] Taking place on December 6 at Kleinhans Music Hall, *Chopin Pops* was a benefit show for the Society sponsored by the *Buffalo Evening News* and WBEN. For the first half of the concert the Buffalo Philharmonic Orchestra, conducted by Melvin Strauss, played a three-song set that included two works by Chopin, "Nocturne Op. 15, No. 1" and

---

[111] Herman, Ray. "Crime Problem Stressed." *Buffalo Courier-Express*, 17 Jan. 1968, p. 39.

[112] Herman, Ray. "Gronouski Blasts Nixon on Issues." *Buffalo Courier-Express*, 18 Oct. 1968, p. 15.

[113] "'Cowboy in Africa' For the Young." *Buffalo Courier-Express*, 6 May 1968, p. 8.

[114] Allen, Clare. "The Chopin Singing Society." *Sunday in the Courier-Express*, 1 Dec. 1968, pp. 8–12.; "Van Cliburn to Appear Here Today, Tuesday." *Buffalo Courier-Express*, 24 Mar. 1968, p. 28.

[115] Putnam, Thomas. "Girl, 16, Places First in Chopin Competition." *Buffalo Courier-Express*, 1 Dec. 1968, p. 33.

"Tarantelle, Op. 43." Before the intermission, Ms. Prior performed the first movement of Edvard Grieg's "Piano Concerto in A." to the great satisfaction of Buffalo Courier-Express music reviewer Roy Sniffen.[116] For the second half, the Society sang works by Chopin and Moniuszko. This was buttressed by two dances from Chopin's Folk Dance Troupe, the "Krakowiak" and "White Mazur," both arranged by Ted Peterson. As the antepenultimate item on the program, Mr. Gorecki played his own original piano concerto, which was as warmly received as Ms. Prior's earlier performance. The evening concluded with Chopins retaking the stage for a rendition of "Lara's Theme" from Dr. Zhivago which the audience of 1,400 thoroughly enjoyed.[117]

The end of the year brought changes to the choir as Ted Mikoll decided not to run for a ninth term as president. In his place Stanley H. Zagora was elected to lead the Society of 900 members with Richard J. Jezuit and Casimer Kedzierski serving as vice presidents.

---

[116] Sniffen, Roy. "Chopin Singing Society, Philharmonic Concert." *Buffalo Courier-Express*, 7 Dec. 1968, p. 20.

[117] Buffalo Philharmonic Orchestra. *Pops Concert - December 6, 1968.* Thorner-Sidney Press, 1968.

Chapter 8

Poland, the Vatican, and Beyond

On March 22, 1969, Stanley H. Zagora became the twenty-third person to hold the title of president of Chopin with his swearing-in ceremony. The festive event with a Chopin Chef Salad, Polonaise Cabbage, and Chicken Marseilles saw Very Reverend James M. Demske, SJ, president of Canisius College, and Richard Eisenstein, Buffalo Philharmonic Orchestra's assistant manager,[1] speak while the Honorable Alois Mazur officially installed the officers.[2]

Chopins returned to the small screen with a televised appearance on Channel 4. The April concert with 100 singers and a 22-piece orchestra was conducted by Gorecki. The concert featured a medley from *Camelot* that spotlighted singer Paul Walker.[3] Another medley heard that night was from the *King and I* with a solo from Teresa Dybas.[4] The next month the Society sponsored the Buffalo Philharmonic Orchestra's *Kern Pops*, a musical selection of works by Jerome Kern.[5] They would close out the month of May by singing at the Adam Plewacki Post 799 Memorial Day remembrance held at St. Stanislaus Cemetery in Cheektowaga.[6]

To start the second half of 1969 the Chopinites played host to Mayor Frank A. Sedita at a reception given by Councilman-at-large Stanley M. Makowski, as part of the mayor's reelection campaign.[7] The political season was followed up by the Chopin Young Pianists Competition. This time held in the auditorium of the Buffalo and Erie County Public Library; the 1969 competition saw the first tie in its five-year history. Judges Livingston Gearhart of the Music Department at the University of Buffalo, piano instructor Hazel Jermoe, and pianist and music critic Ylda Novik could not choose between Lydia Artymiw

---

[1] The Chopin Singing Society. *Frederick Chopin Singing Society Annual Installation Banquet, Saturday March 22, 1969*. The Chopin Singing Society, 1969.

[2] "Demske, Eisenstein to Speak at Dinner." *Buffalo Courier-Express*, 14 Mar. 1969, p. 21.

[3] Shearer, Potter. "Television Highlights." *Union Sun Journal*, 7 Apr. 1969, p. 14.

[4] *Chopin Singing Society Scrapbook, 1967-1974*. Archives, Chopin Singing Society, Buffalo, NY

[5] Sniffen, Roy T. "Kern Pops Concert." *Buffalo Courier-Express*, 7 May 1969, p. 23.

[6] "Post Sets Motorcade." *Buffalo Courier-Express*, 23 May 1969, p. 22.

[7] "Mayor Sedita Denies Favoritism Charge." *Buffalo Courier-Express*, 16 Oct. 1969, p. 8.

and Panayis Lykiardopoulos (Panayis Lyras), instead declaring them both first place winners.[8] At the close of the year, Chopins joined the Polish Choral Ensemble of St. Stanislaus Church, Toronto, and the Polish National Alliance Group at the Polish American Cultural Evening at D'Youville College. Their appearances were part of a larger event sponsored by the International Institute Niagara Frontier Folk Art Council that included Professor Leonard Glowsinski's presentation on the background of Polish culture and the Baja Polonia Band.[9]

With the 1970 elections Zagora was replaced with Casimer J. Kedzierski as president,[10] but in the weeks before the banquet the Society held a testimonial dinner for former President Mikoll at which William B. Lawless, dean of the University of Notre Dame Law School and a former State Supreme Court Justice spoke.[11]

Most of the year was relatively light for the choir. In addition to the Dyngus Day party, the choir had three major events, singing at a memorial service at St. Stan's Cemetery in May, a benefit concert at the Veterans Hospital in June,[12] and the Pulaski Day parade in October.[13] On the other hand, that November was a busy one. It started with a cocktail party and buffet dinner honoring the Pianist Competition judges, an event hosted by co-chairman and Sausage King of Buffalo, Raymond F. Wardynski. The judges for the competition that year were Dr. Kenwyn Boldt, head of the Music Department at Buffalo State College; Frank Glazer, professor of music at the Eastman School of Music in Rochester; and Dr. Dean Boal, chairman of the Music Department and professor of piano at Fredonia State College.[14] The day after the party, 16-year-old Yolanda Liepa of Cincinnati, Ohio was declared the winner of the 6th annual competition.[15] The next Sunday, Chopins was again invited to take part in the Folk Art Council's Polish-American cultural evening, this time singing with the Polish Singing Circle and Kalina Singing Society.[16]

---

[8] "2 Share First Place in Piano Competition." *Buffalo Courier-Express*, 30 Nov. 1969, p. 38.
[9] "Three Music Groups Set Art Event." *Buffalo Courier-Express*, 10 Dec. 1969, p. 10.
[10] *Annual Installation Banquet Frederick Chopin Singing Society 1899-1970.* The Chopin Singing Society, 1970.
[11] "Lawless to Speak at Mikoll Dinner." *Buffalo Courier-Express*, 22 Jan. 1970, p. 11.
[12] *Chopin Singing Society Scrapbook, 1967-1974*. Archives, Chopin Singing Society, Buffalo, NY
[13] Desmond, Michael. "Thousands Parade to Honor Pulaski." *Buffalo Courier-Express*, 12 Oct. 1970, pp. 1–4.
[14] "Fete Chopin Judges." *Buffalo Courier-Express*, 22 Nov. 1970, p. 69.
[15] "Ohio Girl Wins Chopin Prize." *Buffalo Courier-Express*, 26 Nov. 1970, p. 9.
[16] "Choirs Plan Program." *Buffalo Courier-Express*, 26 Nov. 1970, p. 63.

In 1971 Ted Mikoll was again elected as president of the Society.[17] At the installation event Melvin Strauss, the Buffalo Philharmonic Orchestra's conductor in residence, announced that the orchestra and Chopins would be working together on some performances to heighten general interest in music and to unify metropolitan Buffalo culturally. He did so by saying, "I would like to see the cultural as well as the ethnic barriers broken in this town." These concerts would be a joint venture with the entire orchestra and the full choir held at Villa Maria College.[18]

The April that followed would be a busy one for the members of Chopin. The Dyngus Day celebration on April 12 had well over 1,000 people invading the club to enjoy a spread of 220 pounds of Polish sausage, 300 pounds of potato salad, dozens of smokehouse hams, and a full bar of refreshments.[19] To help work off some of the heavy eating, traditional Polish and polka music filled the air to get the crowds moving.[20] A week later the choir performed at Buffalo's Saint Joseph Old Cathedral as part of a Latin High Mass. For the service, Gorecki incorporated several of his original works into the celebration.[21] The Society closed out the month by holding a dinner for pianist Van Cliburn who was visiting for a performance with the BPO. As part of the event, President Mikoll presented Cliburn a remembrance photo album of the virtuoso's 1968 visit to the Queen City.[22]

The members joined the Adam Plewacki Post 799 for their Memorial Day service,[23] before hosting their Annual Brisket Picnic a few months later.[24] In August, the Ladies Auxiliary held a Mexican-themed fashion show and dinner at the Transit Valley Country Club in Clarence.[25] As summer turned to fall, Chopins sang a Mass at SS. Peter and Paul Church before holding their Christmas party at the end of

---

17 The Chopin Singing Society. *Annual Installation Banquet Frederick Chopin Singing Society 1899-1971.* The Chopin Singing Society, 1971.

18 "Orchestra to Play with Chopin Group." *Buffalo Courier-Express*, 7 Mar. 1971, p. 31.

19 Curran, Bob. "It's Great to Be Polish When Dyngus Day Arrives." Buffalo Evening News, 14 Apr. 1971.

20 Dyngus Day Invitation from 1971. *Chopin Singing Society Scrapbook, 1967-1974* Archives, Chopin Singing Society, Buffalo, NY

21 Chopin Society to Sing at Mass in Old Cathedral Article. *Chopin Singing Society Scrapbook, 1967-1974* Archives, Chopin Singing Society, Buffalo, NY

22 Pianist Honored Article. *Chopin Singing Society Scrapbook, 1967-1974* Archives, Chopin Singing Society, Buffalo, NY

23 "Talk Scheduled by Judge Zimmer." *Buffalo Courier-Express*, 27 May 1971, p. 19.

24 Annual Brisket Picnic from 1971. *Chopin Singing Society Scrapbook, 1967-1974* Archives, Chopin Singing Society, Buffalo, NY

25 "Revue Scheduled by Chopin Society." *Buffalo Courier-Express*, 11 July 1971, p. 86.

the year.[26] The Society passed on holding the Pianists' Competition that year choosing to build up their reserves for the fund instead.[27]

Raymond W. Manuszewski was sworn in as the twenty-fifth president of the Society in February of 1972, with Casimer Kedzierski and Stanley Zagora as vice presidents, Richard Jezuit as financial secretary, Lawrence Nagowski as librarian, and Ted Mikoll as a member of the board of directors.[28] That same month, several vocalists joined conductor Gorecki at the Buffalo Athletic Club to sing at the retirement party of longtime friend of Chopins and first Polish American to sit on the city bench, Judge Michael E. Zimmer.[29] At the same time, a small delegation of members had the chance to meet the Honorable Witold Trampczynski, Polish Ambassador to the United States, during his two-day tour of Western New York.[30]

In March, Melvin Strauss's desire to have joint productions between the Chopin Singing Society and the Buffalo Philharmonic Orchestra came true when Chopins relaunched their annual concerts and moved to feature the orchestra as part of the show.[31] In recognition of the 100th anniversary of the death of Stanislaw Moniuszko, Chopins focused on works from the opera *Halka* for the program. With Louis Distel, Theresa Dybas, and Robert Caple as soloists, Polish virtuoso Krzysztof Brzuza on piano, and the orchestra adding the drama needed for many of the songs,[32] the performance was deemed a grand public success.[33]

The concert was followed by another blowout Dyngus Day party at the Chopin clubrooms. With a decade of celebrations, Dyngus Day had truly entered the Buffalo zeitgeist, so much so that Judge Busswell Roberts moved around his calendar in response to attorneys' pleas who wanted to enjoy the party. That year Danny Demyanick was

---

[26] *Chopin Singing Society Scrapbook, 1967-1974* Archives, Chopin Singing Society, Buffalo, NY

[27] *Chopin Singing Society 75th Anniversary, 1899-1974*. The Society, 1974.

[28] Singers Seat Slate Article. *Chopin Singing Society Scrapbook, 1967-1974* Archives, Chopin Singing Society, Buffalo, NY

[29] "Judge Zimmer Given Barrage of Accolades." *Buffalo Courier-Express*, 26 Feb. 1972, p. 21.

[30] "M&T Bank to Host Polish Ambassador." *Lackawanna Leader*, 2 Mar. 1972, p. 1.

[31] Putnam, Tom. "Chopin Society to Present Program." *Buffalo Courier-Express*, 19 Mar. 1972, p. 6.

[32] The Chopin Singing Society. *Annual Concert - Federick Chopin Singing Society Featuring the Buffalo Philharmonic Orchestra March 25, 1972*. Chopin Singing Society, 1972.

[33] Goddard, Grace. "Gifted Piano Virtuoso Excites City with Chopin's Music." *Buffalo Courier-Express*, 28 Mar. 1972, p. 11.

declared "Mr. Dyngus,"[34] while Carol Roth, Michaeline Wyrobek, Phyllis Blonski, Jean Pajda, and Lorrie Graziano were named the "Dyngus Girls."[35]

Moving the piano competition to the spring, the three rounds of judging had again come up with the rare conclusion of two winners. Marion Gaffney of Tonawanda and John Hendrickson of Edmonton, Alberta, Canada both took home first prizes. The third place winner that year was Frederica Prior,[36] younger sister of the 1968 competition winner Kristin Prior, and daughter of Eastman School of Music's organ instructor Evelyn Prior.[37]

The Society closed out their public performances for the year by taking part in the Polish Art and Music festival held on October 8. Sponsored by the Professional and Businessmen's Association of Western New York and held at Villa Maria College, the performers included the Kalina Singing Society, the Polish Singing Circle, Paderewski Singing Society, the Wawel Dancers, the Goral Ensemble and the Echo Singing Society.[38] The last event of 1972 for Chopins was the International Institute's 28th Annual Folk Ball to visit their old friend Jan Sejda. The former dance director for the Society, Sejda was now the director and choreographer of the Kujawiaki Student Dance Group at Alliance College who were in the city to be one of the performers at the ball.[39]

Ted Mikoll returned to the presidency in 1973, starting an unbroken 15-year tenure at the top of the singing society. Jack R. Poczciwinski and Milton F. Bednarek were elected as vice presidents,[40] and Ted's brother James served on the Executive Committee.[41]

To mark the 500th birthday of Nicolaus Copernicus, the Permanent Chair of Polish Culture, the Polish American Congress Western New York Division, the Copernicus Educational Aid Association, and the Felician Sisters held a commemorative program at Villa Maria

---

[34] Curran, Bob. "That Special Day Following Easter - A Polish Festival." Buffalo Evening News, 6 Apr. 1972.
[35] *Chopin Singing Society 75th Anniversary, 1899-1974*. The Society, 1974.
[36] "Chopin-ists." *Buffalo Courier-Express*, 14 May 1972, p. 10.
[37] "'Littlest Dancer' Ready." *Rochester Democrat and Chronicle*, 24 Dec. 1961, p. 5M.
[38] "Polish Art Event to Be Held Oct. 8." *Buffalo Courier-Express*, 9 Sept. 1972, p. 21.
[39] Ott, Betty J. "Student Group Will Perform Dances of Poland at 28th Folk Ball Saturday." *Buffalo Courier-Express*, 10 Nov. 1972, p. 10.
[40] "Society Elects." *Buffalo Courier-Express*, 11 Jan. 1973, p. 28.
[41] The Chopin Singing Society. *74th Annual Concert*. Chopin Singing Society, 1973.

College's Auditorium. While Dr. Eugene Kusielewicz, president of the Kosciuszko Foundation was the keynote speaker, it would be the singing of Chopins that opened and closed the program.[42] Doctor Kusielewicz returned to Western New York in November as the Permanent Chair of Polish Culture at Canisius College hosted their own celebration for Copernicus. Starting with a special Mass led by the Most Rev. Edward D. Head, Bishop of Buffalo the service saw several distinguished concelebrants including Canisius College President James M. Demske, SJ and Rev. Cornelian M. Dende, the host of the *Father Justin Rosary Hour*. The ceremony was then followed by a dinner and program where Dr. Kusielewicz spoke on the significance of Copernicus in modern times.[43]

In April the choir presented its 74th Annual Concert and once again was able to incorporate the BPO into the program.[44] To honor Copernicus, the Society sang an original work by Gorecki entitled, "The Wonderful World" dedicated to the great astronomer.[45] That May, they sang at Erie Community College North as part of a State University of New York Conference, *The University, the Community, and the Arts*. The singers also held their piano competition in which California native Aglaia Koras took home the first prize of $500 while Yumiko Morioka of Tokyo, Japan placed second, securing a $200 scholarship.[46]

As they ended the year, the singers sponsored a Polish American Cultural Night on behalf of Niagara Frontier Folk Art Council. With President Mikoll as the program director, the choir took the stage at the auditorium of the State University College at Buffalo as the headliners of the show. The Society then retired for the rest of the year as they began preparing for their diamond jubilee in 1974.[47]

The Chopinites had a lot on their plate for the 75th birthday celebration. First, they had their April concert, then the anniversary banquet, a program book, and a year full of concerts. As individuals and committees worked away, the board members and directors represented Chopin at functions and events held in their honor. In February the Mikolls attended the Niagara Frontier Folk Art Council's 10th

---

42 "Copernicus Fete Is Set Sunday." *Buffalo Courier-Express*, 1 Mar. 1973, p. 32.
43 "Copernicus' Birth to Be Celebrated at Canisius." *The Griffin*, 5 Oct. 1973, p. 2.
44 "Chopin Unit to Sing." *Buffalo Courier-Express*, 5 May 1973, p. 22.
45 The Chopin Singing Society. *74th Annual Concert*. Chopin Singing Society, 1973.
46 "California Girl Wins Chopin Prize." *Buffalo Courier-Express*, 27 May 1973, p. 31.
47 "Folk Art Program Set." *Tonawanda News*, 27 Oct. 1973, p. 7.

annual awards dinner to accept a scroll on behalf of the singers, in recognition of the decade of dedication of Chopins to the Council.[48]

In March, a project years in the making, finally came to fruition as the Buffalo City Council approved the Society's request to have the bust of Chopin moved to Symphony Circle. It was the culmination of 15 years of campaigning on their part that led to the move, from an isolated spot near the Science Museum, to the prominent place in front of Kleinhans Music Hall. To make sure it was done properly, Alfred Ignaszak, and his firm, Cowper Construction Co., donated the time, labor, and supplies to transport the monument for the city.[49]

On the evening of Saturday, April 6, the 90 singing members of the Chopin Singing Society adorned the stage at Villa Maria College for their 75th Anniversary Concert. Dressed in new formal attire, the choir opened with a composition Gorecki had written in celebration of the big event. Titled "Intro Passa," the chorus finished the new piece and went right into works by Kazuro, Kurpinski, and Zygmunt Noskowski, accompanied by the BPO. For the second act, the Kujawiaki Dancers performed two numbers mixed in with solos from Louis Distel and Theresa Dybas. The songs that followed from the male and female choruses brought much delight to the standing room only audience of 1,500.[50]

Following their concert, the Chopinites took part in celebrating a century of the Felician Sisters in the United States and held its piano competition which Momoro Ono won.[51] In the summer the singers hosted the three day long Hard Times Music Festival and brought their music to the masses with a concert on Broadway near Lombard as part of the first ever Pulaski Day Parade and Festival.[52] In addition to performing a short set of patriotic Polish and American music, Chopins announced to the large crowd before the Broadway Market that they had been approved by both the U.S. State Department and the Polish Government's Ministry of Cultural Affairs to undertake a 14-day tour

---

48 "Folk Art Council Sets Awards Dinner Sunday." *Buffalo Courier-Express*, 23 Feb. 1974, p. 9.

49 "Chopin Bust Is Scheduled to Be Moved." *Buffalo Courier-Express*, 28 Mar. 1974, p. 12.

50 The Chopin Singing Society. *75th Anniversary Concert*. Chopin Singing Society, 1974.; Putnam, Thomas. "Society Concert a 'Tour.'" *Buffalo Courier-Express*, 8 Apr. 1974, p. 6.

51 Zielinski, Adrianne. "Affair in May to Honor the Felician Sisters." *Buffalo Courier-Express*, 14 Apr. 1974, p. 71.; *Chopin Singing Society 75th Anniversary, 1899-1974*. The Society, 1974.

52 The Chopin Singing Society. "Chopin's Hard Times Festival." *Buffalo Courier-Express*, 15 June 1974, p. 6.; "Pulaski Observance to Become Festival." *Buffalo Courier-Express*, 30 Aug. 1974, p. 6.

of Poland in May 1975.[53]

To formally celebrate their 75th birthday, the Society held a grand banquet at the Statler Hilton in October. Besides the food, drink, and impromptu outbursts of song; families who had given greatly and been part of the Society for generations were recognized, including the Czuprynskis, Mazikowskis, Jendrasiaks, Kowalewskis, Chodkowskis, Fincels, Kujawas, Poczekajs, Kolberts, Zawieruchas, Bagienskis, Puchalskis, Duchanskis, Kulwickis, and Poczciwinskis.[54]

The Society ended their year by giving back to the community. As winter fell upon Western New York, the choir hosted an evening of Christmas carols at Luder's Restaurant in Elma. The price of admission for the evening's entertainment was a canned good that would be given to a local food bank. When the night was finished, over $100 worth of goods were donated.[55]

At the start of the year, President Mikoll and a small entourage spent a week in Poland to work out the details of their trip. The late spring tour would include 100 members spending two weeks in Poland and performing in Rzeszow, Czestochowa, and the Palace of Culture in Warsaw. To ensure that the choir could give its best possible performance, each city promised to provide a forty-piece orchestra to accompany the singers. Once the details were finalized, Zbigniew Tomkowski, First Secretary to Wieslaw Adamski, Vice Minister of Cultural Affairs, formally invited the Chopin Singing Society to Poland in February of 1975.[56]

In the weeks leading up to their departure, the members of Chopin practiced fervently for their international tour, while still making the time to take part in some local events. In April they provided the musical entertainment at the Polish Swieconka Feast at Canisius College; while in May, they performed at a Bon Voyage concert held at Villa Maria College's auditorium.[57] As part of their final performance before leaving for Poland, the choir dedicated the concert to Kolko Polek in recognition of their 75th anniversary, as well as singing in memory of longtime board member Eugene Zawadzki.[58]

On May 30 members of Chopin began departing for Poland. As

---

53 "Music Highlights Pulaski Festival." *Tonawanda News*, 25 Sept. 1974, p. 10.
54 *Chopin Singing Society 75th Anniversary, 1899-1974*. The Society, 1974.
55 "Food for Needy Donated at Party." *Buffalo Courier-Express*, 23 Dec. 1974, p. 16.
56 Putnam, Thomas. "Buffalo's 100-Voice Chopin Singing Society Schedules Poland Concert Tour." *Buffalo Courier-Express*, 21 Feb. 1975, p. 4.
57 Allwein, Carole. "Polish Joy at Canisius." *The Griffin*, 11 Apr. 1975, p. 8.
58 The Chopin Singing Society. *"Bon Voyage" Concert*. Chopin Singing Society, 1975.

Mayor Makowski and his wife, Florence, were boarding their flight at the Buffalo International Airport, the Queen City's chief executive said of the upcoming tour, "I think the major purpose of this trip is cultural," and that "we're on this trip to spread peace through music and with the hope that we all can come to a deeper understanding of peace…I'm hoping to chat with some of the public and local officials as I did in Japan," referring to his four-day trip to Kanazawa, Buffalo's sister city in Japan. On the economic development front, Makowski planned to speak with federal officials about establishing Polish factories in Buffalo or elsewhere in the U.S. He went on to say that, "[t]here is some trading going on now between the two countries, and hopefully the trip could stimulate even more."[59]

The tour officially began on the evening of Monday, June 2 when Chopins appeared on stage in Rzeszow, but the group had already taken part in a historic event hours earlier. That afternoon at Rzeszow's city hall with members of the Society looking on, Mayor Makowski and Polish officials signed the formal agreement solidifying Rzeszow and Buffalo as Sister Cities. At the concert, the singers poured their heart and soul into their performance and the audience responded in kind. Tears ran down the cheeks of the Poles while the cheers for multiple encores compelled the singers to repeat songs.[60] In Czestochowa, the English segments of the programs were received with loud applause for the "Battle Hymn of the Republic" and selections from the Broadway musical stage. At the final concert in Warsaw the show concluded with the audience breaking out into song, singing "Sto Lat" and an emotional rendition of the Polish national anthem. The Chopin's board knew that the Warsaw concert would be a special one for the organization and coordinated with a studio to have the show recorded.[61]

With their down time, the members visited Zakopane, the Krakow International Film Festival,[62] and all the famous locations of Warsaw.[63] In the place of Frederic Chopin's birth, Zelazowa Wola, the

---

59 "Mayor, Wife Off for Poland; Chopin Group Goes Today." *Buffalo Courier-Express*, 30 May 1975, p. 1.

60 Witerski, David S. "Audiences Stirred on Chopin Singers Tour, Mayor Says." *Buffalo Courier-Express*, 6 June 1975, p. 1.

61 "Poland for Buffalo's Chopin Singers." *The Courier-Express Magazine*, 10 Aug. 1975, pp. 8–11.

62 "Tours Poland." *Hamburg Front Page*, 5 June 1975, p. 10.

63 "Poland for Buffalo's Chopin Singers." *The Courier-Express Magazine*, 10 Aug. 1975, pp. 8–11.

members enjoyed a private concert by their 1973 guest pianist, Teresa Rutkowska and in Warsaw, they had an audience with Primate of Poland, the now Blessed Stefan Cardinal Wyszyński. Before leaving Poland, the group sang at a Mass at the Church of the Holy Cross, the final resting place of Chopin's heart.[64]

Returning stateside on June 16, the Chopinites took the rest of the summer off to recover from their tour. They began to grace American stages again in late September when the Buffalo Philharmonic Orchestra joined them at Corpus Christi Church as part of the Pulaski Festival. The orchestra played works by Bach and Haydn under its assistant conductor Frank Collura, while Gorecki led Chopins in a medley of Polish songs.[65] In early October the choir revisited Villa Maria for their Encore Concert, a reproduction of their Polish tour set that included music by Gorecki, Sypietynski, and American favorites "The King and I," "Melody of Love," and the "Battle Hymn of the Republic."[66] The singers then closed out the year with a show at the Business and Professional Women's Club of Buffalo's Christmas party.[67]

After proving once again to be one of Buffalo's major cultural ambassadors, and now on the global stage, the choir began fielding concert requests from a variety of local organizations interested in being a part of their 76th Anniversary series. In Buffalo's North Side, the Central Presbyterian Church at Main Street and Jewett Parkway invited Chopins to open the year with a February recital.[68] Following the show, Albany called upon the singers to represent the state as part of the Bicentennial Ceremonies in Washington, D.C.

Arranged to coincide with Congressman Thaddeus J. Dulski's acceptance of the Polish Order of Merit at the Polish Embassy, a delegation that included Buffalo Mayor Stanley M. Makowski; Leonard F. Walentynowicz, United States Assistant Secretary of State for Security and Consular Affairs; New York State Lt. Gov. Mary Anne Krupsak, Erie County Executive Edward V. Regan;[69] and 137 members of Chopins arrived in Washington in mid-March. Once there, the singers had three full days of meetings, receptions, and performances between March 18 and March 21. Dressed in their now signature red blazers

---

[64] Chopin Singing Society Archives, 1987.

[65] Putnam, Thomas. "Philharmonic Joins Chopin Singers." *Buffalo Courier-Express*, 27 Sept. 1975, p. 4.

[66] The Chopin Singing Society. *"Encore" Concert.* Chopin Singing Society, 1975.

[67] "Christmas Program Set for BPW." *Tonawanda News*, 5 Dec. 1975, p. 2.

[68] "Chopin Singing Society Members to Perform." *Lackawanna Leader*, 29 Jan. 1976, p. 11.

[69] "Chopin Group Will Present Bicen Gift." *Buffalo Courier-Express*, 18 Mar. 1976, p. 15.

and donning blue ties for the trip, a highlight had the Chopinites present a silver plate with a portrait of Revolutionary War hero Thaddeus Kosciusko as a Bicentennial gift to the country. In the White House Rose Garden, First Lady Betty Ford and Dr. Theodore C. Marrs, special assistant to the president, accepted the gift on behalf of a grateful nation before the singers gave a brief performance for the president's wife.[70] After a tour of the White House, the Society hosted a reception at the Washington Hilton for the members of the New York congressional delegation as well as the members of Congress who had any Polish ancestry.[71]

Giving a concert on the east steps of the Capital in the morning of March 19, the group later lunched with members of Congress. They would reconvene that evening at the Polish Embassy to watch as Congressman Dulski received his award for promoting close relations between Poland and America. After an evening of festivities, the group of Western New Yorkers arrived at the Kennedy Center for a brief tour before beginning their lunchtime concert for the visitors. A second concert was given at the Lincoln Memorial, garnering an audience that filled out the rest of the memorial steps and part of the National Mall.[72] The last show of the day was held in Silver Springs for the members of the Polish Arts Club of Washington.

As the last act before returning to Buffalo, the Chopinites sang a Latin Mass at the National Shrine of the Immaculate Conception, home to a Chapel of Our Lady of Czestochowa. As the busses containing the singers pulled out of Washington, WGR-TV reporter Rich Kellman and cameraman Harry Marshall agreed that they had captured enough of the weekend to make a great program.

Titled *From Buffalo with Love*, the half-hour television event won a rave review from columnist Jack Allen, who after previewing the show said it was, "[a] joy and an uplift... full of happiness and warmth, and a complete absence of phoniness or overstaging. Kellman and Marshall caught the spirit of the three-day Polish-American adventure with skill."[73] Airing on March 31, the program was popular among both audiences and media critics; so much so that Morality in Media of Western New York recognized the choir for exceeding its

---

[70] Chopin Singing Society Archives, 1987.
[71] "Chopin Group Will Present Bicen Gift." *Buffalo Courier-Express*, 18 Mar. 1976, p. 15.
[72] "Chopin Singers Take Capital by Storm." *Buffalo Courier-Express*, 23 Mar. 1976, p. 14.
[73] Allen, Jack. "Chopin Group's Visit Wins Praise." *Buffalo Courier-Express*, 31 Mar. 1976, p. 16.

tenets of truth, taste, inspiration and love.[74]

After a month of rest, Chopins staged their own bicentennial concert at Villa Maria College. The concert named *To America with Love* was divided into three segments. The first was dedicated to the group's Polish heritage, the second was focused on the songs sprung from America, and the third was American music birthed from dramatic times. Accompanied by the Buffalo Philharmonic Orchestra the musical highlights of the evening were Gorecki's original work "Bicentennialiana," selections from *Oklahoma*, and their internationally acclaimed rendition of the "Battle Hymn of the Republic."[75] One of the most moving performances before the overflowing crowd was the group rendition of "Beautiful Dreamer" which was to be sung by soloist Evelyn Rubach. Sadly, Rubach was tragically killed in an automobile accident the week before.[76] Following the show, the choir released their privately pressed album, *The Chopin Singing Society of Buffalo, New York.* The live recording of their performance from Warsaw National Philharmonic Hall in Poland was not widely available, but those with a connection could pick up a copy for only $5.00.[77]

The singers would represent New York State again, this time with an October tour of Massachusetts. Taking part in the Boston 200 celebration, the group performed at an event attended by Mayor Kevin White, Senator Edward M. Kennedy, and Governor Michael Dukakis.[78] Then they traveled to Salem where they gave a concert at the location where Pulaski first stepped foot in America.[79] Chopins also took part in a number of other Bicentennial events around Western New York, including a Mass at St. Agatha Roman Catholic Church and joined the Plewacki Post at the Memorial Day parade.[80] As part of the *Know Your Neighbor* series, a two-week Bicentennial salute to Polish Americans,[81]the singers held a concert at St. Stanislaus Church before heading a performance at Corpus Christi presented by the Pulaski

---

74 "Reservations Open for April 25 Morality in Media Awards Dinner." *Tonawanda News*, 5 Apr. 1976, p. 5.

75 The Chopin Singing Society. *Bicentennial Concert*. Chopin Singing Society, 1976.

76 "Chorus Sings to America, With Love." *Buffalo Courier-Express*, 18 May 1976, p. 15.

77 The Chopin Singing Society. *Bicentennial Concert*. Chopin Singing Society, 1976.

78 "Chopin Society to Fill Boston Date." *Buffalo Courier-Express*, 15 Oct. 1976.

79 Chopin Singing Society Archives, 1987.

80 "St. Agatha Mass." *Front Page,* 17 June 1976, p. 4.; "Memorial Rites Held Under Gloomy Skies." *Buffalo Courier-Express*, 1 June 1976, p. 15.

81 "Polish-American Salute Is Planned." *Tonawanda News*, 21 Sept. 1976, p. 9.

Association of the Niagara Frontier.[82]

Among all the excitement and programs surrounding the Bicentennial, Chopins still found time to host their Young Pianists Competition. With another strong field of candidates, 17-year-old Brian Ganz was selected the winner of the annual scholarship prize.[83]

In March of 1977, the Society announced that they had received a return-engagement invitation from the People's Republic of Poland. To work out the details the singers dispatched President Ted Mikoll, Vice President David Rutecki, and Marian Strzelczyk, the owner of Pomoc Travel Agency on Fillmore Avenue, to Poland for a week.[84]

While planning was underway for their second European trip, the singers of Chopin took on few engagements. One was a return appearance at the Central Presbyterian Church, which they had visited the year before. The late April concert was highlighted with Polish and American music, with soprano Theresa Dybas and tenor Louis Distel serving as soloists.[85]

After months of practicing, a new wardrobe that embraced America's Wild West image,[86] and a flight delay, Chopins finally departed for their Polish trip on August 18, 1977.[87] Documenting the entire adventure, embedded *Courier-Express* reported Rita Smith captured firsthand the overwhelming enthusiasm the Polish people had for the Buffalo singers. From exclamations of "[t]hey are professionals! I never heard anything so marvelous from amateurs," to the thunderous applause that followed the singing of "God Bless America," Smith was able to record an uncensored account of the people's reaction to the group.[88]

Following their opening show in Krakow, the singers visited Bydgoszcz, Poznan, and Warsaw. At each venue they opened with a set of Polish music before donning six shooters on their hips, vests on their chests, and cowboy hats on their heads, for their America-themed

---

[82] "Two Concerts to Highlight Pulaski Day Parade Weekend." Front Page, 25 Sept. 1976, p. 12.

[83] "'Classical Favorites' Top Philharmonic Program." *Tonawanda News*, 29 Mar. 1977, p. 3.

[84] "Chopin Singers Set Return to Poland." *Buffalo Courier-Express*, 16 Mar. 1977, p. 10.

[85] "Concert Set by Chopin Society." *Tonawanda News*, 21 Apr. 1977, p. 4.

[86] Chopin Singing Society Archives, 1987.

[87] Smith, Rita. "'Chopin Singers' Departure Delayed by Jet Breakdown." *Buffalo Courier-Express*, 20 Aug. 1977, p. 3.

[88] Smith, Rita. "Chopin Singers Stir Krakow Audience to Cheers, Tears." *Buffalo Courier-Express*, 23 Aug. 1977.

second act. Seeing this costume change, Carol Brown, the Charge d'Affaires of the American Embassy in Poland said, "[t]his is diplomacy at its effective best."[89] The show then closed with highlights from their American Bicentennial shows, including "America" and "Bicentennialiana."[90]

On September 3, after being away for more than two weeks, Chopins arrived home. While still on the jet bridge several of the members told reporters of their experience in Poland. Singer Geraldine Szemraj was humbled by the plenty she had in America saying, "I could kneel down and kiss the earth here after seeing how little the people have there. I'm glad our parents came to America." Tour captain James Jankowski spoke of their acceptance by the Poles, "I'm proud our concerts were as successful as they were and the people received us so warmly. I think we did ourselves proud."[91] Two weeks later the group gave a *Welcome Home* street concert at the corner of Broadway and Gibson where they sang a few selections from their shows in Poland. Mayor Makowski acted as Master of Ceremonies, while the Adam Plewacki American Legion Post 799 served as color guard with the American Legion Post 264 of the Tonawandas providing a band.[92]

In addition to Ms. Smith, Channel 2 anchorman Rich Kellman and cameraman Harvey Marshall accompanied Chopins on their trip, and after a month of editing, presented *Beyond the Curtain,* a series of ten short documentaries. The documentaries looked not just at the tour of Chopins but also the lives of the singers, peoples' reaction to having the group in the country, and showed how the great cities of Poland had recovered from the Second World War. Surprisingly, the communist government gave the newsmen free access to the country and even provided archival footage.[93]

In late summer, as the choir was beginning to prepare for their end of year *Encore* concert, a quagmire was developing. That August the philharmonic musicians went on strike for better pay, better

[89] Chopin Singing Society Archives, 1987.

[90] The Chopin Singing Society. *Koncert Choru Imienia Fryderyka Szopena*. Chopin Singing Society, 1977.

[91] Smith, Rita. "Chopin Singers Return to Exultant Welcome." *Buffalo Courier-Express*, 4 Sept. 1977, p. 1.

[92] "Saturday Celebration Is Planned to Honor Chopin Society Singers." *Buffalo Courier-Express*, 17 Sept. 1977, p. 6.

[93] Baker, Jim. "'Chopin Singers' Trip Makes Fine TV." *Buffalo Courier-Express*, 3 Oct. 1977, p. 15.

conditions, better oversight, and more organizational openness. With their October 16 concert fast approaching there was a real threat that the show would not go on. On October 13, the musicians gathered to vote on whether they should play the concert, knowing it would be without pay and might give the philharmonic board the upper hand. When all the votes were counted, it was unanimous, the musicians would play the concert for free.[94] As a sign of appreciation and coming down solidly on the side of the musicians, Chopins handed out a flyer explaining the laborers' side of the struggle and included a full-page ad in the program so patrons could donate to the musicians' cause. As they had in 1975, the 1977 *Encore Concert* was made up of highlights from their tour of Poland, from "Maki and Biale Roze" to singing "Home on the Range" in cowboy hats.[95]

February 1, 1978, was a red-letter day in the history of the Chopin Singing Society with the release of its first studio album, *From Poland with Song.* Produced by Mark Records of Buffalo, the album included remastered of tracks from the group's privately released LP, along with new songs from their 1977 tour of Poland. Launched at a reception at Shea's Theater, the record earned a favorable review in the *Courier-Express*'s "Rock Rack" column and sold briskly in the early weeks of its release.[96] Buffalo Mayor Jimmy Griffin even recognized the accomplishment of the group by signing a proclamation honoring the singers and the release of the album.[97] *From Poland with Song* would also lead to the Society's biggest production of the year with a spring Florida concert tour.

In late 1977 Blanka Rosenstiel, president of the Miami-based American Institute of Polish Culture, had heard about the Society's two successful tours of Poland. Wanting to know more about the singers, she reached out to President Mikoll, who in turn sent her a copy of *From Poland with Song* to demonstrate the group's style and fun approach to Polish music. After listening to the record, Ms. Rosenstiel extended an invitation to the Buffalonians to perform in Florida.[98]

---

[94] "Musicians Vote to Play Chopin Society Concert." *Buffalo Courier-Express*, 13 Oct. 1977, p. 1.

[95] The Chopin Singing Society. *'Encore' Concert*. Chopin Singing Society, 1977.

[96] "Chopin Singers Go on Record." *Buffalo Courier-Express*, 2 Feb. 1978, p. 20.; "Rock Rack." *Buffalo Courier-Express*, 27 Jan. 1978, p. 12.

[97] "Mayor Griffin to Note Chopin Society Record." *Buffalo Courier-Express*, 2 Feb. 1978, p. 14.

[98] "Chopin Society to Sing at Miami Festival on May 6." *Buffalo Courier-Express*, 12 Apr. 1978, p. 14.

Before jetting off to the Magic City, Chopins had a few engagements closer to home to take care of. After throwing one of the biggest Dyngus Day parties to date, the singers held an April concert with the Buffalo Community Orchestra at the Polish Community Center and headlined the Como Park Mall's Second Annual Polish Festival.[99]

Landing in Miami in May, the singers undertook three major performances, one at the Konover Hotel, the second at Miami's Polish Home, and a third at the Bayfront Theater with the Miami Symphony. Wanting to add some local flavor to their Polish repertoire, Chopins incorporated Latin and Jewish works into their concerts. Besides being the first tour in the American South,[100] the Miami concerts were historic for the Society as it included the first non-Pole, Louis Molisani, as a featured soloist. A proud Italian American, Molisani had just been elected to the board of Chopin after serving as a technical assistant for many years.[101]

While the Chopinites were singing their hearts out in Florida, teenagers Marc-Andre Hamelin, Mary Watanabe, and Eun Soo Son were playing their hearts out in Baird Hall at the University of Buffalo for the judges of the Chopin International Competition for Young Pianists. After tallying up the scores 14-year-old Eun Soo Son was awarded the $1,000 scholarship.[102]

Returning from Florida, the choir scheduled the rest of their year. They would take part in St. Andrew's Polish Festival Lawn Fete in Sloan,[103] perform for the Lockport College Women's Club,[104] accompany the Amherst Symphony Orchestra, and prepare for an April 1979 tour of Arizona.[105] But first they had to hold their annual concert.

Having already learned the music and seeing how popular it was with audiences, the choir incorporated much of their Florida program into the annual concert. Held at Kleinhans Music Hall, the evening included selections from *Fiddler on the Roof,* with Dolores

---

99 "Dyngus Day: End to Austerity." *Buffalo Courier-Express*, 28 Mar. 1978, p. 5.; "Como Park Polish Fete Begins Today." *Buffalo Courier-Express*, 19 Apr. 1978, p. 23.
100 Chopin Singing Society Archives, 1987.
101 Smith, Rita. "Chopin Singers Tap First 'Non-Pole' Soloist." *Buffalo Courier-Express*, 30 Apr. 1978, pp. 1-E.
102 "Girl, 14, Wins Chopin Piano Contest." *Buffalo Courier-Express*, 28 May 1978, p. 5.
103 "St. Andrew's Parish to Hold Polish Fete." *Buffalo Courier-Express*, 21 June 1978, pp. 23-D.
104 "Chopin Unit to Sing in Lockport." *Buffalo Courier-Express*, 11 Oct. 1978, p. 21.
105 "Chopin Singers Will Perform." *Tonawanda News*, 6 Dec. 1978, p. 2.

Bielinski performing the solo for *My Cuba* and Theresa Dybas, Daniel Kij, Adam Malik, and Louis Distel singing a medley of Am-Pol Military Airs. The standing room only show was greatly enjoyed. The Society also recognized their longtime member and soloist Ludwik "Louis" Distel, the Singing Barber of East Buffalo,[106] by dedicating the concert to him.[107] As the show concluded, half a world away a cloud of black smoke could be seen rising from the chimney above the Sistine Chapel. Little did the members of Chopin know they were only 12 hours away from a moment that would affect them, Polonia, and the world.

On October 16, Wadowice-born, Cardinal Karol Jozef Wojtyla was elected the 263rd successor to St. Peter, becoming Pope John Paul II. The members of Chopin were ecstatic as a great number of them had met the young prelate during his 1969 and 1976 trips to Western New York.[108] Within days many in the Society cleared their schedules and were booking flights to Italy. Music Director Peter Gorecki canceled the choir's scheduled appearance for the opening of Buffalo's new convention center and Justice Ann Mikoll moved her docket around to accommodate the trip.[109] At the Vatican, both had front row seats to the papal inauguration, where Mikoll was able to shake the pontiff's hand and Gorecki called him the most important Pole since Copernicus.[110] Once back in the U.S., the members flew the Polish flag high once again when they sang at the 60th Anniversary Mass of Polish Independence at St. Stanislaus Church, a service that held new meaning with a Polish pope.[111]

Before wrapping up their 80th concert year and prepping for Dyngus Day, the women of Chopin enjoyed a fashion show and dinner in early April. Sponsored by the Rique Fashion Studio of Cheektowaga and the Riverside Men's Shop, the theme of the evening was *Singing in the Rain*. Chaired by Ms. Michaeline A. Wyrobek the event not only allowed the singers to have some social time, but it also

---

[106] Smith, Rita. "Chopin Society to Honor East Side Singing Barber." *Buffalo Courier-Express*, 8 Oct. 1978, pp. E-1-E-9.
[107] The Chopin Singing Society. *79th Annual Concert*. Chopin Singing Society, 1978.
[108] Witul, Gregory L. "A Saint in Our Midst - Cardinal Wojtyla's 1969 Visit to Buffalo." *Am-Pol Eagle*, 24 Apr. 2014, p. 19.
[109] Smith, Rita. "Five Youngsters Part of WNY Delegation to Rome." *Buffalo Courier-Express*, 22 Oct. 1978, pp. E-7.
[110] Smith, Rita. "Pope, Buffalo Poles Mix Emotionally." *Buffalo Courier-Express*, 24 Oct. 1978, p. 1.
[111] "Area Poles to Celebrate Freedom Day." *Buffalo Courier-Express*, 11 Nov. 1978, p. 2.

worked as an effective fundraiser as well.[112]

Once back to performing, the singers had engagements with Dom Polski in North Tonawanda,[113] SS. Peter and Paul Church's Polish Cultural Festival in Depew,[114] and one for the opening of the Recreation Center at Hilbert College in Hamburg.[115] The group also took part in Polish Singers Alliance's sacred concert at which Chopins performed with the Kalina Singing Society, the Polish Singing Circle, and the Paderewski Singing Society at St. Stanislaus Church.[116] As they were closing out the year, the members congratulated Hayuru Taima as the winner of the 1979 piano competition.[117]

Now on their 80th season the Chopins had a full schedule to see them into the next year. They started out with a grand celebration at their clubhouse on Flag Day. As part of a joint celebration with the Adam Plewacki Post, a mini parade was held from the unit's home on Memorial Drive to Kosciuszko Street where a flag raising ceremony was held. The two groups partied well into the night with music by North Tonawanda's own Sikora Post American Legion Band.[118]

For their 80th birthday party the Chopinites rented out the Golden Ballroom of the Statler and invited a who's who of Buffalo to attend their first ball since 1975. Erie County Executive Edward Rutkowski, industrialist Paul Redlinski, Congressman Jack Kemp, Dr. Matt A. Gajewski and Buffalo Common Council President Delmar Mitchell were all patrons of the ball. The members also took this opportunity to honor their musical director, Peter Gorecki.[119]

While the singers had planned to sing in America's Southwest in 1979, they instead accepted an invitation to sing in Philadelphia as part of that city's unveiling of a statue of General Thaddeus Kosciuszko. A gift from the Polish nation, the bronze statue by Marian Konieczny was given to the city of brotherly love in recognition of the Bicentennial in 1976. This statue was one of two that the people of Poland gave to American cities; the other statue was of Pulaski and was

---

[112] "Chopin Unit Style Show Is April 4." *Buffalo Courier-Express*, 28 Feb. 1979.
[113] "Singers Plan NT Concert." *Tonawanda News*, 25 Jan. 1979, p. 5.
[114] "Polish Festival Set at Depew Church." *Buffalo Courier-Express*, 18 May 1979, p. 18.
[115] "Chopin Singing Society to Perform on May 6th." *Lackawanna Leader*, 26 Apr. 1979, p. 3.
[116] "Music." *Buffalo Courier-Express*, 7 Apr. 1979, p. 9.
[117] "St. Louis Pianist Wins UB Chopin Competition." *Buffalo Courier-Express*, 27 May 1979, p. 1.
[118] "Year of Events Set by Chopin Society." *Buffalo Courier-Express*, 14 June 1979, p. 20.
[119] The Chopin Singing Society. *80th Anniversary Program*. Chopin Singing Society, 1979.

given to Buffalo.[120] The group began the festivities by holding a concert for 300 at the Marriott Hotel the evening before the unveiling. They were then the guests of honor at a reception on the *Dar Pomorza,* the Polish sailing ship that took part in 1976's Operation Sail.[121] On the way home, the group sang at a Mass for the Pauline Fathers at the National Shrine of Our Lady of Czestochowa in Doylestown, PA.[122]

Chopins sang for yet another statue dedication, Kazimierz Danilewicz's monument of Casimir Pulaski at the Church Street Arterial Park in Buffalo. Like its brother statue in Philadelphia, the solid bronze monument of Pulaski was given to Buffalo by the people of Poland and was unveiled five days before the bicentennial of the general's death. Following the songs by the Chopinites and the unveiling, Stephen Larrabee of the U.S. National Security Council; Theodore W. Striggles, executive director of the New York State Council of the Arts; and Councilman-at-large Richard F. Okoniewski all spoke about the importance of the occasion. The event concluded with a reception at the Buffalo Naval Park Museum sponsored by the Pulaski Society.[123]

The October events continued for the singers when they took part in a Mass celebrating the first anniversary of the Investiture of Pope John Paul II. Held at Villa Maria College Auditorium, Chopins was responsible for choral arrangements for the service. On the stage, 22 priests from around the diocese and across Polonia took part in celebration of the Polish American Congress-sponsored Mass.[124]

At the end of October, Chopins held their 80th anniversary concert at Kleinhans Music Hall. They chose Polish songs loved by the new pope and Peter Gorecki's "Cantata to Saint Stanislaus" in honor of its 20th anniversary. A special arrangement of the Hallelujah chorus from Handel's *Messiah* was also performed to "celebrate the joy of the 80th Anniversary of the Chopin Singing Society."[125]

Continuing their anniversary celebration, the group took part in St. John Kanty's Polish Heritage Week, singing a brief program and later joined the Cheektowaga Symphony in their Christmas concert. The winter themed show saw the symphony under the direction of

---

[120] "Chopin Society to Sing in Philly." *Buffalo Courier-Express*, 1 July 1979, pp. B-3.

[121] "Chopin Singers Being Honored." *Buffalo Courier-Express*, 3 July 1979, p. 4.

[122] Chopin Singing Society Archives, 1987.

[123] "Pulaski Statue Erected in Church St. Arterial Park." *Buffalo Courier-Express*, 6 Oct. 1979, p. 2.

[124] *First Anniversary of the Investiture of Pope John Paul II*. Polish American Congress, 1979.

[125] The Chopin Singing Society. *80th Anniversary Concert*. Chopin Singing Society, 1979.

Marylouise Nanna open with a bevy of holiday favorites, before Gorecki guided the singers through some Polish and American standards.[126] The Society closed out the year with a special 80th anniversary Mass and reception at St. Stanislaus Church in Buffalo.[127]

Rolling into the new decade the singers took part in the annual Polish Carnival of Assumption Church in Black Rock,[128] the 75th Anniversary celebration of Annunciation Church in Elma,[129] and later hosted the "granddaddy" of all Dyngus Day parties at the clubhouse.[130]

Wanting to acknowledge the invaluable work the International Institute had done in assisting immigrants who came to Buffalo and helping them find a new and meaningful life, the Society presented the organization a bust of Chopin in May of 1980. A replica of the bust the Society had commissioned Kazimierz Chodzinski to create in 1909, the one gifted to the Institute had been crafted by local artisan Benedict A. Rozek.[131] This would not be the only artistic undertaking they took on that year.

In 1947 John and Florence Raczynski opened the Polish Village Restaurant at 1163 Broadway in Buffalo's East Side. The decor of the restaurant was meant to evoke "a little bit of old Europe" with exposed hand-hewn beams, a kitchen fireplace, and Polish objets d'art. To complete the look, the Raczynski's hired local artist Joseph C. Mazur to create nine large murals depicting Polish holidays and celebrations. For over a quarter century the paintings hung on the wall as the Polish Village became an institution of Buffalo's Polish community. In 1976 the Raczynskis closed their Polish Village, and it shortly became another Polish restaurant. When this bistro also closed, new owners purchased the building with plans to turn it into a disco.[132] Seeing that the now historic Mazur murals were under threat, the Chopinites single-handedly funded the removal, restoration, and relocation of the works to their hall.[133] While the conservation work on the paintings

---

126 "Cheektowaga Symphony, Chopin Society to Join." *Buffalo Courier-Express*, 12 Dec. 1979, pp. 22-B.
127 "Singers to Mark 80th Anniversary." *Buffalo Courier-Express*, 26 Nov. 1979, p. 5.
128 "Philharmonic to Kick Off 10-Day Polish Carnival." *Buffalo Courier-Express*, 28 Jan. 1980, p. 7.
129 "75th Anniversary Events Scheduled." *Buffalo Courier-Express*, 2 Apr. 1980, pp. 22-B.
130 "Dyngus Day!" *Buffalo Courier-Express*, 7 Apr. 1980, p. 1.
131 Ott, Betty J. "International Institute to Get Bust of Chopin." *Buffalo Courier-Express*, 2 May 1980, p. 15.
132 "The Polish Village." *Polonia Trail*, Polish-American Congress WNY, 29 Jan. 2016, poloniatrail.com/location/the-polish-village.
133 "Mural Preserved." *Buffalo Courier-Express*, 8 May 1980, p. 22.

was happening, Seung-Hee Hyun of Cherry Hill, NY was selected as the winner of the 15th annual Young Pianists Competition.[134]

The group kept a minimal schedule for the rest of 1980, instead choosing to practice for the International Singers Alliance Competition in New York. One event they did take part in was the Bassett Park Concert Series in Amherst, performing with the mid-summer Buffalo Pops Orchestra.[135] At the Alliance Competition the extra work and practice paid dividends as the group took home third place at the event.[136]

While Chopins had a light summer, the workers at the Gdansk Shipyard began organizing and striking for workers' rights. These protests culminated on August 31, 1980, when the government of Poland signed the agreement recognizing independent trade unions and giving birth to the first independent labor union, Solidarity.

Back in America, Chopins used their annual October concert to open their 81st year. The theme of the show was music from around the world and included works by French, German, Hungarian, Irish, Cuban, Italian, Jewish, Polish, and American composers. The Society also took the opportunity to remember longtime member Ed Szarek, and dedicated the program to the Halicki brothers, Stan and Ed.[137]

The year 1981 would see foundational changes come to Chopin and the early indication of how the young membership, full of vim and vigor, had begun to age similar to their predecessors a half century earlier. The personification of these early inklings was the passing of board member James E. Mikoll.[138] James helped to bring Chopins out from under near extinction in the late 1950s and helped transform them into the thriving organization of the 1960s and 70s. Passing at age 48 the loss of Mikoll would be indicative of the change the Society would experience over the next decade.

The loss of the prominent leader, although devastating, didn't debilitate Chopins from their engagements. In March, they appeared at a concert celebrating St. Josaphat's diamond jubilee and in April

---

[134] Putnam, Thomas. "N.J. Girl Captures Chopin Piano Competition." *Buffalo Courier-Express*, 25 May 1980, pp. A-6.

[135] "Amherst Park Sets Concerts on Sunday." *Buffalo Courier-Express*, 21 May 1980, pp. 18-C.

[136] Chopin Singing Society Archives, 1987.

[137] The Chopin Singing Society. *81st Anniversary Concert*. Chopin Singing Society, 1980.

[138] "Rites Set Monday for J.E. Mikoll." *Buffalo Courier-Express*, 24 Jan. 1981, p. 24.

hosted 2,000 revelers at their 20th annual Dyngus Day party.[139] In the summer, as they were preparing for the Polish Soldiers Day celebration and Cheektowaga's Polish American Arts Festival a postcard arrived in the mail.[140] The seemingly benign postcard carried startling news. While on vacation in West Germany, Music Director Gorecki decided to stay on the continent to improve his health. He also resigned from Chopins effective immediately. While Mikoll's death was heartbreaking, Gorecki's resignation was devastating. The singers were able to complete their scheduled engagements, and the search for a new musical director began in earnest. It quickly became clear that it would be impossible to hold their annual concert even if a conductor could be found before then. After much deliberation the board made the painful decision to cancel the 1981 annual show.[141]

In mid-October, when the annual concert was traditionally held, Chopins announced that Carl Druba, the director of the Master Chorale of Western New York, would be the eighth musical director of the Chopin Singing Society.[142] One of the first performances Druba would lift his baton for would be at Villia Maria College where Chopins took part in a Mass celebrating the third anniversary of John Paul II's election to the papacy.[143]

On January 1, 1982, the City of Buffalo swore in Mayor Jimmy Griffin and 12 of the city's 15 Common Council Members. Wearing a red Solidarity ribbon, the mayor called for austerity in the budget while trying to mend fences with the council he had been battling with for the last four years. After all the speeches were made and the politicians glad-handed, the group went down to the lobby of City Hall and launched Buffalo's Sesquicentennial Celebration. The Chopin Singing Society greeted Buffalo's 150th birthday with song.[144]

As martial law was instituted in Poland, food shortages soon developed, and quickly intensified. To try and relieve some of the suffering in their ancestral homeland, Chopins worked with the Polish

---

[139] "Chopin Chorus to Sing for Church Jubilee." *Buffalo Courier-Express*, 11 Mar. 1981, pp. 23-D.

[140] "Polish Soldier's Day to Be Celebrated." *Buffalo Courier-Express*, 14 Aug. 1981, pp. A-6.; "Polish Arts Fest Starts Friday." *Buffalo Courier-Express*, 19 Aug. 1981, pp. S-1.

[141] Chopin Singing Society Archives, 1987.

[142] Putnam, Thomas. "Music Notes." *Buffalo Courier-Express*, 21 Oct. 1981, pp. B-5.

[143] "Groups to Celebrate Pope's Anniversary." *Buffalo Courier-Express*, 24 Oct. 1981, pp. A-10.

[144] Billington, Mike. "Griffin Begins 2nd Term, Vowing More Budget Cuts." *Buffalo Courier-Express*, 2 Jan. 1982, pp. A-1-A-12.

American Congress and 23 other Polish organizations from across New York State to sell Food Bonds for Poland. A five-dollar donation would ensure that one food package would be prepared and delivered to the people of Poland. Tops Friendly Markets joined in and accepted cash donations at all their locations and made a matching contribution of $10,000.[145] The Chopinites raised more money for humanitarian assistance to Poland by performing and volunteering at telethons put on for the cause by both Channel 2 and Channel 7.[146]

While the presidents, board of directors, conductors, and soloists grab most of the headlines for Chopins much of the real work of the organization has been done by committees and individuals. In February the *Am-Pol Eagle Newspaper* recognized Walter A. Szwajda as the Citizen of the Year for Music due to his work as temporary choir director for Chopins and guiding the group through the difficult time following Gorecki's departure.[147]

In May, the Society, along with Congressman Jack Kemp, his wife, and a delegation of 300, left Buffalo for Newport News, VA. There they were to take part in the launch of the Los Angeles class submarine, the USS *Buffalo* (SSN-715). Named after the city because of Congressman Kemp's work, the *Buffalo* was sponsored by his wife Joanne and launched on May 8. After the speeches and the handing out of Talking Proud stickers, the members of Chopin sang patriotic songs while the blocks were knocked out and the submarine took to the James River.[148]

As summer rolled in, the Society was planning on a low-key season. The only programs their schedule included was a 35th anniversary Mass for St. Joseph Church in North Tonawanda and their *Summer Under the Stars* event.[149] The singers hoped to use this extra time to be better prepared for their annual concert. While the Mass went off without a problem, the opportunity to practice was missed when maestro Carl E. Druba unexpectedly passed away on June 19, 1982.[150]

---

145 Tops Friendly Markets. "Supplement to Finger Lakes Times - Week Ending Han. 23, 1982." *Finger Lakes Times* [Geneva, NY], 1982.
146 The Chopin Singing Society. *A Salute to Buffalo on Their Sesquicentennial Year! From the Chopin Singing Society.* Chopin Singing Society, 1982.
147 "*Am-Pol Eagle* Selects 'Citizens of the Year.'" *Buffalo Courier-Express*, 7 Feb. 1982, pp. A-6.
148 Turner, Douglas. "Buffalo Showers Nuclear Namesake with a Flood of Pride at Launching." *Buffalo Courier-Express*, 9 May 1982, pp. A-10.
149 "Chopin Society to Lead Mass at St. Joe's." *Tonawanda News*, 11 June 1982, p. 4.; "'Summer Under the Stars.'" *Buffalo Courier-Express*, 17 July 1982, pp. CI-1.
150 "Carl E. Druba." *Buffalo Courier-Express*, 23 June 1982, pp. A-6.

With their program only four months away, the board of Chopin reached out to conductor and violinist Marylouise Nanna. They prayed that the camaraderie they had developed with Nanna from working with her years before and the fact she was a good friend of Carl would help convince her to be their musical director, even temporarily.[151] Knowing their plight and not wanting to let the work Druba invested in the show go to waste, Nanna agreed to take on the group for the year. She also promised to have them in singing shape for their October show.[152] One of the first performances Nanna would oversee was the official closing of the Buffalo Sesquicentennial Celebration held on September 19. Held at the City Court Building on McKinley Square, Chopins sang as the Sesquicentennial Time Capsule was sealed, marking the official end of the celebration.[153]

On October 24, 1982, the Chopin Signing Society held their first annual concert in two years. For the show, the music committee and Nanna selected Kurpinski's Czesc ci Polski, tangos by Jerzy Petersburski, and in honor of the 100th anniversary of his birth, Karol Szymanowski's "Roxanne's Aria" from *King Roger,* performed by Theresa Dybas. Chopins also took the time to recognize the many important members they had lost in the last two years including James E. Mikoll, Lawrence Nagowski, Virginia Angielczyk, Walter Wrobel, and Maestro Druba.[154]

Having Marylouise temporarily in place allowed Chopins to do an extensive search to find her replacement, Ireneusz Lukaszewski. Born in Poland and a graduate of conservatories in Gdansk and Poznan, Lukaszewski was still a recent immigrant when he accepted the position as music director. Almost as soon as Ireneusz was hired, he and the rest of the Chopinites were on a plane to the Vatican. Once at the Holy See, the singers had the honor of singing for the pope at a November 23 Wednesday Audience[155]. The group performed a medley of Polish folk songs and hymns, as well as an original work by Lukaszewski, "Stanislaus," which was composed using some of the

---

151 Osinski, Bill. "City's Ethnic Choral Groups Still Singing Strong." *Buffalo Courier-Express*, 16 Aug. 1982, pp. A-1

152 Putnam, Thomas. "Music Notes." *Buffalo Courier-Express*, 5 Apr. 1982, pp. B-5.

153 "Sesqui Closing." *Buffalo Courier-Express*, 11 Sept. 1982, pp. CI-2.

154 The Chopin Singing Society. *A Salute to Buffalo on Their Sesquicentennial Year! From the Chopin Singing Society.* Chopin Singing Society, 1982.

155 The Chopin Singing Society. *85th Anniversary Concert.* Chopin Singing Society, 1984.

poems of John Paul II.[156] The group then traveled south to sing at Monte Cassino and finally at a Mass at San Stanislao Kostka.[157] They would repeat their concerts for American audiences, but added a second act of Polish Christmas carols at a show at the University of Buffalo's Slee Hall in December.[158]

Back home, the Society undertook some much-needed renovations of their Kosciuszko Street clubhouse. Wanting to create a better space to display the Mazur collection, they hired local artisan Henryk Jarosz to redesign the interior. Jarosz envisioned Tatra inspired rooms, highlighted with wood carvings that would complement Mazur's murals. Outside Chopins purchased an additional property to add a parking lot for their space, which brought their total investment in the area to $250,000.[159]

To go along with their already exceedingly popular Dyngus Day, Chopins added a second Polish Festival to their calendar in 1984, Noc Kupaly or St. John's Eve. Held in June at the Delaware Park Casino the evening of singing and merry making was concluded with floating the candlelit wreaths worn by women during the festivities.[160] Tradition holds that the young men retrieve the wreath of the girl they hope to court. The rest of their 85th anniversary season saw the singers travel to Olean, NY to take part in a fundraiser concert for Transfiguration's church choir, perform at a Mass for Solidarity at St. John Gualbert's and hold its annual, Gay Nineties-themed concert at Villa Maria. To truly embrace the year's theme, the sold-out crowd heard not just the first act of Polish songs, but a second act that included the songs, "While Strolling in the Park One Day," "Daisy Bell," "Sidewalks of New York," and "The Band Played On." To really bring the nostalgia home, For Pete's Sake, Buffalo's premier barbershop quartet gave a medley of Irving Berlin works.[161] The singers ended their 85th year with a Christmas concert at the University of Buffalo that featured Kashubian carols, a first for the Society.[162]

---

[156] The Chopin Singing Society. *In Concert - Chopin Singing Society - Slee Hall - December 14, 1983.* Chopin Singing Society, 1983.
[157] Chopin Singing Society Archives, 1994.
[158] The Chopin Singing Society. *In Concert - Chopin Singing Society - Slee Hall - December 14, 1983.* Chopin Singing Society, 1983.
[159] The Chopin Singing Society. *The 85th Anniversary Ball of the Frederick Chopin Singing Society.* Chopin Singing Society, 1985.
[160] "'Wianki' Set in Delaware Park." *Tonawanda Evening News*, 22 Jan. 1984.
[161] The Chopin Singing Society. *85th Anniversary Concert.* Chopin Singing Society, 1984.
[162] "Chopin Singers Christmas Program Set." *Tonawanda Evening News*, 11 Dec. 1984, p. 6.

In July of 1983 Martial Law was finally lifted in Poland. In an effort to legitimize itself, the Polish government began reopening the country for cultural exchanges. Once again, an invitation was extended to the Chopin Singing Society to make a trip to Poland with a target date of 1985. As was customary for these tours an advance team was sent to the communist nation to scout out locations, set the itinerary, and make all the necessary travel arrangements. But this time the planning trip was different; the members of Chopin were going to dive deep into the world of international affairs and attempt to make a clandestine drop of funds to Solidarnosc (Solidarity), the first independent trade union in the communist world.

As preparations for the trip were underway David Rutecki, vice president of the Society, and longtime singer Michaeline Wyrobek were establishing a connection with Solidarity supporter, Lane Kirkland, the president of the National AFL-CIO. At the time Wyrobek served as secretary to the Buffalo AFL-CIO President George Wessel and Rutecki saw an opportunity to tap the resources of the National AFL-CIO through this excellent Buffalo connection.

Serving as president of the AFL-CIO from 1979 to 1995 Joseph Lane Kirkland was vehemently anti-Communist. With the unexpected birth and rapid growth of Solidarity in Poland, he saw an opportunity to support fellow laborers and put an early nail in the coffin of the communist control of Central and Eastern Europe. In this way he was truly prophetic, which was highlighted in his *New York Times* obituary. "During the…1980's, he worked tirelessly to help Solidarity topple the Communist government, surreptitiously channeling organization money and fax machines to the movement led by Lech Walesa. 'The success of Solidarity owes a lot to Lane,' said Henry A. Kissinger, a close friend of Mr. Kirkland. 'He supported it with funds and organizers, and he had a big effect on American policy makers.'"[163] At the time this put him at odds with the official policy of the U. S. Government, but in the end his path was proven to be the correct one.[164] The lasting critique of Kirkland's actions came from his own members for his focus and interest on foreign affairs over energizing American workers.[165]

---

[163]Serrin, William. "Lane Kirkland, Who Led Labor in Difficult Times, Is Dead at 77." *New York Times*, 15 Aug. 1999, p. 1.
[164]Puddington, Arch. *Lane Kirkland: Champion of American Labor*. Wiley, 2005.
[165]Serrin, William. "Lane Kirkland, Who Led Labor in Difficult Times, Is Dead at 77." *New York Times*, 15 Aug. 1999, p. 1.

With these powerful connections the plot was soon underway. The intrigue began with Mr. Rutecki and fellow board member, Peter Sloane volunteering to be the financial couriers. With some unofficial help from the State Department, the duo strategically strapped cash to themselves before boarding the flight to Poland.

Fortunately for Rutecki and Sloane, "getting money through the border control to Solidarity presented few problems since it was relatively simple to conceal cash in clothing or luggage or to squirrel it away in automobiles."[166] For the Chopin couriers, the first transfer of funds went smoothly. Once on the ground and past customs, Sloane and Rutecki were contacted, then picked up and delivered to St. Stanislaus Church in Warsaw where they made the cash drop.[167] An estimated $150,000 was transferred to Solidarity from the AFL-CIO in part through this Chopin endeavor during the planning trip and later during the actual concert tour.[168] Because of the sensitivity of the endeavor, no other Chopin officers or members were aware of this plan. Wyrobek, as an employee of the AFL-CIO, did not join the choir in their concert tour to avoid raising suspicions, despite being a regular on past choir trips.

If there were any problems for the group they arose from the AFL-CIO's favor of sending printing materials, which presented a larger but manageable dilemma.[169] This and some other money transfers proved to be a bit more challenging when the entire ensemble of singers had to go through the custom inspections. But in the end both customs encounters were successful.

For Sloane and Rutecki the final delivery of Chopin funds was especially memorable as it was completed in the undercroft of St. Stanislaus Church in Warsaw, meeting clandestinely with members of Solidarity and utilizing a private and trusted taxi driver for transportation.[170]

While generally considered a low estimate, official dollar amounts of support to Solidarity by the AFL-CIO are listed as $4

---

[166]Puddington, Arch. *Lane Kirkland: Champion of American Labor*. Wiley, 2005.
[167] Witul, Gregory L, et al. "Interview of Peter Sloane about Chopin Singing Society Smuggling Money to Poland in Support of Solidarity." 21 Sept. 2022.
[168] Witul, Gregory L, "Interview of Peter Sloane about Chopin Singing Society Smuggling Money to Poland in Support of Solidarity." 8 Aug. 2023.
[169]Puddington, Arch. *Lane Kirkland: Champion of American Labor*. Wiley, 2005.
[170]Interview with Peter Sloane, July 28, 2023.

million.[171] Congress' National Endowment for Democracy, instigated by AFL-CIO lobbyists, funneled an estimated $10 million in the mid- to late 1980s.[172]

Besides their funding of the underground social moment, Sloane and Rutecki participated in the "mass for the homeland," which began in February of 1982 at St. Stanislaus Kostka Church in Warsaw by Father Jerzy Popieluszko. The future saint would be brutally murdered by three security police officers in October 1984 for his uncompromising support for Solidarity. During their visit both Chopinites were keenly aware of the security, surveillance, and counter- surveillance activities from both the church and the government. Church security patrolled the area identifying spies inside the church and watched out for provocateurs who attempted to slash tires and incite the crowds. In the buildings surrounding the church, government agents moved into apartments to photograph all those coming and going 24 hours a day. Sloane would later visit the freshly prepared grave of Popieluszko while other choir members afterward recalled their visit to his grave calling it "one of the most powerful memories of their 1985" concert tour. Poignantly, Mr. Kirkland and his wife also visited the grave of Popieluszko in April of 1990 with the former president's biographer describing the day as such:

> "…Kirkland, his wife, and a delegation from the AFL-CIO traveled to Warsaw and Gdansk to attend the second Solidarity congress... During the visit, the Kirklands stopped at the grave of Father Jerzy Popieluszko…They placed flowers at the gravestone; as they turned to leave, a church caretaker approached. 'You should know something,' he said. 'At each mass during martial law, Father Popieluszko included the name of Lane Kirkland in his prayers.' 'I could not reply,' Kirkland wrote later. 'On Judgment Day, I would be willing to settle for that account in my book of life.'"[173]

Following their contribution to free Poland, the singers performed in Copernicus's birthplace, opened the Dominican Fair, and

---

171 Chenoweth, Eric. "Conference on AFL-CIO Foreign Policy." *AFL-CIO Support for Solidarity: Moral, Political, Financial.*

172 Schuhrke, Jeff. "From Solidarity to Shock Therapy: The AFL-CIO and the Fall of Soviet Communism." *LAWCHA*, 22 Nov. 2022

173 Puddington, Arch. *Lane Kirkland: Champion of American Labor.* Wiley, 2005.

took part in the International Convocation of Choirs with a program in Gdansk's town square, which was broadcast on Polish television. The Society also took part in the Polonian Choirs competition held in Koszalin, going head-to-head with groups from over twenty nations. At the event, the Buffalo singers took home grand winner awards with soloists Adrienne Tworek-Gryta, Cynthia Przybyl, Dorothy Braniecki, and Ludwik Distel securing four of the six solo awards. The finals, which took place in Koszalin's concert pavilion, were viewed by 10,000 in-person audience members and thousands more on television. Returning to the U.S., the Chopinites participated in the Cheektowaga Folk Festival,[174] entertaining the 6,000 spectators attending the event. As winter set in, the singers held two Christmas concerts, one for themselves at the University of Buffalo and a second at St. Stanislaus Church in conjunction with the Polish Singers Alliance. [175]

In the early part of 1986, Chopins planned a heavy schedule of engagements. January opened with the Martin Luther King Celebration at Shea's,[176] followed by the 150th Anniversary Mass for SS. Peter and Paul in Williamsville. In March, "Dyngus Mania" overtook all of Buffalo as the Society celebrated the 25th anniversary of their modern take on the Polish tradition.[177] This influence of Chopins on Polish America was seen as more and more Dyngus Day parties popped up across the region. That spring the group toured Rochester singing at Nazareth College and St. Stanislaus Church and in the summer, they visited Lackawanna and Black Rock.[178]

As part of Polish American month celebrations in October, the group sang at a Polish American Congress-sponsored Mass at St. Stanislaus honoring the Polish Pioneers of Western New York. Uniquely, this program was broadcast live on Stanley Jasinski's radio program. The group made a second radio appearance at the close of the year with their staging of *Jaselka*, the traditional Polish Nativity play, on WBFO. Done in lieu of their Christmas Concert, the pageant, under the direction of Raymond Fleszar, featured the Chopin singers and the Krakowiak dancers under the direction of Eugenia Zastempowska-

---

[174] "Month of Festivity Honoring Polish-American Heritage." *Tonawanda Evening News*, 3 Aug. 1985, p. 3.

[175] "Christmas Carols Planned at U.B." *Tonawanda Evening News*, 6 Dec. 1985, p. 5.; Chopin Singing Society Archives, 1994.

[176] "Tribute to Dr. King Set for Shea's Buffalo." *Tonawanda News*, 8 Jan. 1986, p. 8.

[177] "Dyngus Day Food and Dancing Slated." *Tonawanda News*, 26 Mar. 1986.

[178] "Choral Group." *The Fairport Herald-Mail*, 9 Apr. 1986, p. 6.; "Ethnic Festival Schedule Set." *Front Page*, 23 Apr. 1986, p. 5.

Smith.[179] The Society repeated this performance in the following years at St. Josephat parish and the Lancaster Opera House.[180]

The singers returned to the Martin Luther King Celebration in 1987 and added St. Casimir's Kazik Folk Celebration to their calendar.[181] The decades of Chopins proving themselves to be a cultural institution began to pay dividends as the Society began receiving a number of grants from the New York State Council on the Arts, Erie County, and the City of Buffalo. These grants, and the fundraising efforts of Mr. and Mrs. Raymond Wardynski, helped the Chopinites purchase new portable risers and baffles, as well as put on even more free programs and events than before.[182]

One of the notable events that summer was the Society's first trip to South America. Accepting an invitation from the Juventus Society of Curitiba, they traveled to Brazil in August and put on performances in Rio de Janeiro and Curitiba for their Polish Brazilian brethren. The group also added Brazilian songs to their annual concert that year to reflect their trip.[183]

The members of the Society were back in Buffalo in time to take part in the 50th birthday of the Polish Singers Alliance District 9. Held at Marygold Manor, Chopins joined the Echos, Kalinas, Paderewskis, the Circle, St Hyacinth's Men's, and Symfonia Singing societies to hear PSAA President Eugene Pilis and founding District 9 member, Clara Lohr, speak of music while enjoying their dinner.[184]

Nineteen eighty-eight would mark the end of an era for Chopin as Theodore V. Mikoll chose not to stand for the presidency of the Society. This decision ended a quarter century of leadership under the lawyer. To recognize him as the longest serving president of the choir, Mikoll was granted the title of Honorary President at the elections that year. The same elections saw longtime member Richard Jezuit rise to the presidential position.[185]

At Jezuit's installation banquet that March, the choir honored

---

[179] The Chopin Singing Society. Chopin *Singing Society in Concert St. John Kanty December 10, 1986*. Chopin Singing Society, 1986.

[180] Chopin Singing Society Archives, 1994.; "Wanakah Seniors Hear Dentist Speak." *The Sun*, 15 Dec. 1988, p. 9.

[181] "School to Hold M.L.K., Jr. Tribute." *The Buffalo Criterion*, 8 Jan. 1987, p. 1.

[182] Chopin Singing Society Archives, 1994.

[183] The Chopin Singing Society. *88th Annual Concert*. Chopin Singing Society, 1987.

[184] *50th Anniversary Polish Singers Alliance of American Circuit IX 1937-1987*. Polish Singers Alliance of American Circuit IX, 1987.

[185] The Chopin Singing Society. *Installation Banquet Frederick Chopin Singing Society 1899-1988*. Chopin Singing Society, 1988.

two of their most loyal members. The first was Edward Kasprzak, the club's recording secretary who also moonlighted as the singer's official photographer during his fifty years of membership. The second was Michaeline Wyrobek, the Society's administrative assistant, who, in her twenty years with the club, served on the board of directors, headed fundraising efforts, represented Chopins at the Polish Singers Alliance, and coordinated the smuggling in of money to Poland in support of Solidarity. Both were given engraved silver platters in recognition of their work.[186]

The summer highlights for the singers that year were the 10th Annual Polish American Arts Festival in Cheektowaga where the group served as the opening performers and singing at the Quaker Arts Festival in Orchard Park.[187]

In the fall, the Society appeared at St. Patrick's Cathedral in Manhattan as part of the premier presentation of the *Litany of Our Lady of Ostra Brama* by Moniuszko. The one-day event saw dignitaries from across the state, the country, representatives of three foreign nations, and leaders of the Armenian, Antiochian Orthodox, and Melkite-Greek Churches come together as part of the national observance of John Paul II's 10th anniversary as pope. For their part, Chopins closed the program by singing the Hallelujah Chorus from Handel's *Messiah*, with the Silesian Opera Orchestra.[188]

Celebrating their 90th anniversary, the singers took on nearly a dozen performances and appearances. They joined Western New York's African American community for the January MLK celebration, held a sacred music concert at Annunciation Church, and hosted a blowout Dyngus Day party.[189] In May, the singers traveled to Hamilton, Ontario to compete in the 42nd convention and 100th anniversary of the Polish Singers Alliance. Under the skilled direction of professor Lukaszewski the singers entered the mixed choir category with high expectations. Putting their hearts and souls into the songs, the men and women of the Frederick Chopin Singing Society scored an unbeatable 96.2 out of 100 points, coming first in their category. With so many points, the singers were declared best overall and brought home the

---

[186] "Kasprzak, Wyrobek Honored by Chopin's." *Am-Pol Eagle*, 7 Apr. 1988, p. 1.
[187] Cheektowaga Polish-American Festival Committee. *10th Annual Polish-American Arts-Festival.* Polish-American Festival Committee, 1988.; "Community Datebook." *The Sun*, 23 June 1988, p. 9.
[188] *Sacred Music 1988 Gala Concert to Honor the 10th Anniversary of the Elevation of Pope John Paul II.* Polstar Publishing Corp., 1988.
[189] The Chopin Singing Society. *90th Anniversary Concert.* Chopin Singing Society, 1989.

Cardinal Hlond Trophy,[190] the championship cup of the Singers Alliance.[191]

Rounding out the rest of the year the group made an appearance at Orchard Park's Middle School, held a joint concert with the Buffalo Philharmonic, and took part in a Polish Folk Mass at St. David Church in Ontario.[192] The singers also performed at the Federal Court House as part of the Naturalization Ceremony, where scores of foreign residents took the Oath of Allegiance to become American citizens. This started a decades-long tradition of the Chopinites singing at the ceremony.[193]

The Society began the new decade as the inaugural performers for a series of concerts held at Niagara University. Sponsored by the Justice and Peace Council at Niagara, the group gave a spring concert in NU's Alumni Hall to raise funds for Holy Spirit Parish in Gdansk, Poland. Additional funds from the event went to support the Theological Institute in Krakow. The show of Polish Folk songs was conducted by Lukaszewski, while Ann Mikoll explained the meaning of the works and their context within Polish culture.[194] The event included works by Chopin, Moniuszko, Paderewski, and Polish folk songs arranged by Lukaszewski.[195] Gdansk Mayor Jacek Starosciak thanked the group for their efforts when he visited the club later in the year.[196]

Chopins returned to Niagara County in the summer for the Niagara Falls Experience series. As part of the Polish Experience at the convention center plaza, there were Polish vendors and food, with entertainment by the Krakowiacy Polish Folk Dancers, the Steel City Brass, and Chopins.[197]

In the spring the 1990 Young Pianists Competition was held in Rockwall Hall Auditorium at Buffalo State University. In a close competition between local Heath Miller, and Singapore native May Phang,[198] Ms. Phang took home the competition prize.[199]

The group would have one last act of charitable giving that

---

190 "Chopin Singing Society Celebrates 90th Anniv." *Am-Pol Eagle,* 26 Oct. 1989, p. 7.
191 "Polish Singers Competing for the 'Cup'." *Buffalo News*, 29 May 2010,
192 Community Datebook." *The Sun*, 22 June 1989, p. 9.
193 The Chopin Singing Society. *90th Anniversary Concert.* Chopin Singing Society, 1989.
194 "Chopin Singing Society to Perform At NU." *Island Dispatch*, 4 May 1990, p. 11.
195 *The Chopin Singing Society Concert.* Niagara University, 1990.
196 "Gdansk Mayor Will Visit Buffalo Over the Weekend." *Buffalo News*, 25 Oct. 1990.
197 "Niagara Summer Experience." *Island Dispatch*, 29 June 1990, p. 13.
198 *1990 Chopin Young Pianists Competition Finals*. Chopin Singing Society, 1990.
199 "About." *May Phang, Pianist*, www.mayphang.com/about.html.

year with a sizable donation to the Buffalo Philharmonic who were trying to close a $1.3 million deficit. When presenting the check to the Philharmonic, President Jezuit stated what many knew to be true, "the Philharmonic is a very valuable asset to the Western New York community."[200] To end the year, Chopins joined the rest of the Polish Singers Alliance of America District 9 to present a sacred concert at St. Stanislaus Church.[201]

Holding smaller performances in the start of 1991, Chopins held their Gala Spring Concert featuring the Cheektowaga Community Symphony Orchestra. The concert at Villa Maria served as a fund-raiser for the usually free orchestra. The evening event also brought conductor Marylouise Nanna and the Chopinites together again as Nanna led the orchestra and Lukaszewski directed the choir.[202]

Later in the year, Chopins brought out something new for a show at the Buffalo Museum of Science, a Dozynki festival. As part of the Museum's *Traditions of Poland* series, the half concert, half party drew out hundreds of Western New Yorkers to the former home of the Chopin Monument.[203]

As 1991 ended the Society decided that the year would be the last for the Young Pianists Competition. In its 27-year run, the competition had many winners who would go on to have illustrious musical careers including Diane Walsh, Claudia Hoca and Lydia Artymiw.[204]

For Buffalo's Polonia, 1992's marquee event was the Greater Buffalo Opera Company's staging of Karol Szymanowski's *King Roger*. Sponsored in large part by the Kosciuszko Foundation, many members of Chopin worked in helping this opera premier at Shea's and several members appeared on stage as citizens of Sicily.[205]

As spring turned to summer, the members of Chopin installed a new musical director, Thomas Witakowski.[206] A graduate of the University of Buffalo, Indiana University, and a student of Genia Las, Witakowski brought youth and energy to the position that Chopins had not seen in generations.[207] Assisting Witakowski that year was former Transfiguration organist and future vice president of the Polish Singers

---

200 "Chopin Singing Society Gives Philharmonic $1,000." *Buffalo News*, 4 Oct. 1990.

201 "Music Notes." *Buffalo News*, 27 Nov. 1990.

202 "Concert In Cheektowaga Will Highlight Polish Music." *Buffalo News*, 2 May 1991.

203 "Buffalo Museum of Science." *Island Dispatch*, 27 Sept. 1991, p. 14.

204 "Behind the Scenes." *Buffalo News*, 3 Nov. 1991.

205 *King Roger*. Greater Buffalo Opera Company, 1992.

206 "Music Notes." *Buffalo News*, 2 June 1992.

207 The Chopin Singing Society. *94th Anniversary Concert.* Chopin Singing Society, 1993.

Alliance, Edward J. Witul.[208]

In the fall, the singers had the great honor of providing a free concert at St. John Kanty as part of the parish's 100th anniversary. The show concluded a month's long celebration that included a Centennial Mass of Thanksgiving celebrated by Bishop Edward D. Head and a banquet in the Golden Ballroom of the Statler Tower.[209]

With the St. Hyacinth's Men's Choir hosting the 44th annual convention of Polish Singers Alliance District 9, Chopins chose to send a sizeable delegation to the Lackawanna event including Michaeline A. Wyrobek, who had been elected president of the district. Seven other singing groups of the region participated in the event which featured an address by Mr. Michael J. Kogutek, a past national commander of the American Legion and a United States presidential delegate who accompanied the disinterred remains of Ignacy Jan Paderewski to Poland.[210]

Later in March, the group traveled north to Medina to sing at a benefit concert for the Orleans Habitat for Humanity. Held at the town high school the program of Polish and American songs drew a large crowd from the region's Slavic population.[211]

For their annual concert, the singers decided on Rockwell Hall at Buffalo State College. To enhance the experience, the choir was joined by the Krakowiaki Dancers while Theresa Dybas, Irene Gutowski, Susan Malik, Timothy Schuman, Fred Wesolowski and Thomas Witakowski were the soloists for the evening.[212] The singers also debuted a new logo for the Society designed by Eileen Koteras Elibol which featured Chopin in shadow with his right hand over his heart.[213] The Chopinites ended the year by joining District 9 at St. Stanislaus Parish in Buffalo to present a festival of Christmas songs. For the evening each group sang a selection of koledy concluding with a combined performance under the direction of James Kendall, the organist and choirmaster at Resurrection R.C. Church.[214]

While the Society began their year with a return to the Martin

---

[208] "Come Sing Along..." *Cheektowaga Times*, 8 Oct. 1992, p. 20.

[209] "Authority On Holocaust Will Deliver Gellman Lecture." *Buffalo News,* 10 Oct. 1992.

[210] "St. Hyacinth's Men's Choir to Host Circuit IX Convention." *Front Page*, 3 Mar. 1993, p. 4.

[211] "Chopin Singing Society to Perform Here" *The Journal-Register*, 25 Mar. 1993, p. 6.

[212] Chopin Singing Society Archives, 1994.

[213] "Chopin Concert Is October 15." *Am-Pol Eagle*, 6 Oct. 2017, p. 1.

[214] "Polish Singers Society Present Holiday Songs." *Front Page,* 24 Nov. 1993, p. 9.

Luther King Jr. Celebration,[215] and performances with the Buffalo Philharmonic,[216] a number of changes were happening behind the scenes. Since the end of the nineteenth century Poles had been settling east of the Buffalo city line. From a group of fifty individuals in 1890, to hundreds of families by the end of the First World War, the Town of Cheektowaga was becoming home to a growing Polish community. The suburbanization of Western New York exploded in the years following the Second World War, and over the course of fifty years, the traditionally Polish East Side home of Chopins lost both the Polish American population density and the economic stability that went with it.[217] It was under this backdrop that President Jezuit began looking for a new clubhouse for the singers. After reviewing the available properties, the board chose the location of the former Dubel's Restaurant's at 2155 Old Union Road in Cheektowaga.[218]

As the plans for the move were coming together and a press release was being prepared, Chopins took advantage of another invitational tour of Florida. Arriving in Palm Beach, the singers appeared at many venues including the Eissey Theatre, entertaining the ever-growing Polish American population of South Florida.[219]

Within the club it was believed that the announcement of the new home, going public after their Dyngus Day celebration, would be the biggest Society news of the year. Sadly, it was an unexpected headline that would rock both Chopins and Buffalo's Polonia, "Theodore V. Mikoll, Attorney, Polish Arts Leader, Dies At 65."[220] The startling loss of the club's longtime leader was felt not only by the organization but by the whole region. Having served as a chairman for St. Joseph Hospital Ambassadors, a judge advocate for the American Legion, and as part of the legal community for half a century, Mikoll's roots ran deep in Western New York. The emotional reserves of the singers were further depleted when longtime soloist Ludwik J. Distel

---

[215] Palazzetti , Agnes, and Carl Allen. "Program Honoring King's Ideals Is Revived Participants Cite Need to Invoke Teachings Amid Rising Tide of Violence." *Buffalo News*, 10 Jan. 1994.

[216] Kunz-Goldman, Mary. "Philharmonic, Schulze Cook Up a Hearty Serving of Ethnic Stew." *Buffalo News*, 31 Mar. 1994.

[217] Witul, Gregory L. "The History of Polish Americans in Cheektowaga." Cheektowaga Historical Museum, 20 Feb. 2014, Cheektowaga, NY, Cheektowaga Senior Center.

[218] "Dubel's Is New Chopin Singers Headquarters." *Am-Pol Eagle,* 14 July 1994, p. 1.

[219] *Musical Interlude*. The Polish Cultural Society of the Palm Beaches, 1994.

[220] "Theodore V. Mikoll, Attorney, Polish Arts Leader, Dies At 65." *Buffalo News*, 8 July 1994.

passed away a few weeks later.[221]

The loss of these two pillars of the Society in July affected the performance schedule for the remaining part of the year, and in lieu of performing, the group focused on setting up their new clubhouse. The choir was emotionally prepared by the end of the year to take the stage again as they put on return performances of their *Jaselka* at the Lancaster Opera House and Corpus Christi Church.[222] They ended the year by taking part in the Polish Singers Alliance District 9 Christmas concert.[223]

---

221 "Ludwik J. Distel, Known As 'Singing Barber.'" *Buffalo News*, 28 July 1994.
222 The Chopin Singing Society. *96th Anniversary Concert*. Chopin Singing Society, 1995.
223 "St. Hyacinth's Men's Choir to Sing Christmas Song." *Front Page*, 23 Nov. 1994, p. 9.

Chapter 9

The New Millennium

On April 8, 1995, a new chapter of the Chopin Singing Society began with the grand opening of their Cheektowaga clubhouse. The all-night party saw polka legends Big Steve and the Bellaires, Hunky Hoppers, The New Yorkers, New York Transfer, and Scrubby and the Dynatones take the stage as the food and drinks freely flowed.[1] The space reached its 1,000-person maximum again a week later when the Society held its first Dyngus Day party at the Old Union Road location.[2] As with their Kosciuszko Street address, the new clubhouse became the hub for not just the singers, but other organizations of Polonia including the Kalina Singing Society and the General Pulaski Association.[3]

That summer Chopins had two return engagements. The first was a choral presentation at the USS *Little Rock* for the swearing in ceremony of America's newest citizens,[4] and the second was a trip to Medina, NY for a fundraiser benefiting Habitat for Humanity.[5] In the autumn, Chopins hosted a reception and dinner for Jerzy Surdykowski, Consul General of the Republic of Poland in New York. The playwright, author, and future ambassador was first feted by the singers, who then entertained him with an informal program following the banquet.[6]

In October the Society held their annual concert at Villa Maria College. While the show offered up its usual selections of Chopin, Moniuszko, and Polish folk songs, one area of the event that was changing was the growing memorial page of the program. What once only had a name or two, had grown to well over a half dozen members and included important figures such as singers Marianna Sadus and

---

[1] "Grand Opening Set at Chopins." *Am-Pol Eagle*, 6 Apr. 1995, p. 1.

[2] Curran, Bob. "Dyngus Day Has New Home, Same Old Spirit Chopin Singing Society to Open Bigger Clubhouse." *Buffalo News*, 2 Apr. 1995.

[3] Curran, Bob. "Dinner To Honor WW II Vets, Raise Money for Pulaski Parade." *Buffalo News*, 27 Aug. 1995.

[4] The Chopin Singing Society. *96th Anniversary Concert*. Chopin Singing Society, 1995.

[5] "Chopin Society to Sing for Habitat." *The Journal-Register*, 15 Sept. 1995, p. 5.

[6] "Consul General to Visit Chopin Clubrooms." *Am-Pol Eagle*, 14 Sept. 1995, p. 15.

Sigmund Sloane, and board members Cynthia Kroll and Theodore Wozniak.[7] In response to the now post-peak membership, Secretary Adrienne Dados sent out a release saying that the Society was looking for singers in every age group for a new program for the holidays. Highlighting a desire for a youth choir, she also noted that a background in the Polish language is not necessary to join.[8]

The appeal worked; and by the time of the inaugural Wigilia celebration in December, a few adults signed up and the children's choir had nearly two dozen members.[9] The formation of the Chopin Singing Society's Children's Choir would earn the group some accolades the next year when the *Am-Pol Eagle Newspaper* awarded Chopins their Citizen of the Year Award for Culture.[10] The singers would close out their year at the Lancaster Opera House with their *Joys of the Season* show.[11]

In the new year, a new board member joined the ranks of the Society. The young Gary Bienkowski was selected to serve as treasurer, replacing Walter Kaminski. The rest of Chopin's leadership stayed much the same; Richard Jezuit was elected to his tenth term as president, and Robert Ciesielski, Ann Mikoll, and James Jankowski returned to the board. As for the Ladies Auxiliary, Mary Jager remained president, and Betty Skrok and Eleanor Angielczyk became vice president and secretary respectively.[12]

Early 1996 saw the Chopinites celebrate an *Evening of Chopin Music* in honor of the birth of their namesake, hold a concert at Buffalo's oldest Roman Catholic parish, St. Louis, and host their Dyngus Day party with over 3,000 attendees.[13]

While preparing for the second half of their season, Chopins invited the Wroclaw Technical University Choir to Buffalo to sing at St. John Gualbert Catholic Church. The choir, already in the country to take part in the Missoula Festival of Missouri, gave a wide-ranging show from Polish hymns to African-American spirituals.[14]

Once summer set in, the choir appeared at Cheektowaga's 18th

---

[7] The Chopin Singing Society. *96th Anniversary Concert*. Chopin Singing Society, 1995.
[8] "Reporters' Notebook." *Buffalo News*, 13 Nov. 1995.
[9] The Chopin Singing Society. *A Wigilia Celebration*. Chopin Singing Society, 1995.
[10] "Citizen of the Year - Culture." *Am-Pol Eagle*, 25 Jan. 1996, p. 13.
[11] "Theater Notes." *Buffalo News*, 14 Dec. 1995.
[12] The Chopin Singing Society. *Installation Banquet*. Chopin Singing Society, 1996.
[13] The Chopin Singing Society. *97th Anniversary Concert*. Chopin Singing Society, 1996.
[14] "Touring Polish Choir to Perform in Cheektowaga." *Buffalo News*, 27 June 1996.

Annual Polish American Festival,[15] performed at the USS *Little Rock* for *New Citizen's Day* and began rehearsals for their annual concert. The 97th annual show featured classical and contemporary Polish works, with soloists Adrienne Tworek-Gryta, Corinne Dziedzic, Adrienne Dados, Fred Wesolowski and Thomas Ronan. The special guests of the evening were the Docenko String Orchestra, and Dr. Peter Gessner of the Polish Arts Club was the honoree.[16]

That same year, the singers returned to New England, the Athens of America, after a twenty-year hiatus at the invitation of the Moniuszko Musical Society of Boston. On a joint concert tour with Buffalo State College Choir, the group opened the celebration of Boston's Polish American Festival at a noontime event at City Hall. They took the stage the next day with a program at Faneuil Hall with Governor William F. Weld, Senator John Kerry, and former Polish President Lech Walesa in attendance. The groups then traveled to St. Stanislaus's parish in Chelsea for another set of shows.[17]

That autumn, Chopins began working with the Western New York Chapter of the Kosciuszko Foundation to bring Moniuszko's opera, *The Haunted Manor* to a Buffalo stage. A festival committee of twelve organizations was formed with President Jezuit representing Chopins, Joseph Macielag of the Polish American Congress and Janusz Nieduzak of the Polish Veterans.[18] The groups hoped to have everything set for the Greater Buffalo Opera Company to put on the performance in the fall of 1997.[19] As the Christmas season set in, Chopins ended the year with their well-attended annual Wigilia at the clubhouse.[20]

The singular focus of 1997 for the choir and many other organizations of Polonia, was getting the production of *The Haunted Manor* off the ground and onto the stage of Shea's Performing Arts Center. For their part the singers performed at a March fundraising concert, while another handful of them sang at the *Cabaret Night in Warsaw* program at the Statler Hotel. The Society also donated the use of their clubhouse for the opera committee's meetings.[21]

---

[15] Rey, Jay. "Christmas Is New Tradition at Polish-American Festival." *Buffalo News*, 16 Aug. 1996.

[16] "Music Notes." *Buffalo News*, 24 Sept. 1996.

[17] "Reporters' Notebook." *Buffalo News,* 17 Oct. 1996.

[18] *Straszny Dwor*. Greater Buffalo Opera Company, 1997.

[19] "Reporters' Notebook." *Buffalo News*, 13 Nov. 1996.

[20] "Wigilia Held at Chopin's - Members Honored." *Am-Pol Eagle*, 12 Dec. 1996, p. 1.

[21] "Volunteers Welcome at Haunted Manor Opera Meeting." *Am-Pol Eagle*, 2 Jan. 1997, p. 1.

On September 19, after some funding hiccups and nearly a half dozen fundraisers and events,[22] the curtain lifted on the Greater Buffalo Opera's production of *The Haunted Manor.*[23] Running for two days, the show proved to be popular with audiences and critics alike. Herman Trotter of the Buffalo News said of the evening, "[o]ne of the most ingratiating musical aspects are the ensembles, in which the singers truly try to blend and sing to the soul of the music rather than indulging in virtuoso competition. Choral work and dancing are first rate, with the festive Mazurka at the close conveying disciplined choreography and folk spontaneity."[24] The two shows were dedicated to the memory of deceased president Ted Mikoll.

For their own productions, the Society hosted a birthday party for Chopin, sang at their Dyngus Day party, welcomed new citizens with song on the USS *Little Rock*, and presented two concerts at St. John Kanty and Our Lady of Czestochowa.[25] Playing off the *Cabaret Night in Warsaw* idea, the choir put on their own evening of entertainment with the title, *Chopin Cabaret Night.* Featuring vocalist Ania Piwowarczyk, the show blended ballroom dancing, polka music, and the Latin sound for a night of entertainment.[26] The group also sponsored a nonperforming tour of Europe in the summer which took the singers and friends alike to Budapest, Vienna, Krakow, and Warsaw.[27] At the end of the year, the Chopinites combined their annual concert and their annual *Jaselka* presentation into a single performance at St. Joseph's Cathedral. Two weeks later they held their Wigilia and ended December with a New Year's Eve party at their clubhouse.[28]

Besides their usual annual appearances at the King Festival,[29] Chopin's Birthday,[30] Dyngus Day, and Wigilia, the singers added a May Crowning ceremony at Holy Mother of the Rosary Cathedral to their schedule.[31] This was followed by a fashion show that included an

---

22 Trotter, Herman. "An Opera That Sings the Praises of Polish Patriotism." *Buffalo News*, 16 Sept. 1997.

23 *Straszny Dwor*. Greater Buffalo Opera Company, 1997.

24 Trotter, Herman. "Company's 1865 'Flag' Opera Is Vindication of International Effort." *Buffalo News*, 20 Apr. 1997.

25 The Chopin Singing Society. *98th Anniversary Concert*. Chopin Singing Society, 1997.

26 "Chopin Cabaret Night Planned." *Am-Pol Eagle*, 16 Oct. 1997, p. 1.

27 "Chopin Singing Society Sponsoring Trip to Europe." *Am-Pol Eagle*, 13 Feb. 1997, p. 1.

28 The Chopin Singing Society. *98th Anniversary Concert*. Chopin Singing Society, 1997.

29 "Tribute to King Set for Jan. 18 In Shea's." *Buffalo News*, 8 Jan. 1998.

30 "Reporters' Notebook." *Buffalo News*, 6 Feb. 1998.

31 "Chopin Singing Society to Perform at Holy Mother of the Rosary." *Am-Pol Eagle*, 7 May 1998, p. 8.

evening of music.[32] While there was a lot of preparation underway for their upcoming centennial anniversary, the group carved out time for some fun and sponsored a trip to the Mediterranean.[33] They were also able to take part in a special Mass to observe the 20th anniversary of Pope John Paul II's election as pontiff.[34] As the weather chilled the singers moved their *Jaselka* to Buffalo's Kaisertown neighborhood, holding the event at St. Casimir Church.

As the Society began its centennial celebration, it chose to present Ira Wilson and Marion Wakeman's rarely staged operetta, *The Enchanted Isle*. Based on the melodies of Chopin, the opera is a fictitious account of a romantic drama based on the composer's visit to the island of Mallorca.[35] The cold February weather helped garner a large audience for the evening with music, by not only Chopins, but the Buffalo State College Chamber Choir as well.[36] The Society held a more low-key event a month later with the fashion show, *Into a New Era – Chopin 1899 – 1999*. The dinner and cocktail evening highlighted the latest in fashion trends presented by the Jacqueline Shoppe for women and Stein-Mart for men.[37]

In a historic year, March was a historic month for Chopins. Citing his declining health President Richard J. Jezuit stepped down from his role as head of the Society. Rising to replace him was the sitting vice president, the Honorable Ann T. Mikoll. With her swearing in, Ann Mikoll became the first woman to lead the organization.[38] Mikoll also used the announcement of her installation to lay out some additional events that would be held as part of the centennial. These would include a memorial Mass at St. John Gualbert, a gala dinner at the Statler Towers, and a possible tour of Poland in 2000.

For the May 2 anniversary concert, Chopins sang a range of works from the traditional with compositions by Chopin and Polish folk music to the modern with a new song composed by Peter Gorecki for the special occasion. Entitled "Piosenka Szopenistow," the work celebrated a century of the Chopinites and how music has lifted the spirits and strengthened their resolve to preserve Poland in America.

---

32 "Fashion Show Set at Chopin Singing Society." *Am-Pol Eagle*, 2 Apr. 1998, p. 23.

33 "Chopin's Sponsors Trip Turkey, Greece." *Am-Pol Eagle*, 30 Apr. 1998, p. 1.

34 "'Grand Celebration' Planned at North Park Lutheran Church." *Buffalo News*, 17 Oct. 1998.

35 "St. Mary's High School Glee Club to Present 'The Enchanted Isle'." *The Orange Leader*, 24 Feb. 1957, p. 21.

36 "An Evening Honoring Chopin Planned." *Am-Pol Eagle*, 11 Feb. 1999, p. 1.

37 "Fashion Show Is Part of Chopin Centennial." *Am-Pol Eagle*, 25 Feb. 1999, p. 2.

38 "Judge Mikoll Heads Chopin." *Am-Pol Eagle*, 25 Mar. 1999, p. 1.

The group dedicated the concert to St. Stanislaus Church in recognition of the 125th birthday of the parish and acknowledged the now honorary president, Richard Jezuit.[39] On the evening of August 29, their members and friends poured into the Statler Golden Ballroom for the Society's Centennial Ball. Chaired by Adrienne Dados the evening saw a cocktail hour, hors d'oeuvres, a full dinner and a night of dancing. The birthday party program included cabaret singer Ania Piwowarczyk, members of the Radosc Dancers, and Art Kubera's Continental Orchestra who each gave a full set of entertainment, while a few members of the choir performed some traditional songs.[40]

That summer the group sang for their tenth consecutive year at Buffalo's immigration ceremony. They followed up the modern tradition with a large *jarmark* (Polish market) held in their clubrooms. It was hoped that the market event would be able to help defer some of the space's ever-increasing costs. While the turnout for the food, arts, crafts, and flea market was good, the overhead of 2155 Old Union Road continued to grow.[41] The group tried to rent out the hall more often and grow its bingo program, but soon that began to fall apart. With the mounting expenses the board decided to sell their Cheektowaga clubhouse in early November.[42]

Despite the question about the future of the clubhouse, the group was still able to enjoy their Christmas holiday season and hold their 1999 Wigilia on Old Union.[43] They also returned to District 9's Koledy, a Festival of Christmas Carols, at St. Stanislaus Church.[44] As the year closed out, the choir was hit by the unexpected passing of Vice President Adam Malik.

In the last year of the twentieth century, Chopins settled into a steady routine of shows and events. They had their namesake's birthday,[45] Dyngus Day, the annual concert, the naturalization ceremony,[46] Wigilia,[47] Koledy, and *Jaselka*.[48] The stable engagements gave the

---

[39] The Chopin Singing Society. *Centennial Concert*. Chopin Singing Society, 1999.
[40] "Plans Centennial Ball." *Buffalo News*, 21 Aug. 1999, p. C–8.
[41] "Jarmark, Polish Country Market Comes to WNY." *Am-Pol Eagle*, 17 June 1999, p. 13.
[42] "Chopin President Explains Reason for Sale of Clubhouse." *Am-Pol Eagle*, 24 Nov. 1999, p. 1.
[43] "Chopin Singers Wigilia Is Dec. 12." *Am-Pol Eagle*, 2 Dec. 1999, p. 1.
[44] *Koledy Festival of Christmas Carols*. Polish Singer Alliance of America District IX, 1999.
[45] "A Chopin Birthday Celebration." *Am-Pol Eagle*, 23 Mar. 2000, p. 7.
[46] *U.S. Immigration and Naturalization Service Naturalization Ceremony at Buffalo & Erie County Naval & Servicemen's Park U.S.S. Little Rock.* U.S. Department of Justice, 2000.
[47] "Chopin Singing Society Will Hold Wigilia." *Am-Pol Eagle*, 30 Nov. 2000, p. 7.
[48] "Chopin Singing Society to Present Jaselka." *Am-Pol Eagle*, 23 Nov. 2000, p. 3.

group the opportunity to add some interesting and novel engagements during the year. The choir began with a recital featuring pianist Ivan Docenko and cellist Brian Eckerode. The day was enhanced by vocalists Susan Malik, Adrienne Dados, and Mary Jane Masiulionis, who all performed works based on the themes of Chopin.[49] The Society followed up the concert with a members' fashion show and dinner before some members jetted off to Poland for a leisurely tour of Krakow, Zakopane and Czestochowa.[50]

Always working to spread Polish culture in Western New York, Chopins joined Canisius College's Permanent Chair of Polish Culture in bringing Boguslaw Szynalski and Maria Knapik to the Montante Cultural Center for a united concert. Ms. Knapik had previously won the Greater Buffalo Opera Company's International Vocal Competition in 1996, leading to the role of Hanna in the production of *The Haunted Manor*. This brought her onstage with Szynalski, who was already cast as Maciej for the production. At the Center, the Krakow natives gave rousing performances of works by Chopin, Rozycki and Moniuszko.[51]

For their 101st annual concert the members dedicated the event in honor of the Polish and Polish Americans of the World Wars, crafting a musical program around that theme. The sung works that evening included "Marsz, Marsz Polonia" the unofficial theme song of Haller's Blue Army, "Czerwone Maki na Monte Cassino" in recognition of the Polish blood spilled at Monte Cassino, and "Let There Be Peace on Earth" in prayerful hope that there would be no future wars.[52]

In the summer the singers took part in a very special Cheektowaga Polish American Arts Festival as the committee declared Judge Mikoll the festival's honoree. President Mikoll was recognized at an opening reception on the first day of the festival while the singers took the stage on day three for an afternoon set.[53]

The joy of summer was met with a twinge of sadness that fall as the Society closed the deal on their clubhouse, selling it to Resurrection Life Fellowship.[54] Not to be undone by the sale, the group went on with their season, singing at the Dozynki festival of St. Casimir in

---

[49] "Society to Hold Chopin Recital." *Am-Pol Eagle*, 17 Feb. 2000, p. 11.
[50] "Chopin Singers Plan Trip to Poland." *Am-Pol Eagle*, 24 Feb. 2000, p. 11.
[51] Trotter, Herman. "Song Fest." *Buffalo News*, 27 Oct. 2000.
[52] The Chopin Singing Society. *A World of Music.* Chopin Singing Society, 2000.
[53] Cheektowaga Polish-American Festival Committee. *Polish-American Arts Festival*. 2000.
[54] "Real Estate Transactions." *Buffalo News*, 16 Oct. 2000.

Rochester and holding two *Jaselkas* that year: one at Sacred Heart Church in Medina, NY and the second winter program the following day at St John Gualbert Parish in Cheektowaga.[55] The group also held their Wigilia at St. John Gualbert before moving into their new home at the Leonard Post, Jr. VFW Post at 2450 Walden Avenue.[56]

With the birth of the new millennium, the Chopinites added a few extra appearances to their usual performances. At a Corpus Christi service at the Holy Mother of the Rosary Cathedral, the group was the featured musical performer.[57] In October they took part in the centennial of the Pan-American Exposition. Sponsored by Buffalo and Erie County Historical Society, Chopins resurrected several Polish American songs audience members would have heard in Fillmore Hall or along the Expo midway, a century earlier.[58]

For their annual concert the singers dedicated the event to Villa Maria College and its predecessor, Villa Maria Academy. Chaired by Gary Bienkowski and Michaeline Wyrobek, the musical focus of the program was Polish dance themes. To achieve this, they touched on polonaises, polkas, mazurkas, and waltzes in the form of song.[59] As it had in years past, the event sold out and was the talk of Polonia for the following weeks.[60]

The annual concert would be the last event hosted by lifelong member and Polish patriot Michaeline Wyrobek who passed away in January of 2002.[61] Her loss was amplified by the death of former President Richard Jezuit later that year. They were the most prominent members of the once young generation who revitalized the organization but were now passing on.

While the membership was getting grayer, Chopins still worked to engage with younger singers. In March the members of the Chopin Chamber Ensemble performed with the Buffalo State College Chamber Chorus in the Canisius Chair of Polish Culture-sponsored concert, *Hidden Polish Musical Treasures*.[62] Chopins worked with the students again in October at a second concert at the Canisius College

---

55 Beach, Heather. "Chopin Singing Society to Perform in Medina." *The Journal-Register*, 30 Nov. 2000, p. 1.; The Chopin Singing Society. *Jaselka*. Chopin Singing Society, 2000.
56 The Chopin Singing Society. *102nd Anniversary Concert*. Chopin Singing Society, 2001.
57 "Nuns' Leadership Team to Be Installed." *Buffalo News*, 16 June 2001.
58 "Pan-Am Celebration." *Am-Pol Eagle,* 4 Oct. 2001, p. 4.
59 The Chopin Singing Society. *102nd Anniversary Concert*. Chopin Singing Society, 2001.
60 "102nd Concert." *Am-Pol Eagle*, 10 May 2001, p. 3.
61 "Michaeline Wyrobek, Union Secretary." *Buffalo News*, 25 Jan. 2002.
62 "A Musical Treasure." *Am-Pol Eagle*, 7 Mar. 2002, p. 1.

Montante Cultural Center.[63] The second performance also saw Ivan Docenko present several Chopin works on piano. A third and final complementary program was presented the following April with the Buffalo State Chamber Orchestra joining the two choirs. The focus of the final show was the music of Karol Szymanowski, as well as Baroque composers Mikolaj Zielenski, and Grzegorz Gorczycki.[64]

Following their standing annual engagements, including the 40th Dyngus Day celebration, Chopins held their 103rd Anniversary Concert in late May. Dedicated to the memory of Michaeline Wyrobek and Teddy Konieczek, the show focused on the works of Moniuszko as well as folk works of Eastern Europe. One of the standout performances of the night was the singing of "W Zelazowej Woli." Sung by Susan Malik and accompanied by Docenko, the poem from Wanda Chotomska's children's book *Muzyka Pana Chopina* describes how a little girl hears the music of nature at Chopin's birthplace.[65] The other noteworthy selection from the evening was Russell Morgan IV's trumpet performance of "Hejnal," the five-note Polish bugle call heard every hour on the hour from Saint Mary's Basilica in Krakow. Keeping with the tradition of the call, Witakowski had Morgan end his performance abruptly.[66]

On stage for the first time with Chopins that night was a woman who would rise to the upper echelons of the singers in a few short years, Frances Cirbus. As a child, Frances Szymanski fell in love with music by plunking away at the toy piano her father gave her. A desire to play in a band led her to learn to play the bass while at Kensington High School. Picking up some gigs around town as time went on, happenstance would find her filling in at a practice session on a borrowed bass with the jazz great, Count Basie, conducting. Her lovely soprano voice got her accepted as part of the Intercollegiate Women's Chorus who joined the Buffalo Philharmonic under the guest-conductor's baton of Leopold Stokowski. She eventually joined the Paderewski Singing Society for two different stints where she sang in their energetic performances. Her passion for performing music was put on hold to make room for her life with husband Robert Cirbus and

---

63 The Chopin Singing Society. *Chamber Series - Concert II*. Chopin Singing Society, 2002.
64 The Chopin Singing Society. *Chopin Chamber Series: Concert III*. The Chopin Singing Society, 2003.
65 The Chopin Singing Society. *103rd Anniversary Concert*. Chopin Singing Society, 2002.
66 Wiater, Edward S. "Chopin Concert Is Tribute to Wyrobek, Konieczek and Polish Soldiers." *Am-Pol Eagle*, 30 May 2002, p. 5.

her medical career as a researcher and Pulmonary Unit manager at Millard Fillmore Hospital. It was after the passing of Robert that Fran joined the ranks of Chopins. From a humble singer she would rise through the ranks of the Society until she arrived on the board as the financial secretary.[67] Cirbus would go on to serve as the treasurer for the Polish Singers Alliance Central Administration and also District 9, sing with Kalina and the St. Stanislaus Choir, and sit on the board of the *Farewell to Summer* benefit committee. In 2010 the Am-Pol Eagle recognized Cirbus with a Citizen of the Year award for her dedication not only to Chopin but Polonia as a whole.[68]

In autumn Chopins held a harvest festival at St. Casimir in Rochester while the Christmas season, as always, was a hectic one for the singers. Starting with District 9's *Festival of Christmas Carols* at St. Stanislaus on December 1, followed quickly by their Wigilia at the Leonard Post, and then two performances of *Jaselka* at Holy Mother of the Rosary Cathedral in Lancaster and the next weekend, at Assumption Church in Buffalo.[69]

The year 2003 kicked off with the annual birthday celebration for Chopin, a Chamber Concert, and the famous Dyngus Day party. Their annual concert presentation drew on the theme of a night in Krakow (a la Madrid) focused on the influence of Latin rhythms on Polish music.[70] As examples, the show included the Andalusian folk song "Con el vito!" the piece "Ciribiribin" by Pestalozza, and from the opera *Carmen* the "Toreador Song" sung by Chopin musical director Thomas Witakowski.[71]

For the rest of the year, Chopins took part in singing for the newly declared American citizens, performing their robust Christmas schedule, and one unique event, an observance of the 750th anniversary of the canonization of St. Stanislaus Bishop and Martyr. The featured piece was former Chopin director, Peter Gorecki's, "Cantata to St. Stanislaus Bishop and Martyr," composed in 1953 in honor of the 700th anniversary of the canonization. Sponsored by the Polish Singers Alliance and held at St. Stanislaus Church in Buffalo, the program

---

67 Wiater, Ed. "There Are Many Dimensions to Cirbus' Musical Career." *Am-Pol Eagle*, 28 Oct. 2009.

68 Gramigna, Glenn. "'10 Individual in Organizations – Frances Cirbus" *Am-Pol Eagle*, 10 Feb. 2011.

69 Wiater, Edward S. "Polish Chamber Music Tops Chopin's Lineup." *Am-Pol Eagle*, 3 Oct. 2002, p. 7.

70 "Chopin Singing Society Plans 104th Annual Concert." *Am-Pol Eagle*, 8 May 2003, p. 12.

71 The Chopin Singing Society. *104th Anniversary Concert*. Chopin Singing Society, 2003.

featured additional sacred music and included performances by the Chopin Singing Society, Kalina Singing Society, Paderewski Singing Society, Symfonia Singing Society of Hamilton, Ontario, and the St. Stanislaus Church Choir.[72]

The group launched their 105th year by returning to Shea's to take part in the 25th Anniversary of Buffalo's Martin Luther King Jr. celebration. As part of the silver jubilee the singers shared the stage with the New Beginnings Ensemble, the AACC Dance and Drum Performance Company, and the Jus' Different Step Team, all honoring the spirit of harmony and brotherly love Dr. King strived for.[73]

As a prelude to the upcoming Paderewski Festival, the singers used their own annual Chopin birthday celebration as an opportunity to highlight the works of the former composer and statesman. As the special guest for the evening, Chopins hosted Igor Lipinski.[74] The recipient of the Grand Prix for Young Pianists at the Paderewski Festival in Kasna Dolna, Poland in 1999 and in 2000, Lipinski was a popular pick with Western New York audiences.[75] At the recital Igor demonstrated his mastery of the piano with Paderewski's "Cracovienne Fantastique" as well as his own composition "Letter to Love."

As the weather warmed, the Society took part in a two-day concert at Our Lady of the Blessed Sacrament in Depew. The event focused on the sacred music of Beethoven, Chopin, and Moniuszko. At the end of May, the singers traveled to Michigan to participate in the 47th International Convention of the Polish Singers Alliance. While not joining in the official competition, Chopins did participate in the Convention meetings which elected Dr. Thomas Witakowski as General Choral Director of the Polish Singers Alliance[76], a position he would hold through 2017 and the 125th anniversary of the organization. Additionally, with help from members of Kalina, Chopins was the buzz of the conclave. All anyone could talk about for days was District 9's concert performance of Peter Gorecki's "Cantata to St. Stanislaus"

---

[72] "Hilbert College Continues Its Prayer Vigil for Mideast Peace." *Buffalo News*, 21 June 2003.

[73] *25th Anniversary Celebration*. The Dr. Martin Luther King Jr. Celebration Committee, 2004.

[74] The Chopin Singing Society. *A Celebration of the 194th Birthday of Fryderyk Chopin with the Chopin Singing Society and Special Guest: Igor Lipinski*. Chopin Singing Society, 2004.

[75] "History of Polish Chair." *Detailed History of the Permanent Chair of Polish Culture*, Canisius College - Buffalo, NY, www.canisius.edu/node/2252.

[76] Minutes of the 47th International Convention of the Polish Singers Alliance of America." Polish Singers Alliance of America, 27-30 May 2004, Detroit

under the baton of Dr. Witakowski with Gorecki on the organ, a reprise of their special program at St. Stanislaus Church in Buffalo in 2003. The concert at the Warren Woods Fine Arts Auditorium featured performances by the combined female, male and mixed choruses, as well as this special performance by District 9 and finally the whole retinue of choruses in performance. The general consensus was that, despite not being one of the nine choruses participating in the competition, Chopins was definitely one of the best choral groups present, even if it wasn't proven with a score sheet.[77]

In June, the members were the musical guests for the Corpus Christi Mass at Holy Mother of the Rosary Cathedral.[78] At the end of the month the singers held their 105th anniversary dinner and ball at Samuel's Grande Manor which was chaired by Robert Ciesielski and Evelyn Pietrzak. The evening's entertainment included music by Rare Vintage, a selection of dances by the White Eagles of Toronto, and songs by a slice of Chopin chorus membership.[79]

The group concluded the year singing at District 9's *Festival of Christmas Carols*, Wigilia, and the Christmas in Poland event at the Lancaster Opera House, but not before they held their annual concert. For the October show, Witakowski selected works by Zygmunt Noskowski, Wladyslaw Zelenski, Tadeusz Sygietynski, and a smattering of American composers.[80] Following their show the Polish American Congress feted Chopins, along with the Polish Falcons Nest 6, SWAP Post #1, and other organizations of Polonia, as part of the congress's 60th anniversary.[81]

As the Chopinites marched into the New Year, planning was underway to recognize the 150th anniversary of the death of Poland's greatest poet, Adam Mickiewicz. Part of a global celebration of the wordsmith's work, Chopins coordinated with the Polish Cultural Foundation, Buffalo State College Chamber Choir and Ensemble, the Polish Saturday School, and Canisius College to produce a bilingual program on the life of Mickiewicz.[82] Written and directed by Kazimierz Braun, the role of Mickiewicz was taken up by Polish actor Pawel

---

77 Wiater, Edward S. "The Chopin Singing Society Does It Again." *Am-Pol Eagle,* 10 June 2004, p. 10.

78 "Religion Notes/News from Area Churches." *Buffalo News*, 12 June 2004.

79 "Plans Chopin Dinner." *Buffalo News*, 24 June 2004.

80 The Chopin Singing Society. *105th Annual Concert*. Chopin Singing Society, 2004.

81 Polish American Congress Western New York Division. *60th Anniversary Banquet*. Polish American Congress, 2004.

82 "Local News Briefs - Final." *Buffalo News*, 26 Oct. 2005.

Chomczyk for what was the cultural highlight of Buffalo's Polonia in 2005.[83]

To celebrate Chopin's 195th birthday, the singers put on an evening of music under the banner of *Chopin in Paris* at their Leonard Post home. The group rendered the works of Hedwige Chretien, Jules Massenet, and Gabriel Faure, while pianist Emma Ziskind served as the special guest for the show.[84] Following her engaging work on the piano, Ziskind became the accompanist for the group.[85]

While the Society had much of their year planned out by February, including a group concert at Our Lady of the Blessed Sacrament Church, their Dyngus Day at Hearthstone Manor, celebrating the 100th Anniversary of Annunciation Church in Elma, and their Christmas concert with the Polish Singers Alliance,[86] as well as at the Erie County Home.[87] Chopins would have to take some time to grieve. After nearly two months of mounting health crises, Karol Wojtyla, the 263rd successor to Peter, and friend of the Chopin Singing Society said, "[l]et me go to the house of the Father," and passed away.

After providing some of the history and background music for WNED's production of *Polonia: Western New York's Polish-American Legacy,*[88] the members of Chopin took part in *Sharing the Music*, a Buffalo-Rzeszow Sister Cities-sponsored concert at Villa Maria College. This concert brought Ewa Lewandowska, Karina Kalczynska, Pawel Staszczyszyn, and sisters, Kasha and Anna Karkowska, from Poland to sing in the United States.[89]

For their annual October concert, the singers titled their show *On the Wings of Polish Song* and focused on music from the Tatra Mountains.[90] To accomplish this they included Alojzy Kluczniok's "Gonia juz Gorale Trzody," "Czerwony Pas" by Karol Kurpinski, and Maklakiewicz's "Beskidzki Harnasiu" in the program. The rest of the

---

[83] *Poetry and Prophecy: A Remembrance of Adam Mickiewicz*. Polish Cultural Foundation, 2005.

[84] The Chopin Singing Society. *A Celebration of the 195th Birthday of Frederic Chopin: "Chopin in Paris."* Chopin Singing Society, 2005.

[85] "Ziskind Departs from Chopin Singing Society." *Am-Pol Eagle*, 30 Oct. 2020.

[86] The Chopin Singing Society. *A Celebration of the 195th Birthday of Frederic Chopin: "Chopin in Paris."* Chopin Singing Society, 2005.

[87] Minutes of the 47th International Convention of the Polish Singers Alliance of America." Polish Singers Alliance of America, 27-30 May 2004, Detroit

[88] "Polonia: Western New York's Polish-American Legacy." Performance by Christine Baranski, WNED, 2005.

[89] "Talent From Poland, WNY To Join in Concert." *Buffalo News*, 6 Apr. 2005.

[90] "Chopin Singing Society Plans Concert." *Am-Pol Eagle*, 8 Sept. 2005, p. 16.

recital was rounded out with works by American and European composers including Paderewski and his "Chorus of Gypsies" from the opera *Manru.*[91] The evening of music won universal adulation for those in attendance which was best summarized by Dr. Frederick Fleszar who said, "[t]hat's the best composition of songs and performance I've seen from all the Chopin concerts I've attended." This was very high praise indeed from the former member of the famous Boys' Choir of Poznan.[92] The group also joined the Buffalo State College Choir at St. John the Baptist Church where both had the privilege of premiering Peter Gorecki's "Stabat Mater."[93]

At the start of the Society's 107th year, the Honorable Ann Mikoll was elected to her sixth term as president, with James Jankowski, and Genevieve Zielinski also being selected to serve on the board.[94] With their first performance of the year celebrating their namesake's 196th birthday, the choir sang a number of seldom heard Polish songs. Andrew Kowtalo served as the soloist for Maria Szymanowska's "Switezianka" or in English "The Mermaid of Lake Switez," based on a work by Adam Mickiewicz. The choir went on to sing Piotr Perkowski's "Chopinowi" which speaks to the sorrowing face that Poland's great composer sleeps in Paris, with only his heart in his motherland. [95]

On the first anniversary of John Paul II's passing, Chopins coordinated with Christopher Weber of the Camerata di Sant'Antonio Chamber Orchestra, and joined the Buffalo State Chamber Singers, the Buffalo State Chorus, the St. Stanislaus Parish Choir under the direction of Tom Borowski, and the Camerata di Sant'Antonio Chorus under Gary Sage, in a memorial concert at both St. Stanislaus Church on April 2 and at St. Anthony of Padua Parish two days later.[96]

In the summer, the Society sang at the Pontifical High Mass

---

[91] The Chopin Singing Society. *106th Anniversary Concert*. Chopin Singing Society, 2005.
[92] Wiater, Edward S. "Getting Better with Age." *Am-Pol Eagle*, 27 Oct. 2005, p. 2.
[93] Minutes of the 48th International Convention of the Polish Singers Alliance of America." Polish Singers Alliance of America, 24-27 May 2007, Albany
[94] Wiater, Edward S. "Mikoll Reviews Chopin's Progress, Re-Elected President." *Am-Pol Eagle*, 19 Jan. 2006, p. 6.
[95] The Chopin Singing Society. *A Celebration of the 196th Birthday of Frederic Chopin*. Chopin Singing Society, 2006.; "Chopin Bash to Feature Hunting Chopinowi." *Am-Pol Eagle*, 2 Feb. 2006, p. 5.
[96] *St. Stanislaus Bishop and Martyr Parish Memorial Concert Honoring Pope John Paul II on the 1st Anniversary of His Death*. St. Stanislaus Bishop and Martyr Parish, Buffalo NY, 2006.; *In Memory of Pope John Paul II*. Camerata Di Sant'Antonio, 2006.

celebrated at the Polish Heritage Festival in Hamburg,[97] welcomed 46 new Americans aboard the USS *Little Rock,*[98] and took part in a memorial Mass of the living and deceased members of the Polish Roman Catholic Union.[99]

In the later part of the year Maestro Witakowski spent a semester teaching in Poland. In his stead, Adrienne Tworek-Gryta, a soloist and instructor at Villa Maria took up the baton as his substitute. Under her hand the Society sang at St. Stanislaus Parish at an event celebrating the completed renovations of the church, their annual Wigilia celebration, and the Polish Singers Alliance Christmas concert.[100] As the year drew to a close the group traveled to North Tonawanda for a concert of Christmas carols at Our Lady of Czestochowa Church for the benefit of the North Tonawanda History Museum,[101] as well as a concert for the Beechwood Nursing Home.[102]

Following their February salute to Chopin, the Society held their annual elections. With over a half century of proven leadership and the lack of palace intrigue, Ann T. Mikoll was elected president for another term. The rest of the board elected was Gary Bienkowski, Paul Kosek, Thomas Pawlak, Evelyn Pietrzak, Ronald Smith, Henry Superczynski, and Geraldine Szemraj. These seven members joined the already serving Stephanie Borkowska, Fran Cirbus, James Mrozek, Genevieve Zielinska, Andrew Kowtalo, and Robert Ciesielski.[103]

While the Chopinites held another blowout Dyngus Day party at the Hearthstone Manor, the style of Easter Monday celebration they pioneered reached a new height in Western New York. On April 9, 2007, Dyngus Day Buffalo, LLC hosted the inaugural Dyngus Day Parade. Snaking around Buffalo's Old Polonia District the parade would become an annual event and would inspire similar Dyngus Day parties

---

97 *Festival Vigil Mass Book*. Polish Heritage Festival, Inc., 2006.

98 *Naturalization Ceremony at Buffalo and Erie County Naval & Servicemen's Park U.S.S. Little Rock.* United States Citizenship and Immigration Services, 2006.

99 *Fraternal Memorial Mass in Honor of the Living and Deceased Members of the Polish Roman Catholic Union of America*. Polish Roman Catholic Union of America, 2006.

100 The Chopin Singing Society. *108th Annual Concert*. Chopin Singing Society, 2007.

101 Kunz-Goldman, Mary. "GIFT LIST The Shelves Are Full of Great Concerts - and More - to Stock up on This Holiday Season." *Buffalo News*, 24 Nov. 2006.

102 Minutes of the 47th International Convention of the Polish Singers Alliance of America." Polish Singers Alliance of America, 27-30 May 2004, Detroit

103 Wiater, Edward S. "Mikoll, Tota Re-Elected for Chopin, Pomost." *Am-Pol Eagle*, 29 Mar. 2007, p. 1.

across the U.S. for decades to come.[104]

Recuperated from the festivities, Chopins joined the other choirs of the Polish Singers Alliance for their convention in Albany. While not singing in the competition, the group did take part as a demonstration choir at the gala concert, singing Jan Maklakiewicz's "Beskidzki Harnasiu."[105]

The summer brought a return performance at the Polish Heritage Festival and an autumn event at St. Stanislaus Church in Buffalo. With their annual concert, Witakowski focused on the works of Stanislaw Niewiadomski, Antoni Szalinski, Feliks Nowowiejski, and, of course, Chopin. The evening's program was dedicated to the memory of soloist and board member Susan Malik who unexpectedly passed away that May.[106]

As their winter concert series gave way to the New Year, the singers returned to the stage with their birthday party for Chopin, this time with special guest Dr. Bryan Boyce. This was followed by a performance at Corpus Christi Church and their Dyngus Day festivities.[107] Maintaining their usual schedule of annual events, the Society did add a show at Most Precious Blood Church in Angola. The one major departure for the singers in 2008 was the format of their annual concert. For most of the past 108 years the group sang a variety of numbers from different composers to make up the program. But in recognition of the 150th anniversary of the premier of Moniuszko's opera *Flis*, Music Director Witakowski completely retranslated the libretto. The Society, with a small orchestra, staged the entire one act production.[108] In recognition of the monumental undertaking of the opera, the *Am-Pol Eagle* newspaper rewarded the singers with their 2008 Citizen of the Year Award in the category of Art & Drama.[109]

Their 2009 celebration of Chopin's birth utilized their member's talents with Nicole Pawlik and Andrew Kowtalo, both soloists in *Flis*, serving as soloists on works by Moniuszko and Kuchen

---

[104] "Inaugural Dyngus Day Parade to Showcase Buffalo's Historic Polonia District." *Am-Pol Eagle Celebrate Dyngus Day*, 2007, p. 3.; Zeigler, Connie. "Unspoken Rules: Dyngus Day at the Chatterbox." *Indianapolis Monthly*, 2017

[105] *Gala Concert.* Polish Singers Alliance of America, 2007.

[106] The Chopin Singing Society. *108th Annual Concert.* Chopin Singing Society, 2007.

[107] The Chopin Singing Society. *A Celebration of the 198th Birthday of Frederic Chopin.* Chopin Singing Society, 2008.

[108] The Chopin Singing Society. *109th Annual Concert.* Chopin Singing Society, 2008.

[109] "*Am-Pol Eagle* Citizen of the Year Award." *Wikipedia*, Wikimedia Foundation, 5 May 2021

respectively. This evening was made possible with grants from New York State and Erie County and was followed up with a March performance at St. John Gualbert Church in Cheektowaga.

In late May Chopins returned to St. Adalbert to take part in a special reunion and Mass at the Basilica. This was the first time the singers had returned to the place of their birth since the Diocese of Buffalo moved to close and suppress St. Adalbert two years earlier.[110] The reunion was followed up with an early June concert at Our Lady of Victory Basilica as part of the City of Lackawanna's centennial celebration.[111] After again singing for America's newest citizens aboard the USS *Little Rock*, Chopins took part in the Pulaski Day Parade, where they won top prize as a marching unit.[112]

For the 110th annual concert, the singers decided to stage one of their largest productions in decades. In three parts, the group covered over a half dozen Polish composers, four works from Paderewski alone, including sections from two of his opuses, and closed with a medley of patriotic American music.

Closing out their year with the 29th Annual District 9 Koledy, the singers soon began preparing for an event they were largely the host of, the 49th International Convention of the Polish Singers Alliance.[113]

Officially sponsored by District 9, Chopins was well represented in the organization of the event, with members serving as the chair of the pre-convention committee, the convention ball, the Mass, hotel, concert, and competition committees. The Society was equally represented on the PSAA board with members Mary Lou Wyrobek serving as president, Adrianne Kusmierczyk as assistant Secretary, the position of treasurer taken up by Theresa Rogowski, and Fran Cirbus, Charlotte Harris, Ronald Smith, and Gary Bienkowski sitting as regular board members. Leading the international organization musically was Dr. Thomas Witakowski.

Under the theme of "Honoring the Musical Geniuses of Frederic Chopin and Ignacy Jan Paderewski" whose 200th and 150th birthdays, were being celebrated, Chopins took part in the competition

---

[110] The Chopin Singing Society. *A Celebration of the 199th Birthday of Frederic Chopin*. Chopin Singing Society, 2009.

[111] O'Brien, Barbara L. "Centennial Activities to Begin Today." *Buffalo News*, 29 May 2009.

[112] The Chopin Singing Society. *110th Annual Concert*. Chopin Singing Society, 2009.

[113] *29th Annual Festival of Christmas Carols - "Koledy."* Polish Singers Alliance District IX, 2009.

taking place at the Millennium Hotel in Cheektowaga, placing third in the Mixed Chorus Category. In addition, they were joined by the ladies of Kalina at the Convention Mass held at St. Stanislaus Church on May 30 where they sang "Ziemia Polska, tam dom moj!"[114] Of the ten groups going head-to-head for what the local media dubbed the "Stanley Cup of the Polish Singers Alliance of America," it would be the mixed-voice choir, Aria from New Jersey, who got to lift the Cardinal Hlond Trophy above their heads.[115]

But even before the convention began, the Chopinites had already seen a hectic year. To celebrate Frederic Chopin's 200th birthday, the Society put on a full concert of not just Chopin and Paderewski, in anticipation of the convention, but lesser-known Polish composers as well, including holocaust victim Jozef Krudowski. At the end of March, the group held a dinner and dance in celebration of the close of their 110th anniversary and got just enough rest to host their Dyngus Day party a week later.[116]

That summer, Chopins performed at Assumption Church and the Naval and Military Park in Buffalo as well as Holy Mother of the Rosary Cathedral in Lancaster. It also saw the singers bid a sad farewell to longtime board member and community leader Ronald M. Smith who passed away that August.[117]

To celebrate the 50th anniversary of the founding of Villa Maria College and to recognize the 20th anniversary of John Landis as the music director of the Cheektowaga Symphony, Chopins transformed their annual concert into a dual show with the Symphony at the College.[118] Serving as the season opener of the Symphony, Landis began the evening with works by Frederick Loew, Samuel Barber, and Beethoven. Chopins then staged their award-winning production of Moniuszko's *Flis*, for their part of the evening's entertainment.

The singers ended the year with their usual bevy of Christmas shows and with help from a grant from the Margaret Frank Rofat Trust, the Society was able to revive their *Jaselka* for a performance at

---

[114] *Polish Singers Alliance of America 49th International Convention.* Polish Singers Alliance of America, 2010.

[115] "Polish Singers Alliance of America Holds 'Festival Concert'." *Buffalo News*, 30 May 2010.

[116] The Chopin Singing Society. *A Celebration of the 200th Birthday of Frederic Chopin.* Chopin Singing Society, 2010.

[117] "Ronald M. Smith, Active in Polish Community; April 15, 1937 -- Aug. 4, 2010." *Buffalo News*, 22 Apr. 2010.

[118] "Happy 50th, 65th!" *Buffalo News*, 22 Oct. 2010.

St. Stanislaus Church in early 2011.[119]

The new year marked an important anniversary for both Chopins and Polonia, as it was the 50th anniversary of Chopins modern take on Dyngus Day. But before they could partake in the post-Easter celebration, they had to hold their annual birthday party for their namesake.

For the late February event, the singers gave a performance of works by Chopin, Johann Strauss, and Franz Lehar.[120] To highlight the skill and artistry of their accompanist, Emma Ziskind gave a stunning rendition of Chopin's "Polonaise #8 in d-minor Op. Post. 71, no. 1," "Nocturne #19 in e-minor, Op. 72" and "Ballade #1 in g-minor, Op. 23."[121]

At the April 2011 election, the members saw fit to re-elect retired New York State Supreme Court Justice Ann Mikoll as president. Gary Bienkowski, Thomas Brucz, Paul Kosek, Adrianne Kusmierczyk, Thomas Pawlak, Kathleen Pawlowski and Geraldine Szemraj each also received two-year terms to the board. In her inaugural address for the year, President Mikoll said of the group, "I am most proud to head this group of singers because I know they work hard and those who attend our concerts will get an enjoyable evening or afternoon of extremely fine singing."[122]

For their golden Dyngus Day celebration, Chopins went all out decorating the Hearthstone Manor for the all-day party. Opening with Father Czeslaw Krysa's blessing of the food, Chopins performed a few songs before a program of Polish dancing and singing by the White Eagle Dancers of Toronto, Canada. With the festivities in full gear, the polka bands took the stage as the Rare Vintage Orchestra, Buffalo's City Side, and DynaBrass from Waterford, MI played into the wee hours of Tuesday morning.[123] Chopins would see Father Krysa again later in the Easter season when they led St. Casimir's parish in a series of vibrant and inspiring Polish Easter hymns.[124]

---

[119] The Chopin Singing Society. *111th Annual Concert*. Chopin Singing Society, 2010.

[120] The Chopin Singing Society. *A Celebration of the 201st Birthday of Frederic Chopin*. Chopin Singing Society, 2011.

[121] Wiater, Edward S. "Fans Celebrate Chopin's Birthday in Style." *Am-Pol Eagle*, 3 Mar. 2011, p. 5.

[122] Wiater, Edward S. "Chopin Singers Elect Officers, Prepare for Coming Year." *Am-Pol Eagle*, 21 Apr. 2011, p. 17.

[123] Mroziak, Michael J. "Dyngus Day 2011: Revelry in the Rain." *Am-Pol Eagle*, 28 Apr. 2011, p. 1.

[124] Krysa, Rev. Czeslaw. "We're Still On…25 Days of Easter to Go." *Am-Pol Eagle*, 19 May 2011, p. 5.

The Society came back to their mother church of St. Adalbert on September 18 to sing at a Mass celebrating the 125th anniversary of the parish, and the 120th anniversary of the Basilica's July 1891 dedication.[125] From the position of the Diocese of Buffalo, this would be the last parish sponsored event of St. Adalbert as the parish was joined with St. John Kanty Church in Buffalo's far East Side.[126]

After singing at the Dozynki Festival of Holy Mother of the Rosary Cathedral, Chopins returned to Buffalo's Broadway-Fillmore neighborhood for the blessing of a reliquary and shrine dedicated to John Paul II at St. Stanislaus's parish.[127] Singing "Gaude Mater Polonia," "Be Not Afraid," and "Bogarodzica Dziewico," the singers earned the praise of not just the laity attending, but Buffalo's bishop as well.[128] The group was back at St. Stan's a few months later for the Polish Singers Alliance *Festival of Carols*, and closed out the year with their Wigilia and a concert at North Presbyterian Church with the Amherst Chamber Orchestra.[129]

Building up the celebration of Chopin's birth over the course of a decade, the party for "Freddy's" 202nd packed the hall at the Leonard Post. Led by Vice President Gary Bienkowski, who stepped in for an ill President Mikoll, the show opened with a rarity, "Trabka Bojowa" by Antoni Jax. The singers then dove headfirst into Chopin's "Zal Szopena" and Tadeusz Sygietynski's "Cyt, Cyt" before finishing out their set. The afternoon closed with a piano presentation by Emma Ziskind that featured Chopin polonaises.[130] After their Dyngus Day party, the singers took to the loft of the Oratory of St. Casimir to sing at a Mass for Father Krysa.[131]

In the months leading up to their annual concert, Chopins had to say goodbye to three longtime friends and colleagues. First, former Music Director Peter Gorecki passed away, followed shortly thereafter by St. Stanislaus' organist Thomas Borowski.[132] In the month that followed, onetime vice president, former Polish revolutionary and eternal

---

[125] "St. Adalbert Basilica Plans Anniversary Celebrations." *Am-Pol Eagle*, 16 July 2011, p. 16.
[126] "Saving St. Adalbert's." *Am-Pol Eagle* [Cheektowaga, NY], 14 July 2011, p. 2.
[127] "Polish Harvest Festival Set." *Am-Pol Eagle*, 18 Aug. 2011, p. 8.
[128] Radomski, Jaroslaw K. "Relic and Shrine of Blessed John Paul II Blessed by Bishop Edward U. Kmiec." *Am-Pol Eagle*, 27 Oct. 2011, pp. 1–5.
[129] The Chopin Singing Society. *113th Annual Concert*. Chopin Singing Society, 2012.
[130] Radomski, Jaroslaw K. "Chopin's 202nd Birthday Celebrated." *Am-Pol Eagle*, 1 Mar. 2012, p. 1.
[131] "Nestled in the Choir Loft." *Am-Pol Eagle*, 3 May 2012, p. 5.
[132] The Chopin Singing Society. *113th Annual Concert*. Chopin Singing Society, 2012.

stalwart of Chopins, David Rutecki, unexpectedly died from a stroke.[133]

Despite these losses, the Society put on their 113th annual concert with the theme of "On Wings of Polish Song." Highlighting works by Milek, Maszynski, and Ketelby, Adrienne Kusmierczyk, Mary Lou Wyrobek, James Mrozek, and Paul Kosek each sang a solo with the Amherst Chamber Orchestra accompanying. The choir also performed a new translation of Moniuszko's "Verbum Nobile" completed by Dr. Witakowski.[134]

As always, the singers ended their year with the Koledy festival and their Wigilia but also took up Father Krysa's invitation to participate in St. Casimir's *40 Days of Christmas,* singing a Mass there in early 2013.[135]

With the support of the New York State Council of the Arts, the choir held a 203rd birthday bash for Frederick in late February. The Leonard Post was filled as the singers entertained their guests with "Gora Piesn Polska" by Eugeniusz Walkiewicz, the motto of both Chopins and the Polish Singers Alliance. They also included three Polish folksongs for winter by Zygmunt Noskowski and the "Warsaw Polonaise" by Tadeusz Sygietynski. A wonderful departure for the classical set was a cabaret-style production by alto Susan Peters, accompanied by pianist Sherrie Morris. The duo reworked the lyrics of "What Are You Doing New Year's Eve?" to "What Are You Doing Tuesday Night?" This original piece was sung to encourage members of the audience to enroll as singers of Chopins and join them for their Tuesday night practices.[136] Pianist Emma Ziskind closed out the evening with a concert of five compositions by Chopin, with maestro Witakowski giving a little context and history of each work between the pieces.[137]

The spring took the singers to Annunciation Church in Elma, NY for a Lenten concert while accompanist Emma Ziskind took part in the Permanent Chair of Polish Culture at Canisius College's presentation, *An Afternoon with Chopin*.[138] For the program, Ms. Ziskind

---

[133] "Contributing Editor Rutecki Dies." *Am-Pol Eagle*, 29 Nov. 2012, pp. 1–16.

[134] The Chopin Singing Society. *113th Annual Concert*. Chopin Singing Society, 2012.

[135] "Celebrating the Days." *Am-Pol Eagle*, 24 Jan. 2013, p. 8.

[136] Szemraj, Edward R. "Chopin's Birthday Observed in Grand Style." *Am-Pol Eagle*, 28 Feb. 2013, p. 1.

[137] The Chopin Singing Society. *A Celebration of the 203rd Birthday of Frederic Chopin*. Chopin Singing Society, 2013.

[138] *A Lenten Concert with the Chopin Singing Society*. Annunciation Church, 2013.

played the works of Chopin while ethnographer Amy Smardz read letters written by the composer.[139]

Returning to Hearthstone Manor, the Dyngus Day program featured the White Eagle Dancers of Toronto with polka music by Rare Vintage, City Side with Ted Szymanski, and DynaBrass.[140] They followed up their post-Easter party with a Mother's Day concert sponsored by the Chopin Singing Society Ladies Auxiliary. Dedicated to the memory of the late, longtime president of the auxiliary, Evelyn Pietrzak, the evening had members reflect on the roles their mothers played in their individual lives. To achieve this, the group sang a mother themed set that included "Gwiazdo Sliczna," "Czarna Madonno," and "O Matko Moja."[141]

In the middle of May, the Chopinites returned to their role as an ambassador of Western New York's Polonia. Serving on the welcoming committee that opened the Polish American Historical Association board meeting in Buffalo, the group performed "Goralu Czy Ci Nie Zal" to open the event and "Patrz Kosciuszko, Na Nas Z Nieba" to close it.[142]

The summer took the singers from one end of Buffalo to the other. Their first major engagement of the season was the 140th anniversary Mass and celebration of the founding of St. Stanislaus Bishop and Martyr parish. Held on the last day of June, the service had every major Roman Catholic dignitary, politician, and organization of Polonia present. Completely responsible for the music of the Mass Chopins perfectly executed the hymns in both Polish and English.[143] The group then traveled to Buffalo's Black Rock neighborhood for the 125th anniversary of Assumption parish. Again, every major Roman Catholic dignitary, politician, and organization of Polonia was present, and again the choir executed a perfect performance of the sacred music.[144]

At the end of 2013, the Permanent Chair of Polish Culture at Canisius College; Polish Legacy Project of the Polish American

---

139 "An Afternoon with Chopin Set." *Am-Pol Eagle*, 17 Mar. 2013, p. 10.
140 "Chopin Singing Society Continues Dyngus Day Tradition." *Am-Pol Eagle*, 28 Mar. 2013, p. 16.
141 Szemraj, Edward R. "Chopin Singing Society Observes Mother's Day." *Am-Pol Eagle*, 16 May 2013, p. 5.
142 *The Polish Arts Club Welcomes the Board of Directors of the Polish American Historical Association to Buffalo*. Polish Arts Club of Buffalo, 2013.
143 *140 Years of Glory, Praise, and Wisdom*. St. Stanislaus Bishop and Martyr Parish, 2013.
144 "Black Rock Readies for Assumption Church 125th Anniversary Celebration Mass, Dinner." *Am-Pol Eagle*, 18 July 2013, p. 5.

Congress, WNY Division; Polish Arts Club of Buffalo; the Chopin Singing Society; Msgr. Peter Adamski Polish Saturday School; Ars Nova Musicians Chamber Orchestra; and the Canisius College Fine Arts Department took several of their major programs and events and united them under the banner of the Polish Cultural Festival 2013. For their part, Chopins moved their 114th annual concert to St. Casimir Church and hosted it under the title, *Journey Down the Wisla from the Mountains to the Sea.*[145] Accompanied by the Amherst Chamber Orchestra, the first half of the concert featured the classical, religious, and folk music of Poland while the second half highlighted a poem by John Paul II set to music. The day ended with a couple of popular American melodies and an arrangement by the former Chopin Director Peter Gorecki.[146]

The choir ended their 114th performance year with the Kalina Singing Society and Ludowa Nuta of Canada at the 33rd Festival of Koledy at St. Stanislaus Parish. They then hosted their ever-popular Wigilia, now at the Millennium Hotel.[147]

After hosting Chopin's birthday party in February 2014, the singers ran into some complications as they prepared for their Dyngus Day party.[148] In March their longtime venue Hearthstone Manor unexpectedly shut down. The Society was able to salvage the event by quickly rescheduling with the Adam's Mark Hotel and brought the Easter Monday party to Buffalo's downtown for the first time ever.[149] In the week that followed, Wanda Pakula, Susan Peters, and James Mrozek were the featured soloists for the annual Mother's Day performance at the Millennium. The singers then traveled to Detroit where they took part in the Polish Singers Alliance 50th International Convention, celebrating 125 years. While in the Motor City, the group scored third place in the mixed-choir category.[150]

At the end of May, Chopins were the performers for a Mass and gala dinner marking the 70th anniversary of the founding of the Polish American Congress. While the guests from across the country,

---

[145] The Permanent Chair of Polish Culture at Canisius College. "Polish Cultural Festival 2013." *Am-Pol Eagle* [Cheektowaga, NY], 5 Sept. 2013, p. 12.

[146] Szemraj, Edward R. "Chopin Singing Society Takes Its Audience Down the Wisla." *Am-Pol Eagle*, 7 Nov. 2013, p. 1.

[147] "The Festival of Koledy." *Am-Pol Eagle*, 5 Dec. 2013, p. 1.

[148] The Chopin Singing Society. *115th Annual Concert*. Chopin Singing Society, 2014.

[149] Watson, Stephen T. "Hearthstone Manor Customers Await Refunds as Venue Shuts Down." *Buffalo News*, 6 Mar. 2014.

[150] The Chopin Singing Society. *115th Annual Concert*. Chopin Singing Society, 2014.

and around the world were enjoying their filet mignon and herb crusted salmon, the singers serenaded them with the classical works of Poland and the folksongs of the homeland.[151]

The summer had the group returning to the USS *Little Rock*, once again singing for the new Americans. This time was special for the Society as it marked the silver anniversary of their taking part in the occasion. The choir then sang for another national convention held in Buffalo, this time for the American Council for Polish Culture.

In the fall, the members traveled to Niagara Falls to celebrate the 100th anniversary of Holy Trinity School. Closed by the Diocese of Buffalo in 2008, the nonprofit that took over the complex, Historic Holy Trinity, still engaged the former members and students of the parish in recognizing the important milestones of the site.[152] They also sang at a Mass of Thanksgiving for the 133rd anniversary of the Felician Order working in Western New York.[153]

For their annual concert, the Society returned to St. Casimir Church. With the Amherst Chamber Orchestra, Chopins aimed for an evening of the *Best of Polish Music and Song*. With fifteen musical selections, the *Am-Pol Eagle* music reviewer summed up the importance of the performance saying "the concert continued the distinctive tradition of the Chopin Singers – that of promoting, highlighting and pridefully passing on the musical heritage of the Polish people."[154]

Some of the musical heritage passed on that night was the Society's theme song, "Gora Piesn Polska" and the solemn hymn "O Boze Moj." Sung by Adrienne Kusmierczyk and Paul Kosek the hymn was composed by Reverend Antoni Hlond-Chlondowski, a Salesian priest and brother of the Polish primate Cardinal August Hlond, the namesake of the Polish Singers Alliance's Hlond Trophy. The piece de resistance that evening was Emma Ziskind's "Warsaw Concerto."[155]

As always, the end of the year was a busy one for the singers. Their ever-growing Wigilia saw over 300 guests partake in the traditional Christmas-Eve meal, and the Polish Singers Alliance of America

---

[151] *Celebrating the 70th Anniversary of the Polish American Congress*. Polish American Congress, 2014.

[152] Sharp, Teresa. "School, Now Closed, Is More than a Memory." *Buffalo News*, 21 Sept. 2014.

[153] The Chopin Singing Society. *115th Annual Concert*. Chopin Singing Society, 2014.

[154] Szemraj, Edward R. "Chopin Singing Society, Amherst Chamber Orchestra Fill St. Casimir's with Music." *Am-Pol Eagle*, 6 Nov. 2014, pp. 1–16.

[155] Szemraj, Edward R. "Chopin Singing Society, Amherst Chamber Orchestra Fill St. Casimir's with Music." *Am-Pol Eagle*, 6 Nov. 2014, pp. 1–16.

District 9's Festival of Koledy always brought out an enthused audience.[156]

The Chopinites had a busy start to their 116th year with three major engagements. In the first Sunday of the New Year, they displayed their skill at St. Gregory the Great Church in Williamsville where they gave a Koledy prelude to the afternoon Mass. Everyone made sure to pack their passports to travel to Hamilton, Ontario for a Koledy celebration at St. Stanislaus Kostka Church with the rest of District 9. As guests of the Symfonia Choir all the singers put on a rousing show which was followed by a traditional Polish Canadian dinner.[157]

The Society retuned to Buffalo to serve as the singers for the eighth Buffalo Mass Mob at St. Casimir Church. The Mass Mob, a Buffalo-born project that draws people to attend a religious service at historically and architecturally important churches, gave Chopins one their largest audiences in years with over 800 attendees. Sporting their signature red blazers, keeping them both warm and fashionable, the Society gave stirring renditions of "Bog Sie Rodzi," Gdy Sie Crystus Rodzi," "Dzisiaj w Betlejem," and "O Swieta Noc." As soon as the service finished, praise for Chopins from those attending the service began to rain down. Mobbers who never heard a note from Chopins before were saying the music was like "a trip to Europe at holiday time," "the singing was absolutely wonderful," and "my mother said it was the best music she's ever heard."[158]

For their 54th Dyngus Day celebration, Chopins moved the party closer to home, arranging it at the Millennium Hotel. With a spread of delectable Polish food, the singers really shined with their musical lineup. The set included Lenny Gomulka & Chicago Push, Rochester's Tommy Brunett, Larry Trojak and Scrubby Seweryniak of the Dynatones, to name only a few of the acts.[159]

The summer heat couldn't stop the singers from their events at the USS *Little Rock* or prevent them from marching in the Pulaski Parade at the Cheektowaga Polish American Festival. The summer was capped off by President Mikoll, who was honored by the Buffalo

---

[156] Szemraj, Edward R. "Chopin Wigilia – the Power of Nostalgia and Cherishing a Polish Custom." *Am-Pol Eagle*, 11 Dec. 2014, pp. 1–16.; "Wrapped Up with A Bow." *Am-Pol Eagle*, 11 Dec. 2014, p. 1.

[157] Facebook Archives, Chopin Singing Society, Buffalo, NY

[158] Buffalo Mass Mob Archives, 2023.

[159] McNeil, Harold. "Thousands Flock to Old Polonia for Annual Dyngus Day Revelries." *Buffalo News*, 7 Apr. 2015.

Bisons at the team's annual Polish Night.

In the autumn the singers relocated their annual concert once again, this time to Assumption Church in North Buffalo. With the theme of On Wings of Polish Song and held with the Amherst Chamber Ensembles, Chopins presented a program of folk and religious music. The October afternoon presentation filled the Black Rock church with friends and fans of Polish music.[160] The Society then ventured to Holy Mother of the Rosary Cathedral for a mid-November concert that featured Shirley Byczynski, Nicole Chodaczek, and Joanna Brown. For their part, Chopins performed classical and Polish folk songs as well as modern works by Edward Bury and Henryk Wars.[161]

As the singers prepared for their holiday concerts, the winds of change were in the air. The leadership that the Society had depended on for the last two decades was starting to tire and slow. A visit from St. Nicholas still filled the Wigilia partygoers with delight, and the Society would still sing their hearts out at the Koledy, but the year 2016 would see a new order of familiar faces rise to the top of Chopins.[162]

---

[160] Pietruszka, Michael "Pulaski Association Honors Pol-Am Educators." *Polish American Journal*, Oct. 2015, p.8.

[161] *Holy Mother of the Rosary Cathedral presents in concert: The Chopin Singing Society.* Holy Mother of the Rosary Cathedral, 2015.

[162] Facebook Archives, Chopin Singing Society, Buffalo, NY

Chapter 10

Chopin at 125

Chopins started the year of 2016 by completing their Christmas season. They first held a program at St. Stanislaus Kostka Church in Hamilton before returning and visiting St. Casimir Church in Buffalo. While in Canada Chopins were joined by their friends Symfonia for a day of caroling koledy.[1]

To celebrate Frederic Chopin's 206th birthday, the singers serenaded the audience with songs at their clubhouse. The special guests of the evening were cellist Barbara Cordaro and pianist Ivan Docenko who played one of Chopin's first published works, 1831's "Introduction et polonaise brillante, Op.3."[2]

On Monday March 28, the Society celebrated its 55th Dyngus Day, hosted at the Millennium Hotel. The event started with Chopins giving a lunchtime program as the White Eagle Dancers of Toronto added some cultural flair to the day. Ed Guca and Franek Zosia & the Polkatowners kept attendees dancing to polka music until the next day.[3]

Led by President Mikoll, the Chopin Singing Society and White Eagle Dancers returned to Buffalo, sponsoring a fundraiser for St. Stanislaus's parish that May. As she had all her life, Ann worked overtime to fill the auditorium at Villa Maria College for her parish. When the receipts were counted the two groups raised over $4,400 for the church.[4]

Later in the month, the singers took part at the Camerata Di Sant' Antonio chamber orchestra's *Slavic Soul* program at Corpus Christi Church. Their pre-concert program included the thirteenth century Polish hymn to St. Stanislaus, "Gaude Mater Polonia," a work by Otton Mieczyslaw Zukowski followed by the folksong "Jak Dobrze

---

[1] Facebook Archives, Chopin Singing Society, Buffalo, NY

[2] Chopin Singing Society. "Commemorating the Genius of Frederic Chopin." 2016.

[3] Chopin Singing Society. "Chopin Singing Society Dyngus Day." 2016.

[4] Dlugosz, Steve. "Community Leader and Former Judge Ann T. Mikoll Advocates for St. Stan's Church." *Am-Pol Eagle*, 27 May 2016.

Nam."[5]

In the spring of 2016, for the first time in her life, President Ann T. Mikoll felt her age. With an ever-growing tapestry of health concerns, a desire to slow down, and having full faith in the abilities of Vice President Gary Bienkowski, Mikoll decided to step down as president of the Society she had helped lead for a half century.[6] As the choir was preparing for the transition of leadership, they hosted a St. John's Eve celebration at Cheektowaga Town Park. The late June festival featured Chopins in song and the White Eagles in dance. The Eagles also demonstrated some of the traditions of St. John's Eve celebration including the custom of wreath floating.

For that year's Polish American Festival, the singers appeared onstage with the Cheektowaga Community Symphony Orchestra. Both musical groups were part of the official kickoff of the three-day event that began July 14.[7] The Society closed the Cheektowaga Town Park event on Sunday by marching in the General Pulaski Parade down Harlem Road.[8]

While Witakowski, the singers, and the Amherst Chamber Ensembles, gave stirring renditions of the "Polonaise Militaire Op. 40 No. 1" and Peter Gorecki's "Dobra noc, spij" Chopin's 117th annual concert is remembered for Ann Mikoll's farewell address. From the lectern of St. Stanislaus church Ann said in part,

> As we enter a new presidency, I would like to hearken back in a recollection of what Chopin's meant to Ted, my husband, who led the society for 30 years with his brother Jim's help as choir chairman and to me its president for 20 years. These were the most happy occasions of our life. Song lightens the heart and invigorates one's life…[w]hen one dedicates oneself to presenting the 'best in Polish music' this adds another positive dimension to one's joy. There is happiness in joining a choir – new friendships and great experiences waiting for the taking.[9]

---

5 Pitas, Jeannine. "Photo Gallery: Slavic Soul at Corpus Christi Church." *Broadway Fillmore Alive*, 28 May 2016,

6 Dlugosz, Steve. "Judge Mikoll Looks Fondly upon Tenure in Chopin Singing Society." *Am-Pol Eagle*, 2 June 2016.

7 Facebook Archives, Chopin Singing Society, Buffalo, NY

8 Staff. "Polish American Festival Held in Cheektowaga." *Wgrz.com*, WGRZ, 18 July 2016,

9 "Ann Mikoll Feted at 117th Annual Chopin Singing Society Concert." *Am-Pol Eagle*, 21 Oct. 2016.

Besides dedicating the program to the retired justice, the singers also bestowed the title of President Emeritus on the woman who led them for the better part of two decades.

As the new president Gary A. Bienkowski planned for a busy, but predictable end of the year. The Society would hold their Wigilia, join in the *Festival of Carols*, and take part in *Polka Buzz*'s Christmas episode. Everything was going smoothly until word reached Gary that Music Director Tom Witakowski suffered a devastating stroke and was in critical condition. Knowing that Witakowski wouldn't want them to cancel the events on his account, Bienkowski appointed Andrew N. Kowtalo music director pro tem, as the Society and all of Polonia prayed for Tom.

With Witakowski on their minds, Chopins made a triumphant return to the television screen with a featured appearance on WBBZ's *Polka Buzz*. On a special December 18 Christmas edition of the Ron Dombrowsk hosted show, Chopins presented a medley of koledy, bookended with Christmas polkas by The Buffalo Touch.[10] In the years to come Chopins would become a fixture of the Christmas episodes looking dapper in their red jackets or festive in traditional Polish costume.[11]

As had become tradition, the singers opened 2017 by singing for the koledy Mass at St Casimir in late January. The cold, wintery weather didn't deter the faithful from attending the always popular service. In the month that followed the singers held their annual birthday party for Chopin which featured a piano performance by Emma Ziskind and songs by the choir.

As April approached the singers began preparing for their annual Dyngus Day extravaganza. With the Millennium Hotel hosting the party, the Society organized a four-act program for their 56th annual post-Lenten event. The singers would get the party started performing during a lunch buffet, then New Jersey's own Heroes featuring Polka Hall of Famer Eddie Biegaj took over. A new band at the time, Heroes focused on an Eastern Style polka not often heard over the past few decades. To showcase traditional Polish dance, the Rodzina Folk Group of the Polish Cadets took to the floor to show off a step or two. The evening was then led by Polka master John Gora and his band,

---

[10] "WBBZ-TV Presents 'Yule Log' & Special Christmas Programs." *Niagara Frontier Publications*, 24 Dec. 2016,

[11] Facebook Archives, Polka Buzz TV Show on WBBZ, Buffalo, NY

trading off sets with Heroes all night long.[12]

In the month after their post-Lenten celebration, the Society traveled to Philadelphia to take part in the 51st International Convention of the Polish Singers Alliance of America. Under the direction of temporary conductor Andrew Kowtalo, the singers secured fourth place in their category at the competition.[13] The win gave the singers a little extra pep as they sang for the joyful occasion of Father Cole Webster's First Mass at Assumption Church the weekend after their return.

That summer the choir took part in several community events. The first was the Pulaski Day Parade and the second was helping to greet Polish Secretary of State Anna Maria Anders Costa on her visit to the Niagara Frontier.[14] While the events worked as a bit of a distraction, what was really on everyone's mind was the status of the annual concert and who would be leading it? In a recovery that can only be described as miraculous for a stroke survivor,[15] Dr. Witakowski informed the singers that he would be ready to lead them for the October performance.

In front of an enthusiastic crowd at St. Stanislaus Bishop & Martyr Church, Witakowski led the singers and the Amherst Chamber Ensembles through a "program spanning the centuries of Polish music and tapping into the depths of emotion of Polish song."[16] The evening of music, dedicated to TV personality and friend of Polonia Eileen Koteras Elibol, brought more than one standing ovation for the performers and their director.[17] In support of the event, the Polish American Congress sponsored a reception for its member organization that was greatly appreciated by both the attendees and singers.[18]

In the first weekend of December the singers held back-to-back events with their Wigilia at the Millennium Hotel and the Festival of Carols at St. Stanislaus.[19] Inclement weather put a damper on the start of Chopin's next year, forcing the cancellation of their appearance at

---

[12] Pasierb, Mike. "Millennium Hotel and Chopin Singing Society's 56th Annual Dyngus Day." *Am-Pol Eagle*, 21 Apr. 2017.

[13] Facebook Archives, Chopin Singing Society, Buffalo, NY

[14] "Polish Singers Alliance of America Newsletter." Feb. 2018.

[15] "Stroke Recovery: A Music Miracle." Catholic Health, 3 June 2018,

[16] "Chopin Concert Is October 15." *Am-Pol Eagle*, 6 Oct. 2017, p. 1.

[17] Facebook Archives, Chopin Singing Society, Buffalo, NY

[18] Lawicki, James. "Your Polish American Congress in Action." *Am-Pol Eagle* [Cheektowaga, NY], 3 Nov. 2017.

[19] Chopin Singing Society. "Would like to Wish All of Polonia a Merry Christmas and a Happy Joyous New Year!" 2017.

St. Gregory the Great.[20] But things did clear up in time for the annual celebration of Chopin's birth at the Pvt. Leonard Post. For those who attended the free evening of entertainment, they enjoyed a few songs by the choir, a solo by Andrew Kowtalo, and some folk dances by the Rodzina of the Polish Cadets.

With an early Easter, the choir had to start getting everything in order for Dyngus Day shortly after the party. With Robin Pegg in the Twigs Lounge and the choir, John Gora & Gorale, Stacy Morris & the NuTones,[21] and the Rodzina in the ballroom, the Millennium Hotel would be shaking in its foundation on Dyngus Day 2018.[22] The all-night party saw hundreds of guests, drinking kegs of beer, all celebrating their Polish heritage.

As the spring's Chopin Auxiliary's Mother's Day celebration ended and summer rolled in, the singers took part in the biggest event of the season, the Mass at St. Stanislaus for the 80th Annual General Pulaski Parade. Members later joined in the parade that stretched from Walden Avenue down Harlem Road to Cheektowaga Town Park.[23]

That fall, Daemen College hosted a one-day conference, *For Your Freedom and Ours: Symposium on Polonia and the Struggle for Polish Independence*. The keynote speech was by noted Polish American historian James Pula entitled, "The Fourth Partition and the Restoration of Polish Independence" and Chopins closed out the conference with a performance of selected Polish works.[24]

The singers followed up their college appearance with their own 119th annual concert at St. Stanislaus parish that October. Under the banner of *The Pride of Poland*, the program was dedicated to the Buffalo Philharmonic Orchestra and their Music Director JoAnn Falletta. For the show the singers gave an afternoon of Polish religious, folk, and patriotic music with the help of the Amherst Chamber Ensembles.[25] Ms. Falletta was then presented with a plaque and one of Joseph Mazur's original models for the Chopin monument residing in

---

[20] Facebook Archives, Chopin Singing Society, Buffalo, NY

[21] Kushner, Matthew. "Which Bands Are Coming to Town for Dyngus Day?" *Am-Pol Eagle*, 29 Mar. 2018.

[22] Chopin Singing Society. "Millennium Buffalo Presents Chopin Singing Society's 57th Annual Dyngus Day Celebration." 2018.

[23] Facebook Archives, Chopin Singing Society, Buffalo, NY

[24] "Polish Independence to Be Explored at Symposium: Daemen University." *Polish Independence to Be Explored at Symposium*, Daemen University, 13 Sept. 2018,

[25] Anderson, Dale. "Reporters' Notebook: Oct. 12, 2018." *Buffalo News*, 12 Oct. 2018.

Symphony Circle.[26]

To celebrate the 100th Anniversary of Poland's Rebirth, the Permanent Chair of Polish Culture sponsored a centennial concert and Mass at Assumption Church in Black Rock. With a sanctuary full of veterans in uniform, their families, friends of Polonia, and the faithful, Chopins sang to a century of Poland's freedom.[27] The Amherst Ensembles joined the group again in December for *A European Christmas*, a concert of Polish, American, and European Christmas carols sung at Holy Mother of the Rosary Cathedral.[28] The Society ended the year with their always popular Wigilia and a special celebration of the 100th birthday of longtime member Genevieve Zielinski. Chopins filled the halls of the Weinberg Campus with song and joy for the rare occasion.[29]

The weather ruined Chopins new year once again, forcing them to cancel their Mass at St. Casimir Church,[30] but were able to host their birthday to Chopin that February. The party served as a triple celebration, first in commemorating Chopin, second the 120th anniversary of the founding of the Society, and third honoring the 200th birthday of composer Stanislaw Moniuszko. The celebration of Stanislaw was part of an international movement lead by the United Nations and the Republic of Poland who declared 2019 as the Year of Moniuszko. To mark the event, the singers performed works by Moniuszko and Chopin along with piano pieces presented by Emma Ziskind. The Rodzina Dance Group also demonstrated their skills for the at capacity crowd.[31]

For their 58th Dyngus Day celebration the singers secured both John Gora and Gorale as well as Western New York favorite 90 West.[32] But Dyngus Day wouldn't be the end of Easter for the group as they would go on to sing a few Easter hymns before Mass at St. Gregory the Great Church in Williamsville on April 28.[33]

May 18 was another day of triple celebration for Polonia as a

---

[26] "Chopin Singing Society Concert Honoring BPO and JoAnn Falletta." *Am-Pol Eagle*, 18 Oct. 2018.

[27] Chopin Singing Society. "Future Events." 2018.

[28] Anderson, Dale. "Reporters' Notebook: Dec. 18, 2018." *Buffalo News*, 18 Dec. 2018.

[29] "Chopin Singers Celebrate Zielinski's 100th Birthday." *Am-Pol Eagle*, 9 Jan. 2019.

[30] Facebook Archives, Chopin Singing Society, Buffalo, NY

[31] "Chopin, Moniuszko Celebrations Intermingle." *Am-Pol Eagle*, 21 Feb. 2019.

[32] Kushner, Matthew. "Which Bands Are Coming to Town for Dyngus Day?" *Am-Pol Eagle*, 18 Apr. 2019.

[33] Facebook Archives, Chopin Singing Society, Buffalo, NY

special Mass was held at St. Adalbert Basilica. The service recognized the saint's feast day, the 120th birthday of the Chopin Singing Society, and the 60th anniversary of the founding of the "Voice of Polonia," the *Am-Pol Eagle Newspaper*. With Chopins singing, Roger Puchalski and Renee Harzewski of the *Eagle* presenting the gifts and Father Bryan Zielenieski wearing vestments bearing an image of Our Lady of Czestochowa, the event was one of Polish Buffalo's high points of the year.

At the start of June, the group took part in another anniversary Mass, this one marking the diamond jubilee of the Polish American Congress at St. Stanislaus Church. Born in Buffalo in May of 1943, the Polish American Congress worked to free Poland, pressed the U.S. Congress to investigate the Katyn Massacre, and assisted Poland in joining NATO.[34] At the conclusion of the Mass the Congress presented a plaque to the parish, marking it as one of the founding locations of the esteemed body.[35] In the summer, the singers again sang on the USS *Little Rock* for the Naturalization service and took part in both the Mass and parade of the Pulaski Festival in Cheektowaga. In Hamburg, the Society saw their history highlighted at the Erie County Fair with a display at the Historical Building.[36] The exhibit put on by the *Am-Pol Eagle* even garnered an Honorable Mention Ribbon by the judges.[37]

In October, keeping with the theme of Moniuszko, the Society titled their 120th anniversary concert and dinner, *Mostly Moniuszko*. Staying on point, Chopins, along with the Amherst Chamber Ensembles, presented pieces from Moniuszko's Opera, *Flis*. They also included works by Chopin, a few folk songs, and a cabaret selection.[38] The choir also used their 120th anniversary concert to honor one of Western New York's most influential, musically talented, and humble Polish Americans, Joseph Macielag. In addition to dedicating the concert to the former president of the Polish American Congress and member of the International Polka Hall of Fame, Chopins presented Macielag an award as a token of their appreciation for the "many musical, cultural and social contributions [he] has made to Polonia and

---

34 "Buffalo Memorial Auditorium." Polonia Trail, Polish-American Congress WNY, 29 June 2016,

35 Facebook Archives, Polish American Congress WNY, Buffalo, NY

36 "120 Years in the Making." *Am-Pol Eagle*, 8 Aug. 2019.

37 Facebook Archives, Chopin Singing Society, Buffalo, NY

38 The Chopin Singing Society. *120th Annual Concert*. Chopin Singing Society, 2019.

beyond."[39] The harsh winter slowed the singers down a little to close out their year, but they still held their annual Wigilia with great holiday cheer and joined in District 9's Festival of Carols.

To open 2020, the Society sang a Mass at St. Gregory the Great on the first Saturday of the year and held a concert at Blessed Sacrament Church of Buffalo eight days later.[40] Entitled, *Farewell to the Manger*, the Blessed Sacrament concert featured Christmas carols in both English and Polish, as well as selections from the previous year's *Mostly Moniuszko*.[41] In the days leading up to the show, the World Health Organization begins using a new phrase for a disease outbreak in China calling it the "2019 Novel Coronavirus."[42]

Chopins returned to Kleinhans Music Hall on February 8 as the "Community Spotlight" pre-concert performers for the BPO's *Mahler & Bernstein.* At the ticketed event exclusively available to those attending the Philharmonic, the red jacketed singers magnificently executed works by Zygmunt Karasinski, Stanislaw Moniuszko, Alfred Schutz, and Eugeniusz Walkiewicz in the Mary Seaton Room. Andrew Kowtalo's solo performance of "Czerwone Maki" was particularly noteworthy that evening.[43]

In later February, as the outbreak was renamed COVID-19 and began to show up on American shores, not yet considered a threat, Western New York's Polonia announced that 2020 would be a musical celebration of the centenary of Pope John Paul II's birth. To kick off the year of festivities the Chopin Singing Society dedicated their annual birthday concert to the first Polish pontiff. On March 3 a fairly substantial crowd filled the Leonard Post where the singers premiered the piece "Pasterze z Polskiej Krainy (Poland gave us a Shepherd)" composed by Parisian Georges Nawrocki and Algerian born Jean-Pierre Stora. The rest of the evening was dedicated to the music of the Polish mountains before a reception of coffee and cake.[44]

On March 11, 2020, the World Health Organization declared COVID-19 a pandemic with the White House declaring the disease a

---

39 "Joseph Macielag Honored by Chopin Singing Society." *Am-Pol Eagle*, 19 Oct. 2019.
40 Facebook Archives, Chopin Singing Society, Buffalo, NY
41 "Chopin Singers to Bid Farewell to the Manger." *Am-Pol Eagle*, 9 Jan. 2020.
42 "CDC Museum Covid-19 Timeline." Centers for Disease Control and Prevention, Centers for Disease Control and Prevention, 15 Mar. 2023
43 "In The Spotlight at Kleinhans." *Am-Pol Eagle*, 13 Feb. 2020, p. 1.
44 "Chopin Concert and Reception Begins JPII Centenary Celebrations." *Am-Pol Eagle*, 20 Feb. 2020.

national emergency two days later.[45] On March 16, the Society canceled all rehearsals until the end of the month. Eight days later the board announced that Dyngus Day 2020 was canceled and that all rehearsals and programs would be put on an indefinite hiatus. In May Chopins was going to help host the Polish Singers Alliance of America's convention in Buffalo, but that too was rescheduled. The break was first extended through the summer, then to the winter, and then into the next year.[46]

While there were no public appearances at the time, behind the scenes changes were happening at Chopins. In late 2020 singer and board member Diana Kniazuk passed away, and longtime accompanist Emma Ziskind retired shortly thereafter, leaving the Buffalo area.[47]

As 2020 gave way to 2021, the world began to tentatively open up and members of Chopin started taking part in some small events and receptions. In January, Dr. Thomas Witakowski was presented with the Bronisław Durewicz Memorial Award from the Polish American Congress of Western New York,[48] while one of the group's younger singers Anna Pascucci was the winner of the 2020-2021 Leokadia Dombroska/Polish Singers Alliance of America Scholarship.[49] While the group didn't hold their Dyngus Day party that spring, they were able to take part in the limited Dyngus Day parade that wound through Buffalo's East Side.

On August 17, the choir was able to gather for its annual outdoor Mass for deceased members. The service at Stiglmeier Park concluded with a picnic where their newly refurbished bust of Chopin was unveiled. Created by Kazimir Chodzinski in 1909 while he resided in Buffalo, Chodzinski had already garnered international fame for his Tadeusz Kosciuszko Monument in Chicago and his equestrian statue of Casimir Pulaski in Washington, D.C.[50]

By October, COVID-19 vaccines were distributed, and the group felt comfortable enough to test the in-person, indoor waters and

---

[45] United States, Congress, Biden, Joseph R. *Continuation of the National Emergency with Respect to the Novel Coronavirus Disease (Covid-19) Outbreak: Message from the President of the United States, Transmitting a Continuation of the National Emergency with Respect to the Coronavirus Disease 2019 (Covid-19) Pandemic, Declared in Proclamation 9994 of March 13, 2020, Is to Continue in Effect beyond March 1, 2021, Pursuant to 50 U.S.C. 1622(d); Public Law 94-412, Sec. 202(D); (90 Stat. 1257).*

[46] Facebook Archives, Chopin Singing Society, Buffalo, NY

[47] Facebook Archives, Chopin Singing Society, Buffalo, NY

[48] Facebook Archives, Polish American Congress WNY, Buffalo, NY

[49] "PSAA Names Pascucci Its Scholarship Winner." *Am-Pol Eagle*, 11 Mar. 2021.

[50] "Polish Singers Alliance Newsletter." 2022.

hosted *Calling All Singers* a launch event for their 123rd year. Starting with a print and broadcasting media blitz,[51] the group encouraged members of the Polish American community, and Western New York to come out to a meet and greet, and maybe even try out with the choir. The event was also the first held in their new headquarters at Potts Banquet Hall in Cheektowaga, just outside Buffalo's Kaisertown neighborhood.[52]

With the success of the launch event, a delegation of Covid-masked Chopin Singers performed for the unveiling of the Jozef Slawinski sgraffito at Canisius College in Buffalo on October 19. Slawinski, a Polish artist who settled in Niagara Falls worked in the ancient Etruscan art of sgraffito. This technique utilized layers of pigmented cement which the artist etches away to form the picture. The Canisius College work features Chopin, Copernicus, Madame Curie and Mickiewicz, as well as the Jagiellonian University.[53]

The Society then returned to form with their television stint singing koledy for the WBBZ Polka Buzz program and their well attended 2021 Wiliglia. Other organizations also began opening up and in January of 2022 the singers joined their fellow members of District 9 of the Polish Singers Alliance of America for the relaunching of the *Festival of Carols*, now held at St. Gabriel's Church in Elma. With Dr. Thomas Witakowski in charge of Chopins and maestro Edward Witul directing the Kalina Singing Society, the limited audience of 200 raved about the singing saying it was "great," "wonderful," and "inspiring."[54]

That March, Chopins brought back their celebration of their namesake's birthday, but this time limited it to a members only event. Those who did have the privilege to attend heard Polish-Ukrainian-American member Andrew Kowtalo give a sobering rendition of the Ukrainian national anthem "Shche ne vmerla Ukrainy," in recognition of the Russian invasion of Ukraine that commenced a month earlier. The second half of the program included some Polish hymns and works by Chopin.

Due to the pandemic, board elections were not held, meaning for the first time in over three generations every board seat was open.

---

[51] Golebiowski, Andy. "Polish Mountain Music, Classical, Pop, Guests." *Polish American Radio Program,* 2 Oct. 2021.

[52] "Chopin Singers Prepare for New Season in New Location." *Am-Pol Eagle*, 24 Sept. 2021.

[53] "Polish Singers Alliance Newsletter." 2022.

[54] "Festival of Carols Finds New Fans." *Am-Pol Eagle*, 14 Jan. 2022.

Those victorious in this historic election were Joanna Brown, Thomas Brucz, Robert Ciesielski, Frances Cirbus, George Kania, Irene Kmiotek, Adrianne Kusmierczyk, Karen Macris, David McElroy, James Mrozek, Thomas Pawlak, Susan Peters, Geraldine Szemraj, and Mary Lou Wyrobek. Gary Bienkowski was re-elected as president with Christine Witkowski winning the presidency of Chopin's Auxiliary.[55]

While their spring schedule passed on Dyngus Day 2022, the Auxiliary held a highly successful fundraiser honoring the Mothers of Ukraine that May, raising $4,000 for St. Gabriel's Angels of Elma, an aid organization assisting Ukrainian war refugees in Ukraine and Poland. Later in May, they took part in the closing reception for the Galicia Jewish Museum's travelling exhibit, *The Girl in the Diary – Search for Rywka from the Lodz Ghetto* at the Karpeles Manuscript Library Museum.[56] At the end of the season the choir sang at St. Stanislaus Church, the religious heart of Buffalo's Polish East Side, at the Mass of Thanksgiving that marked the start of the sesquicentennial celebration of the parish.[57]

In the summer Chopins held their picnic and participated in the mini-parade at the now-revamped Cheektowaga Polish Festival. They sang at the rededication ceremony of the Polish Armed Forces Exhibit aboard the USS *Little Rock* at the Buffalo and Erie County Naval and Military Park.[58] With Consul General of the Republic of Poland in New York City, Adrian Kubicki as the keynote speaker of the rededication, the singers opened the program with the national anthems and closed it with Polish patriotic songs.

Their summer schedule only got busier from there. The group offered a performance at the West Seneca Pavilion entitled *The Music Festival for all Ages*, a concert that also served as a fundraiser for St. Gabriel's Angels of Elma[59] and then they took part in downtown Buffalo's Pulaski Parade & Festival.[60] This was then followed by the

---

[55] "After Yearlong Hiatus, WNYers Celebrate Chopin's Birthday." *Am-Pol Eagle*, 18 Mar. 2022.

[56] "Closing Reception Planned for Girl in the Diary Exhibit." *Am-Pol Eagle*, 20 May 2022.

[57] "Heading toward an Historic 150th!" *Am-Pol Eagle*, 3 June 2022.

[58] "The Topic of War, Past and Present to Bring Polish Consul General to Buffalo." *Am-Pol Eagle*, 29 July 2022.

[59] "Chopin Singers Get Ready to Perform at Exhibit Opening, Music Festival, Tour." *Am-Pol Eagle*, 29 July 2022.

[60] Dlugosz, Steve. "Pulaski Parade & Festival Incorporates Multi-Cultural Theme, Interests." *Am-Pol Eagle*, 19 Sept. 2022.

inaugural concert for Explore Buffalo's Doors Open Buffalo Houses of Worship Music Series with a free event at Assumption Church on Amherst Street in Buffalo.

In the fall the group announced that a book on their history would be written and launched as part of the choir's quasquicentennial in 2024, with the author giving a brief overview of the text at that September's meeting.

October held Chopin's 123rd anniversary concert at St. Stanislaus Church in Buffalo. Under the title of *Golden Polish Folk Songs for One and All*, the choir was accompanied by the Amherst Chamber Ensembles and featured Moniuszko's "St. Stanislaus Hymn" in honor of the parish's 150th anniversary year. The group also recognized Russia's ongoing attempt to conquer Ukraine by performing Mykola Lysenko's 1885 "Prayer for Ukraine" and folk song "Hej Sokoly," made popular by Polish and Ukrainian soldiers during the Polish–Soviet War. The show included featured member, pianist Melanie Bebak, the winner of the Leokadia Dombrowska/Polish Singers Alliance Scholarship,[61] who gave a superb rendition of Chopin's "Nocturne in G-minor, Op. 37, no. 1." The program was further highlighted by George Kania, Paul Kosek, James Mrozak and Michael Zachowicz, who performed as a featured quartet during the ever popular "Precz, Precz." The entire event was held in honor of longtime husband and wife members Geraldine and Edward Szemraj, and in memory of member Wanda Pakula.[62]

After celebrating their founder Boleslaus Michalski by decorating his grave for Zaduszki, in the 150th year of his birth and 75th year of his death,[63] the singers returned their Wigilia to its pre-COVID glory. Held at the Depew Polish Falcons Hall, the evening saw the full Polish Christmas Eve dinner served with a few rounds of koledy and a visit from St. Nicholas.[64]

Almost 200 guests attended the 2023 *Festival of Carols* at St. Gabriel's Church. Opened by the Kalina Singing Society led by Edward Witul, the group presented a selection of koledy and the Alsatian lullaby "Schlaf, Kindlein, Schlaf." They were followed by the Polish Saturday School Children's Choir who delighted audiences with "Gdy

---

61 "Chopin's to Feature Golden Polish Folk Songs." *Am-Pol Eagle*, 7 Oct. 2022.
62 "Chopin Singing Society Provides a Crowd-Pleasing Anniversary Concert." *Am-Pol Eagle*, 31 Oct. 2022.
63 "Chopin Founder Remembered." *Am-Pol Eagle*, 14 Nov. 2022.
64 Facebook Archives, Chopin Singing Society, Buffalo, NY

Sliczna Panna," "Lulajze Jezuniu," and "Jingle Bells" sung in Polish and English directed by the vice president of Chopins, Mary Lou Wyrobek. Soprano Haley Brunstad offered two Christmas songs, Chopins added their selections, including three works presented by the men of Chopins and ending with the full choir rendition of "O Swieta Noc" featuring soloist Andrew Kowtalo.[65]

Chopins and Kalina took the show on the road a week later, traveling to St. Stanislaus Kostka parish in Hamilton, Ontario. There they were joined by the Symfonia and Cantabile choirs for another day of Christmas music.[66]

In recognition of the 550th birthday of Copernicus and the 213th birthday of Chopin, the Permanent Chair of Polish Culture at Canisius College joined with the Society and the Polish Arts Club of Buffalo in presenting *Chopin & Copernicus: The Art of the Heavens*. Under Witakowski's skillful hand, the Chopin singers presented two renaissance pieces and an arrangement created by Dr. Witakowski of *De Revolutionibus* with narration by Fr. Benjamin Fiore, S.J. honoring Copernicus. The audience of the packed Montante Cultural Center then enjoyed pianists Maria Chomicka and Melanie Bebak in selections by Chopin while images from the Webb and Hubble Telescopes were projected as a backdrop to the heavenly music. The Strassenburg Planetarium's Paul Krupinski prepared the projection. The afternoon concluded with some light refreshments.[67]

Teaming up with St. Stanislaus Bishop & Martyr Church for 2023, Chopins brought their legendary Dyngus Day to the parish's social hall. Speaking of the return to Broadway-Fillmore after a 29-year absence, Chopin president Gary Bienkowski said, "Returning to the East Side is returning to the heart of old Polonia, the place where it all began. It is where the Polish immigrants first came in the 1870s to gather, worship and celebrate. Now, we want to continue the tradition for the old and perhaps introduce it to another generation."[68]

Opening the post-Lenten program, the singers performed a medley of Polish songs before giving way to a lineup of the Polka Country Musicians, John Gora & Gorale, and the Piatkowski Brother All Star Band. The Polka music only broke for the fancy footwork of

---

65 "Festival Fills Elma Church with Carols." *Am-Pol Eagle*, 12 Jan. 2023.

66 "Solidarity in Song." *Am-Pol Eagle*, 20 Jan. 2023.

67 *Chopin & Copernicus: The Art of Heaven*. The Chopin Singing Society and the Polish Arts Club of Buffalo, 2023.

68 Dlugosz, Steve. "WNY Gets Ready for Dyngus Day 2023." *Am-Pol Eagle*, 8 Apr. 2023.

the Krakowiacy Polish Dancers from Eugenia's Studio. With a ten-hour block of entertainment, the revelers arrived early and stayed late, and even the mother of the modern Dyngus Day, the Honorable Ann T. Mikoll made an appearance to take in the good time and to be honored, along with St. Stanislaus volunteer Theresa Gonciarz.[69]

After a three year delay the 52nd International Convention of the Polish Singers Alliance of America was held at the Buffalo Marriott Niagara in suburban Western New York, hosted by Chopin and Kalina Singing Societies of District 9. For their part, Chopins presented "Aleć Nade Mną Wenus" and "A w Tej Naszej Dolinie" as their competition numbers which earned them third place in the Mixed Chorus category.[70] The Society then joined the rest of the choirs in a joint concert at the closing event held at Black Rock's Assumption Church.[71]

The next week on June 4, the Society was in the limelight again this time taking part in the Mass celebrating the 150th anniversary of St. Stanislaus Bishop & Martyr's parish in Buffalo. At the church the singers, under the direction of Dr. Thomas Witakowski, sang for the Feast of the Holy Trinity which celebrant Bishop Michael Fisher said was so magnificent it was "lifting us to heaven." The Society then had the honor of closing out the yearlong celebration by singing "Jak Szybko Mijaja Chwile" at the end of the anniversary banquet held later in the day at Kloc's Grove.[72]

The members would get a slight reprieve before being in front of Polonia again, this time in their honored slot at the Cheektowaga Polish American Arts Festival.[73] Besides leading the Saturday Mass with song, which festival organizer Eddy Dobosiewicz described as "phenomenal," the group entertained the crowds with a selection of secular and religious Polish songs during the three day event.[74]

The members took some time for themselves later in the summer with their annual outdoor Mass and picnic before helping

---

69 Facebook Archives, Chopin Singing Society, Buffalo, NY

70 Witul, Gregory L., and Michael Szafranski. "Polish Singers Alliance of America Award Dinner 2023." 28 May 2023.

71 Facebook Archives, Chopin Singing Society, Buffalo, NY

72 Wyrobek, Mary Lou. "Joyful Mass, Banquet Mark St. Stan's 150th Anniversary." *Am-Pol Eagle*, 8 June 2023.

73 "Cheektowaga Gets Ready for This Summer's Pol-Am Arts Festival." *Am-Pol Eagle*, 22 June 2023.

74 Dlugosz, Steve. "Despite Rain, Expanded Cheektowaga Polish American Arts Festival Is a Thunderous Hit." *Am-Pol Eagle*, 3 Aug. 2023.

Assumption church celebrate their 135th anniversary.[75] Led by organist Bruce Woody and buttressed by trumpeters Ray Domin and Cedric Wrobel, the singers brought the music of the event to a level worthy of the momentous occasion.[76]

As summer turned to fall, the vocalists joined much of the rest of Polonia at the General Pulaski Association's 85th Annual parade. Returning the event to downtown Buffalo the singers were led by parade Grand Marshal Robert Sienkiewicz from Edward Street down Delaware Avenue to Niagara Square, greeting people along the route and enjoying the festivities at the heart of the Queen City.[77]

Following the parade, the Society journeyed up to Niagara County on October 7 to take part in the Polish Day at the Basilica of The National Shrine of Our Lady of Fatima in Lewiston. Returning for the first time since the start of the COVID pandemic, the Chopinites joined the Kalinas in singing for the Mass celebrated by Father Mariusz Dymek of the Pauline Fathers. The rest of the day was highlighted by a viewing of the film *Joseph's World* about the beatified Ulma Family and a crowning of Our Lady of Czestochowa in the Gallery of Saints.[78]

With the month drawing to a close, the Society hosted their 124th Annual Concert on October 29 at St. Stanislaus Church in Buffalo. Under the banner of "Songs of Yesterday and Today" guest director Dr. Bradley Wingert led the Society through the works of Eugeniusz Fierla, Chopin, and Peter Gorecki's arrangement of "Tango Milonga." Founder of the Nickel City Opera Valerian Ruminski and Vocal Fellow at the Tanglewood Music Center Emily Helenbrook were the guest soloists, along with singer and pianist, Melanie Bebak, while Karen Swietlik-Schmid served as the accompanist. The entire performance was dedicated to Adrienne Tworek-Gryta.[79] The magnificence the singers displayed that evening could be heard by the raves they received at the reception following the performance. While "excellent," "awesome," and "wonderful" were apropos, the praise of the "best one yet" was especially high for the annual event that was now well into its second century.[80]

---

[75] Facebook Archives, Chopin Singing Society, Buffalo, NY

[76] "Assumption Congregation Celebrates Its Past and Looks Ahead with Optimism." *Am-Pol Eagle*, 17 Aug. 2023, p. 1.

[77] "Sienkiewicz Is Pulaski Parade Grand Marshal." *Am-Pol Eagle*, 21 Sept. 2023, pp. 1–7.

[78] "Polish Day Returns to Fatima Shrine." *Am-Pol Eagle*, 12 Oct. 2023.

[79] The Chopin Singing Society. *124th Annual Concert*. Chopin Singing Society, 2023.

[80] "Chopin Anniversary Concert Showcases Local Talent." *Am-Pol Eagle*, 2 Nov. 2023.

The singers started their Christmas season by recording a selection of Koledy for WBBZ TV's *Polka Buzz Christmas* program at the Matthew Glab post in Lackawanna. Split over the episodes airing in December the group delivered renditions of "Wsrod nocnej ciszy," "Lulajze Jezuniu," and "Dzisiaj w Betlejem" to the enthused Polka audience.[81] The singers followed up their television show with their annual Wigilia on December 7 at the Polish Falcons hall in Depew. Besides the traditional pre-Christmas meal, the evening included a sharing of the oplatek, strolling musicians, and a short program by the Chopinites.[82] In keeping with the Christmas spirit several Chopin members worked on the Heavenly Pillow Collection, a project which collected new bed pillows to be distributed to the needy by the Response to Love Center.[83]

After the Christmas break and working towards their 125th birthday, the singers traveled to Elma to take part in the Polish Singers Alliance of America District IX's Festival of Carols on the first Sunday of 2024. Held at St. Gabriel's Church the choir was joined by the Kalina Singing Society and the Polish Saturday School Children's Choir, as well as the Symfonia Choir and Cantabile Choir from Ontario, Canada.[84] The crowd of over 350 heard the Chopin's Men Choir opening the program with "Przy onej gorze" and "Triumfy," a nod to their founding as an all-male singing group. The ladies then joined the men for "Witaj, Jezu Dzieciatko," "Kolysanka Goralska" and the call and response Koleda "O, Jozefie!"[85]

Two weeks later, the group returned to their former tradition of celebrating Martin Luther King, Jr. at a Permanent Chair of Polish Culture at Canisius University and Polish Arts Club of Buffalo event honoring Revolutionary War Heroes Thaddeus Kosciuszko and his aide-de-camp Agrippa Hull, a free black man. The choir then reprised their presentation from St. Gabriel Church at a snow-delayed Koledy at St. Stanislaus Kostka Church in Hamilton, where on the eve of their 125th year, early February of 2024 brought a great change to Chopin when the music director of 32 years Dr. Thomas Witakowski announced his decision to step down as the active director and assumed

---

[81] Facebook Archives, Polka Buzz TV Show on WBBZ, Williamsville, NY
[82] Facebook Archives, Chopin Singing Society, Buffalo, NY
[83] "Providing Help with Heavenly Pillows." *Am-Pol Eagle*, 14 Dec. 2023, p. 5.
[84] Facebook Archives, Chopin Singing Society, Buffalo, NY
[85] "Over 350 Attend District IX PSAA Annual Festival of Carols." *Am-Pol Eagle*, 11 Jan. 2024.

the title of Director Emeritus.[86]

To celebrate the 214th birthday of Chopin and the 225th birthday of Adam Mickiewicz, the Permanent Chair of Polish Culture at Canisius University, the Chopin Singing Society, the Polish Arts Club of Buffalo, and the Adam Mickiewicz Library & Dramatic Circle hosted *Celebrating the Arts: A Birthday Bash for Chopin & Mickiewicz*. For their part of the multimedia event held at the Montante Cultural Center at the newly renamed Canisius University on the afternoon of February 25, Chopins joined with the Canisius University Chorale and gave a performance under the direction of Dr. Wingert. The Society also arranged for Claudia Hoca, the second winner of their Young Pianists Competition, to perform a number of Chopin's piano pieces as well as their assistant director Melanie Bebak.[87] Shortly after the concert the board of directors announced they had chosen their twelfth choral master to lead them, Mr. Nicholas John Steltzer. As March 2024 came to a close, the Frederick Chopin Singing Society of Buffalo, NY officially entered its 125th year. With a special Mass, the release of a book of their history, a concert, and the popular Wigilia, the Society's quasquicentennial promised to be a memorable year.

When the near dozen men gathered at St. Adalbert's at the behest of the parish organist, it's hard to imagine that any one of them thought that the meeting would lead to an organization that would become a cultural standard bearer for Polonia in the twenty-first century. That from that cold March day the members of the group would sing at the Vatican and the halls of Warsaw and Krakow, work to undermine an oppressive regime's grip on Poland, rise to prominence in every corner of life in the Niagara Frontier and New York State, and launch a post-Lenten party that is celebrated across the country. And as this generation's Chopinites perform, sponsor events, recruit, and adapt to an ever-changing community, the song started by those men a century and a quarter ago will go ever on.

[86] Facebook Archives, Chopin Singing Society, Buffalo, NY
[87] "Chopin/Mickiewicz Birthday Bash Planned for Feb. 25." *Am-Pol Eagle*, 15 Feb. 2024.

Boleslaus Michalski (1872-1947),
founder and first director (1899-1902)
and president of the Chopin
Singing Society.

Leon Olszewski (1872-1919), Chopin director
(1902-1919) pictured with Chopin Singing Society 1902.

Jan Nadolny directs the Chopin and Kalina Singing Societies in the operetta *Sylvia*, selling out the house twice and receiving high praise.

To celebrate the 25th anniversary of the Chopin Singing Society, a bust of Frederick Chopin was commissioned by the Chopin Board, headed by President Zdzislaw Krysztafkiewicz, from artist Joseph Mazur to be a gift to the City of Buffalo unveiled June 7, 1925.

The Board of Directors for the Silver Jubilee of the Chopin Singing Society, Zdzislaw Krysztafkiewicz, president.

Arnold Cornelissen and the Chopin Singing Society at their 35th anniversary concert.

Chopin Clubrooms purchased 1947 and home to the Society until its move to Cheektowaga in 1994.

Peter Gorecki directs the Chopin Singing Society Mixed Choir at Kleinhans Music Hall with the Merry Tatra Dancers and members of the Buffalo Philharmonic. c. 1961

In 1965 President Ted Mikoll, with help from the Villa Maria Institute of Music, inaugurated the Chopin Young Pianist Competition. here is the 1986 winner John Noel with Ted Mikoll.

The first European trip by the Chopin Singing Society to Poland in 1975.

Representing New York State as part of the Bicentennial Ceremonies in Washington, D.C. Chopin Singing Society performed from March 18-21, 1976, including singing on the Capitol steps joined by First Lady Betty Ford, Congressmen Henry Nowak, Jack Kemp and Thaddeus Dulski. Justice Ann T. Mikoll and Director Peter Gorecki flank Mrs. Ford.

In 1977 the Chopin Singing Society returned to Poland for another grand tour complete with cowboy outfits.

Under the direction of Dr. Ireneusz Lukaszewski, Chopin Singing Society travelled to Rome, singing for Pope John Paul II and at Monte Casino. Chopin members pictured as they greet Pope John Paul II at the Vatican Audience Hall in June 1983.

Justice Ann Mikoll, Peter Sloane, and Ted Mikoll represent Chopin at the 1985 World Competition of Polonian Choirs in Koszalin where the choir and their soloists garnered numerous awards.

In the planning trip of 1984 and the 1985 concert tour to Koszalin, Vice President David Rutecki and Board Member Peter Sloane clandestinely carried monies from the National AFL-CIO to Solidarity, the banned Polish independent trade movement, coordinated by local AFL-CIO President George Wessel and his secretary, Michaeline Wyrobek, a long-time Chopin member. Pictured (l-r): George Wessel, Peter Sloane, Michaeline Wyrobek, AFL-CIO President Lane Kirkland.

The awards won by the Chopin Singing Society and their soloists in the Koszalin Music Competition line the stage at the choir's performance in Cheektowaga.

Under the direction of Dr. Ireneusz Lukaszewski, the Chopin Singing Society attained the top score among all competing choirs at the 1989 PSAA Competition, gaining the Cardinal Hlond Trophy, a first for the choir.

Members Mary Lou and Michaeline Wyrobek show off the choir's awards at the PSAA Centennial Competition in Hamilton.

Teresa Dybas and Susan Malik, regular soloists and members of the Chopin Singing Society pictured with Dr. Ireneusz Lukaszewski.

Under Director Dr. Thomas Witakowski, the Chopin Singing Society travels to Palm Beach in 1994 to serenade the growing South Florida Polonia.

The Chopin Singing Society sang for the Oath of Citizenship ceremony aboard the USS Little Rock for many years.

The 100th anniversary banquet was a grand celebration at the Statler Golden Ballroom.

Beginning in 1986 and staged numerous times afterward, the Society has presented Jaselka, a traditional Polish Christmas Morality Play.

Board of Directors c. 2004
Standing l-r: Evelyn Pietrzak, Thomas Pawlak, James Jankowski, James Mrozek, Gary Bienkowski, Marcia Pszeniczny, Henry Superczynski, Stefania Borkowski, Paul Kosek, Ronald Smith, Susan Malik, Frances Cirbus, Walter Kaminski; seated: President Ann T. Mikoll.

Chopin Singing Society Wigilia (traditional Christmas Eve Dinner) celebrations have continued for many years.

Robert Fronckowiak and Sr. Blaise, CSSF sharing oplatek at Wigilia celebration.

In 2008, the Chopin Singing Society and Buffalo State Chamber Chorus under Dr. Thomas Witakowski performed Moniuszko's Flis, garnering them their second Am-Pol Eagle Citizen of the Year Award.

Dyngus Day in the Kosciuszko Street Clubrooms.

Dyngus blessing of Swieconka food.

Dyngus:
Multi-generational fun.
The Wyrobek-Shemik
families

Dyngus: Dancing

The Original! The First! The Best!

2024 Dyngus Day at St. Stanislaus Social Hall

The Society privately celebrated the birthday of their namesake each year in the clubrooms.

The public celebration of Chopin's birthday began under Dr. Thomas Witakowski's reign as director.

The celebration of Frederick Chopin's birthday.

Beginning in 2023, the birthday celebration is hosted by the Permanent Chair of Polish Culture at Canisius University.

2023 Chopin Singing Society Anniversary Concert with interim Director Dr. Bradley Wingert

2024 Board Photo (missing Thomas Pawlak)
1st row seated: Frances Cirbus, Mary Lou Wyrobek, Gary Bienkowski, Joanna Brown
2nd row: Thomas Bruch, Adrienne Kusmierczyk, Christine Witkowski, Irene Kmiotek, Karen Macris, George Kania
3rd row: James Mrozek, Susan Peters, Robert Cieselski, Michael Zachowicz, David McElroy.

Appendix I

Presidents

1. Boleslaus Michalski (Founder 1899)

By the time Boleslaus Michalski became the founder and first president of Chopin Singing Society, he was already a known figure in America's Polonia. Born near Poznan on the April 21, 1872 Boleslaus arrived on America's shores by age 17. A proven organist, Michalski first found work in Pittsburgh before heading out to Poniatowski, Wisconsin. After a brief stay in the Midwest, Boleslaus finally settled in Buffalo after accepting a position at St. Adalbert Church in 1898.[1] The next seven years were a whirlwind for the maestro. Playing at Adalbert's, Michalski formed the Chopin Singing Society in 1899 staying on as conductor until 1902, marrying Agnes Mulka a year later. This was soon followed up with the family welcoming their daughter Cecelia three years later, all while Boleslaus was starting a real estate and insurance business.

With his family growing, Boleslaus took a position serving as organist for St. Barbara Church. His stay in Lackawanna was brief and in less than a year Michalski moved his focus back to the Rother, Walden, and Sycamore neighborhood of East Buffalo. He was soon behind the organ again, now for St. Luke Church. A pillar of the community, serving as a member of the Polish National Alliance, the Polish Association of America, the Woodmen of the World, the Fraternal Order of Orioles and the Polish Singers Alliance, Boleslaus tried his hand in politics. He laid the groundwork for this venture by serving as president of the Sycamore Street Business Men's and Taxpayers Association and vocally opposing the Lackawanna Terminal in downtown Buffalo. With this polished resume, Boleslaus ran for the County Board of Supervisors from the Sixteenth Ward on the Democratic ticket in 1913.[2] With his wide circle of friends, his reputation as a civic-minded individual, his strong connection to the Catholic Church, and a $10 campaign contribution from his wife,[3] Michalski easily

---

[1] "The Choir of St. Adalbert's..." *Buffalo Courier*, 15 Dec. 1901, p. 26.
[2] "Citizens' Union Will Work on Ticket Tonight." *Buffalo Evening News*, 12 Aug. 1913, p. 7.
[3] 'Jackson Spent $301.99 Only to Be Defeated." *Buffalo Courier*, 11 Nov. 1913.

trounced Republican incumbent Samuel G. Koch.[4] A strong advocate for home rule, fiscal responsibility, and making sure Poles had access to county services,[5] Alderman Michalski served until 1916 when Joseph W. Becker took over the Sixteenth Ward.

While Boleslaus was focused on flipping real estate and selling insurance, his heart was still in music. At the 1918 annual convention of the Polish Singers Alliance, Michalski sat on the planning committee and had the honor of directing the combined mixed choirs of Buffalo. He was also entrusted with closing the program in which he directed the united Buffalo and Cleveland Choirs in a rendition of "America."[6] Staying on the East Side, Boleslaus continued to play organ, now for Queen of the Rosary Church on Sycamore Street.[7] As with his music, Michalski kept a hand in politics endorsing George S. Buck for mayor of Buffalo over Frank X. Schwab in the 1921 elections.[8] In Polonia, Boleslaus was still as active as ever. In the 1920s he served as the state vice president of the Polish Association of America,[9] served as host to Polish American dancer and actress Gilda Gray during her visit to Buffalo and began a fifteen-year tenure as organist at Precious Blood. [10]

Like many prominent Americans, the Great Depression left Michalski financially, legally,[11] and emotionally scarred.[12] 1933 was particularly devastating with the passing of Agnes. It would be music that would sustain Michalski through the troubled times. Moving to Jones Street, Boleslaus spent the rest of his career behind the keys and pedals of Precious Blood's organ. Retiring in 1942, Boleslaus Michalski passed away on February 22, 1947.[13] Despite all he completed in his life, the focus of his obituary was his contribution to Buffalo's music scene, from being an organist, to directing the Polish Singing Society, and most importantly his founding of the Chopin Singing

---

[4] "Democrats Win Majority of Supervisors." *Buffalo Evening News*, 5 Nov. 1913, p. 15.
[5] "Michalski Looks Like a Sure Winner." *Buffalo Courier*, 3 Nov. 1913, p. 9.
[6] "Polish Singers' Alliance Will Convene Sunday." *Buffalo Evening News*, 24 Aug. 1918, p. 11.
[7] "Hymns of Poland Sung at Special Easter Services." *Buffalo Courier*, 24 Apr. 1916, p. 5.
[8] Michalski, B. "Why I Am for Mayor Buck." *Buffalo Evening News*, 7 Nov. 1921, p. 1.
[9] "Young Women Win as Polish Delegates." *Buffalo Evening News*, 12 Sept. 1928, p. 3.
[10] "Mayor Refuses to Pose with Shimmy Queen 'I'm Father of Seven Children," His Reason." *Buffalo Evening News*, 29 Jan. 1925, p. 3.; Jablonski, Fred F. *Precious Blood Church; 75th Diamond Jubilee, 1899-1975*. Precious Blood Church, 1974.
[11] "Michalski Gets Year." *Buffalo Evening News*, 17 June 1932, p. 36.
[12] "Lives But Arrested." *Buffalo Courier-Express*, 14 June 1932, p. 1.
[13] "Boleslaus Michalski." *Buffalo Courier-Express*, 24 Feb. 1947, p. 18.

Society.[14]

2. Michael Bilicki (1900-1901)

From the establishment of Chopins in early 1899, Boleslaus Michalski was all things to Chopins, president, choir master, librarian, and cashier. On March 26, 1900, the first elections for the group were held, and of the nine men who were at the first meeting, Michael Bilicki was chosen as the Society's first elected president.[15] As the first president, Bilicki would be a model for the early presidents, while still having a perspective and background that would be all his own.[16]

Born in Poland in September of 1871, Michael moved with his family to America in 1873. In 1891 he married Cecelia and became a tailor. While his occupation would be the same as many future presidents of Chopin, his involvement in politics would make him an outlier. In the early 1890s, Michael began making his way through the East Side's Democratic Machine. In 1894 and 1895, while living at 44 Loepere Street, he was named Inspector of Elections for the Fifth District of the 14th Ward, an important local position that came with a nice honorarium.[17] At the same time Bilicki was also doing well professionally, becoming a key employee at Jacob Cohn's Tailor Shop at 474 Sycamore[18].

Eighteen Ninety-Nine was an important year for Bilicki, he moved to 377 Sweet Avenue, become secretary of the 14th Ward Democratic Club, and joined eight other men at St. Adalbert's Hall to start the Chopin Singing Society. As secretary of the Democratic Club, Michael was a vital conduit for English speaking politicians trying to reach the Polish vote since Bilicki was a master of both languages. When Police Justice Thomas S. King came through the East Side to campaign, it was noted how he would give an impassioned speech in English to the silent Polish crowd, who all then turned to Bilicki for translation. When Michael was finished, the group would react with

---

[14] "Boleslaus Michalski Dies; Church Organist 40 Years." *Buffalo Evening News*, 24 Feb. 1947, p. 17.

[15] "Srebrny Jubileusz Tow. Spiewu Chopin." *Dziennik Dla Wszystkich*, 18 May 1924, p. 3.

[16] *Towarzystwo Śpiewu Fryderyka Chopina 1899-1949*. Buffalo, NY: Tow. Śpiewu Fryderyka Chopina, 1949. Print

[17] "List of Names." *Buffalo Evening News*, 27 Aug. 1894, p. 4.; "List of Names." *Buffalo Evening News*, 9 Sept. 1895, p. 4.

[18] Album Pamiatkowe I Przewodnik Handlowy: Osady Polskiej W Miescie Buffalo, Z Dolaczeniem Okolicznych Miejscowosci Ze Stanu New York. Buffalo, 1906.

delayed cheers, roars, and thundering applauses.[19]

Bilicki was active at Chopins during its first year and the start of his presidency, but by the end of 1901 Michael decided to step back from a leadership position.[20] Bilicki continued in his tailoring career after moving to 279 Woltz Avenue, but his life was tragically cut short on March 2, 1908.[21]

3. John A. Zelechowski (1901-1902, 1905-1906, 1916-1918)

Filling out the rest of Bilicki's term, Jan Zelechowski was the first leader of Chopins who wasn't present at the founding of the organization with his election in 1902.[22] John was born in the village of Kikol, in the district of Plock, Poland around 1869 to Antoni and Jozefa Zelechowski. He received his primary education in the village before taking up an apprenticeship as a horticulturist which sent him to the manor house in Dzialyn. In 1891 John completed his apprenticeship in the gardens and palaces of Warsaw and returned to Dzialyn, to marry Julia Kurowska. Within a month the newlyweds were aboard the *Columbia* and steaming towards the Americas.

The couple's first destination was the borough of Mansfield in Pennsylvania's Northern Tier. There they found an established, but not bustling Polonia. By the mid-1890s, the Zelechowskis had had enough of the simple life and moved to Buffalo, NY first settling on Warren Avenue. John's earliest jobs in the city were basic; he worked as a laborer for the Buffalo Car Manufacturing Co., a clerk, and debt collector. But his choice of work had a hidden value. It allowed him to master English so he could secure better opportunities when they presented themselves.[23] By 1908 John had served one term as the president of Chopins,[24] sat on the local committee of the Polish Singers Alliance of America,[25] had a position with Prudential Life Insurance Co., and was working as a wholesaler for a line of vodkas, wines, and liqueurs.

In the intervening years, Zelechowski tried his hand at other

---

[19] "Poles Are Enthusiastic." *Buffalo Courier*, 27 Oct. 1899, p. 5.
[20] "Minutes of the Chopin Singing Society 1900-1904." Buffalo, NY.
[21] "Michal Bilicki (1872-1908) - Find A Grave..." *Find a Grave*, 29 May 2017, www.findagrave.com/memorial/179822751/michal-bilicki.
[22] "Minutes of the Chopin Singing Society 1900-1904." Buffalo, NY.
[23] Album Pamiatkowe I Przewodnik Handlowy: Osady Polskiej W Miescie Buffalo, Z Dolaczeniem Okolicznych Miejscowosci Ze Stanu New York. Buffalo, 1906.
[24] *Towarzystwo Śpiewu Fryderyka Chopina 1899-1949*. Buffalo, NY: Tow. Śpiewu Fryderyka Chopina, 1949. Print
[25] "Polish Singers to Contest Here." *Buffalo Courier*, 27 Aug. 1906, p. 3.

careers, opening a butcher shop behind Sattler's Store on Beck Street and running a saloon at 1068 Broadway, but his heart was always with Polish culture and the Society. In 1916 he was elected to serve as president of Chopins again and was selected for the steering committee of the Henryk Sienkiewicz Memorial Celebration.[26] Serving alongside architect Wladyslaw H. Zawadzki, and real estate developer Stanislaus S. Nowicki, the region-wide memorial included Polonias ranging from Niagara Falls to Albion, Batavia to Perry, Olean to Salamanca, and everywhere in between, and became the banner event of the year.[27]

In his later years, John worked as a Buffalo City firefighter, but never let up on his devotion to Chopins. He would go on serve as a director of the board and as the club cashier, receiving a special recognition for his work from the Polish Singers Alliance of America in 1936.[28] On the morning of Saturday, March 29, 1941, Jan A. Zelechowski passed away, delivering a devastating blow to both his wife and the Society he so loved. All 65 singers stayed with Julia during the wake at the Zelechowski home at 252 Person St., and before leaving, sang a lamentation over the coffin.[29] Jan's funeral was held on April 1 from Transfiguration church, and he was buried at St Stanislaus Cemetery in Cheektowaga.[30]

4. Stanislaus E. Mrugowski (1903)

Stanislaus Edmund was born on October 14, 1870, in the city of Gniezno to Stanislaus and Franciszka Mrugowski. He received his primary education in the city and entered a trade school where he focused on tailoring. After graduating, Mrugowski first worked in the shops of Poznan before moving to the German capital of Berlin to master his craft. In 1891 with some experience under his belt, Mrugowski's father beckoned him to join the family which had relocated to Buffalo, NY some time earlier.

Once in America, Stanislaus quickly found work and eventually became a manager at Janke & Tepe Merchant Tailors on Seneca Street. Working on Seneca Street by day, Mrugowski spent his nights and weekends at 1112 Broadway where he opened a shop to make

26 "Polish Societies Elect Officers." *Buffalo Courier*, 12 Dec. 1915, p. 59.
27 "Arrange To Pay Honor to Great Polish Author." *Buffalo Courier*, 3 Dec. 1916, p. 66.
28 "Tow. Spiewu Fryderyka Szopena." *Dziennik Dla Wszystkich*, 23 May 1936, p. 3.
29 "Chopini Uczcili Zasluzonego Sp. Kol. Jana Zelechowskiego." *Dziennik Dla Wszystkich*, 31 Mar. 1941, p. 13.
30 "Sp. Jan Zelechowski." *Dziennik Dla Wszystkich*, 29 Mar. 1941, p. 10.

bespoke pieces for Polonia's more discerning gentleman.[31] On top of all that, he helped establish the forerunner to Polish Falcons Nest 6,[32] was active in the Association of Polish Tailors, the Polish Merchants Association, and the Chopin Singing Society. Mrugowski's work ethic and popularity secured him the position of president of Chopins in 1903, but the many jobs, personalities, and activities would also be his undoing. Work obligations mounted forcing Stan to be less attentive to Chopins and their needs. He decided it would be best to resign mid-term and let Vice President Constantine Nowakowski take over, rather than attempt to muddle through the rest of the year.[33]

One of the reasons Mrugowski lost focus at Chopins was that his personal shop on Broadway was taking off. He quit Janke & Tepe as orders poured in and by 1907, Stan was looking for ways to expand both his business and his workforce. He found a partner in the form of John F. Zimms, a Hamburg developer, and the two formed Zimms & Mrugowski setting up offices at 21 West Eagle. As merchant tailors, they provided wholesale fabric, supplies, and patterns to the Western New York market. The endeavor found some successes, but after a move to Washington Street and Mrugowski's desire to go back to hands on tailoring, the firm closed by 1910.

Back on Broadway, Mrugowski expanded his horizons and transformed his tailoring workshop into a full-blown haberdashery, first at 1152 and then 1277 Broadway. With stable and predictable business, Stan was able to dedicate himself once again to his Polish pursuits. He became heavily involved with Polish Falcons Nest 58 and by 1915 was elected president.[34] As a devoted Falcon, Mrugowski traveled the area and addressed other nests on subjects ranging from history to politics. He also served as president of the Prosperity Club which organized and filed naturalization papers for members of the Polish community. It also advocated for improvement projects around the East Side, including better lighting along Fillmore and around the Broadway Market.[35]

When Polish Falcon's Nest 6 on Playter Street burned to the

[31] Album Pamiatkowe I Przewodnik Handlowy: Osady Polskiej W Miescie Buffalo, Z Dolaczeniem Okolicznych Miejscowosci Ze Stanu New York. Buffalo, 1906.

[32] "Polish Falcons of America Nest 6." Polonia Trail, Polish-American Congress WNY, 29 June 2016, poloniatrail.com/location/polish-Falcons-of-america-nest-6/.

[33] *Towarzystwo Śpiewu Fryderyka Chopina 1899-1949*. Buffalo, NY: Tow. Śpiewu Fryderyka Chopina, 1949. Print

[34] "Polish Falcons Nest 58 Celebrate Anniversary." *Buffalo Evening News*, 8 Feb. 1915, p. 4.

[35] "Six Pole Societies Work to Assist Their Countrymen." *Buffalo Courier*, 2 Apr. 1916, p. 75.

ground in 1915, several of the regional nests, including Nest 58, joined with Nest 6 to help secure a new building spot. Moving to the corner of Sycamore and Fillmore, and banding all the Nests together, Mrugowski went from being the president of a small local nest, to the vice president of one of the most powerful nests in the nation.[36]

Stan took his lesson about overstretching himself as president of Chopins to heart, so before he ran for the Nest 6 president in 1918, he made sure he was ready. Under his tenure as president, the Falcons sold Polish Government Liberty Bonds, raised monies for Polish war orphans, and celebrated their silver jubilee. As a Falcon, he would later serve as head of the organizational committee for the official visit of Gen. Joseph Haller to Buffalo in 1923.[37] Stan also reunited with the singers in 1925 at the formal dedication of the Chopin monument, serving as both a former president of the Society and as a representative of the Falcons.[38]

On the home front, Mrugowski's tailor shop continued to be a great success, almost too much so. The 1920s would see some daring break-ins to the store. Burglars sawed through four, half inch bars to steal $2,000 worth of suits, while another time over a hundred yards of fabric disappeared in a single night.[39] But the appetite for new and fashionable clothing helped Stan to weather these storms.[40]

Beyond his service to the Falcons, the late '20s would see Mrugowski's profile continue to rise. He was elected president of the Polish Welfare Council and from this post he was one of three representatives, including Dr. Francis E. Fronczak, and the Right Reverend Alexander Pitass to formally welcome Ignacy Jan Paderewski during his 1926 visit to Buffalo.[41] In the 1930s, Mrugowski decided he no longer wished to be a confirmed bachelor and married Ms. Pelagia Pilichowska. The younger Pelagia was the perfect companion to the more seasoned Stanislaus at Falcons events or just around town. One of the last major events Mrugowski would work on was the 15th anniversary of the American recruitment for Haller's Polish Army is 1932.[42]

---

36 Welcome to the Polish Falcons of America Nest 6 Centennial 1896-1996. Buffalo, NY: Polish Falcons of America, 1996. Print

37 "Buffalo Pours Out Glowing Greeting to Gen. Haller, Poland's 'Man Of The Hour.'" *Buffalo Courier*, 26 Nov. 1923, p. 3.

38 "To Present Chopin Monument Sunday." *Buffalo Courier*, 3 June 1925, p. 14.

39 "Thieves Rob Home as Woman Testifies." *Buffalo Evening News*, 19 Feb. 1921.

40 "Thieves Saw Iron Bars." *Buffalo Courier*, 21 Apr. 1922, p. 16.

41 "Paderewski Here to Give Concert." *Buffalo Evening News*, 8 Jan. 1926, p. 25.

42 "East Side to Honor Polish Army Vets." *Buffalo Evening News*, 29 Sept. 1932.

After a long career, Mrugowski retired in the late 1930s. The couple moved to Black Rock and Stan spent as much time with his family as he could. On December 21, 1942, Stanislaus Edmund Mrugowski passed away. His funeral was held at St. Florian Church, and he was buried at St Stanislaus Cemetery in Cheektowaga.[43] Pelagia joined her husband in 1948.

5. Constantine Nowakowski (1903)

With the resignation of Stanislaus Mrugowski in 1903, Konstanty Nowakowski became the fourth president of the Chopin Singing Society. Born in Otorowo, Poland in 1872, Constantine was much like his direct predecessor as he also trained as a tailor. Just shy of the age of twenty, Nowakowski moved to America, settling in Buffalo's East Side. Almost as soon as he arrived Nowakowski teamed up with Charles Rutkowski, Anthony Jedrzejewski, Stanley Dzienyski, and Frank Zielezinski to form the Polish Tailors Society Group 194 of the Polish National Alliance on January 29, 1891.[44] This would be one of the first non-religious Polish societies in Buffalo and would be one of the founding members of the Dom Polski building.[45] Nowakowski would further join almost two score other men in September of 1897 to form the Polish Singing Circle, Buffalo's second major Polish singing society, after Moniuszko.

Located at 1013 Sycamore, Constantine's first tailor shop was in the heart of Polish Sycamore Street in the 1890s, with Transfiguration Church at one end and the intersection of Sycamore and Walden at the other. An excellent tailor best known for his high-quality suits, Nowakowski created clothing for daily wear and special occasions. Nowakowski's ascension to the presidency of Chopins came quickly. In 1902 he was listed only as a member, in early 1903 he was elected vice president and by the end of the year he was at the helm of the Society.[46] In his term as president, Constantine effectively played the role of a caretaker until the elections. While he never was elected president

---

43 "Mrugowski - Stanislaus E." *Buffalo Evening News*, 22 Dec. 1942, p. 34.

44 Album Pamiatkowe I Przewodnik Handlowy: Osady Polskiej W Miescie Buffalo, Z Dolaczeniem Okolicznych Miejscowosci Ze Stanu New York. Buffalo, 1906.

45 "Srebrny Jubileusz Krawcow Polskich." *Dziennik Dla Wszystkich*, 4 Mar. 1916, p. 3.; Pamietnik 50-Cio Lecia Stowarzyszenia Domu Polskiego, 1905-1955. Dom Polski Association, 1955.

46 *Towarzystwo Spiewu Fryderyka Chopina 1899-1949*. Buffalo, NY: Tow. Spiewu Fryderyka Chopina, 1949. Print/

again, he would serve the role of cashier for years.[47]

In the years that followed his presidency, Constantine purchased 1180 Broadway and moved his merchant tailor shop in the upper part of the building, while renting out the lower half.[48] He also invested in the Polska Spolka Akcyjna, commonly known as Spolka Clothing Shop, where he became a director.[49] To free up additional workspace on Broadway, Nowakowski purchased a home on Bissell Avenue and moved in. Constantine's business acumen became well known and led to a leadership position in the Polish Business Men's Association, where he served as sergeant-at-arms under the leadership of President Maxwell M. Nowak and alongside Polonia luminaries as Leon Olszewski, James M. Rozan, Dr. Francis E. Fronczak, and Anthony Schreiber. This in turn led to some highly visible positions outside of Polonia. During the Great War, Constantine sat on the Fourth Liberty Loan Committee of Buffalo as part of the Tailors and Drapers Subcommittee.[50] He was one of only about a dozen Poles to serve on the city-wide committee and a rare public face of the Slavic people.

On the home front, Constantine married Antonina Kaluzna and had five children, Adam, Edmund, Leon, Eugenia, and Angeline. In the shop Nowakowski was almost continuously expanding, eventually employing 18 men and women.[51] Much of Constantine's success came from the fact he drafted customized patterns for each customer to ensure a perfect fit every time.[52]

As Nowakowski grew older many of the organizations he was involved with started lauding him for his service.[53] As early as 1916 he was issued a special diploma from the Polish Singing Circle during the installation of Vincent Zawadzki, and a few years later a silver medal

---

47 Album Pamiatkowe I Przewodnik Handlowy: Osady Polskiej W Miescie Buffalo, Z Dolaczeniem Okolicznych Miejscowosci Ze Stanu New York. Buffalo, 1906.
48 "K. Nowakowski." *The Enterprise-Times*, 20 Sept. 1928, p. 11.; "Pedestrians Chase Thieves Who Rifle Show Windows." *Buffalo Courier*, 11 Dec. 1908, p. 6.
49 Album Pamiatkowe I Przewodnik Handlowy: Osady Polskiej W Miescie Buffalo, Z Dolaczeniem Okolicznych Miejscowosci Ze Stanu New York. Buffalo, 1906. 458-461 Print.
50 "Trades and Professions Committees." *Report of Director of Publicity, Third Liberty Loan, April 1918*, by A. G. Bartholomew, Matthews-Northrup Works, Buffalo, NY, 1918, pp. 64–79.
51 "K. Nowakowski." The Enterprise-Times, 20 Sept. 1928, p. 11.
52 Album Pamiatkowe I Przewodnik Handlowy: Osady Polskiej W Miescie Buffalo, Z Dolaczeniem Okolicznych Miejscowosci Ze Stanu New York. Buffalo, 1906.
53 *Pamietnik 50-Cio Lecia Stowarzyszenia Domu Polskiego, 1905-1955*. Dom Polski Association, 1955.; "Founders Are Honored by Polish Group." *Buffalo Courier-Express*, 17 Nov. 1941, p. 5.

was presented to him for helping to establish the organization.[54] In 1933, Council 19 of the Polish National Alliance celebrated its ruby anniversary, and as part of the celebration, John Romaszkiewicz national president of the PNA presented gold pins to Nowakowski and the other surviving founding members of the Polish Tailors Society Group 194.[55]

Constantine watched his children grow, welcomed the grandchildren, and lived to see a fourth generation added to the family. In October of 1957 Antonina passed away, with Constantine joining her on December 30, 1964, at age 92.[56]

6. Michael J. Stefanski (1904)

Present at the first meeting of the Chopin Singing Society,[57] Michael Stefanski served as a caretaker president of the group for the first six months of 1904.[58]

Born near Posen, Poland on September 17, 1876, Michael was still a child when he immigrated to America with his family. In Buffalo, Stefanski trained as a carpenter and at age 21 married Anastasia Zandrowicz.[59] Settling at 130 Sears Street, Michael would join Boleslaus Michalski and seven other parishioners of St. Adalbert to form the Chopin Singing Society.

At the height of the First World War, the Stefanskis relocated to North Tonawanda, where in time, Michal would find work at the American District Steam Company.[60] In North Tonawanda, Stefanski quickly rose to a leadership position in the city's Polonia. In 1927 Michal was selected to serve on the building committee for the new Our Lady of Czestochowa Church and eight years later, he was elected a director of the parish's Holy Name Society.[61]

After the opening of North Tonawanda's semi-Polish parish St.

---

54 "Poles Fittingly Observe Singing Circle Birthday." *Buffalo Courier*, 11 Sept. 1922, p. 16.
55 "40th Anniversary Observed by Polish National Alliance." *Buffalo Evening News*, 22 May 1933, p. 19.
56 "Nowakowski - Antonina." *Buffalo Evening News*, 10 Oct. 1957, p. 46.; "Konstanty Nowakowski." *Buffalo Courier-Express*, 1 Jan. 1965.
57 *Towarzystwo Spiewu Fryderyka Chopina 1899-1949*. Buffalo, NY: Tow. Spiewu Fryderyka Chopina, 1949. Print.
58 "Minutes of the Chopin Singing Society 1900-1904." Buffalo, NY.
59 "Michael Joseph Stefanski." *FamilySearch*, www.familysearch.org/tree/person/details/LCJG-1NB.
60 "Stefanski." *Tonawanda News*, 10 Mar. 1955, p. 15.
61 "Will Break Ground for New Church in Ironton Sunday." *The Evening News*, 20 Sept. 1927, p. 2.; "Holy Name Officers Elected." *The Evening News*, 16 Dec. 1935, p. 5.

Joseph, Michal and his family joined the church. As he entered retirement, Stefanski spent more time with his friends at the Oliver Street Dom Polski, and more time with his family at his Jackson Avenue home. On March 9, 1955, at age 79, Michael J. Stefanski passed away suddenly at his home. He was buried at Mt Olivet Cemetery and was survived by 8 children, 27 grandchildren, and 13 great-grandchildren.[62]

7. Stanislaus Nadolny (1904)

At the very end of 1904, Stanislaus Nadolny served as president of the Society. The Nadolny name would be an important one in the early history of Chopins, as a Stanislaus and Ignatius Nadolny were present at the first meeting of the Society, and John Nadolny served as the group's third musical director. Confusingly, there are two men named Stanislaus listed on the 1903 club registry,[63] and no way to differentiate which one served as president. All that can be added is that a Stanislaus served on the board after 1904 and stepped in and out of leadership roles over the next quarter century.[64]

8. Stanislaus F. Kujawa (1907-1908)

The election of Stanislaus F. Kujawa in 1907 marked a sea change for Chopin, as Kujawa would be the first American-born president of the Society. Born on November 9, 1881, Kujawa was the third president to be a professional tailor. A bass singer, it was no surprise that he won the election of 1907, as Stanley had proven himself to be a dedicated and devoted member of Chopin.[65] As early as 1903 Kujawa was prominent enough to represent the Society at the Congress of the Polish Singers Alliance of America in Chicago and in 1905 he secured the position of vice president.[66]

Born and raised in Buffalo's East Side, Kujawa came from a squarely skilled and working-class background.[67] His father, Michael, was a mason and his other family members, Teofil and Victoria,

---

62 "Obituaries." *Tonawanda News*, 10 Mar. 1955, p. 15.

63 Chopin Singing Society. "Meeting Minutes." Buffalo, NY, 1900.

64 *Towarzystwo Spiewu Fryderyka Chopina 1899-1949*. Buffalo, NY: Tow. Spiewu Fryderyka Chopina, 1949. Print.

65 *Towarzystwo Spiewu Fryderyka Chopina 1899-1949*. Buffalo, NY: Tow. Spiewu Fryderyka Chopina, 1949. Print.

66 Blejwas, Stanislaus A. *The Polish Singers Alliance, 1888-1998: Choral Patriotism*. University of Rochester Press, 2005.

67 Registration Card, Serial Number 1610 Order Number 1897 - Stanley Francis Kujawa 1918

became a button maker and a dressmaker, respectively. In 1906 Kujawa married Magdalena Chrzanowska and soon welcomed daughter Irena to the family. She was followed by her brothers Norbert and Ryszard.[68]

In both marriage and business Magdalena and Stanislaus were a team. While Stan was a great tailor, serving as managing tailor at the George W. Puls Factory on Franklin Street, working with Constantine Nowakowski at his shop on Broadway, and running his own store, Magdalena was a truly gifted milliner. While Stan left the house to go to work, Magdalena began making and selling hats out of their 66 Houghton home. By 1917 she had her own store at 1210 Broadway with Stanislaus assisting her. Magdalena's venture succeeded for years until the growing needs of her family took over.

Besides his family, Stanislaus' other great love was the Chopin Singing Society. If something had to be done, Kujawa was ready, willing, and able. If a joint concert was being planned with the Singing Circle, the Kalina Singing Society, or the Philharmonia Singing Society, Stanley was ready to coordinate it. When there was an effort to combine all the Polish singing societies, Kujawa worked to keep Chopins independent.[69] If a speaker from Chopins was needed at an event at the Dom Polski,[70] Stanley had a talk prepared. If there was a dinner or event, the entire Kujawa family would have tickets for the night.[71]

When Stanislaus F. Kujawa passed away on April 30, 1934, at the age of 51, Magdalena and their children were devastated. Equally moved by the loss were the members of the Chopin Singing Society who lost a friend, a colleague, and a true leader.[72] Kujawa's impact on the Society was so meaningful that his life was celebrated and death lamented at Chopin's 50th anniversary, a full 15 years after his passing.[73]

9. Jan F. Nowak (1909-1910)

On the verge of their tenth anniversary, the Chopin Singing

---

[68] "Sp. St. Kujawa Zmarl Nagle Dzis Nad Ranem." *Dziennik Dla Wszystkich*, 1 May 1934, p. 9.

[69] "Initiate Plan to Unite Polish Singing Societies." *Buffalo Courier*, 24 May 1916, p. 3.

[70] "Concert at Dom Polski." *Buffalo Evening News*, 16 Nov. 1914, p. 14.

[71] "Chopin Society's Hall Opened with Ceremony." *Buffalo Evening News*, 23 Apr. 1928.

[72] "Sp. Stanislaw F. Kujawa." *Dziennik Dla Wszystkich*, 1 May 1934, p. 9.

[73] *Towarzystwo Spiewu Fryderyka Chopina 1899-1949*. Buffalo, NY: Tow. Spiewu Fryderyka Chopina, 1949. Print.

Society selected Jan F. Nowak as their new president. Born in Buffalo and educated at Transfiguration School, Nowak was a musical prodigy. A protégé of Leon Olszewski, John became a professional organist by age 16. His first job behind the keys was in Bay City, Michigan and after a year he took a position with a parish in Meriden, Connecticut. Nowak married Leocadia Slesinski in 1905, and before the decade ended, moved to Depew to play at SS. Peter and Paul Church.[74]

Upon his return to Western New York, John joined the singing society, and his musical talents endeared him to the membership. In 1909 Nowak won his first of two terms which were highlighted by the anniversary and the purchase of a bust of Frederic Chopin by Casimir Chodzinski.[75]

Shortly after finishing his terms at Chopins, Nowak took a new position playing at St. Luke Church on Sycamore. Over the next 40 years, Jan played masses, weddings, and funerals at the church while directing the Kalina, Lirnik and Harmonia societies. He was also instrumental in the establishment and operation of the Polish Organists' Society where he served as president and secretary.[76] At home, John and Leocadia had seven children. In his later years Nowak took a job at Queen of Peace Church on Genesee Street,[77] playing there until the day of his death on March 4, 1962.[78]

10. Kazimierz Nowak (1911-1915)

The election of Kazimierz Nowak as the ninth person to hold the title of president would come as no surprise to anyone who had been involved in the Society in its first decade. A member of the first constitution committee and delegate to the Congress of the Polish Singers Alliance, Kazimierz knew the organization better than many, and was more devoted to it than most.

Born in the village of Srebrna Gora in the Grand Duchy of Posen on February 23, 1878, Kazimierz, his parents Stanislaus and Mary, and siblings, settled in Buffalo when he was still a boy. Finished with school, Nowak took simple labor jobs, working as a buffer and

---

74 "John Nowak, Organist at Church, Dies." *Buffalo Courier-Express*, 5 Mar. 1962, p. 8.; Zloty Jubileusz Parafii Sw. App. Piotra I Pawla. Depew, NY. 1947.

75 *Towarzystwo Spiewu Fryderyka Chopina 1899-1949*. Buffalo, NY: Tow. Spiewu Fryderyka Chopina, 1949. Print.

76 "Polish Organists Plan to Provide Better Music." *Buffalo Courier*, 14 Apr. 1912, p. 45.; "Polish Organists' Choir Society Elects Officers." *Buffalo Evening News*, 1 Mar. 1932, p. 25.

77 "John F. Nowak." *Buffalo Evening News*, 5 Mar. 1962, p. 23.

78 "Nowak - John F." *Buffalo Courier-Express*, 6 Mar. 1962, p. 20.

polisher for a local tin works. The year 1900 was a big year for Kazimierz as he married his fiancée Pelagia Helminiak and joined the Chopin Singing Society.[79] As the young couple welcomed their first child Joseph to the family, Kazimierz was bitten by the entrepreneurial bug and opened a bar supplies store at 947 Broadway in 1907. The venture was short-lived, but it would leave a lasting impression on the family. Returning to his job as a nickel plater, Nowak divided his free time between his home family which grew to include children Thaddeus, Monica, Wladyslaw, Regina and his singing family, Chopins.[80]

After serving for years in the role of president, Kazimierz was happy to see the position taken back over by his friend John A. Zelechowski. Soon after the election, Kazimierz's health began to decline and on January 19, 1917, at 6:15 in the morning, Kazimierz Nowak passed away. Like his family, the members were grief stricken. As per their custom they sang at Nowak's funeral, but they also withdrew from several public performances to grieve, including the masquerade ball for the Polish Singing Circle.[81] The members of Chopins took their mourning a step further, publishing a resolution in the Dziennik Dla Wszystkich, highlighting Nowak's work in organizing the choir, his zealous efforts in growing it,[82] and their sympathies to the family.[83] The Kosciuszko Camp of the Woodmen of the World would honor Nowak's efforts at Chopin by carving a special grave marker for him, and unveiling it as part of a large parade and ceremony six months after his death.[84]

Kazimierz's entrepreneurial spirit would be passed down to his oldest, Joseph who opened Nowak's Funeral Home at 947 Sycamore Street, and then later Nowak's Camera.[85]

11. John A. Mikolajczak (1918)

Following Zelechowski's second tenure as president of Chopin Singing Society, the members next selected an up-and-coming star of the organization, John Mikolajczak. John A. Mikolajczak was born in

---

[79] "Casimir Nowak." *The Buffalo Times*, 20 Jan. 1917, p. 5.

[80] "Kazimierz Nowak." *Dziennik Dla Wszystkich*, 17 Jan. 1917, p. 3.

[81] "Sp. Kazimierz Nowak." *Dziennik Dla Wszystkich*, 19 Jan. 1917, p. 5.

[82] "Chopini Bacznosc!" *Dziennik Dla Wszystkich*, 19 Jan. 1917, p. 5.

[83] "Chor Chopina Dziala." *Dziennik Dla Wszystkich*, 19 Jan. 1917, p. 5.

[84] "Polish Camps Pay Their Tribute to Deceased Members." *Buffalo Courier*, 9 July 1917, p. 4.

[85] "Joseph C. Nowak Is Dead; Was Former Little Mayor." *Buffalo Evening News*, 10 Jan. 1948, p. 8.

Buffalo to Stella and Andrew Mikolajczak on January 2, 1893. Growing up between Stanislaus Street and Broadway, John attended school and played with his brothers Joseph, Frank, Bernard, Edward, Vincent, and younger sister Charlotte. As a young man John trained as barber and soon after starting to work, joined the Chopin choir.[86] When the First World War broke out, Mikolajczak as much as the rest of Polonia took interest as it could potentially lead to a free Poland.

In 1918 John was elected president of the Society, but he wouldn't be able to see his term out as on March 12 he signed up to serve Uncle Sam.[87] In less than four months Mikolajczak was trained and sent overseas to fight the Germans. John would spend a year in Belgium and France, seeing the war being wrapped up five months after he landed. Almost as soon as he arrived home, Mikolajczak joined the newly formed Adam Plewacki Post No. 799 and married his sweetheart, Lucy Rejent.[88]

Mikolajczak threw himself into 799 and by 1921 was elected an executive officer of the post, along with Plewacki founder, Victor B. Wylegala, Dr. Francis E. Fronczak, and Michael Borowczyk.[89] John's activity at the post gave him the first taste of politics when he became a director of the non-partisan Veteran's Political League in an effort to elect Victor B. Wylegala to the position of Buffalo City Commissioner.[90] Wylegala would stay focused on politics through the 1920s, so much so that he chose not to run for the commandership of 799 instead choosing to run for Buffalo's Councilman at Large seat in 1927. To fill Wylegala's vacancy his former vice commander, John Mikolajczak, ran and easily won the commandership election, becoming only the second person to hold the position of commander of the Adam Plewacki Post.[91]

Being a prominent member of Polonia helped Mikolajczak in his job as an advertising salesman for the Polish language *Everybody's Daily* newspaper and as a caterer with his brother Vincent. This prominence would also help John as he began to embrace his political aspirations. Mikolajczak first worked on the campaigns for congressional candidate C. Hamilton Cook and state senator Leonard R. Lipowicz in

---

86 "Military Funeral Planned for John A. Mikolajczak." *Buffalo Evening News*, 28 Oct. 1949, p. 49.

87 "Chopin Singing Society." *Buffalo Morning Express*, 2 Nov. 1919, p. 8.

88 "Mikolajczak-Rejent." *Buffalo Evening News*, 18 Jan. 1921, p. 10.

89 "Post Elects Officers." *Buffalo Evening News*, 20 Jan. 1921.

90 "Candidates For Council Make New Appeals for Votes." *Buffalo Courier*, Oct. 1923, p. 4.

91 "Mikolajczak Chosen Plewacki Post Head." *Buffalo Evening News*, 31 Oct. 1927, p. 28.

1928.[92] Although both candidates lost, it deepened John's appetite for politics. Later that year, Mikolajczak chose to not run for the commandership of 799, allowing Victor Wylegala's younger brother, Leon to become the third commander of the post.[93] No longer in a leadership role, but still active in the post, John was free to run for 9th ward supervisor for the City of Buffalo. With name recognition, a solid track record of public service, and the support of the Republican Party, Mikolajczak easily won the 1929 election.[94]

Sitting on the Lodging House Committee and the Committee on Forestry, Mikolajczak would also work diligently on trying to land a veterans' hospital in Buffalo early in his tenure. Not wanting to leave his friends behind, John continued to play an active role in the Plewacki Post.[95] Following his time with the city, and the end of Prohibition, John became the East Side sales representative for the George F. Stein Brewery and then the Iroquois Brewing Company.

As he got older, John became less involved in public events, making a rare exception to praise his good friend Francis Fronczak at the good doctor's retirement party in 1946.[96] On October 26, 1949, a heart attack took John A. Mikolajczak's life. The men and women at of Post 799 held a special service for him before his funeral at Transfiguration and interment at St. Stanislaus cemetery.[97]

12. Joseph A. Siudzinski (1919)

Joseph Siudzinski was born on February 9, 1885 in Gniezno, Poland, and at age two his family relocated to Buffalo. At age 23 Siudzinski joined the Post Office as a substitute letter carrier at Station A on William Street, and in 1912 he was promoted to full letter carrier for Station F on Fillmore Avenue. In his personal life, Joe married Victoria Kujawa, and the couple had three children, Alice, Florence and Jerome.

In March of 1902, Sidudznski joined the Chopin Singing Society, along with two other highly influential Poles at the time, editor and publisher of the *Album Pamiatkowe I Przewodnik Handlowy:*

---

92 "Cook and Lipowicz Committees Named." *Buffalo Evening News*, 2 Oct. 1928, p. 5.
93 "355 Men Accepted by Plewacki Post." *Buffalo Evening News*, 6 Dec. 1928, p. 36.
94 "Orlowski Will Bear G.O.P. Flag in Lovejoy Zone." *Buffalo Courier-Express*, 20 May 1931, p. 3.; "Republicans Again Hold Large Majority in City Council." *Buffalo Evening News*, 6 Nov. 1929, p. 18.
95 "Buffalo Group Plans Tribute to Washington." *Buffalo Courier-Express*, 21 Feb. 1932, p. 7.
96 "Retiring Health Officer is Feted." *Buffalo Courier-Express*, 26 Mar. 1946, p. 14.
97 "Rites Today for Former Supervisor." *Buffalo Courier-Express*, 29 Oct. 1949, p. 16.

Osady Polskiej W Miescie Buffalo, Z Dolaczeniem Okolicznych Miejscowósci Ze Stanu New York Joseph Smolczynski and photographer Ignatz Romaszkiewicz.[98] In his early years with the Society, Joseph was content with just being a member and a singer. After a decade with the group, he decided to become more involved and was elected host of the clubhouse.[99] In 1916, there was an effort to unite all the Polish singing societies of Buffalo into a single organization, and Sidudznski served as both a representative of Chopins and on the organizing committee.[100] After it was decided to keep all the singing organizations separate, Joe worked on an experimental project for the Chopin's quartet with fellow singers Vincent Kwiecikowski, Stanislaus Kujawa, and Teofil Kujawa.[101]

With limited membership because of the Great War and everyone focusing on a new Polish state, Siudzinski's profile was just high enough to rise to the board and then the presidency. It would be under his watch that Leon Olszewski would pass away, and Poland would return as a nation. Following his brief presidency, Joseph stayed with the choir serving on committees, and helping to oversee the silver anniversary and other special events of the club.[102]

In 1947 illness forced Siudzinski to retire from the post office. It was hoped that less strenuous work and stress would lead to a recovery, but it did not.[103] On March 25, 1948, Siudzinski died in his bed at 18 Bissell Avenue. The funeral was held out of the family home as well as St. Adalbert Church, where Joseph was a longtime member of the parish choir. His burial was held at St. Adalbert Cemetery.[104]

13. Vincent E. Kwiecikowski (1920)

Wincenty Eugene Kwiecikowski was born on March 12, 1884, in Buffalo's East Side. Attending parochial school, Kwiecikowski attended high school and eventually graduated from St. Bonaventure University.[105] With a focus on education, Vincent was brought on to

---

98 "Polish Editor Dead Fillmore Avenue." *Buffalo Courier*, 5 Dec. 1915, p. 71.; "Nowi Czlonkowie." Harmonia [Buffalo, NY] 15 Mar. 1902: 8. Print.
99 "Z Tow. Spiewu Chopin." *Dziennik Dla Wszystkich*, 9 Jan. 1912, p. 5.
100 "Initiate Plan to Unite Polish Singing Societies." *Buffalo Courier*, 24 May 1916, p. 8.
101 "Co Sie U Nas Dzieje." *Dziennik Dla Wszystkich*, 5 June 1917, p. 5.
102 "Polish Societies Join in Concert." *Buffalo Courier*, 19 May 1924, p. 4.; "Uczczono Bardzo Pieknie p. Feliksa Kulwickiego." *Dziennik Dla Wszystkich*, 9 Mar. 1931, p. 10.
103 "Joseph A. Siudzinski." *Buffalo Courier-Express*, 27 Mar. 1948, p. 16.
104 "Siudzinski." *Buffalo Evening News*, 26 Mar. 1948, p. 35.
105 Alumni Directory. 1859/1928-... St. Bonaventure University., n.p, 1930.

Buffalo's Department of Public Instruction as an attendance officer in late 1910.[106] At about the same time, Kwiecikowski began serving on the board of the Polish-American Liberty Club, a social and political organization based around St. Stanislaus Church.[107] Vincent's political involvement would peak in the 11th Ward, where he served as a committee man for the Democratic Party in 1911.[108] With a steady job and an excellent reputation, Kwiecikowski married Hedwig E. Matuszak of Mohr Avenue in August of the next year.[109]

Soon the family expanded with the addition of two daughters Wanda and Adela, as Vincent focused more of his efforts at Chopins. In 1915 he was elected as the recording secretary,[110] holding that position for three terms.[111] It would be during this time that Kwiecikowski was selected to sit on the committee that attempted to unify all the Polish singing societies of Buffalo.[112] Vincent also served as a public face of Chopins, gave presentations to his fellow members on the history of Polish song,[113] and volunteered for the preconvention committee of the Polish Singers Alliance's 18th Annual Meeting at Dom Polski on Broadway.[114]

In mid-1919 Vincent left the school district and entered the financial industry by taking a position with Liberty Bank. As bank manager of the Broadway-Fillmore branch it was his hope to bring the banking services that the rest of Buffalo enjoyed to the Poles of the East Side.[115]

In 1920 Vincent was elected president of Chopins. During his single term, Kwiecikowski worked to secure a larger clubhouse for the organization and to find a new choir master, even going so far as taking up the baton himself as they searched.[116] His efforts paid off as he was able to secure John Nadolny for the big May 1920 production of

---

[106] "Eligible List for Truant Officer Announced." *Buffalo Courier*, 5 Oct. 1910, p. 8.
[107] "Official Staff of the Polish American Liberty Club." *Buffalo Courier* Week Ending, 18 Dec. 1910, p. 11.
[108] "Wright Essays Reply to Critics at Mass Meeting." *Buffalo Courier*, 29 Oct. 1911, p. 46.
[109] "Vincent E. Kwiecikowski, No. 83..." *Buffalo Courier*, 22 Aug. 1912, p. 8.
[110] "Chopin Singing Society Holds Its Installation." *Buffalo Courier*, 11 Jan. 1915, p. 7.
[111] "Polish Societies Choose Officers For 1920." *Buffalo Express*, 21 Dec. 1919, p. 8.
[112] "Initiate Plan to Unite Polish Singing Societies." *Buffalo Courier*, 24 May 1916, p. 3.
[113] "Two Speakers to Address Polish Societies Today." *Buffalo Courier*, 1 Apr. 1917, p. 76.
[114] "Polish Singers Will Hold Big Convention." *Buffalo Evening News*, 17 Aug. 1918, p. 14.
[115] "Liberty Bank Powie Ksza Sztab." *Dziennik Dla Wszystkich*, 5 Sept. 1919, p. 2.
[116] "Kin of Soldier Dead Receive French Tribute." *Buffalo Evening News*, 24 Feb. 1920, p. 16.

Maude Elizabeth Inch and W. Rhys-Herbert's operetta *Sylvia.*[117] When nominations came around for the 1921 elections, Kwiecikowski declined to run, citing his workload at the bank, saying that he could not offer the Chopinites the time and energy needed to lead the organization. He then endorsed his friend Zdzislaw F. Krysztafkiewicz for president, who went on to easily sweep the election.[118]

With the family expanded to include Vincent Kwiecikowski Jr., the draw of education returned to the senior Kwiecikowski. Ready for a new adventure the family moved from Buffalo to Detroit, MI in 1924, eventually settling in Hamtramck. There, Kwiecikowski taught at the Senior High School where he was affectionately known as "Mr. Kaye." At the start of World War II Vincent transferred to Copernicus Junior High.[119] In Michigan, Kwiecikowski was still very involved in music and helped the choir at St. Ladislaus church transform from a religious organization into a formal club, becoming its first president in the process.[120]

Vincent would go on to have a long teaching career until retiring to La Jolla to spend time with his six grandchildren and eight great grandchildren. Wincenty E. Kwiecikowski died January 23, 1970, and was buried at Holy Sepulchre Cemetery in Southfield, MI.[121]

14. Zdzislaw F. Krysztafkiewicz (1921-1926, 1931, 1934-1939) (Krystafkiewicz, Krystaf)

Zdzislaw Francis Krysztafkiewicz was born on March 3, 1892, in Poznan, Poland. Before his first birthday his parents, Joseph and Helen, gathered Zdzislaw and his brothers, Romuald and Edmund, and set sail for America.[122]

In his new country, Joseph, after finding employment as a barber, felt compelled to keep his Polish culture alive. In 1893, Krysztafkiewicz, along with Stanislaus Mrugowski, Mr. Olbratowski, Jan Nowak, and a handful of others started the Polish National Athletic

---

117 *Operetka Sylvia Chor Chopina z Udzialm Choru Kalina Poniedzialek 10 Maja 1920.* Chopin Singing Society, 1920.

118 "Nominacy U Chopinow." *Dziennik Dla Wszystkich*, 6 Nov. 1920, p. 2.

119 Local Board No. 51 - Wayne County. "D.S.S. Form 1 Registration Card - Vincent Eugene Kwiecikowski." Hamtramck, MI, 27 Apr. 1942.

120 Golden Jubilee of St. Ladislaus Parish, 1920-1970: The Growth of a Community, St. Ladislaus Parish, 1970, p. 49.

121 "Vincent Kwiecikowski." *The Clarkston News*, 5 Feb. 1970, p. 3.

122 "Celebrate Their Silver Wedding Anniversary." *Buffalo Courier*, 19 June 1916, p. 4.

Club, electing Krysztafkiewicz as their president.[123] The Polish Athletic Club survived for three years with little growth and in 1896 was reorganized into Polish Falcons Nest 6.[124]

While Joseph was bringing athleticism to Polonia, Zdzislaw was getting an education. Finishing primary school, Krysztafkiewicz attended Masten Park High School. There, Zdzislaw and fellow student Stanislaus N. Puchalski, with some assistance from Principal Fosdick, would establish the Polish Literary Circle. The circle would grow to become a robust organization with a clubhouse at the corner of Detroit and Peckham Streets with over 100 members and 50 sponsoring businesses. The mission of the circle laid out by Krysztafkiewicz was for the examination and perpetuation of Polish history, literature, and language arts.[125] Later, while attending Canisius College, Krysztafkiewicz was recognized with distinction for excelling in his religion, English, and bookkeeping classes.[126] The bookkeeping classes would be most useful to Krysztafkiewicz as his first job was in the insurance industry.

Following in his father's footsteps, Zdzislaw joined the Polish Falcons Grunwald Nest 255 shortly after it formed in 1911.[127] Having already been raised as a junior member of various nests in Buffalo, Zdzislaw was well respected in the Falcon community, so much so he was selected as one of the negotiators in the unification between Nest 255 and Thaddeus Kosciuszko Nest 58. Because of Krysztafkiewicz's youth and community connections, he was able to perfectly bridge the gap between the two nests. Nest 255 was popular and growing with younger members but lacked the funds for equipment. On the other side, Nest 58 was well established, with a full range of equipment, but a dwindling number of members to use it.[128] Separate, the two nests would not amount to much, but together they could be a force.[129] To

---

[123] "Polish Athletic Club." *Buffalo Evening News*, 27 Nov. 1893, p. 5.

[124] "Polish Falcons of America Nest 6." Polonia Trail, Polish-American Congress WNY, 29 June 2016, poloniatrail.com/location/polish-Falcons-of-america-nest-6/.

[125] "Polish Circle Will Entertain Tonight For 150 Graduates." *Buffalo Courier*, 29 June 1913, p. 65.

[126] Canisius College Buffalo, N.Y. 1905-1906 Thirty Sixth Annual Catalogue. Canisius College, 1905.

[127] "Former Nests of the Polish Falcons of America." One Hundred Years Young: A History of the Polish Falcons of America, 1887-1987, by Donald E. Pienkos, East European Monographs, 1987, pp. 235–275.

[128] "Lectures and Gymnastics Planned for Winter Season." *Buffalo Courier*, 15 Sept. 1912, p. 49.

[129] "Will Make Final Plans to Merge Polish Societies." *Buffalo Courier*, 14 July 1912, p. 49.

reach an accord that would appease both sides Krysztafkiewicz helped hammer out a deal where the name Grunwald would be married to the Nest 58. This way the history and heritage of both groups would be honored and preserved.

Like other men of his time, Zdzislaw had a great interest in Polish culture and the education of Polish youth. As the movement to establish an institute of higher learning, informally known as Copernicus College was underway, Krysztafkiewicz joined some of Polonia's other intelligentsia, including Wladyslaw H. Zawadski and John Slisz, in formally incorporating the effort as the Copernicus Educational and Aid Association.[130] To promote Polish culture, Zdzislaw spoke at public events including the 1913 remembrance of the 1863 Uprising, the first event where he shared a program with the Chopin Singing Society.[131]

As Krysztafkiewicz's career as an insurance agent thrived, so too did his role in the Polish Falcons. By 1913 he was the vice president of the Third Circuit of the Falcons and would be the standard bearer of the organization when representing the Falcons across the region.[132] When a number of smaller nests, numbers 58, 135, 144, 306, 313, 400, 551, 630, and 685, merged with Nest 6 so they could purchase a new building in 1916, Zdzislaw was one of the inaugural 21 directors of the one thousand member organization.[133] Of the 58 other nominees, Dr. Francis E. Fronczak, Alexander Cwiklinski, and Maxwell Chudy would join him on the board.[134] This was a big move for Nest 6, especially as Polish Americans were gearing up for the Great War. For his part, Krysztafkiewicz joined the 65th Regiment of the National Guard of the State of New York under Lt. Stanislaus Schoen but would not see any action due to some heart issues.[135] While Zdzislaw's heart kept him away from Europe, it brought him closer to

---

[130] "Polish Educational and Aid Association Seeks Incorporation." *Buffalo Courier*, 15 Nov. 1912, p. 8.

[131] "Polish Citizens to Commemorate Uprising Of '63." *Buffalo Courier*, 15 Jan. 1913, p. 55.

[132] "Falcon Alliance Begins Two-Week Course of Drills." *Buffalo Courier*, 2 Oct. 1913.; "Poles Pay Tribute to Kosciuszko and Abraham Lincoln." *Buffalo Courier*, 14 Feb. 1916, p. 9.

[133] This is most likely a typo for Nest 143 in Lackawanna, NY as Nest 144 was formed in Detroit, MI.

[134] "Poles Subscribe $2,500 To Home at Falcon Election." *Buffalo Courier*, 29 May 1916, p. 5.

[135] "Buffalo Poles Anxious to Go to Front Under Flag of U.S. Government." *Buffalo Courier*, 26 June 1916, p. 5.; Registration Card, Form 1 Number 36 - Zdzislaw Francis Krysztafkiewicz 1917.

Ms. Stefania M. Cielesz who he married with great fanfare in 1917.[136]

With a new wife, a new real estate and insurance venture with Stanley Puchalski in Black Rock, and a heart condition, Krysztafkiewicz began looking for something less strenuous than the Falcons to become involved with, and in 1918, joined the Chopin Singing Society. The well-respected Zdzislaw was welcomed with open arms by the Society, and he was quickly elected to the role of recording secretary. At the 1921 elections Krysztafkiewicz's name was placed on the ballot for president, and although he was only with the organization for three years, he was elected to the position.[137]

As president, Krysztafkiewicz would help the Society settle into their new home at 1212 Broadway, celebrate the choir's silver anniversary, dedicate the statue of Chopin in Humboldt Park, secure Arnold Cornelissen as musical director, work to make the Buffalo Philharmonic Orchestra a permanent cultural attraction, navigate the club through the Roaring Twenties, the Great Depression and the invasion of Poland.[138] As part of the larger singing world, Zdzislaw, through Chopin, would serve as chairman of the Polish Singers Alliance Western New York Circuit.[139]

Shortly after Zdzislaw took as president, he and his wife, Stephanie, welcomed their only child, Olga to their family. Krysztafkiewicz also took a position with the Employers Liability Assurance Company, whom he would work for through the rest of his professional career. Outside of Chopins, Krysztafkiewicz was an avid fisherman, known for handing out his catch to his friends after a day on the Niagara River.[140]

In the handful of years that Krysztafkiewicz wasn't president, he was heading other major initiatives in Polonia. In 1932 Zdzislaw served on the Polish Centennial,[141] the organization that planned how the Polish community would celebrate the City of Buffalo's Centennial.[142] As part of the group, Krysztafkiewicz worked on a plan to hold

---

136 "Polish Falcon Leader to Wed Miss Cielesz." *Buffalo Evening News*, 11 Aug. 1917, p. 5.
137 "Head Of Chopin Singing Society to Be Honored." *Buffalo Courier-Express*, 22 Nov. 1936, pp. W-5.
138 "Campaign for Orchestra to Be Citywide." *Buffalo Courier-Express*, 21 Feb. 1936, p. 13.
139 "Head Of Chopin Singing Society to Be Honored." *Buffalo Courier-Express*, 22 Nov. 1936, pp. W-5.
140 Argus. "Grave to Gay." *Buffalo Evening News*, 6 July 1937, p. 26.
141 "Last Session Tonight." *Buffalo Evening News*, 27 May 1932, p. 29.
142 "Polish Colony Pays Honor to Stadnicki." *Buffalo Evening News*, 1 July 1932, p. 5.; "Polish Citizens Plan Centennial Campaign." *Buffalo Evening News*, 14 Apr. 1932, p. 34.

a celebration on Humboldt Park that July but funding for the project fell through and the group dissolved. A second committee was formed, the Polish Citizens' Centennial Committee, where Zdzislaw served as secretary. This group decided the best representation for Polonia would be as an overwhelming force in the July first parade, with a grand float and a great number of marchers.[143] This solution proved to be both economical and practical.

In 1940 Krysztafkiewicz chose not to run for president, ending nearly two decades of leadership of Chopins. Despite stepping down from presidency, Krysztafkiewicz did not remove himself completely from Buffalo's Polish music community, as he became president of the Ninth Circuit of the Polish Singers Alliance.[144] Zdzislaw maintained his association with Chopins but in a more honorary role.[145] With more free time, Krysztafkiewicz involved himself with other organizations outside Polonia including the Casting and Fishing Club. Truncating his name Z. Francis Krystaf, Zdzislaw served as secretary of the club for many years.[146] Krysztafkiewicz would also be tapped by Governor Dewey to serve on the Second Selective Service Appeals Board for Buffalo,[147] where he again he was secretary.[148]

Following the war, Krysztafkiewicz remained active in Polonia, but in a much-limited capacity. On June 19, 1949, Zdzislaw F. Krysztafkiewicz passed away. His funeral was held out of his Amherst Street home before his interment in St. Stanislaus Cemetery.[149]

15. Albert L. Widzinski (1927-1929)

Al Widzinski was born Albert Leonard Widzinski in Poznan, Poland on April 23, 1883. At age 22, Albert left Poland for America and eventually settled in Buffalo. Living near Sycamore Street, Albert met Ms. Stella Helmicki and in September of 1907 married her in Transfiguration Church.[150]

With a home on Reed Street, Al and Stella began expanding their little family with the addition of two daughters, Frances and

---

143 "Centennial Committee Plans Float in Parade." *Buffalo Evening News*, 18 June 1932, p. 13.
144 "Banquet Observes Society Birthday." *Niagara Falls Gazette*, 23 Nov. 1937, p. 7.
145 "Polish Group Here to Honor Chopin." *Buffalo Courier-Express*, 4 Feb. 1945.
146 "Troop I Casting Club Re-Elects Al Jarecke; Trophies Are Awarded." *Buffalo Evening News*, 25 Oct. 1941, p. 11.
147 "Graduates Get Bids to Try Air Cadet Test." *Buffalo Courier-Express*, 24 June 1943.
148 "Walczak Heads Appeals Board." *Buffalo Courier-Express*, 25 Jan. 1943, p. 13.
149 "Krystaf." *Buffalo Evening News*, 20 Jan. 1949, p. 35.
150 "Golden Years." *Buffalo Evening News*, 11 Sept. 1957, p. 81.

Helen. To provide for his growing family, Albert took work as an independent bricklayer. Settling into the rhythm of life, Widzinski continued as a contractor before taking a similar position with the Lackawanna Steel Company for many years. Tired of working for companies and architects, Al formed his own construction company in 1922.

In 1924, while his new firm was working on the Crooker residence, across from the Wanakah Country Club, and a French colonial home on North Lincoln for Frank Piekarski, Widzinski began rising through the ranks at Chopins.[151] That spring, Albert along with Jan Dulski, Tadeusz Puchalski, Jan Zelechowski, and sixteen others formed the committee that oversaw the 25th anniversary of the Society.[152]

As his business prospered, Widzinski purchased a Chevrolet Coupe and began constructing a new home at 95 Walden Avenue for his family of five.[153] At Chopins, Widzinski's popularity and devotion to the Society earned him the presidency starting in 1927.[154] It would be under Al's tenure that the Ladies' Auxiliary was formed in 1927 and organized in 1929, and the 30th anniversary of the Society was held in Genesee Park.[155] Albert would also be the president that would squelch the rumors that the Society and the Polish Singing Society were planning to merge in 1928.[156]

While Prohibition was the law of the land, it wasn't well recognized in the Polish East Side. Just about every home had some wine fermenting in the cellar, every corner had a speakeasy on it, and the City of Buffalo even elected an indicted bootlegger for mayor, twice. Despite all this, Widzinski is one of the few unlucky souls to be charged with whiskey smuggling. On May 17, 1931, while returning from a night out in Canada, Al's car was pulled aside and searched by customs at the Peace Bridge. The agents patted down Al and found nothing, but when they searched his two passengers, three bottles of Canadian Whiskey were found hidden under their clothes. Being the driver, Widzinski was detained but quickly released by U.S.

---

151 "Spring Building Plans Under Way." *Buffalo Courier*, 13 Feb. 1924, p. 7.

152 "Srebrny Jubileusz Tow. Spiewu Chopin." *Dziennik Dla Wszystkich*, 18 May 1924, p. 3.

153 "Stolen Automobiles." *Buffalo Evening News*, 11 May 1925.; "File Nine Proposals for New Construction; Cost to Be $269,000." *Buffalo Courier*, 28 Apr. 1926, p. 5.

154 "Albert Widzinski Elected Head of Singing Society." *Buffalo Evening News*, 11 Dec. 1928.

155 "Chopin Society Meeting." *Buffalo Evening News*, 9 Jan. 1929, p. 12.; "Weather Fails to Stop Chopin Society Outing." *Buffalo Courier-Express*, 8 July 1929, p. 4.

156 "Merger Reports Denied by Two Singing Clubs." *Buffalo Evening News*, 5 Oct. 1928, p. 38.

Commissioner Harry E. Harding with a $1,000 bond.[157] As with many of those caught by the Dry Agents, Widzinski's brush with Prohibition had no impact on his life, so little, in fact, he performed at the inaugural Chopin concert conducted by Arnold Cornelissen two weeks later.[158]

As a bricklayer and then president of Widzinski Construction Co., Albert worked on several important structures across Polonia. His most notable religious projects included Joseph Zakrzewski's Lyceum for St. John Kanty,[159] the Convent for Transfiguration Church,[160] and St. Francis High School in Athol Springs, while his most notable secular structure was 1931's Public School 9 in Sloan.[161] The ongoing Second World War would hurt nonessential construction, and in 1943 Widzinski was forced to declare bankruptcy.[162] To keep their family close to home, Al and Stella lent out an upstairs apartment at 95 to their daughter Frances Mikolajczak and grandsons Theodore and James.[163] Theodore would truncate his name to Mikoll and take Ann Skulicz as his bride, all while continuing to live at the Walden Avenue address.[164]

In September of 1957, the Widzinskis celebrated their golden anniversary with a wedding renewal Mass at Transfiguration with their son, five daughters, and all their grandchildren in the pews.[165] Two months later the family returned to Transfiguration for a much more somber event. On November 14, 1957, Albert L. Widzinski passed away.[166] Amongst the bereaved that day were his family, some rank and file from the Bricklayer's Union, several representatives of the Polish Union of America, and the great mass of the singers he once led from the Chopin Singing Society.[167]

---

157 "Raid Lake Shore Taverns; Twelve Arrested." *Buffalo Courier-Express*, 18 May 1931, p. 1.
158 "Chopin Society Choir to Present Concert." *Buffalo Evening News*, 22 May 1931, p. 38.
159 "Lyceum Is Dedicated Before Large Crowd." *Buffalo Evening News*, 14 Sept. 1931, p. 5.; "New Parish Lyceum to Be Started Soon." *Buffalo Evening News*, 3 June 1930, p. 32.
160 "Joseph Zakrzewski, 72, East Side Architect." *Buffalo Evening News*, 12 Jan. 1953, p. 24.
161 "School Addition Contracts to Be Let." *Buffalo Evening News*, 31 Mar. 1931, p. 12.; "Albert L. Widzinski." *Buffalo Courier-Express*, 16 Nov. 1957, p. 10.
162 "Bankruptcy Petitions." *Buffalo Evening News*, 5 Apr. 1943, p. 17.
163 "Commendation Ribbon Is Won by Buffalo Artilleryman." *Buffalo Evening News*, 6 Feb. 1953, p. 17.
164 "Woman Is Among 21 From the Area Admitted to Bar." *Buffalo Evening News*, 9 Mar. 1955, p. 59.
165 "Golden Years." *Buffalo Evening News*, 11 Sept. 1957, p. 81.
166 "Albert L. Widzinski." *Buffalo Courier-Express*, 16 Nov. 1957, p. 10.
167 "Albert L. Widzinski." *Buffalo Evening News*, 15 Nov. 1957, p. 38.

16. Stanislaus M. Jendrasiak (Jedrasiak) (1930, 1932, 1941-1942)

Like Krysztafkiewicz before him, Jendrasiak came from a family of humble beginnings in Poland but would have an outsized impact once they arrived in the New World.

At age 25, Ignacy Jendrasiak took his young bride Anastazya and fled the German partition of Poland for Buffalo. Settling on Loepere Street Ignacy soon began practicing his trade as a tailor, and in 1892 their family expanded with the birth of their daughter, Jadwiga. The family grew over the next decade and two months before the Pan-American Exposition in Buffalo opened, Anastazya gave birth to the second son of the family, Stanislaus. While Stanley was still a toddler, Ignacy was securing his place in the firmament of Polonia.[168]

One of the first Polish organizations Jendrasiak joined was the Czytelnia Polska (The Polish Reading Room) at the corner of Broadway and Sweet. His dedication to Polish literature and history earned him the presidency of the organization in 1902, a position he would hold for the next fourteen years.[169] As Ignacy's notoriety grew, so too did his finances, and by 1908 he was a major shareholder and director of Polska Spolka Akcyjna.[170] After serving a year as president of Polish Falcons Nest 6,[171] Jendrasiak's influence would reach its zenith with his election as president of the Dom Polski Association in 1910, winning a number of reelections over the next decade.[172]

As a member of a prominent family in East Buffalo, Stanislaus was expected to excel. Luckily for him, the whole world wasn't watching his every move like they were with his older brother Telesfor, who became an electrical engineer and son-in-law to banker Stanislaus S. Nowicki.[173] When the U.S. entered the Great War, Stanley enrolled and was ready to serve his nation and free Poland, but was never called

---

[168] "Ignacy Jedrasiak." Album Pamiatkowe I Przewodnik Handlowy : Osady Polskiej W Miescie Buffalo, Z Dolaczeniem Okolicznych Miejscowosci Ze Stanu New York , Wydane Staraniem i Nakładem Polskiej Spółki Wydawniczej, 1906, p. 572.

[169] Towarzystwo Czytelnia Polska w Domu Polskim Buffalo, New York 1889 1964. 1964.

[170] Album Pamiatkowe I Przewodnik Handlowy: Osady Polskiej W Miescie Buffalo, Z Dolaczeniem Okolicznych Miejscowosci Ze Stanu New York, Wydane Staraniem i Nakladem Polskiej Spolki Wydawniczej, 1906, p.458-461.

[171] Rozek, Ben, and Norma Wujcikowski. "History." Polish Falcons of America Nest #6 100th Anniversary Oct. 5, 1996, Polish Falcons of America Nest #6, Buffalo, NY, 1996, pp. 29–32.

[172] Pamietnik 50-Cio Lecia Stowarzyszenia Domu Polskiego, 1905-1955. Dom Polski Association, 1955.

[173] "Mrs. H. M. Jendrasiak Dies in St. Mary's Hospital." *Buffalo Evening News*, 29 Jan. 1924, p. 6.

up, staying home for the duration of the conflict.[174] After the war, Stan took a job as a clerk, eventually becoming a salesman for one of the local dairy companies. Looking for his own place in Polonia, Jendrasiak joined the Chopin Singing Society in the early 1920s and by the middle of the decade was leading committees within the Society.[175] At the end of 1928 Stanley was elected vice president.[176] For two years he served the role, and when John A. Mikolajczak and Zdzislaw F. Krysztafkiewicz refused to run for the presidency after the stock market crash, Jendrasiak agreed to lead the organization in 1930.

For his term of 1930, Jendrasiak had only three jobs, find a new conductor to replace John F. Nadolny which he did with Prof. Jan Karol Kapalka, work to keep money flowing into the coffers,[177] and be the public face of the choir.[178] During his second tenure as president, Stan was able to do more with and for the club, including holding concerts,[179] and hosting Polish singers once again.[180] Stan's second term also brought him the opportunity to spend an evening with Paderewski during the pianist's 1932 concert in Buffalo.[181]

Between the end of his second term in 1932 and his second tenure as president from 1940 to 1942, Stan focused on his career selling foodstuffs. He stayed active in Chopins, sitting on committees and working as needed. When World War II broke out, Jendrasiak was too old to fight for the freedom of Poland this time, so he took a job at Bell Aircraft and resumed the role of president, so Chopins would survive the war.

A Democrat in politics,[182] Stan worked for the City of Buffalo for a time after the Second World War,[183] served as Steward for Chopins once they moved their clubhouse to Kosciuszko Street, and starting in 1954, worked as a deputy of the sheriff's department, stationed in

---

174 "Boards Rapidly Enrolling Men for New Army; Sixty Percent Pass Physical Test." *Buffalo Courier*, 4 Aug. 1917, p. 4.
175 "To Celebrate Hallowe'en." *Buffalo Evening News*, 28 Feb. 1927.
176 "Installation Planned." *Buffalo Evening News*, 23 Jan. 1929, p. 19.
177 "East Side Briefs." *Buffalo Evening News*, 13 May 1930, p. 18.
178 "Plan To Welcome Envoy." *Buffalo Courier-Express*, 27 Mar. 1930, p. 11.
179 "Chopin Singing Society to Give Concert in April." *Buffalo Evening News*, 17 Feb. 1932, p. 23.
180 "Chopin Society Engages Contralto for Concert." *Buffalo Evening News*, 19 Feb. 1932, p. 29.
181 "Reception Is Planned." *Buffalo Evening News*, 15 Mar. 1932, p. 26.
182 "Leaders Assail Dubinsky Choice." *Buffalo Evening News*, 2 Oct. 1936, p. 1.
183 "Commissioner Appoints 35." *Buffalo Courier-Express*, 15 Aug. 1950, p. 22.

the County Court. Jendrasiak served for 15 years, retiring in 1969.[184] On November 25, 1971, Stanislaus M. Jendrasiak passed away and was interred at St. Stanislaus Cemetery in Cheektowaga.[185]

17. Boleslaus "William B." Lemanski (1933, 1940, 1945-1949, 1954, 1959)

Boleslaus Lemanski's influence over Chopins would stretch over three decades and lead the organization at major turning points in the history of America. He would oversee the choir at the height of the Great Depression, as the U.S. prepared for war, and the beginning of the postwar boom. William would also have the honor of heading the Society during its golden jubilee and live long enough to see the next generation take the Society in a new and exciting direction.

A lifelong Buffalonian, Boleslaus was born to Joseph and Frances Lemanski on May 19, 1896, between Broadway, Fillmore, and Curtis Streets in Buffalo's East Side. The son of a laborer, Lemanski played in the streets and ran along the tracks of the neighborhood with his brothers John and Wladyslaw until he graduated from the eighth grade and entered the workforce. Anglicizing his name to William, Boleslaus held several jobs until he became a car repairman and helper for the railroad. His work helped Boleslaus avoid being drafted in the Great War, but he was ready to fight if called upon.

Lemanski spent most of the 1920s working hard and earning a living. By 1927 Will had been promoted to a painter with the New York Central Railroad, a position he held for the next 35 years. As his brothers and friends settled down and got married, Boleslaus the eternal bachelor, found himself with a lot of free time on his hands. One of the first organizations he became heavily involved with Central Council of Polish Organizations. Lemanski's dedication and devotion to the advocacy group for Polonia saw him elected to the board of directors in 1929.[186] The 1920s also saw Boleslaus become involved with Democratic politics when he ran to be the representative of the Sixth Ward's Third District and worked on Alexander A. Patrzykowski's 1929 run for Lovejoy's district councilman. [187]

---

184 "Stanley M. Jendrasiak." Buffalo-Courier Express, 27 Nov. 1971, p. 4.

185 "Jendrasiak - Stanley M." *Buffalo Courier-Express*, 27 Nov. 1971, p. 20.

186 "Council Re-Elects Stanley Puchalski." *Buffalo Evening News*, 21 Feb. 1929.

187 "Fair Vote Polled in First Primary Under New Charter." *Buffalo Evening News*, 12 Sept. 1929, p. 32.; "Expect Higgins to Give Answer by Next Week." *Buffalo Courier-Express*, 15 Aug. 1929, p. 24.

As the Great Depression set in, Lemanski headed up a committee at the Central Council to encourage enrollment in the organization. It was hoped that as funds became scarce, the council could work to keep its members afloat.[188] It was around this time that William's stock at Chopins began to rise as well and when the choir had the opportunity to elect the well-known leader as its president in 1933, they took it.[189] As a first-time president of an organization, Lemanski did well to make sure Chopins was well represented in greater Polonia. He personally sponsored part of the 1933 Polish art exhibition at the Albright Art Gallery and worked the room on opening night to make sure everyone attended the Chopinites' performance that weekend.[190] While Boleslaus didn't stand for president again in the 1930s, he did stay highly involved in the choir, heading up fish fry fundraisers and helping to organize President Krysztafkiewicz's 12th anniversary tribute.[191]

In the years between his presidencies, Boleslaus was a leader of the John W. Kraska Political and Social Club. Named after the owner of the Mills Street tavern where they met,[192] the J.W.K. focused on the betterment of Polonia by advocating for community centers and parks.[193]

Returning to the presidency of Chopins in the 1940s Lemanski was a delegate to the District 9 convention of the Polish Singers Alliance,[194] represented Chopins on a Red Cross committee,[195] and oversaw the purchase of 18 Kosciuszko Street that would be the home of Chopins for a generation.[196] Following his second stint as president, Boleslaus sat on the board before returning to the head of the organization in the 1950s.[197]

In 1962 William retired from the railroad and on the morning

---

188 "Campaign Planned by Central Council." *Buffalo Evening News*, 18 Nov. 1931, p. 36.

189 "Six Large East Side Units Pick Officers." *Buffalo Evening News*, 12 Dec. 1932, p. 6.

190 "Polish Exhibit to Be Featured at Art Gallery." *Buffalo Courier-Express*, 23 Nov. 1933, p. 7.

191 "Chopin Singing Society to Hold Fish Fry Tonight." *Buffalo Evening News*, 2 Feb. 1935, p. 3.; "Chopin Society Pays Tribute to President." *Buffalo Courier-Express*, 21 Dec. 1936, p. 9.

192 "Polish Groups Back Marlinski." *Buffalo Courier-Express*, 28 Feb. 1936, p. 24.

193 "Seek Recreation Center." *Buffalo Courier-Express*, 3 Mar. 1939, p. 15.

194 "Convention Delegates Named by Chopin Society." *Buffalo Evening News*, 22 Jan. 1940, p. 21.

195 "Benefit Show Aides Chosen." *Buffalo Courier-Express*, 11 Jan. 1940, p. 8.

196 "Chopin Singing Society." Polonia Trail, Polish-American Congress WNY, 29 June 2016, poloniatrail.com/location/chopin-singing-society/.

197 "Netzel Elected Board President by Chopin Singers." *Buffalo Evening News*, 26 June 1957, p. 63.

of Monday March 20, 1966, he passed away in Deaconess Hospital after a long illness. His funeral was held at Corpus Christi with burial at St. Adalbert's.[198]

18. Rev. Joseph J. Winnicki (1943-1944, 1958)

In the middle of World War II, the membership of Chopins selected a Roman Catholic priest to lead them. Under his guidance the Society transformed part of its clubrooms into housing for Polish war refugees,[199] supported the members that signed up for military service, and tried to find a home the Chopinites could call their own.[200]

Joseph John Winnicki was born March 6, 1885, in Sanok, Poland. Joseph heard the call to the priesthood early in life and while still in his youth, he geared his education towards that goal. At age 19 he met with two priests from Buffalo traveling through Poland who convinced Winnicki to attend seminary in America. By the end of the year, he boarded a ship and set sail for Western New York.

He enrolled at St. Bernard's Seminary in Rochester and finished his studies at St. Bonaventure. On December 18, 1908, he was ordained and was assigned to Holy Trinity in Niagara Falls to serve as an assistant. After a few years, Father Joe was transferred to the countryside parish of Sacred Heart in Batavia, NY.[201] In his short time there, Father Joe traveled to the Vatican for a papal audience with Pope Benedict XV,[202] resisted attempts by a faction in the parish to have the church property signed over to them,[203] and served as first chaplain of Polish Falcons Nest 493.[204] After five years in the rural Genesee county church, Joseph was sent to Buffalo's East Side to take a census of the Polish people around the city's meatpacking district. When the numbers came in, Bishop Dougherty placed Winnicki at Precious Blood Church and charged him with converting the former

---

198 "B. Lemanski Dies; Headed Male Chorus." *Buffalo Courier-Express*, 21 Mar. 1966, p. 25.

199 Blejwas, Stanislaus A. The Polish Singers Alliance, 1888-1998: Choral Patriotism. University of Rochester Press, 2005.

200 *Towarzystwo Spiewu Fryderyka* Chopina 1899-1949. Tow. Spiewu Fryderyka Chopina, 1949.

201 "Buffalo Once Wild as West, Priest for 50 Years Recalls." *Buffalo Evening News*, 11 Dec. 1959, p. 31.

202 "Priest Imparts Papal Blessing." *Rochester Democrat and Chronicle*, 19 Oct. 1914.

203 "Batavia Priest Tells Police He's Annoyed." *Buffalo Evening News*, 10 Aug. 1915, p. 12.

204 "Falcons Recall 60-Year History in Preparing for Anniversary." *The Daily News*, 27 Sept. 1973, p. 12.

Irish parish into a Polish one.[205]

During his long tenure at Precious Blood, Father Winnicki was very active in the community surrounding his parish. An early ongoing problem the new urban priest tackled was the use of city streets for cattle drives to the stockyards. The cows, as well as sheep and pigs, would destroy private property and interfere with solemn events such as processions and funerals. Father Joe took on the cattle barons and by the 1920s beat them as the city passed an ordinance forbidding the use of public streets for the open air movement of animals.[206] Father Joe was also involved in other East Side events and organizations including the formation of the Aurora Singing Society, traveling regularly to Poland, and in 1934 was presented an award by General Jozef Haller for his dedication to Polish culture.[207] A lot of Joseph's cultural interest was in music and his devotion to the art earned him a seat on the board of the Polish Singers Alliance District 9 as chaplain.[208]

On May 4, 1938, while driving home from downtown Buffalo Father Winnicki was in a terrible automobile accident. Heading south on Pearl Street he reached Terrace and didn't see the "must turn sign." Moving forward Joseph crashed down a 15-foot embankment and landed on the tracks of the New York Central. Once settled an oncoming train sideswiped his car further injuring the priest. His admission to the emergency hospital listed a fractured skull, missing teeth, lacerations, and shock as his major injuries.[209] Following the accident and with a long and tenuous recovery, Winnicki was removed from Precious Blood Church and became a liaison for the diocese to the Polish people.

One of the first projects Father Joe worked on was setting up the welcome party and meet-and-greet for Colonel Alexander Bobkowski, Poland's vice minister of communications. Joining Alexander that day was his wife Helena, the daughter of President Ignacy Moscicki.[210] Following the invasion of Poland in 1939, Reverend Winnicki, as president of the Buffalo Polish Citizens Committee became an activist for American relief for Poland. He also called for the nation

---

205 Kobielski, Milton J. Millennium of Christianity of the Polish People, 966-1966: Buffalo Diocesan Observance. Millennium Committee of the Diocese of Buffalo, 1966.

206 "Buffalo Once Wild as West, Priest for 50 Years Recalls." *Buffalo Evening News*, 11 Dec. 1959, p. 31.

207 "Win Coveted Order." *Buffalo Courier-Express*, 13 May 1934, p. 6.

208 "Polish Singers Alliance Meets." The Evening News, 9 Mar. 1938, p. 3.

209 "Injured Buffalo Priest Reported Improving." *The Daily News*, 5 May 1938, p. 7.

210 "Polish Visitors Greeted." *Buffalo Evening News*, 15 May 1939, p. 30.

to apply pressure to the Nazi regime to stop the slaughter of the Polish populace.[211] At the same time, Reverend Joseph maintained his strong interest in Polish song and music. When the elections for president of Chopins began in 1943, Winnicki was quickly selected to fill the position. Maintaining his role at the Citizens Committee and now leading the Society, Father Joe remained committed to seeing Poland, and now the whole of Europe, free from Nazi rule. In 1944, he rallied the members to raise over $1,750 for the war effort.[212]

After the war and his first tenure as Chopins' president Winnicki stayed in Polonia's cultural scene, supporting the efforts of the Arion Singing Society of North Tonawanda,[213] working to have Chopin's clubrooms house Polish refugees, and becoming the chaplain of Buffalo's Polish Falcons.[214] Joe's profile was growing nationally as well. The Polish Singers Alliance chose him to serve as an honorary president and in 1956, the Polish Falcons of America selected him as their national chaplain.[215] In 1958 Father Winnicki felt ready to lead a parish again and was sent to SS. Peter and Paul parish in Depew. Father Joe would regularly celebrate Mass in the suburban parish, but it would be two of his Masses in Poland that would grab international attention.

In 1960 Father Winnicki went on a musical excursion to Poland as part of the 150th and 100th anniversary of Chopin's and Paderewski's births, respectively. In his homeland the priest laid wreaths at each of their monuments while choruses from across Poland sang under the direction of Dr. Jan Niezgoda, president of the Union of Polish Choral and Music Society. Father Winnicki concluded his time in Warsaw by celebrating Mass at Holy Cross Church, where Chopin's heart is housed. He then traveled to Czestochowa, where on August 26, he celebrated the Mass for the Feast of Our Lady of Czestochowa. As the main celebrant he observed, "[t]wo hundred thousand pilgrims sang together like one choir."[216]

---

211 "Polish Leaders Urge U.S. Protest to Nazis." *Buffalo Courier-Express*, 28 Feb. 1940, p. 7.

212 "Chopin Society Buys $500 Bond." *Buffalo Courier-Express*, 24 Jan. 1944, p. 7.

213 "Arion Society President Announces Concert Patrons." *The News*, 26 Apr. 1951, p. 8.

214 "Rochesterian Named Falcons President." *The Daily News*, 6 July 1953, p. 9.

215 Blejwas, Stanislaus A. The Polish Singers Alliance, 1888-1998: Choral Patriotism. University of Rochester Press, 2005.; "Chaplains of the Polish Falcons Alliance and the Polish Falcons of America." *One Hundred Years Young: A History of the Polish Falcons of America, 1887-1987*, by Donald E. Pienkos, East European Monographs, 1987, pp. 226.

216 Folger, Bill. "Depew Priest Awed by Polish Hymnody." *Buffalo Courier-Express*, 24 Sept. 1960, p. 6

In 1964 Father Joseph retired from SS. Peter and Paul and returned to Poland to live out the rest of life. On June 27, 1969, Joseph J. Winnicki passed away in Strachocina, Poland.[217]

19. Raymond A. Fabiniak (1950-1953)

Raymond was born to Stanley and Stella Fabiniak of Titus Avenue in Buffalo, NY on December 10, 1923. Educated at St. Luke parochial school, Ray demonstrated he was a bright and talented boy. At age eight he represented his school at an oratorical contest sponsored by the Polish Union of America and at age 10 took part in city-wide youth singing competition at the Elmwood Music Hall. [218] Fabiniak continued to develop his musical skills as a student at East High, singing in the 1939 annual concert.[219]

In 1940 Ray joined Chopins as a tenor and within a year was serving on the concert committee.[220] Around the same time he joined one of Buffalo's finer singing groups, the Guido Chorus. With the U.S.'s entry to the Second World War, Fabiniak signed up to serve in the Air Force.[221] With the completion of his service in 1946 Ray returned to Buffalo and was elected the vice president of Chopins the following year.[222] He would hold this position until his election as president in 1950. As president, the young Fabiniak did all he could to inject energy into the waning organization. He did his best to recruit new members and was able to give the choir a little more life that would help it see the 1960s.[223] After his tenure as presidency, Ray stayed active in Chopin and was bestowed the title Honorary President. By the late 1950s other musical ventures, life, and work took Fabiniak away from the Society.

On the musical front Ray deepened his involvement with his parish of St. Luke. By the time of the church's golden jubilee in 1958 he had been appointed musical director of the choir and chorale.[224] Over the next two years, Fabiniak became involved with the

---

217 "Rev. Joseph J. Winnicki." *Buffalo Courier-Express*, 1 July 1969, p. 31.
218 "Oratorical Series Will Begin Friday." *Buffalo Evening News*, 26 Oct. 1932, p. 29.; "First School Solo Contest Nearing Semi-Final Stage." *Buffalo Evening News*, 8 May 1934, p. 6.
219 "Doroczny Koncert Szkoly 'East High'." *Dziennik Dla Wszystkich*, 11 Mar. 1939, p. 3.
220 The Chopin Singing Society. *41-Szy Koncert*. Chopin Singing Society, 1940.; The Chopin Singing Society. *43-Ci Koncert Chopina*. Chopin Singing Society, 1942.
221 "Local Flier Training as Pilot of Fortress." *Buffalo Courier-Express*, 21 May 1944, p. 1.
222 The Chopin Singing Society. *48th Annual Concert.* Chopin Singing Society, 1947.
223 *Chopin Singing Society 75th Anniversary, 1899-1974*. The Society, 1974.
224 "Church Anniversary Marked by Concert." *Buffalo Courier-Express*, 14 Apr. 1958, p. 8.

Choirmasters Guild of the Diocese of Buffalo and became their men's choir director.[225] By the middle of the 1960s Ray took the position of organist-choirmaster of the prestigious Christ the King Church in Amherst.[226]

In his family life, Fabiniak met and married Ms. Lorraine J. Kwiatkowski and the couple had a son, Michael.[227] Outside of his family life and music, Ray worked with his brother Alfred in his growing grocery businesses.[228] Owning a store on Broadway since the 1950s, the Fabiniaks joined up with the Bells Supermarket group. By 1976 Ray owned and operated the stores in Hamburg, East Aurora, Orchard Park, and was elected vice president of the Bells Franchise Owners Organization.[229] He would assume the presidency two years later at the Annual Bells Retailers Convention in Washington, D.C.[230] In time the stores would be rebranded as Jubilees and when Ray wanted to slowdown, the stores fell under the watchful eye of his son, Michael.[231]

After retiring Ray devoted himself to bettering the community, improving the Chestnut Ridge Conservancy, and lowering his golf score. Raymond A. Fabiniak passed away August 8, 2015.[232]

20. Frederick S. Netzel (1955-1957)

In his early 40s at the time of his election as president of Chopin, Frederick Stanislaus Netzel was one of the younger members of the aging organization. While no great expansions or performances were undertaken during his tenure, Netzel's greatest accomplishment as president would be to see that the organization survived for three more years.

Born May 7, 1914 in Buffalo, Fred attended St. Andrew's Parochial School and graduated from East High.[233] Even as a young man Fred demonstrated a natural ability to entertain. Although not the

---

[225] "Diocese Choirmasters to Offer 1st Festival." *Buffalo Courier-Express*, 26 Mar. 1960, p. 4.
[226] "Organist Says Choir Adds to Beauty of Mass." *Buffalo Courier-Express*, 26 Mar. 1966, p. 15.
[227] "Deaths: Fabiniak — Lorraine J." *Buffalo Courier-Express*, 18 Mar. 1979, p. 29.
[228] "Alfred Fabiniak - Sunday, May 15th, 2011." *Kolano Funeral Home*, May 2011 www.kolanofuneralhome.com/memorials/alfred-fabiniak/743798/obituary.php.
[229] "Hamburg Bells Owner Named Group Officer." *The Hamburg Sun*, 23 Dec. 1976, p. 16.
[230] "Pawlak Elected V-P by Bells Retail Assoc'n." *Medina Journal-Register*, 22 Dec. 1978, p. 3.
[231] Gavin, Jennifer. "Jubilee Opens in Former Quality Store." *The Sun*, 9 Dec. 1999, p. 17.
[232] "Raymond A. Fabiniak's Obituary (2015) *Buffalo News*." *Legacy.com*,
[233] "Frederick Stanislaus Netzel (1914-1990)." Find a Grave, 30 Sept. 2020.; "Chopin Staff." May 1966.

winner, Netzel garnered the biggest laughs at an Amateur Show at Shea's where he did a spot-on impression of the American comedian and actor, George Givot, with a Greek accent and red sash.[234]

Before joining Chopins in 1941 Fred married Ms. Irene Grabski in October of 1938 and was an active member of the Perla Dramatic Circle.[235] In his professional life, Netzel worked as a salesman at R. W. Jones Dairy and would stay with the dairy as it became the Jones-Rich Milk Company where he worked as a supervisor before retiring.[236]

As a member of the Society, Netzel performed as a tenor and for much of the 1940s was happy to be just a singer. In 1948 he began his rise within the organization with his election as buffet secretary, overseeing the clubhouse and its menu.[237] Two years later he was elected vice president and in 1955, he ascended to the presidency.[238] As the old guard gave way to the new, Fred stayed active in the leadership working on the club newsletter, *The Chopin Staff,* and serving as financial secretary.

As he got older Fred worked hard to keep up with the younger Chopinites, even if it meant overextending himself. During the choir's 1977 tour of Poland, Netzel's high blood pressure got the better of him and he had to spend four days in a Warsaw hospital.[239] In the 1980s Fred did finally slow down and enjoyed time with his wife, son, and four grandchildren. On June 24, 1990, Frederick Netzel passed away and was interred in St. Stanislaus Cemetery. Irene joined him two years later.[240]

21. John A. Kedzierski (1960-1961)

John A. Kedzierski would be the last transitional president of the Chopin Singing Society, seeing the Society go from the old guard of Father Winnicki and Boleslaus Lemanski to the next generation in the form of Theodore V. Mikoll.

---

234 "Amateur Show First Prize Won by Novelty Musician." *Buffalo Evening News*, 24 Apr. 1935, p. 32.

235 Staff. "Mr. and Mrs. Frederick S. Netzel." Buffalo News, 19 Dec. 1988.; "Officers Inducted." *Buffalo Evening News*, 1940, p. 29.

236 Buffalo City Directory 1941

237 The Chopin Singing Society. *49th Annual Concert*. Chopin Singing Society, 1948.

238 The Chopin Singing Society. *51st Annual Concert*. Chopin Singing Society, 1950.

239 Smith, Rita. "Chopin Singers Return to Exultant Welcome." *Buffalo Courier-Express*, 4 Sept. 1977, p. 1.

240 "Frederick Stanislaus Netzel (1914-1990)." Find a Grave, 30 Sept. 2020,

John Kedzierski was born in the closing months of the Great War, April 27, 1918, to Joseph and Anna Kedzierski.[241] Growing up in Buffalo he would marry Stella before joining the Army. Shortly after deploying, Stella welcomed their daughter Christine, while John reached the rank of staff sergeant before being discharged in 1946.[242]

Following the war, John found work in a grocery warehouse and soon joined Chopins.[243] Singing as a second bass he started just in time to take part in the Society's large 50th annual concert.[244] Kedzierski demonstrated a particular devotion to the singers, working on the annual concert and making sure everyone fit into their wardrobe. In 1953 he was first elected to the board as a director,[245] and then in 1955 as vice president.[246] Following Lemanski's last term as president in 1959, Kedzierski garnered enough support to be elected president.

While he was president for only two years, John oversaw the production that would usher in a new era for the choir, *A Festival of Folk Songs and Dance*. The performance would become the prototype for the extravagant and entertaining programs the Society would put on for the next quarter century. Kedzierski also had the foresight to put Theodore V. Mikoll in charge of 1961's *The Many Faces of Poland*, giving the young lawyer another feather in his cap,[247] and helping him reach the presidency the next year.

After his presidential win in early 1962 a grateful Mikoll presented Kedzierski a plaque on behalf of the entire Society.[248] John would stay on the board of the group for the first few years of Mikoll's tenure,[249] but stepped away from the board completely by 1966. Kedzierski would visit the Society again in 1974, this time for a group photo of all the surviving presidents, including his brother Casimer, as part of the diamond jubilee celebration.[250]

After decades of working, John and Stella finally retired. Wanting to live closer to their daughter in Florida, the couple moved

---

241 "Kedzierski - Anna F." *Buffalo Evening News*, 20 Sept. 1954, p. 25.

242 "Discharged From Service." *Buffalo Evening News*, 7 Sept. 1946, p. 7.

243 "United States 1950 Census," Entry for John A Kedzierski and Stella Kedzierski, 10 April 1950.

244 The Chopin Singing Society. *50th Annual Concert*. Chopin Singing Society, 1949.

245 "Singing Society Head Re-Elected." *Buffalo Courier-Express*, 22 Dec. 1952, p. 26.

246 The Chopin Singing Society. *56th Annual Concert*. Chopin Singing Society, 1955.

247 "Concert To Show 'Faces of Poland'." *Buffalo Evening News*, 19 Jan. 1961, p. 32.

248 "Zimmer Cites Role of Songs in Poland." *Buffalo Evening News*, 12 Feb. 1962, p. 18.

249 "Relate Truth About Reds, Keating Asks." *Buffalo Courier-Express*, 16 Feb. 1964, pp. 11-A.

250 *Chopin Singing Society 75th Anniversary, 1899-1974*. The Society, 1974.

to Sarasota in the mid-1980s. On January 21, 1999, John A. Kedzierski passed away, with Stella passing ten years later.[251]

22. Theodore V. Mikoll (Thaddeus V. Mikolajczak) (1962-1968, 1971, 1973-1987)

Not since Boleslaus Michalski and the founding of the Chopin Singing Society was there a president of the organization as important as Theodore V. Mikoll. With his grandfather and uncle having already served as president of the singers, Ted was practically royalty within Chopins. But instead of trying to repeat what had been successful for the previous generation, Mikoll and his wife Ann forged a new path for the singers that would see the Society thrive well into the next century.

Thaddeus was born August 24, 1928, to Frances and Vincent Mikolajczak of Stanislaus Street in Buffalo's East Side. Married a year earlier, both Vincent's and Frances's family had been involved with Chopins for years. Thaddeus's uncle John had been president shortly after the First World War, and his grandfather Albert was the sitting president at his birth.[252] Chopins was even an important part of his parents' wedding as the clubrooms hosted the reception following their ring ceremony at Transfiguration Church.[253]

As a child, Ted along with his younger brother James would often be dragged to the singers' headquarters, either accompanying their mother to prepare for a women's auxiliary card party or to fete President Krysztafkiewicz.[254] As he grew, Thaddeus's father opened a butcher shop in the Broadway Market and helped Widzinski incorporate his construction business,[255] while his mother became active in Kolko Polek Charity Organization.[256] The brothers first attended Transfiguration School before graduating from East High School.

In September of 1948, Vincent V. Mikolajczak was tragically swept away by the Niagara River, widowing Frances, and leaving

---

251 "John A. Kedzierski." *Sarasota Herald-Tribune*, 23 Jan. 1999, p. 5B.; "Stella T. Kedzierski." *Sarasota Herald-Tribune*, 22 Apr. 2009.

252 *Chopin Singing Society 75th Anniversary, 1899-1974*. The Society, 1974.

253 "Dzis Zaslubiny - Widzinski-Mikolajczak." *Dziennik Dla Wszystkich*, 15 Aug. 1927, p. 5.

254 "Chopin Singing Society to Hold Party Sunday." *Buffalo Evening News*, 28 Mar. 1930, p. 35.; "Chopin Society Plans Banquet." *Buffalo Courier-Express*, 17 Dec. 1936, p. 11.

255 "Five Buffalo Concerns Are Incorporated." *Buffalo Courier-Express*, 15 June 1930, p. 2.

256 "Kolko Polek Christmas Fete to Aid Charity." *Buffalo Courier-Express*, 22 Nov. 1945, p. 33.

Thaddeus and James fatherless.[257] With the loss of Vincent, Frances and James moved back to her parents' home as Ted went to Olean to attend St. Bonaventure University. It would be as a student at the School of Arts & Science that Thaddeus Mikolajczak began going by Theodore Mikoll.[258] While in Olean, Ted would travel back to Buffalo to take part in the East Side's active social scene. It would be on one of these excursions that Mikoll was reintroduced to a girl from his youth, the young Miss Ann T. Skulicz at a dance at Dom Polski Hall.[259]

Ted and Ann's romance would be put on hold as Mikoll joined the U.S. Marine Corps and was sent to North Carolina for training. With a lieutenant's commission, he was sent to Cherry Point as an adjutant and legal officer. It would be from this position that Ted's love for the law would grow.[260]

In 1954, Mikoll left the Marines, and that September, entered the University of Buffalo's School of Law. One month later Ted professed his love to Ann in front of their friends and family at a High Nuptial Mass in St. Stanislaus Bishop & Martyr Church.[261]

Needing to earn some money while both he and Ann were at university, Ted often considered becoming a professional piano player. His skill at the instrument would allow him to be a session musician from jazz to rock and roll, classical to polka. However, his wife advised him to stay focused on the law. As their budget tightened, Ted decided that he would attend classes in the morning and find a company that would let him work in the afternoon and evenings. The company he ended up with was ACF Industries, where he had to troubleshoot production control in the company's top-secret atomic energy division.[262]

Theodore parted ways with ACF so he could work on his wife's 1957 election for Associate City Judge for Buffalo.[263] With her

---

[257] "Victim of Falls Is Identified as Buffalo Man." *Buffalo Courier-Express*, 29 Sept. 1948, p. 13.

[258] "Eight-Buffalo Area Students on St. Bonaventure List." *Buffalo Evening News*, 1 Apr. 1950, p. 7.

[259] Smith, H. Katherine. "Judge Ann Mikoll's Husband Preps for Bar Exam." *Buffalo Courier-Express*, 9 Feb. 1958, pp. 15-A.

[260] "Commendation Ribbon Is Won by Buffalo Artilleryman." *Buffalo Evening News*, 6 Feb. 1953, p. 17.

[261] "Mikoll-Skulicz." *Buffalo Evening News*, 26 Nov. 1954, p. 44.

[262] Smith, H. Katherine. "Judge Ann Mikoll's Husband Preps for Bar Exam." *Buffalo Courier-Express*, 9 Feb. 1958, pp. 15-A.

[263] "Young Woman Judge Greeted at City Court." *Buffalo Courier-Express*, 12 Sept. 1957, p. 9.

victory and placement on the bench, Ted took over the day-to-day necessities of running the home when he wasn't at school. He could be found shopping at Sattler's or over at the Broadway Market scrutinizing the cuts of meat, and being jokingly referred to as "His Honor" by friends and acquaintances. Taking it in stride with those close to him, Ted was far more firm with the media when they tried to make light of the situation, stating, "[b]eing married to the judge is worth all the responsibility and ribbing. My pride in her achievement compensates for any of these minor inconveniences."

When not attending school, taking care of the home, or being active in Polonia, Ted and Ann could be found at Bisons baseball games, and basketball and football games from their alma maters. On his own, Ted took an interest in golf and proved to be a natural on the links. Within the first few years of picking up a club, Mikoll won his first tournament at the Port Colborne Country Club.[264]

Finishing law school, Ted found himself with a little more free time. After talking with his brother and some old friends and still having a warm spot for the aging singers, Ted joined the Chopin Singing Society in time for their 1958 annual concert.[265] As a second tenor the young "Thaddeus" was appreciated by the old guard that watched him grow up and respected by the younger members who saw what he had already accomplished in life. In the next year, Mikoll was elected to the board of directors and his brother James joined the singers as a bass.

In his professional life, Mikoll opened his own private practice specializing in business, estate, and real estate law, in his grandfather's old home on Walden. Otherwise, Ted was a member of several organizations including the Adam Plewacki Post where he was chairman of the constitution and by-laws committee, the Hank Nowak Post, and an active member of the Polish Falcons.[266]

At Chopins, the Society was heading to its last legs with Boleslaus Lemanski as president and less than twenty singers in the ranks. To try and turn the page, John Kedzierski was elected president in 1960 and with it a new generation took the reins of the singers. This would be the beginning of the three-year transformation from an old men's society to a thriving youthful organization.

---

264 Smith, H. Katherine. "Judge Ann Mikoll's Husband Preps for Bar Exam." *Buffalo Courier-Express*, 9 Feb. 1958, pp. 15-A.
265 The Chopin Singing Society. *59th Annual Concert*. Chopin Singing Society, 1958.
266 Kay, Denis. "Personality Profile." *Am-Pol Eagle*, 25 Apr. 1974, p. 13.

First would come the all singing, all dancing *Festival of Folk Songs and Dances* in the fall of 1960 and then the *Many Faces of Poland* production the next year. In 1962, the change would be complete with the election of Theodore V. Mikoll to the presidency of the Chopin Singing Society.

Young, sociable, energetic, and free from the responsibility of children, the Mikolls put their hearts and souls into Chopin. They would give birth to the modern American Dyngus Day, a daylong festival of food, drink, and polka music. Their social standing in not just Polonia, but Buffalo, New York State, and national politics made the Chopin clubrooms a place to see and be seen. Ted's passion for nurturing the next generation of musicians would take physical form when he launched the Chopin Society Young Pianists Competition. For the better part of a quarter century Thaddeus Mikolajczak would lead Chopins to a greater prosperity and cultural significance than his uncle, his grandfather, Boleslaus Michalski, or even maestro Leon Olszewski could have imagined.

Beyond Chopins, Mikoll's star would rise in other public and social organizations. By 1965 he was the national president of the National Advocates Society, an organization of Polish American lawyers,[267] and was serving on the board of the Professional & Businessmen's Association, Polonia's leading Chamber of Commerce.[268] Three years later he would be an organizer and serve as counsel to the Buffalo Broadway Market Merchants Corporation. This new organization would lease the market from the city and rent it out to the merchants, giving them more control of the market's operation, free the city from the ongoing maintenance of the building, and resolve some of the ongoing issues around the parking ramp.[269] He would shortly thereafter be appointed to the Buffalo Sewer Authority,[270] a department he would be a part of for the next quarter century.

During the 1970s, Buffalo Mayor Stanley Makowski tapped Ted to be chairman of the Buffalo-Rzeszow Sister City Committee. The group achieved its goal of uniting the two metropolitans in 1975 when the cities signed a pact during a Chopin tour of Poland.[271] That

---

[267] "Two Groups Plan for Convention." *Buffalo Evening News*, 18 Jan. 1963, p. 21.

[268] "Amvets to Install." *Buffalo Courier-Express*, 15 Apr. 1965, p. 21.

[269] "Tenants Offer to Lease Mart." *Buffalo Courier-Express*, 25 Mar. 1969, p. 15.

[270] "Lawless Almost Says He'll Run." *Buffalo Courier-Express*, 31 Jan. 1970, p. 28.

[271] Witerski, David S. "Audiences Stirred on Chopin Singers Tour, Mayor Says." *Buffalo Courier-Express*, 6 June 1975, p. 1.

decade Mikoll also became one of St. Joseph Hospital Ambassadors serving as the chairman of the debutantes' ball and raising hundreds of thousands of dollars.[272]

After multiple trips to Poland, two albums, and two score Dyngus Days, Ted Mikoll stood down as president of the Chopin Singing Society in 1987. Two years later the Society conferred the title of Honorary President upon Ted, a title he held for the rest of his life. This would be but one of many accolades that Ted would receive for his many contributions to Western New York. The Am-Pol Eagle awarded him their "Man of the Year" award twice, with both the Professional and Businessmen's Association and the Polish Arts Club bestowing similar honors. Hilbert College presented Mikoll their President's Medal, and Chopins even gifted Ted a commissioned portrait early in his presidency.[273]

On July 7, 1994, Mikoll passed away in his Depew home. Days later, hundreds of mourners, including Erie County Executive Dennis Gorski, Congressman Jack Quinn, and former Congressmen Henry Nowak, packed St. Stanislaus Church to pay their respects to Theodore. Serving as pallbearers were Adam Malik, Walter Kaminski, Stan Zagora, John Zabinski, Max Czamecki, and Richard Jezuit, all officers and directors of the Society. The full choir, under the direction of Dr. Witakowski, sang the funeral Mass, while radio star Stanley Jasinski and Sue Wardynski, the former chairwoman of the Chopin Society Young Pianists Competition, eulogized their friend in Polish and English, respectively.[274]

Following his interment, Mikoll's memory was kept alive by both his widow and the Society. The singers dedicated many programs in honor of Mikoll, and the larger community recognized Ted's contributions to Polonia by dedicating the 1997 production of *The Haunted Manor* to him.[275] Some of the proceeds from the opera went towards the establishment of the Theodore V. Mikoll Memorial Fund. Administered by the Kosciuszko Foundation, the fund supported the education of students of vocal and choral performance.[276]

---

[272] "Ambassadors Complete $100,000 Hospital Pledge." *Buffalo Courier-Express*, 17 Mar. 1971, p. 25.

[273] "Mikoll Receives Self-Portrait at Chopin Singing Society's Installation." *Am-Pol Eagle*, 14 Feb. 1963, p. 1.

[274] "Ted Mikoll, a Leader in Polonia, Dies." *Am-Pol Eagle*, 14 July 1994, p. 15.

[275] *Straszny Dwor*. Greater Buffalo Opera Company, 1997.

[276] Trotter, Herman. "An Opera That Sings the Praises of Polish Patriotism." *Buffalo News*, 16 Sept. 1997.

23. Stanley H. Zagora (1969)

With Ted Mikoll stepping back from the presidency of Chopins, other members stepped up to lead the Society. The first of the three men who oversaw the singers from the 1960s and into the 70s was treasurer and longtime board member Stanley H. Zagora.

Born in Buffalo's Broadway-Fillmore neighborhood on September 25, 1924, to Stanley and Estelle Zagora, Stan Jr. spent much of his early life stomping around Buffalo's far East Side. Attending St. Luke, School 44, and School 58, Zagora's free time was taken up by working at the Modern Auto and Home Supply, a store run by his mother's side of the family. He attended Hutchinson-Central High School until age 16 when he dropped out to work full-time at the Jankowiak family-owned shop. In October of 1950 Stan married his love, Miss Grace Petti.[277]

Wanting to support his family, Zagora was ready to strike out on his own and took a job selling advertising for the Polish daily newspaper Dziennik Dla Wszystkich. After a couple years, he switched careers and became an insurance broker with Prudential.[278] While he was job hopping, Zagora was slowly building up an impressive political resume. Making a name for himself in the Democratic circles in the East Side, Stan announced in the spring of 1952 that he would seek the Democratic nomination for the Assembly in the Fifth District.[279] While his first attempt at public office didn't succeed, Stan tried again, this time as the candidate for the Tenth Ward Supervisor. Even though he garnered the support of the Young Democrats of Western New York,[280] Stan didn't secure the Democratic nomination, but the Liberal Party chose to provide Stan a platform.[281] When election night came, Stan fell short by a scant 14 points. Undeterred, Zagora took another bite of the apple two years later in the 1957 election for the Tenth Ward, this time losing by a single vote to Vincent J. Cegielski.[282]

In 1959 Stan made another run for the Tenth Ward, now as an

---

277 "50th Celebrated at Salvatore's." *The Lancaster/Depew Bee,* 9 Nov. 2000, p. 11.

278 "Supervisor, Tenth Ward - Liberal." *Buffalo Evening News*, 30 Oct. 1957, p. 67.

279 "Two Men Announce Intention to Seek Office." *Buffalo Courier-Express*, 28 May 1952, p. 17.

280 "Young Democrats Endorse Slate." *Buffalo Courier-Express*, 12 Apr. 1953, p. 17.

281 Meddoff, Jack. "Liberals Predict Sufficient Votes to Swing Election." *Buffalo Evening News*, 11 July 1953, p. 7.

282 "Zagora Granted Order for Tenth Ward Re-Count." *Buffalo Evening News*, 20 Sept. 1957, p. 30.

employee of Buffalo's Law Department, only to lose once again to Daniel A. Buczynski.[283] Looking to shore up support and have a new social outlet, Zagora joined Chopins as a bass singer in early 1960.[284] Over the next decade he sat on the publicity and ticketing committees, then was elected to the board,[285] later as treasurer, before ascending to the presidency.[286]

In 1965 Buczynski stepped down from the Erie County Board of Supervisors and the Buffalo Common Council selected Zagora as his replacement.[287] On the board, Zagora sat on the Public Protection, Public Works, Municipal Relations, Health and Sanitation, and Library committees,[288] the last one being a proper fit considering he worked on having the new Broadway branch library named after Dr. Francis E. Fronczak in 1964.[289] On January 1, 1968, the Erie County Board of Supervisors became the Erie County Legislature and Zagora was amongst the inaugural class of twenty to be sworn in, representing District 5.[290] In time Stan would rise up in the legislature, becoming chairman of the Budget Committee, then the majority leader, and finally in the early 1980s, chairman.

While working for the City of Buffalo for most of his later career, Zagora did take the position of Erie County Commissioner of Personnel under County Executive Edward J. Rutkowski. Outside of work, Stan was a member of the board of directors of the Buffalo Philharmonic Orchestra, Albright-Knox Art Gallery, the Buffalo & Erie County Public Library, and many other organizations.

In his retirement, Stan traveled but slowed down after he lost his wife Grace in 2004. On March 14, 2014, Stanley H. Zagora passed away after a brief illness.

24. Casimer J. Kedzierski (1970)

Born March 14, 1920, Casimer was just old enough to join the U.S. Army Air Corps at the outbreak of World War II. Following his

---

283 "To Oppose Buczynski." *Buffalo Evening News*, 3 Aug. 1959, p. 19.
284 The Chopin Singing Society. *61st Annual Concert*. Chopin Singing Society, 1960.
285 *Frederick Chopin Singing Society, Inc - Chopin Installation Banquet*. The Chopin Singing Society, 1963.
286 *Frederick Chopin Singing Society Annual Installation Banquet, Saturday March 22, 1969*. The Chopin Singing Society, 1969
287 "Zagora Picked for Board Seat." *Tonawanda News*, 4 Feb. 1965, p. 14.
288 "Three Seek District 5 Seat." *Buffalo Courier-Express*, 12 Oct. 1967, p. 8.
289 "Proposal For Library Name Made." *Buffalo Courier-Express*, 21 Nov. 1964, p. 23.
290 Askew, Peter. "County Legislators Sworn In, Officially Tap Leaders Today." *Buffalo Courier-Express*, 2 Jan. 1968, p. 15.

discharge from the conflict, Kedzierski wed Ms. Loretta Burzinski at St. Bernard Catholic Church in Buffalo on July 14, 1945.

Working at a couple of mills around Buffalo and Lackawanna, Casimer eventually found a position with Bethlehem Steel, rising through the ranks to become an inspector. With steady employment, the Kedzierskis moved out to Elma to raise their family.

Following his brother John, Casimer joined Chopins as a first tenor in 1955.[291] Like much of the rest of the membership, Kedzierski worked hard to bring the annual concert to fruition serving on several subcommittees.[292] In 1958 under President Reverend Joseph J. Winnicki, Casimer was elected to the Board as the treasurer.[293] As the old guard made way for the new generation, Kedzierski would be instrumental in this transition. He was recording secretary, when John Kedzierski became president and launched the *Festival of Folk Songs and Dances* at the dawn of Chopins' second golden age.[294] Once Ted Mikoll had ascended to the presidency, Casimer worked with Ann Mikoll to make sure *Springtime in Poland* was a sold-out event, even going so far as to appear on the cover of the *Buffalo Evening News Magazine* in the orange, green, and yellow folk costume of the Lowicz region.[295]

Under Mikoll's leadership, Casimer was active on the board as a director and secretary.[296] After Stanley Zagora's single term as president, Casimer was elected to the post in 1970.[297] Kedzierski's term was a light one, with a handful of concerts, sporadic social events, and a few parties. After his year as their leader, Casimer returned to his seat on the board as a director, a position he held until the early 1980s.[298]

In their retirement, Casimer and Loretta moved to Ohio to be closer to family. Casimer J. Kedzierski passed away on March 3, 2016, with Loretta joining him a year later.[299]

---

[291] The Chopin Singing Society. *56th Annual Concert*. Chopin Singing Society, 1955.
[292] The Chopin Singing Society. *58th Annual Concert*. Chopin Singing Society, 1957.
[293] The Chopin Singing Society. *59th Annual Concert*. Chopin Singing Society, 1958.
[294] The Chopin Singing Society. *61st Annual Concert*. Chopin Singing Society, 1960.
[295] Williams, Bob. "Chopin Society—Their Songs Come from the Heart." *Buffalo Evening News Magazine*, 28 Apr. 1962, p. 1.
[296] "Chopin Society Installs Mikoll." *Buffalo Courier-Express*, 13 Mar. 1966, pp. 11-B.; "Singing Society Dinner Saturday." *Buffalo Evening News*, 6 Feb. 1963, p. 44.
[297] *Chopin Singing Society 75th Anniversary, 1899-1974*. The Society, 1974.
[298] The Chopin Singing Society. *74th Annual Concert*. Chopin Singing Society, 1973.; The Chopin Singing Society. *81st Anniversary Concert*. Chopin Singing Society, 1980.
[299] "Kedzierski, Casimer J." *Buffalo News*, 6 Mar. 2016.

25. Raymond W. Manuszewski (1972)

In the handful of years between Ted Mikoll's two major tenures as president of Chopins, bank executive Raymond Manuszewski was the last of three presidents who held the position for a single year.

The oldest son of Alois and Pearl, Raymond W. Manuszewski was born on January 24, 1925. Growing up in Kaisertown, Ray attended local schools and demonstrated he was a bright child. In his youth, he took up the accordion to much local acclaim and when it came time for him to attend high school, he chose the Roman Catholic Canisius High.[300] Graduating shortly after the U.S. entered the Second World War, Ray joined the Navy where he was assigned to the Marine Corps in the Pacific Theater.

Returning from the war, Ray enrolled at Canisius College and in the fall of 1949 married Ms. Lorraine Kleister.[301] Finishing college, Manuszewski began his long banking career with a management training program at Marine Trust Co. and a placement in the Lovejoy branch. With his understanding of the Polish community, Manuszewski was soon sent to the Broadway Market branch of the bank as an assistant manager and was promoted to manager in 1959.[302] By the mid-1960s the bank became the Marine Midland Trust Company of Western New York and Ray was the regional supervisor of the firm.[303]

As Manuszewski secured his regional position he ingrained himself into the Broadway-Fillmore community. He was a director of the Professional and Businessmen's Association, the treasurer of the Broadway-Fillmore Association, a committee chairman of the Father Justin's Drivers,[304] and by 1971, the financial chairman of Chopins.[305]

Manuszewski's quick ascent in the Society was due to his endless energy and his close association with fellow Professional and Businessmen's Association member Ted Mikoll.[306] It was on the links

---

300 "Accordion Concert Honors Won by Boy." *Buffalo Evening News*, 12 May 1939, p. 32.
301 "Manuszewski-Kleister." *Buffalo Evening News*, 28 Sept. 1949, p. 59.
302 "Appointed by Marine Trust Co." *Buffalo Evening News*, 8 Dec. 1959, p. 45.
303 "Marine Midland Trust Lists Two Promotions." *Buffalo Courier-Express*, 18 Nov. 1965, p. 29.
304 "Marine Trust Announce New Appointments." *Wyoming County Times*, 7 Jan. 1965, pp. 1–2.
305 The Chopin Singing Society. *Annual Installation Banquet Frederick Chopin Singing Society 1899-1971*. The Chopin Singing Society, 1971. Chapter 8
306 "Mikoll Honored." *Buffalo Courier-Express*, 12 Jan. 1969, p. 21.

of the Lancaster Country Club that Mikoll prodded his golfing partner Manuszewski to run for Chopin's presidency and in 1972, Ray ran for and won the position.[307]

During his year as president, Manuszewski was successful in relaunching the annual concerts,[308] saw that the piano competition was moved to earlier in the year and hosted the 10th annual Dyngus Day party.[309] Still active following his term, Manuszewski was the Society's treasurer during its 1974 diamond jubilee, but by the nation's bicentennial, Ray chose to step down from the board.

It's not surprising that Ray had to step away from much of his volunteer work as his responsibilities as work mounted. In 1971 he was placed in charge of loan administration in Branch Departments Administration and by 1973 oversaw Marine Midland's downtown Buffalo operations.[310] While his duties only grew when he was named chairman of the Manufacturers Hanover Corp's Western New York operations,[311] Manuszewski still made time to hit the links with his friend Ted at local golf tournaments.[312]

After settling into his new job, Ray made time to join the Canisius College Board of Regents, joining real estate developer William H. Pearce and insurance executive Harrison R. Naylor.[313] In time he would be elected president of the board of trustees of St. Joseph's Hospital, serve on the President's Council of Villa Maria College, and helm the Buffalo Niagara Industrial Development Corporation.[314]

In the Polish community, Manuszewski teamed up with Assemblyman Dennis Gorski, St. Stanislaus Church, and Daniel Kij, president of the Polish Union of America in Buffalo, to promote the wearing of red ribbons during Christmas of 1981 to show Buffalo's support of the Solidarity movement in Poland. The ribbons representing the Polish flag, the Solidarity union, and the Christmas season, were given away for free to "demonstrate…empathy for the Poles

---

[307] Jankowski, Mike. "Manuszewski Duo Posts 61 for Lead." *Buffalo Courier-Express*, 20 Aug. 1971, p. 19.

[308] Putnam, Tom. "Chopin Society to Present Program." *Buffalo Courier-Express*, 19 Mar. 1972, p. 6.

[309] *Chopin Singing Society 75th Anniversary, 1899-1974*. The Society, 1974.

[310] "Marine Bank Names Aide." *Buffalo Courier-Express*, 21 Jan. 1973, p. 27.

[311] Callahan, William F. "Bank Helm Seen for Manuszewski." *Buffalo Courier-Express*, 21 Sept. 1974, p. 7.

[312] "Simonin Duo Takes Golf Lead." *Buffalo Courier-Express*, 10 Aug. 1974, p. 21.

[313] "Board Members Announced." *Buffalo Courier-Express*, 25 Sept. 1976, p. 3.

[314] "Bank Chief Gets Helm at Hospital." *Buffalo Courier-Express*, 4 Mar. 1979, pp. C-8.

during this tense situation."[315]

After retiring from banking, Ray joined Freed Maxick Sachs & Murphy where he chaired the Financing and Credit Consultation Group. He was able to spend more time volunteering for many of the organizations he was a part of, while spending time with his daughter's family. In 2014 Manuszewski moved to North Carolina, passing away on June 26, 2016.[316]

26. Richard J. Jezuit Sr. (1988-2000)

Born in Buffalo, Richard was the oldest son of Agatha and John Jezuit. Growing up in the Babcock neighborhood, Jezuit attended and graduated from South Park High School.[317] With the bombing of Pearl Harbor Richard joined the U.S. Navy and saw action in Africa, Sicily, Italy, and the Caribbean. Following the global conflict, Jezuit stayed on and took part in the Korean War.

Following his service, he attended the University of Tennessee and received a bachelor's in accounting. With diploma in hand, Jezuit returned in Western New York finding work at a number of firms including, Curtiss-Wright, Twin Industries, and American Standard. In 1953 he married Miss Alice B. Mazikowski at St. Luke's parish, with the couple eventually settling down in Cheektowaga to raise three daughters and a son.[318] In his free time, Jezuit was an avid outdoorsman and enjoyed traveling.

It would be through his wife and the long-time members of the Mazikowski family that Jezuit joined Chopins in early 1961. First as a singer, Richard was selected to serve as the buffet secretary and in 1962 was elected vice president.[319] Through the 1960s and '70s Jezuit handled much of the financial side of the Society serving as treasurer and in 1972 helped get Chopin's bingo program off the ground, a venture he would oversee for the next quarter century.

Following the retirement of longtime president Ted Mikoll in 1987, Jezuit was elected president of the singers when longtime vice president David Rutecki decided not to run.[320] Over the next 12 years Rich led the group through both easy times and through the loss of the

---

315 "Red Ribbons for Poland." *Buffalo Courier-Express*, 16 Dec. 1981, p. 1.

316 "Raymond W. Manuszewski, Retired Bank Executive Jun 28, 2016." *Buffalo News*, 28 June 2016.

317 "Richard J. Jezuit Sr., Singing Society Leader." *Buffalo News*, 1 Sept. 2002.

318 "Venice Lace Trims Bride's Satin Gown." *Buffalo Courier-Express*, 30 Nov. 1953, p. 10.

319 "Vice President Jezuit A Man of Diligence." *Chopin Staff*, Apr. 1966, p. 2.

320 The Chopin Singing Society. *88th Annual Concert*. Chopin Singing Society, 1987.

singers' longtime leader Theodore V. Mikoll. At his retirement in 1999 Jezuit was asked what he felt were his greatest accomplishments as president, to which he replied that taking "first place as best all round choir and best mixed chorus in the Polish Singers Alliance of America's International Choral Competition in 1989 and its performance in St. Patrick's Cathedral of Moniuszko's 'Litany of Our Lady of Ostrobrama' hailed by the New York Times' music critic as 'impressive.'"[321]

Besides his activities with Chopin, Richard was active at Adam Plewacki Post and the Father Justin Council, Knights of Columbus. On August 30, 2002, Richard J. Jezuit Sr. passed away after a long illness.[322]

27. Ann T. Mikoll (Mikolajczak) (2000-2016)

In the second half of the twentieth century no one from Western New York's Polonia reached greater heights than Ann T. Mikoll. From becoming one of the first women to serve as a City of Buffalo Judge and sitting on the bench of the New York State's Supreme Court, to helping to revive the Chopin Singing Society and birthing the modern American Dyngus Day, Mikoll's influence on Polish America will be felt for generations. After a lifetime of dedication to her community, one of her last acts of public service was as the 24th president of the Chopin Singing Society.

Ann was born to Victoria and William J. Skulicz in the early days of America's Great Depression and was one of six children. To support their large family of eight, both Victoria and William were bread winners. William worked as a linotypist for the *Telegram* and the *Everybody's Daily* newspapers,[323] the former Victoria Filar embraced her entrepreneurial spirit and operated several grocery stores throughout the East Side.[324]

In her youth Ann proved to possess both brains and brawn. As a student at St. Stanislaus School and a member of Polish Falcons Nest 6, Skulicz garnered accolades in track and field,[325] basketball,[326] swim,

---

[321] The Chopin Singing Society. *Centennial Concert*. Chopin Singing Society, 1999.
[322] "Richard J. Jezuit Sr. Dies." *Am-Pol Eagle*, 5 Sept. 2002, p. 1.
[323] "W.J. Skulicz, Printer Here, Dies at 75." *Buffalo Courier-Express*, 29 Jan. 1965, p. 9.
[324] "Mrs. William J. Skulicz." *Buffalo Courier-Express*, 17 Aug. 1963, p. 8.
[325] "Defending Champs Retain P.S.A.A. Track Titles; Two Records Set, Three Tied." *Buffalo Courier-Express*, 2 Mar. 1940, p. 18.
[326] "Blue Banner Girls Down Falcons, 44-6." *Buffalo Evening News*, 19 Nov. 1947, p. 48.

and tennis.[327] In school her academic prowess was unmatched. At Immaculate Heart of Mary Academy, Ann was a four-year honor roll student, fluent in French, English, and Polish, the champion of the American Legion elocution contest, and was the only student to receive a perfect score on the New York State Regents exam for American History.[328] When she wasn't in school or on the field, Ms. Skulicz could be found volunteering at Nest 6. She was on the Falcon Festival Day committee,[329] led the dance troop,[330] represented the Nest at the 1948 National Falcon's convention,[331] and at the ripe old age of 18 worked as the women's physical instructor.

It surprised no one that when she finished at Immaculate Heart, Ann enrolled at the University at Buffalo, eventually joining the Law School. In college, Skulicz artfully balanced her studies with social obligations. While never missing an assignment, Ann took part in the school clubs and was even able to serve as one of the hostesses at Dean Jacob D. Hyman's welcome party.[332] It would also be during her school days that Ann became reacquainted with Thaddeus V. Mikolajczak at a Dom Polski dance. The two, smitten with each other, began dating.

Upon her graduation The Counselors, the women lawyers organization of Buffalo and Western New York, feted both of UB's female graduates of 1954, Ann T. Skulicz and Sally E. Peard.[333] In November Ann passed her exam and was admitted to practice law the following March.[334] Between the two events, Ted and Ann were married at St. Stanislaus church.[335]

Now with a young husband to support, Ann joined the City of Buffalo's Law Department as a foreclosure attorney. She wouldn't be in the position long as by the end of 1956 she would be promoted to

---

327 "Franczyks Seek Sweep of Polish Net Titles." *Buffalo Evening News*, 23 July 1948, p. 25.
328 Kowalewski, Ed. "Blonde Instructor of Falcons Has Beauty, Brains and Brawn." *Buffalo Evening News*, 31 Aug. 1948.
329 "Falcons to Hold Annual Festival." *Buffalo Courier-Express*, 12 July 1947.
330 "10,000 Jam Buffalo Version of Ancient Polish Country Fair Third Annual Jarmark Ten Times as Large as Last Year's." *Buffalo Evening News*, 26 Nov. 1951.
331 "600 To Make Excursion to Falcons' Convention." *Buffalo Courier-Express*, 19 July 1948, p. 6.
332 "Reception Honors Dean, Mrs. Hyman." *Buffalo Evening News*, 30 Apr. 1953, p. 42.
333 "Counselors Will Honor Graduates." *Buffalo Evening News*, 22 May 1954, p. 4.
334 "19 Law Students of Buffalo, Area Pass Bar Exams." *Buffalo Evening News*, 30 Dec. 1954, p. 17.
335 "Mikoll-Skulicz." *Buffalo Evening News*, 26 Nov. 1954, p. 44.

Assistant Corporation Counsel.[336]

On Thursday August 29, 1957, City Court Judge Frank A. Sedita announced he would retire from the bench to run for mayor of Buffalo. Upon hearing the news, Mayor Steven Pankow announced that he would select Ann T. Mikoll as Sedita's replacement and a firestorm quickly ensued. By Saturday the Directors of the Bar Association of Erie County unanimously adopted a report declaring that Mikoll was "not qualified" for the bench, while legal experts agreed that there was no way to block the appointment which fell under the authority of the mayor.[337] While the ink was still wet on the Bar's report, the East Buffalo Democratic Junior League issued an endorsement for Ann citing the "approximately 1,500 to 1,750 cases" she had tried over the previous two years.[338] Regardless of what the parties and political observers wanted, Pankow stood by his selection and on September 1, 1957, Ann T. Mikoll became Judge Mikoll to much fanfare at both City Hall and in Buffalo's Polonia.[339] Her selection even reached national attention on October 20, 1957 when she appeared on the CBS game show *What's My Line?* where publisher Bennett Cerf was able to figure out Ann was a "lady judge."[340]

As soon as Mikoll was on the bench, pundits were already saying her tenure would be short. When Sedita stepped down, he only had four months left on his term, meaning Mikoll would have to run in November for the 10-year term if she wanted to keep her job. While the Democrats endorsed Poles Michael E. Zimmer and Mikoll,[341] the Republicans saw Ann as an easy target. To unseat Mikoll the Republicans put up two strong candidates,[342] played up her "lack of qualifications," and tried to portray her as a "little girl" as best they could,[343] because who is going to vote for a little girl? On the morning of November 6,

---

[336] "Three Changes Announced in City Law Dept." *Buffalo Courier-Express*, 18 Nov. 1956, pp. 4-B.

[337] Borelli, George. "Bar Assn. Raps Mikoll Appointment." *Buffalo Courier-Express*, 31 Apr. 1957, pp. 1–2.

[338] "Junior League Endorses Mrs. Mikoll for Bench." *Buffalo Courier-Express*, 1 Sept. 1957, pp. 2-B.

[339] "Mrs. Mikoll Will Take City Court Oath Today." *Buffalo Courier-Express*, 7 Sept. 1957, p. 24.

[340] "Episode 42." *What's My Line?,* season 8, episode 48, CBS, 20 Oct. 1957.

[341] "Judge Mikoll Is Endorsed for a Full Ten-Year Term." *Buffalo Evening News*, 24 Sept. 1957, p. 36.

[342] "Sketches of Candidates." *Buffalo Evening News*, 31 Oct. 1957, p. 39.

[343] Meddoff, Jack. "Capitol Club Has a Field Day With 60 Votes That Got Away." *Buffalo Evening News*, 12 Dec. 1957, p. 45.

they got their answer when Mikoll earned 80,760 votes, beating her closest Republican rival by almost 5,000 votes,[344] and taking 80% of the Polish electorate.[345]

This would be the first step in an illustrious and celebrated legal career for Judge Ann Mikoll. She would win her 1967 reelection before trying for a seat on the Supreme Court of the State of New York, which she secured in 1971. This would make her the first woman outside New York City to sit on the Court. In 1977 she was duly appointed to the Appellate Division, Third Department, making her the first woman to hold that position as well.[346] Mikoll later sat on the State Commission on Judicial Conduct before retiring in 1999.[347]

In the years following her first election to the Buffalo Judgeship, Ann and Ted joined the Chopin Singing Society. With her husband as president, Ann was instrumental in revitalizing the Society into a singing and dancing cultural institution, incorporating the members of the Immaculate Heart of Mary Academy choir into Chopins, and creating the modern American Dyngus Day. She would be at the forefront of the Society's tours of Poland, the recording of their albums, and raising the status of the group on the regional and national stage. For the better part of a half century, the judge had a hand in every accomplishment the choir had. In the years following the death of her husband Ted, Ann eventually took over the presidency, guiding it for nearly twenty years, slowing down only when age caught up with the eternally energetic woman.

The awards and accolades the judge earned in her lifetime are many and include one from about every major Polish American and legal organization in New York State. While she has received much, her greatest gift has been the American style Dyngus Day, with ample food, drink, and polka music, which is now celebrated in every corner of North America. Since stepping down in 2016 Mikoll has settled into retirement making the occasional social appearance, but never missing a Chopin's Dyngus Day party.

28. Gary A. Bienkowski (2016-Present)

---

344 "Election Results." *Buffalo Evening News*, 6 Nov. 1957, p. 1.

345 "East Side Help Counts in Zimmer, Mikoll Victories." *Buffalo Evening News*, 6 Nov. 1957, p. 89.

346 *The Appellate Division of the New York Supreme Court, Third Judicial Department: Over 100 Years of Judicial Service*. 1998.

347 Tarapacki, Thomas. "Ann Mikoll - a Trailblazer." *Am-Pol Eagle*, 30 Dec. 2016.

Following the retirement of longtime president and multi-generational leader of Chopins, Ann T. Mikoll, Vice President Gary A. Bienkowski picked up the mantle of the helm of the Society that had already seen three separate centuries. Well versed in the history of Chopins, Bienkowski would be forced to face the same threats President Zdzislaw F. Krysztafkiewicz confronted almost a century earlier.

A third generation Polish American, Gary spent his early years living in a small Polish enclave in the suburbs of Buffalo. As a young parishioner at St. Augustine in Depew, Bienkowski joined the parish choir, and as an adult served as cantor and was part of the church's Diamond Jubilee choir.[348]

Following his high school education in Lancaster,[349] Gary enrolled at Villa Maria College, eventually graduating from both Villa and Niagara University.[350] Working for Erie County, Bienkowski was part of the Department of Social Services for over two decades. An avid traveller, he visited many parts of the United States and twelve countries, including Poland. Joining Chopins in 1994, Gary was elected to the board in 1996 and became vice president four years later.[351]

With the retirement of Ann Mikoll in 2016, Bienkowski reached the pinnacle of the Society with his election to the presidency. Helming the organization for only a few months, Gary was forced to navigate the possible loss of music director, Thomas Witakowski, when the conductor suffered a stroke. Watching the health situation of Witakowski, Bienkowski placed longtime Chopinite Andrew Kowtalo as temporary music director. With Bienkowski, Kowtalo would see the Society win fourth place at the 51st International Convention of the Polish Singers Alliance of America in early 2017.[352] While having Mr. Kowtalo as a temporary replacement, the miraculous recovery of Tom precluded any need to look elsewhere as Dr. Witakowski was conducting again by the end of the year.

Beyond his involvement in Chopin, Gary has been a notable presence in Buffalo's Polonia. For a decade he served on the Board of District 9 and the Central Administration of the Polish Singers

---

[348] *St. Augustine Parish Depew Diamond Jubilee 1909-1984*. 1984.

[349] "Wigilia Feast to Open Polish Week." *Enterprise-Journal*, 24 June 1976, p. 1.

[350] The Chopin Singing Society. *102nd Anniversary Concert*. Chopin Singing Society, 2001.

[351] The Chopin Singing Society. *Installation Banquet*. Chopin Singing Society, 1996.; The Chopin Singing Society. *A World of Music*. Chopin Singing Society, 2000.

[352] "Polish Singers Alliance of America Newsletter." Feb. 2018.

Alliance of America, becoming vice president of the Central organization in 2017. He has also been an active member of the annual Farewell to Summer fundraiser, is a member of the Polish Arts Club of Buffalo, an adult student at Polish Saturday School, a delegate to the Polish American Congress – WNY Division, and was appointed to the Permanent Chair of Polish Culture at Canisius College in 2022. He received a Polonia leader award from the General Pulaski Association in 2018.

Bienkowski's biggest struggle as president of Chopin would be guiding the 120-year-old organization through the global catastrophe that was COVID-19. Even with the forced cancellation of almost two years' worth of events, Gary and the board were able to manage the organization through the pandemic, keeping it alive even when so many organizations closed permanently.

In the post-pandemic era, Bienkowski has overseen the reintroduction of the Society's Dyngus Day celebration, moving it back to Buffalo's East Side, and a return to normalcy in their events and concerts.[353]

---

[353] Facebook Archives, Chopin Singing Society, Buffalo, NY

Appendix II

Choral Masters

1. Boleslaus Michalski (1899-1902)

See Appendix I - Presidents for biography.

2. Leon T. Olszewski (1902-1919)

In the pantheon of Poles and Americans of Polish decent who have called Western New York home, only Dr. Francis E. Fronczak, international dignitary of Polonia, and Julian Lipinski, a founding member of the Polish National Alliance, have been as influential in America's Polonia as Chopin's second choir master, Leon Olszewski. It would be Olszewski's time as president of the United Polish Singers Alliance of America and editor of their organ *Harmonia* that he would transform the idea of Polish singing societies as social or religious organizations into ones that served to protect and promote Polish nationalism, culture, and identity in America. Writing in *Harmonia* Olszewski declared,

> The hidden agenda is purely political, the recruitment of youth under the national banner – the youth who in a given moment answer the call to sacrifice their health, possessions, and life on the Fatherland's altar. Such is the aim of our choirs. The Falcons and the Polish Youth share the same objectives and in general so do all our societies and organizations that are established not for material profit but which are established and exist for an idea. We no longer play the blind man's bluff. Our youth ought to gather in societies in which, under different pretexts, they ought to prepare themselves for the moment for which our nation has waited a century.

This transition to a "Polish first" movement is still at the heart of the Polish Singing Alliance of America and its 22 member choirs.[1]

Born near Poznan in 1872, Leon fled Poland in 1892 to escape

---

[1] Blejwas, Stanislaus A. The Polish Singers Alliance, 1888-1998: Choral Patriotism. University of Rochester Press, 2005.

forced conscription into the Prussian Army. After landing in New York, Leon took a position writing for the Kuryer Nowoyorski i Brooklynski, became the director of New York's Harmonia Choir, and gave music lessons on the side to make ends meet. After a year he was hired by Father Stanislaus Siedlecki of St. Mary Roman Catholic Church in Blossburg, PA to be the school's parochial teacher. In 1895, Olszewski moved to Buffalo, NY when he was retained to teach and to play organ for St. Adalbert Church.

Almost as soon as he arrived in Western New York, Olszewski established himself as a member of Polonia's intelligentsia. When Father Piotr Wawrzyniak, a papal chamberlain, was dispatched to America in the summer of 1896 to investigate the rising Polish National Catholic Church movement, Olszewski's musical arrangements for his Mass at St. Adalbert's garnered as much attention as the headline grabbing monsignor.[2] Leon further cemented his status as a leader that autumn when he was selected as a delegate and vice secretary for the Polish Roman Catholic Congress held in Buffalo. This put Leon on equal footing as fellow committee members Jacob Johnson, the first Polish Alderman of Buffalo, and future New York State Assemblyman for Erie County 6th District James M. Rozan. It also put him on the dais as the chairman of the executive committee the Very Reverend Dean John Pitass.[3] The next year Olszewski padded his cultural bona fides by working with John M. Chrzanowski, Constantine Nowakowski, and Peter Piotrowski to establish the Polskie Kolo Spiewackie or in English, the Polish Singing Circle. By the end of the decade the circle joined the Polish Singers Alliance as Choir #27 and boasted over 60 members making it the largest singing society in Buffalo, second only to Buffalo's older, larger, and more influential group, the Moniuszko Singing Society and its 200 members.[4]

Now an established luminary in the firmament of Buffalo's Polonia, well respected in Pennsylvania's Northern Tier, and a known name in Brooklyn and Manhattan, Olszewski was ready to launch himself to the national stage of Polish America. In 1900, at the United Polish Singers Alliance of America convention in Detroit, Leon campaigned for and won the selection for director general and newsletter

---

[2] "Father Wawrzyniak." *Buffalo Evening News*, 6 Aug. 1896, p. 6.

[3] "Here Next Week." *Buffalo Courier*, 14 Sept. 1896, p. 6.

[4] *Pamiętnik Z Okazji Złotego Jubileuszu 1897-1947, Polskiego Koła Śpiewackiego, Buffalo, N.Y.* Polskie Koła Śpiewackie, 1947.

editor. Eight years after stepping off a boat in New York harbor, Olszewski became the leading choir director in Polish North America. Leon retained the position for the next three years, and then one more when the United Polish Singers Alliance of America reunited with the Polish Singers Alliance of America. In 1905 Olszewski reached the political peak of the alliance when he was elected president of the organization at the 15th National Convention held in New York City.[5]

In his second term as director general, Leon received the invitation to be the choir master of the Chopin Singing Society, following the resignation of Michalski, with Franciszek Piorczynski filling in.[6] Already a member of the growing group that was filled with friends he had known for years, Leon quickly accepted.

Because of his role as general director, Olszewski was heavily involved in the 1901 Polish Singers convention held in Buffalo. Fresh off the heels of the National German Sangerbund,[7] and the ongoing Pan-American Exposition, the United Polish Singers Alliance gathering garnered a lot of glowing press and attention for the organizations and the Poles of Buffalo. Even Buffalo Mayor Diehl sang the praises of Olszewski for his work with the convention.[8] Leon would make the news again the next year when he, along with Dr. Francis E. Fronczak, Stephen M. Spryszynski, John Krysztafkiewicz, and Vincent Buczkowski held a mass rally to shame the visiting Prince Henry of Prussia, for his brother the Kaiser's treatment of Poles and Poland.[9] Just as he was in the secular world, Olszewski was a rising star in Buffalo's Catholic community. In 1903 he was the only lay Pole to accompany Bishop Quigley on his trip to Chicago to be installed as archbishop.[10] At the same time Leon became the organist for the prominent and increasingly influential Transfiguration Church on Sycamore.[11] It would be from the bench at Transfiguration that Leon would help to establish and become the first president of the Polish Organists' Society.[12]

By the middle of the decade Olszewski was a mainstay at Polish conventions and important gatherings held in Buffalo. He was

---

[5] Blejwas, Stanislaus A. The Polish Singers Alliance, 1888-1998: Choral Patriotism. University of Rochester Press, 2005.
[6] "Srebrny Jubileusz Tow. Spiewu Chopin." *Dziennik Dla Wszystkich*, 18 May 1924, p. 3.
[7] "Music." *Buffalo Courier*, 21 July 1901, p. 21.
[8] "Sons of Plucky Poland." *Buffalo Courier*, 19 Apr. 1901.
[9] "Poles Will Greet Henry with Defies." *Buffalo Courier*, 27 Jan. 1902.
[10] "Departs For Chicago See." *Buffalo Courier*, 10 Mar. 1903, p. 7.
[11] "Beautiful Music and Wealth of Flowers." *Buffalo Courier*, 13 Apr. 1903, p. 6.
[12] "Polish Organists Plan to Provide Better Music." *Buffalo Courier*, 14 Apr. 1912, p. 45.

in attendance for the Polish National Alliance Convention of 1905 where he acted as secretary to Censor Anthony Schreiber,[13] was present at the Eastern Branch of United Polish Singers of America Convention of 1906,[14] served as a committeeman for the Polish-led Independence League for William R. Hearst for governor,[15] sat as a committeeman for the Polish Businessmen's Association,[16] and became a board member of the Niagara Non-Refillable Bottle Company,[17] all while directing the Chopin, Kalina, and Kolo singing societies. On top of all that, Leon served two years as president of the Polish Singers Alliance of America.

As busy as he was in his professional life, so too was Olszewski involved in his home life. Marrying Stella Nowak, the couple had six children, Eugenia, Flora, Leon Jr., Jadwiga, Theodora, and Helen. With so many children, education was always in the mind of Leon. After the crusade for a Polish vocational school in the East Side succeeded and rooms were rented out at the Adam Mickiewicz Library and Dramatic Circle,[18] Leon began campaigning for more space and additional programs.[19] Eventually the school moved to Sycamore Street and became Emerson Vocational High School.[20]

In the middle 1910s, Olszewski continued to dabble in politics, conducted the Chopin Singing Society, and sponsored Frank R. Roberson's Polish Travelogue with the *Buffalo Evening News.* The Travelogue was a monumental undertaking that culminated in a presentation of photographs secretly taken in Russian controlled Poland.[21] In 1913 the first epoch of Buffalo's Polonia ended with the death of Dean Jan Pitass, founder of St. Stanislaus Church. To oversee the music for the funeral that would have thousands attend, the parish chose Olszewski for the task, knowing he would not disappoint.[22]

---

[13] "Annual Convention of the Polish National Alliance Opens Here." *Buffalo Courier*, 23 Oct. 1905, p. 5.
[14] "Tuning Up for Polish Singing Society Contest." *Buffalo Courier*, 2 Sept. 1906, p. 29.
[15] "6th And 7th Name Delegates." *Buffalo Courier*, 7 Sept. 1906.
[16] "Polish Business Men Name Station Committee." *Buffalo Courier*, 10 Mar. 1908, p. 6.
[17] "Glens Falls Real Estate Concern on List." *The Argus*, 2 Apr. 1908, p. 4.
[18] "Polish-Americans Eager to Learn." *Buffalo Courier*, 16 Apr. 1912, p. 6.
[19] "Polish School Needs More Room." *Buffalo Courier*, 23 May 1913.
[20] Bucki, Carl L. "Polish Vocational School Was the Source of Community Pride." The *Am-Pol Eagle*, The *Am-Pol Eagle* Newspaper, ampoleagle.com/polish-vocational-school-was-br-the-source-of-community-pride-p5222-147.htm.
[21] "Buffalo Poles Visit Native Land in Spirit with Frank R. Roberson." *Buffalo Evening News*, 3 Oct. 1913, p. 17.
[22] "Polish Societies to Honor Memory of Father Pitass." *Buffalo Courier*, 14 Dec. 1913, p. 95.

On January 10, 1915, Olszewski was elected as the chairman of the board of directors of Chopins.[23] After the loss of Stella, Leon threw himself into conducting and submerged himself in Polonia.[24] As the Great War raged in Europe, Olszewski worked on concerts and benefits to support his countrymen in Poland.[25] Soon Leon was back in the full swing of things, arranging the music for the dedication of the new Polish Union Home on Fillmore Avenue,[26] endorsing Boleslaus Michalski for the board of supervisors,[27] and even traveling to far off Elmira to address Poles as a well-known newspaper editor for the May 3 celebration.[28]

Olszewski continued his breakneck pace, seeing the Polish soldiers at Camp Niagara off,[29] installing the board of the Polish Singing Circle, and raising money for a second Liberty Loan,[30] all while managing the *Polish Daily News.* As Leon worked, he soon started to feel fatigued, but just pushed through it to make way in his ever-filling schedule. Seeing Poland finally set free, the culmination of his life's work invigorated Leon, but the fatigue persisted. Soon the tiredness gave way to other symptoms and Leon finally met with his doctor, only to find out it was cancer.[31] Always trying to better his Polish brethren, Leon's last act for Polonia would be to organize the Broadway National Bank. From his sickbed Olszewski said, "Poles should have a banking institution conducted by their own people so that they might be induced to save more money and become more prosperous and better citizens."[32] After this last act, Leon T. Olszewski passed away on July 17, 1919, at his home on Parade Street.[33]

Over a century after his passing, his mission to tie Polish nationalism to song still resonates today, and as long as Polish music is sung in America, Olszewski's legacy will live on.

---

[23] "Chopin Singing Society Holds Its Installation." *Buffalo Courier*, 11 Jan. 1915, p. 7.
[24] Noreck Ruppert, Barbara. "Stella Olszewska." Grave Finder at St. Stans, Grave Finder at St. Stans, 31 Dec. 2021, gravefinderatststans.com/details/?PersonID=2697.
[25] "Poles Organize Relief Body to Aid Countrymen." *Buffalo Courier*, 16 May 1915, p. 69.
[26] "Poles Parade to Union's New Home for Dedication and Jubilee Celebration." *Buffalo Courier*, 30 Aug. 1915, p. 7.
[27] "Endorse Michalski." *Buffalo Courier*, 28 Sept. 1915, p. 8.
[28] "To Celebrate Poland's Day." *Elmira Star Gazette*, 18 May 1917, p. 3.
[29] "Polish Patriots Will Leave Today for Camp Niagara." *Buffalo Courier*, 19 Nov. 1917.
[30] "Buffalo Club in Drive for Liberty Loan." *Buffalo Evening News*, 15 Oct. 1917, p. 1.
[31] "Leon Olszewski." *Dziennik Dla Wszystkich*, 16 July 1919, p. 6.
[32] "Leon Olszewski." *Buffalo Evening News*, 17 July 1919, p. 16.
[33] "Leon Olszewski." *Buffalo Express*, 18 July 1919.

3. John F. Nadolny (1920-1923) (1928-1929)

Like his predecessor Olszewski, John F. Nadolny was an immigrant, proved his abilities in the Keystone State, sat behind the keyboard at Transfiguration Church, and passed too soon.[34]

John Nadolny was born in Poznan, Poland in 1876. Before celebrating his thirteenth birthday, John and his family moved to the U.S. Once stateside, John took up music and after years of training became a church organist.[35] Nadolny took his first job playing for a church in Nanticoke, then moving to Dickson City around 1910 and finally in Plymouth, all of which are in Pennsylvania. As the parish of St. John Gualbert in Cheektowaga grew, they needed a new organist and as 1919 ended, hired Nadolny as their musical director.

With the passing of Olszewski in 1919, the Chopin Society took a brief period of mourning as they looked for a proper replacement for their former musical titan. During this time, Franciszek Majerowski and Antoni Grzegorzewski filled in as conductors.[36] In short order the group selected Nadolny who began practicing with the choir by early 1920. It would be the grand May 10, 1920 production of *Sylvia,* put on by a joint Chopin and Kalina choir, in which Nadolny would get his first write up as the director and conductor for Chopins.[37]

Nadolny's service for the Society was brief at only four years but included major accomplishments. In April of 1921 John was praised for the Chopins' highly publicized performance at the Polish Union Hall that included guest vocalists Adamo Didur of the Metropolitan Opera.[38] He also brought the singing society to the radio where they performed Polish folk songs on WGR in May of 1922.[39]

As he grew professionally, Nadolny looked to take on more musical responsibilities in greater Polonia. Having conducted the Fredro Singing Society as part of some Chopin's concerts, John fell in love with the Kaisertown group.[40] He soon parted with Chopin to head the Fredros and was replaced by maestro Seth Clark.

---

[34] "Zany Muzyk Organista J. Nadolny Nie Zyje." *Dziennik Dla Wszystkich* [Buffalo, NY] 23 Oct. 1933: 3. Print.

[35] ibid

[36] "Srebrny Jubileusz Tow. Spiewu Chopin." *Dziennik Dla Wszystkich*, 18 May 1924, p. 3.

[37] "Opertka Slyvia W Domu Pol." *Dziennik Dla Wszystkich*, 7 May 1920, p. 7.

[38] "Polish Society Concert." *Buffalo Courier*, 9 Apr. 1921, p. 7.

[39] "Today's Program. WGR-Buffalo, N.Y." *Buffalo Evening News* [Buffalo, NY] 24 May 1922: 21. Print.

[40] Drabik, Michael. The Aleksander Fredro Library and Singing Society. Drabik, 1992.

While the Fredros were a good choir, they were not overly large and did not have as many engagements as Chopins. To fill the musical space left in his schedule, John accepted the position of choirmaster of the 60 voice Kalina Singing Society in 1924 to fill the position vacated by John Lund.[41] Nadolny would guide the ladies' singing society though some of its most monumental moments, including its 1926 silver jubilee.[42] Nadolny would also take on the responsibility of directing the Philharmonia Singing Society at Transfiguration Church before taking up the console as the parish's organist. [43] It would be as Transfiguration's choirmaster and organist that John would have the opportunity to work with Black Rock's Lirnik Singing Society in their staging of *Peasant Meets Peasant* under the directions of Ksawery (Xavier) Fronczak.[44]

In 1928 when there was discussion of the Polish Singing Circle and Chopins combining, the conductors were realigned. Clark joined the Polish Singing Circle and Nadolny was brought back on to Chopin Singing Society.[45] Over the next couple of years John took up the baton for the Lirnik Singing Society and was elected president of the Polish Organists Association where he served with former Chopin President John Nowak, and longtime organist and oplatek baker at Assumption Parish,[46] Zygmunt J. Kroczynski.[47]

In the early 1930s, John began to feel unwell. After a prolonged illness, John F. Nadolny passed away on October 22, 1933.[48] Having been the leader of a so many Polish singing societies, organizations, and parishes, the outpouring from Polonia was immense. Keeping up with their traditions, both the Chopins and Fredros sang laments over John's body as it lay in state at the family home. In Transfiguration Church the Felician Sisters prepared the altar for Nadolny's

---

[41] Pamietnik Zlotego Jubileuszu 1901-1951 Towarzystwo Spiewu Kalina, Buffalo, New York. 1951.

[42] "Singers End Jubilee with Big Concert." *Buffalo Courier*, 31 May 1926, p. 22.

[43] "City Briefs - The Philharmonia Singing Society..." *Buffalo Evening News*, 27 Oct. 1927, p. 44.; Diamond Jubilee, 1893-1968: Transfiguration R.C. Church, Buffalo, New York. Transfiguration Church, 1968.

[44] "Singing Society Presents 'Peasant Meets Peasant.'" *Buffalo Evening News*, 7 May 1928, p. 14.

[45] "Merger Reports Denied by Two Singing Clubs." *Buffalo Evening News*, 5 Oct. 1928, p. 38.

[46] "Change In Literacy Test Control Is Hit." *Buffalo Evening News*, 8 Apr. 1931, p. 11.; "Zygmunt J. Kroczynski." *Buffalo Courier-Express*, 10 Feb. 1955, p. 9.

[47] "Polish Organists' Choir Society Elects Officers." *Buffalo Evening News*, 1 Mar. 1932, p. 25.

[48] "Zany Muzyk Organista J. Nadolny Nie Zyje." *Dziennik Dla Wszystkich,* 23 Oct. 1933: 3. Print.

funeral taking place on October 25. Flanking the casket were memorial wreaths from the Polish Organist Association, Lirnik, Chopin, Kalina, and Orpheus singing societies. Guests from as far away as Auburn, NY and Pittsburgh, Plymouth, Plains, and Dickson, PA gathered in the church to say their final farewells to the man who meant so much to them. When the morning service concluded, a caravan of cars escorted Nadolny to St. Stanislaus Cemetery in Cheektowaga to return him to the dust from which he came.[49]

4. Seth C. Clark (1923-1928)

The hiring of Seth C. Clark as conductor was a monumental shift for the singing society. For the first time in the quarter century history of the singers, a non-Pole led their musical direction. Under his tenure at the baton, Clark saw the silver jubilee celebration of the Society and the dedication of the Chopin monument in Humboldt Park.

By the time Seth Clark took over in late 1923, he already had one of the most distinguished musical careers in Western New York's history. Born in Sardinia on September 18, 1863, Seth displayed an engrossing passion for music as a child. At age 11 the young Clark began his training on the hardest instrument to master, the organ. Still a child, Seth was behind the console at the Methodist Episcopal Church in Akron and in five years, the boy organist moved to Buffalo,[50] hired by Westminster Presbyterian to serve as their musical director.[51] Once settled, Clark began expanding his repertoire by studying under William Kaffenberger, the organist at Trinity Church.[52] In the next year, Seth took the position of organist at the Episcopal Church of the Ascension and then moved on to Central Presbyterian, First Presbyterian, St. John's Episcopal Church, until finally settling at Trinity Church on May 19, 1901, the same day the future bishop of Western New York, Cameron J. Davis began his rectorship there.[53] In the years leading up to Trinity, Seth traveled to London and Berlin to further his studies of the organ, published the song "The Brook and the Wave,"[54] married Annie Gail in 1892, and then toured Europe to continue his

---

[49] "Podziekowanie Sp. Jana Nadolnego." *Dziennik Dla Wszystkich*, 30 Oct. 1933: 7. Print.
[50] Jarvis, H. P. "Men You Ought to Know." *Buffalo Courier-Express*, 5 Sept. 1926, p. 92.
[51] "Dean of Musicians, Seth Clark Is Dead After Long Illness." *Buffalo Evening News*, 29 June 1941, p. 25.
[52] "Mr. Seth Clark, the Young Organist..." *Buffalo Express*, 13 Mar. 1880.
[53] "Dean of Musicians, Seth Clark Is Dead After Long Illness." *Buffalo Evening News*, 29 June 1941, p. 25.
[54] "Home Items." *Evening Republic*, 21 June 1884.

education.[55] Once he was at Trinity, Clark became the first singing instructor to Metropolitan Opera singer Rose Bampton.[56]

In 1904 Clark established one of the most influential musical organizations in twentieth century Western New York, the Guido Chorus. Named in honor of the father of musical notation in the West, the 11th century Italian monk Guido of Arezzo,[57] the Guido Chorus was made up of businessmen, lawyers, doctors, and white-collar professionals who had a love for music and a desire to sing. In time it would be recognized as one of the outstanding nonprofessional singing groups in America.[58]

Clark took the reins of the Chopin choir in the spring of 1924 and began preparing the group for their silver jubilee concert.[59] On Sunday May 19, at the Polish Union Hall on Fillmore, singing societies from Buffalo, Rochester, and Cleveland celebrated with song the 25th birthday of the Chopin Singing Society. Mayor Schwab, Jacob Rozan, and Jan Zelechowski gave speeches and Professor Ladislaus Sorys, John Lund, and Seth Clark directed the music.[60] Seth finished out his first year with Chopins by conducting a joint concert with the Polish Singing Circle and the Guido Chorus at the Union Hall that featured famed Polish opera singer Ignacy Dygas.[61]

At the start of his second year at the Society, Clark led the chorus on a one hour radio special for WGR while preparing them for their biggest concert of 1925, the dedication of the Chopin monument in Humboldt Park.[62] On June 7, the monument by Joseph Mazur was unveiled and in front of the mayor of Buffalo, the Board of the Chopin Singing Society, and a crowd of thousands, Clark led the singers, joined by the male members of the Fredros, Harmonia, Polish Singing Circle, and Moniuszkos, in a rendition of Chopin's Polonaise Op. 40, No. 1.[63] This performance would be a high point of Seth's illustrious time with Chopins. His later high points with the Singing Society

---

[55] "Illness Fatal to Seth Clark, Noted Organist." *Buffalo Courier-Express*, 20 June 1941, p. 28.

[56] "Dean of Musicians, Seth Clark Is Dead After Long Illness." *Buffalo Evening News*, 29 June 1941, p. 25.

[57] "Chorus Members to Give Concert." *Buffalo Courier-Express*, 12 Mar. 1957, p. 11.

[58] "Guido Chorus Concert Sunday to Star News Voice Winners." *Buffalo Evening News*, 11 Jan. 1950, p. 50.

[59] "Chopin Society to Unite Polish Choirs in Recital." *Buffalo Courier*, 27 Apr. 1924, p. 102.

[60] "Polish Societies Join in Concert." *Buffalo Courier*, 19 May 1924, p. 4.

[61] "The Chopin Singing Society, Seth Clark..." *Buffalo Sunday Express*, 30 Nov. 1924, p. 11.

[62] "Radio." *Buffalo Courier*, 24 Apr. 1925.

[63] Commemorating the Unveiling of the Chopin Memorial by the Chopin Singing Society: Humboldt Park, Buffalo, New York, June Seventh, Nineteen Twenty-Five. The Society, 1925.

would include performances with Eugene Stebelski[64] and Zygmunt Stojowski.[65]

On the eve of the 1930s, Clark left the Society and took the position of director for the Polish Singing Circle and later also took up the baton for Kalinas.[66] Outside of Polonia, Seth was directing the Guido and Orpheus Choirs and playing at Trinity Church.[67] At the Polish Singing Circle, Seth was most noted for leading their 35th anniversary concert.[68]

In the late 1930s Seth began to become weak and run down. He resigned from all his jobs except for playing the organ at Trinity and directing the Guido. By 1939 even that became too much for the man, and he retired from music all together. After two years of battling illness, Seth C. Clark passed away June 19, 1941.[69]

At a memorial service for Clark held a year later at Trinity Episcopal, only two choirs were chosen to perform, the Guido Chorus and the Chopin Singing Society. Under the direction of Arnold Cornelissen, the Guidos sang Rudyard Kipling's "Recessional" which Clark had written music to, while the Chopin choir performed "W Mogile Ciemnej."[70]

5. Jan Karol Kapalka (1930)

Not since Leon Olszewski had Chopins engaged a musical director that was as knowledgeable, as famous, and as nationally respected until in early 1930 they hired Jan Karol Kapalka as their fifth musical director. Like Olszewski, Kapalka was a fervent Polish nationalist who believed that music was a uniting force for both the Poles at home and abroad. However, while Leon was with the choir for nearly two decades, Kapalka's tenure would not last a single year.

Born in Carpathian Foothills town of Ciezkowice, Poland on December 9, 1886, John attended school in Tarnow before graduating from the musical conservatory in Krakow. Mere months before the

---

64 "Choral Concert." *Buffalo Evening News*, 15 May 1926, p. 8.

65 "Stojowski Plays at Concert of Chopin Singing Society." *Buffalo Evening News*, 25 Apr. 1927.

66 "News To Present Jubilee Program." *Buffalo Evening News*, 10 Oct. 1930, p. 43.; "Washington's Day Tribute Is Planned." *Buffalo Evening News*, 18 Feb. 1932, p. 22.

67 "Elks Will Convene in Buffalo Sunday." *Buffalo Evening News*, 1 June 1928.

68 "Circle Anniversary Program Is Opened." *Buffalo Evening News*, 6 Sept. 1932, p. 20.

69 "Illness Fatal to Seth Clark, Noted Organist." *Buffalo Courier-Express*, 20 June 1941, p. 28.

70 "Rector Eulogizes Seth Clark's Work at Trinity Church." *Buffalo Evening News*, 16 Feb. 1942, p. 12.

world descended into the chaos of the Great War, Jan immigrated to the United States and married his sweetheart, Wanda.[71]

Fluent in both Polish and German, John settled in New York City and took a position as a music director for a German choir. When it was discovered that he was a Pole, Kapalka was fired, and he moved to the Polish mecca of Chicago. Once in the Windy City he became director of *Nowe Zycie* a job that garnered him enough notoriety to sign a recording deal with Victor Records. Recording folk, comedic, instrumental, and orchestral works, Kapalka eventually was involved in over 75 albums with Victor, Columbia, Okeh, and Brunswick.[72] John's focus on secular music in recording and in concert made him a point of concern for the parish choirmasters in the cities where he worked. Not only was he overshadowing them musically, but they were afraid he would peel away their best singers, leaving their choirs deficient. While a fitting concern, it was not enough for them to attempt to derail his continuing rise in the consciousness of Polonia.

As his time and influence in Chicago grew, John began directing other choirs. As a member of the Polish Singers Alliance of America he ascended to the position of district conductor before being elected general director in 1926.

When his tenure as general director ended in 1929, Kapalka was ready to leave Chicago and make a home in another great Polish colony. Near the end of that year, the board of Buffalo's Chopin Singing Society contacted him about taking lead of their choir. After securing a position as the orchestra leader of the Fillmore Theater, Kapalka agreed to take the reins of Chopins. On January 22, 1930, John held his first practice with the singing society in the Broadway clubrooms.[73] Impressed with the talent he had on hand he scheduled his first concert with the group on the Rosinski Brothers radio show for March 22.[74]

Living on Fillmore Avenue near the Polish Union of America Hall and the home of Dr. Fronczak, Jan and Wanda were in the very heart of Buffalo's Polonia. Jan took his orchestra around town to play shows and parties while Wanda socialized. In time Kapalka took over

---

[71] Blejwas, Stanislaus A. The Polish Singers Alliance, 1888-1998: Choral Patriotism. University of Rochester Press, 2005.

[72] "Kapalka, Jan." Discography of American Historical Recordings. UC Santa Barbara Library, 2022. Web. 7 March 2022.

[73] "Chor Chopina Zyskal Nowego Dyrygenta." *Dziennik Dla Wszystkich* , 21 Jan. 1930, p. 9.

[74] "Do Chopinow Warto Udac Sie Jutre Na Card Party." *Dziennik Dla Wszystkich*, 1 Mar. 1930, p. 3.

directing the Aleksander Fredro Singing Society as well.[75]

As 1930 closed out, and finances tightened, John began looking for a more stable job instead of juggling a handful of gigs. On November 24, his orchestra played their last show in the Chopin clubrooms and by the end of the year he left for Cleveland.[76]

In Ohio, Kapalka headed the Choru Polsko-Narodowego, as well as a few of the smaller Polish choruses. It was at this time that he was able to indulge his passion for Polish opera, staging a performance of Moniuszko's *Flis*. On December 2, 1931, a week before his 45th birthday, Jan Karol Kapalka died of a heart attack in his Brooklyn Centre neighborhood home.[77] His passing would be noted in the Polish and English press across the country,[78] each one commenting on how his death was a great loss to the sound of the nation.[79]

6. Arnold Cornelissen (1931-1953)

After having two back-to-back Polish conductors with Nadolny and Kapalka, the leadership of Chopins turned to a non-Slavic musician of European birth to lead them with the hiring of Arnold Cornelissen in mid-1931.

Born in Abcoude, a suburb of the Netherlands capitol of Amsterdam on June 1, 1887, Arnold enjoyed the safety of a tightknit community, peppered with the occasional excitement of the big city. The Cornelissens were a family with a penchant for music and encouraged their son's talents. At age 13 the young Arnold won a scholarship to the Royal Music School where he studied composition, counterpoint, harmony piano, violin, and voice.[80]

With his musical education complete, Arnold, his brother Andries, and their friend Jan Geets formed a trio and in 1906 left Holland to take America by storm. With Arnold on piano, Andries on cello and Jan on violin, the Holland Trio booked stages in the U.S., but the crowds didn't pack the halls in the way they expected. Marrying Gerda Rinkel in New York in 1907, Cornelissen and the boys still wanted to make a go of being musicians, but now Arnold needed a change of

---

[75] Drabik, Michael. *The Aleksander Fredro Library and Singing Society*. Drabik, 1992.

[76] "Kapalka i Jego Zespol..." *Dziennik Dla Wszystkich*, 22 Nov. 1930, p. 8.

[77] "Zmarl Znany Muzyk i Dyrygent Jan Kapalka." *Dziennik Dla Wszystkich*, 3 Dec. 1931, p. 6.

[78] "John Karol Kapalka." *New York Evening Post,* 4 Dec. 1931, p. 15.

[79] "Drobne Wiadomosci Ze Stosunkow Polskich Na Wychodztwie." *Dziennik Dla Wszystkich* , 8 Dec. 1931, p. 6.

[80] "Chorus Director Cornelissen Dies In New York City." *Niagara Falls Gazette*, 1 Aug. 1953, p. 1.

plans to bring some stability.[81] Instead of playing concert halls, they decided to move to the smaller hotel circuit. This way they could still tour the States but would trade the possible payday of a sold-out concert hall for the stability of a traveling house band. During their seventh year of hotel touring, the trio picked up a gig at the Lafayette Hotel. After experiencing Buffalo, and their contract ended, the crew decided to make the Queen City their home.[82]

Settling in Buffalo at the dawn of the Great War, Arnold opened a studio on College Street to teach music and compose his own works. With letters of reference from Frederick Stock, the music director of the Chicago Symphony Orchestra; Dr. Ernst Kunwald of the Cincinnati Symphony Orchestra; baritone David Bispham; and his teacher Oscar Saenger,[83] Cornelissen was soon instructing the creme of Buffalo's middle class. While he was setting up his studio, Arnold was brought to the attention of Buffalo attorney, E. Llewellyn Parker. Llewellyn was so enamored with Arnold's work that he became the patron of the fifteen-man Cornelissen String Symphony.

Arnold's friendship with the Cincinnati Symphony Orchestra would pay dividends when they performed his "Rhapsody Characteristique" during their 1917 concert at the Elmwood Music Hall. The symphony debuted the rhapsody earlier in the year at a concert in Ohio.[84] The reviewer of the Buffalo Courier said of the work, "[it's] built upon the famous 'Serenade' by Gabriel Pierne and is a most intricate weaving of the melody into an elaborate piece of musical tapestry. It has sharply defined contrasts and passages of real beauty and displays the genius of its young composer in a manner that promises greater things to come." At the conclusion of the performance Dr. Kunwald brought Cornelissen up to the stage to be acknowledged for the work to enthusiastic applause.[85] With his star rising, Arnold formed the Buffalo String Orchestra that autumn,[86] that gave their premier performance at the Crystal Ballroom at the Hotel Statler.[87] Arnold utilized the orchestra to highlight the greats like Liszt and Bach while also experimenting

---

[81] "Mrs. G. R. Cornelissen." *Buffalo Courier-Express*, 17 Aug. 1948, p. 15.
[82] "Arnold Cornelissen, Conductor, Pianist, Composer, Dies at 63." *Buffalo Evening News*, 1 Aug. 1953, p. 9.
[83] "Arnold Cornelissen Announces That He..." *Buffalo Courier*, 8 Oct. 1916, p. 74.
[84] "Musical News." *Buffalo Courier*, 25 Feb. 1917, p. 31.
[85] "Orchestra Scores Brilliant Triumph with Fine Concert." *Buffalo Courier*, 7 Mar. 1917, p. 5.
[86] "The Recently Organized Buffalo String..." *Buffalo Express*, 17 Nov. 1917.
[87] "Music." *Buffalo Courier*, 27 Nov. 1917, p. 73.

with his own compositions in their first year.[88] Arnold also moved his studio out of his home and into the Art Building of the Alchemists at the corner of Chippewa and Elmwood.[89]

The stature of both the orchestra and Cornelissen quickly rose in the halls and ballrooms of Buffalo, the orchestra for their playing, and Cornelissen for his compositions.[90] The respect that he earned brought Arnold into the upper echelons of Buffalo's elite. Cornelissen would reach the zenith of Buffalo's music world in 1921 when he was named conductor of the Buffalo Symphony Orchestra. For this predecessor of the Buffalo Philharmonic Orchestra, Arnold didn't just lead the music, he pressed the flesh, worked the soirées, and encouraged subscription membership in support of the endeavor.[91] Cornelissen leveraged the immense popularity of the orchestra to form a junior orchestra made up of Buffalo youth in 1925 and then the Pro-Arts Symphonic choir three years later.[92]

Arnold also was involved in Western New York's greater music community. To supplement his teaching income, Cornelissen became a music director for a few local religious organizations. Over the course of his life Cornelissen served at St Mary on the Hill, First Church of Christ Lutheran, Temple Beth Zion, and the First Unitarian Church.[93] He also was on the board of the Musical Institute of Buffalo and acted as a spokesman for Buffalo's Kurtzmann Piano Co. [94]

Arnold produced a massive amount of quality music in the 1920s. One of his symphonies would be performed by the Chicago Symphony Orchestra while his "Eau de Vie" for strings and piano,[95] "Sonata" in F major for viola and piano, and "Trio" in F sharp minor for piano, violin and cello would also be publicly debuted.[96] Of the latter two works, a reviewer from the *Buffalo Evening News* said,

---

[88] "Music." *Buffalo Courier*, 23 Dec. 1917, p. 50.

[89] Arnold Cornelissen. "Accompanist And Coach Teacher the Art of Piano." *Buffalo Courier*, 7 Oct. 1917, p. 37.

[90] "Music." *Buffalo Courier*, 24 Mar. 1918, p. 72.

[91] "Good Support for Orchestra." *Buffalo Courier*, 16 Feb. 1922, p. 12.

[92] "Music." *Buffalo Courier*, 13 Sept. 1925, p. 69.

[93] "Famed Buffalo Musician Dies In New York." *Buffalo Courier-Express*, 2 Aug. 1953, pp. 21-B.

[94] "Music in Buffalo." *Buffalo Evening News*, 29 Jan. 1921, p. 5.; Kurtzmann Piano Co. "Arnold Cornelissen." *Buffalo Evening News*, 21 Feb. 1922.

[95] "Music In Buffalo." *Buffalo Evening News*, 12 Feb. 1921.; "Music." *Buffalo Courier-Express*, 17 Feb. 1929, p. 11.

[96] "Music In Buffalo." *Buffalo Evening News*, 12 Feb. 1921.

> His 'Sonata' in F major for viola and piano, is a worthy contribution to the literature for the latter instrument. It is in four movements, showing interesting and scholarly development of the subject matter and its performance by Moe Balsom and Meyer Balsom won considerable applause. Mr. Cornelissen's beautiful 'Trio,' in F sharp minor, was given an especially advantageous hearing as performed by the composer at the piano, Andries Cornelissen, cellist, and Meyer Balsom. The trio contains valuable material and it reveals continuity of structure and pleasing variety. In both the trio and the sonata the composer has generally avoided expressing himself in modern idiom. Yesterday's audience freely voiced its pleasure, honoring composer and performers with warm applause.[97]

Cornelissen won further accolades for his work with the Buffalo Symphony Orchestra from Willem van Hoogstraten of the New York Philharmonic when he said, "Buffalonians have small idea, of what the orchestra is doing for the city... not only is it making of its fifty-five to seventy players far better men, better musicians and better teachers for Buffalo's coming music students, but the public is deriving great advantages."[98]

At the end of the decade, former Chopin's conductor Seth Clark and future conductor Arnold Cornelissen starred in a much-celebrated radio concert. Performed before a live audience at the Elmwood Music Hall and broadcast on WMAK and WKEN simultaneously, Cornelissen conducted the Buffalo Symphony Orchestra while Clark directed the Guido Chorus.[99] The two men had known each other for years at that point, since at least when Clark became a supporting member of the orchestra,[100] but this was the first time the two worked on a project together. Presented by the *Buffalo News* the April 27, 1928, concert won hearty praises from both the *Buffalo News* and the competing *Courier-Express.* [101] This would be one of the last concerts

---

[97] "Music." *Buffalo Evening News*, 17 Feb. 1921, p. 12.

[98] "New York Conductor Praises Buffalo Symphony Orchestra." *Buffalo Courier*, 10 Apr. 1924, p. 4.

[99] "Buffalo Symphony On Air Friday." *Buffalo Evening News* - Radio Magazine, 21 Apr. 1928, p. 1.

[100] "Good Support for Orchestra." *Buffalo Courier*, 16 Feb. 1922, p. 12.

[101] "Symphony's Concert Presented by News." *Buffalo Evening News* - Radio Magazine, 28 Apr. 1928, p. 1.; "Guido Chorus, Symphony Win Hearty Praise." *Buffalo Courier-Express*, 28 Apr. 1928, p. 4.

Arnold would lead with the Buffalo Symphony Orchestra, as he left later in the year to make room for John Ingram.[102]

At the end of 1930, Jan Kapalka left Buffalo and the Chopin Singing Society for Cleveland. The board put out the word that they were looking for a new musical director and through the work of President Zdzislaw Krysztafkiewicz, Arnold agreed to be the Polish society's musical head.[103] On the evening of Monday, May 25, 1931, Cornelissen directed his first public concert with Chopins at the Polish Union Hall.[104] For the show Arnold chose a selection from *Halka*, "Going Home" by Dvorak, and "Winter Song" by Bullard.[105] For the rest of his life, Arnold directed them through the Great Depression, the Second World War, and into the Atomic Age.

While Arnold was able to take up this new challenge, the financial reality of the Great Depression forced him to triple up his work, becoming the conductor for the Buffalo Civic Symphony,[106] the Canisius College Glee Club, and the Buffalo Ensemble.[107] When he wasn't working, Arnold was composing. He produced a tribute to French composer Gabriel Pierne, the "Rhapsody on the Pierne Serenade,"[108] and "In the Garden of Omar."[109] Cornelissen's work with the Chopinites also brought him in close contact with Buffalo's greater Polonia. Working with Chicago native and Alexander Raab-trained pianist Jeno Swislowski, Arnold also premiered his etude "Aeroplane" at the Twentieth Century Club.[110]

Cornelissen and Clark would work together one last time in the summer of 1939. Along with Joseph Messner, director of the Lyric Chorus, Arnold and Seth were the judges of the German Singing Festival in Genesee Park under the auspices of Male Choir Bavaria.[111] After listening to nine choirs and 2,000 voices, the three maestros selected

---

[102] Van Wagoner, Bob. "Its People Gave Buffalo a Warm Musical Heritage." *Buffalo Evening News* Magazine, 11 Mar. 1950, p. 1.

[103] "Campaign for Orchestra to Be Citywide." *Buffalo Courier-Express*, 21 Feb. 1936, p. 13.

[104] "Koncert Choru Chopina Bedzie Wielka Uczta Dla Milosnikow Muzyki i Spiewu." *Dziennik Dla Wszystkich*, 23 May 1931, p. 5.

[105] "Chopin Society Choir to Present Concert." *Buffalo Evening News*, 22 May 1931, p. 38.

[106] "Civic Orchestra Gives Benefit Performance." *Buffalo Courier-Express*, 12 Jan. 1931, p. 5.

[107] Durney, Edward. "Ensemble Is Heard." *Buffalo Evening News*, 11 Nov. 1932, p. 26.

[108] "Philharmonic Gives a Surprise Number." *Buffalo Evening News*, 22 Apr. 1935, p. 12.

[109] "Philharmonic To Play." *Buffalo Courier-Express*, 17 Mar. 1938, p. 4.

[110] "Chooses Buffalo as Home." *Buffalo Courier-Express*, 24 Jan. 1937, p. 4.; Boris, Theodolinda C. "Opera Again to Seek a Buffalo Audience." *Buffalo Evening News*, 26 Nov. 1938, p. 3.

[111] "9 Singing Societies to Compete Sunday." *Buffalo Evening News*, 23 June 1939, p. 4.

the Buffalo Orpheus for third place, the Liederkranz of Niagara Falls second, and in first, the Frohsinn Ladies' Singing Society directed by Hans Hagen. This would be one of Seth's last public appearances.[112] By the end of the year, Clark would hand over the reins of the Guido to Cornelissen who would head it for the next decade.[113]

As World War II raged in Europe, Arnold garnered regional and national musical accolades. On the local front he served as a guest soloist for the Buffalo Philharmonic Orchestra, while on the national level one of his opuses was performed by the National Philharmonic Orchestra in Washington.[114] The selection of his *First Symphony* was part of a challenge Hans Kindler, conductor of the National Symphony, proposed. Kindler called on all the composers of the United States to submit a symphony, of which a section from the ten best would be performed at a special concert where the public could vote on their favorite. When the ballots were counted, Cornelissen had 751 votes, almost double the second place winner, and his "First Symphony" inspired by a lilac bush in bloom was played at Constitution Hall in early 1942.[115] Music critic Ray Brown of the *Washington Post* said of the piece,

> This symphony is fresh and attractive music, liberal in the matter of harmonic progressions, eclectic in the treatment of instrumentation, solid in structure and technically adroit. It is music from a keen and intelligent mind and from a temperament sanguine, generous and expansive. There is an ever-present humor expressed in glints rather than guffaws, and a sure perception of emotional poignancy when that is needed. The composer's originality is evident not only in such patent places as the unusual endings of the first two movements, but also in the constant tenor of the themes.[116]

Arnold would touch further personal heights when the Buffalo Philharmonic produced his "Serenade Enfantine, Opus 33,"[117] but

---

[112] "Frohsinn Ladies Group Wins Choral Contest." *Buffalo Evening News*, 26 Jan. 1939, p. 6.
[113] Workman-Evans, Isabelle. "Music Review." *Buffalo Courier-Express*, 5 Dec. 1939, p. 10.
[114] "Society :: Teas :: Dinners :: Dances." *Buffalo Courier-Express*, 9 Feb. 1940, p. 10.
[115] Gorham, Nat. "National Orchestra to Play Cornelissen's Work Sunday." *Buffalo Evening News*, 6 Feb. 1942, p. 31.
[116] Brown, Ray C.B. "Cornelissen and Grainger Win Ovation." *Washington Post*, 9 Feb. 1942, p. 16.
[117] "Cornelissen Opus to Have Premiere." *Buffalo Evening News*, 14 Feb. 1944, p. 7.

would also reach new lows with the loss of his beloved Gerdaand his brother Andries.[118] But Cornelissen wouldn't let these personal setbacks sideline him from his compositions or the organizations that relied on his musical wisdom. The one thing they did do was force Arnold to face his own mortality, and he began looking at what his legacy would be. Having produced scores of original works, some of which were already destroyed because the artist became displeased with them, Arnold with the help of his second wife, Bonny Jean Pascoe, began organizing his papers and looking for an organization to act as a repository for them.[119] After much consideration Arnold selected the Music Library of the Buffalo Museum of Science. About his selection Cornelissen said, "the Music Library at the Science Museum has a wonderful collection of material, it is shipped out all over the country. I want to feel that my compositions are placed where they can be of use."[120] The donation would turn out to be an act of providence as Arnold Cornelissen unexpectedly passed away six months later, on August 1, 1953.[121]

The death of Arnold sent a wave of sorrow across Western New York's musical community. Each group he was a part of marked his passing in their own way and in time moved through it. The Guido Chorus chose Herbert W. Beattie and Chopins selected Peter Gorecki to replace Cornelissen.[122] While he is gone, Cornelissen's music lives on as his manuscripts and archives are freely accessible at the University of Buffalo Music Library where they are now part of their archives.

7. Peter J. Gorecki (1953-1981)

With the death of Cornelissen in 1953 the members of Chopins began a task they hadn't had to undertake in over a generation, finding a new musical director. While there were many young and talented

---

118 "Mrs. Arnold Cornelissen, Artist, Horticulturist, Dies." *Buffalo Evening News*, 17 Aug. 1948, p. 29.; "Long Illness Fatal To 'Cello Virtuoso, A.J. Cornelissen." *Buffalo Evening News*, 26 Aug. 1942, p. 41.

119 Gorham, Nat. "National Orchestra to Play Cornelissen's Work Sunday." *Buffalo Evening News*, 6 Feb. 1942, p. 31.

120 "Composer Gives Life's Work to Library." *Buffalo Courier-Express*, 22 Feb. 1953, pp. 25-A.

121 "Arnold Cornelissen, Conductor, Pianist, Composer, Dies at 63." *Buffalo Evening News*, 1 Aug. 1953, p. 9.

122 "Guido Chorus Picks Beattie to Be Director." *Buffalo Courier-Express*, 10 Sept. 1953, p. 27.

musicians that could have handled the position, the search committee quickly gravitated to a rising star in Buffalo's Polonia, Peter Gorecki.

The organist of St. Stanislaus parish in Buffalo at the time of his selection, Peter J. Gorecki was born on the Feast of Saints Peter and Paul in 1924 in the town of Pszczyna, Poland. The son of the parish organist at All Saints Church, the young Peter quickly understood the delicate intricacies of music under his father's tutelage. When he came of age, Gorecki was enrolled at the music conservatory in Katowice. Graduating at age twenty, Gorecki would be forced to wait until the end of the Second World War to complete his education. Once the Allies occupied Germany and the Nazis surrendered, Peter attended the Handel Conservatory in Munich. While at the Bavarian institute, Gorecki studied piano, counterpoint, composition, instrumentation, and orchestration. In his later years, Peter sharpened his skills under Aaron Copland, Carlos Charvez, and Robert Wright.[123] It was at this time that Gorecki met and wed Helena Martusiewicz, who remained his bride for 47 years.

While studying at the conservatory, Gorecki served as the musical director for both the Academic Chorus of Polish Students and the Displaced Persons Men's Chorus of Wildflecken. It would be with the second group that Peter would have the opportunity to immigrate to America in 1949 when the entire chorus was granted entry. While the chorus was becoming a mainstay in Manhattan and Long Island, Gorecki took up residence at St. Ladislaus in Hempstead where he became the parish organist.

In 1951 Peter moved to Buffalo's East Side and was soon behind the console at St. Stanislaus Church. With the passing of Cornelissen in mid-1953, the Chopin board quickly contacted Gorecki and by the beginning of October, he was in place to start rehearsing with the choir.[124]

As the musical director of the Society for nearly a quarter century, Gorecki led the choir through two tours of Poland, the recording of two albums, headed their diamond jubilee, and guided them through a number of television and radio performances.[125]

Slowly, Gorecki became the musical director of other singing

---

[123] *Chopin Singing Society - 80th Anniversary Program.* Chopin Singing Society, 1979.
[124] "From Pole to Pole." *Dziennik Dla Wszystkich*, 6 Oct. 1953, p. 9.
[125] Chopin Singing Society *75th Anniversary, 1899-1974.* The Society, 1974.

societies, starting with the Auroras,[126] then the Kalinas, the Polish Singing Circle, as well as the Bavaria Maennerchor, and the United German Singing Societies.[127] He was also the choral director of the Polish Singers Alliance of America and the conductor for the Buffalo Community Orchestra with their City Parks Summer Concerts. Gorecki described his hectic schedule in his later life saying, "Monday I worked with Kalina, Tuesday was Chopins. Wednesday was the Polish Singing Circle. Thursday was the German choir, and Friday was a different German choir."[128]

It would be this frantic pace that prompted Peter and his wife to take a long restful vacation to Germany in 1981. While in Europe the couple decided to stay on the continent, sent for their things, and Peter resigned as Chopin director by postcard.[129]

In Europe, Gorecki maintained his involvement with music, but at a much more relaxed pace. But after a decade, Peter and Helen missed America and in 1991, they returned to Western New York, this time settling in West Falls. Peter returned to Polonia's musical scene by becoming director for the Paderewski Singing Society and assisted other Polish organizations as needed. As they grew older, the couple wintered in Boynton Beach, Florida until finally retiring in 2009. On June 13, 2011, Peter J. Gorecki passed away and was interred at St. Stanislaus Cemetery in Cheektowaga.[130] Helena joined him three years later.[131]

8. Carl E. Druba (1981-1982)

Following the sudden resignation of Gorecki, the singers wanted to replace him with someone who was both equally as accomplished as Peter and who would be with them for a long time. In October of 1981, they believed they found that person in the form of Carl Druba, only to have him taken from them eight months later.

Carl was born near Poestenkill, NY in the state's capital

---

[126] "300 Voices Will Be Heard in a Massed Concert on Feb. 7th." *Dziennik Dla Wszystkich*, 30 Dec. 1953, p. 11.

[127] *Chopin Singing Society - 80th Anniversary Program.* Chopin Singing Society, 1979.

[128] "Peter J. Gorecki, Choir Director, Organist, Composer." *Polish American Journal*, vol. 100, no. 8, Aug. 2011, p. 18.

[129] Osinski, Bill. "City's Ethnic Choral Groups Still Singing Strong." *Buffalo Courier-Express*, 19 Aug. 1982, pp. A-1.

[130] "Peter J. Gorecki, Choir Director, Organist, Composer." *Polish American Journal*, vol. 100, no. 8, Aug. 2011, p. 18.

[131] "Peter Gorecki (1924-2011) - Find a Grave Memorial." Find a Grave, 5 May 2021, www.findagrave.com/memorial/226480883/peter-gorecki.

district, on September 25, 1927, to John and Rose Druba. The son of German immigrant farmers, Carl grew up in a large family with three brothers and three sisters on the Rensselaer Plateau. After grammar school Carl attended Troy High School, and eventually enrolled at the Potsdam Normal School.[132]

As an undergraduate, Druba majored in voice and trumpet and won the Franklin H. Bishop award as the outstanding senior in the instrumental department.[133] Carl returned to the SUNY School and earned a master's degree in 1950 and shortly thereafter spent a brief time in the U.S. Army. Following his stint in the Army, Druba did graduate work at Northwestern University, NYU, the University of Southern California, and the University of Illinois. It was during his time at USC that Carl became the founding musical director of the Disneyland Carolers and directed the Hollywood Presbyterian Church Choir.[134] Eventually becoming a music professor at the Crane School of Music at the University in Potsdam, Carl was co-conductor of the Crane Chorus and was lead conductor of the Men's Glee Club and Chamber Singers.[135]

After 23 years of teaching at Crane, Druba retired in 1971 to focus on conducting full time. Becoming a traveling conductor, Carl was director of Master Chorales in Long Island, Westchester County, New Jersey, and Buffalo. Driving across the state every other week, Druba was in Buffalo two Tuesdays a month for rehearsals.[136]

Settling in Tonawanda in the late 1970s, Druba began working with the younger Mary Louise Nanna.[137] While Nanna and her Ars Nova Musicians were making a name for themselves, Druba held joint programs with them and his Camerata Singers.[138] In 1977 Carl added the Salem's Chancel and Chapel choir to his schedule, complimenting his work with the Master Chorale and Camerata singers.[139] Then on October 21, 1981 the Chopin Singing Society announced that Carl E. Druba would be their eighth music director.[140]

---

132 "South Cambridge." *The Times Record*, 15 Feb. 1945.
133 "63-Year-Old Wins College Award." *Union-Sun & Journal*, 8 June 1948, p. 7.
134 "Obituaries." *Buffalo Courier-Express*, 23 June 1982, p. A6.
135 "Carl E. Druba." *Courier & Freeman*, 22 June 1982, p. 10.
136 "Carl Druba to Direct WNY Chorale's Show." *Buffalo Courier-Express*, 3 Jan. 1973, p. 5.
137 "Master Chorale to Perform Mozart 'Requiem' Sunday." *Tonawanda News*, 20 May 1978, p. 2.
138 "Camerata Singers." *Buffalo Courier-Express*, 19 Aug. 1978, p. 10.
139 "Salem UCC to Confirm 23 Junior High Members." *Tonawanda News*, 12 May 1978, p. 3.
140 Putnam, Thomas. "Music Notes." *Buffalo Courier-Express*, 21 Oct. 1981, pp. B-5.

Days after the announcement Druba led the singers in a Mass celebrating the third anniversary of John Paul the Second's election to the papacy.[141] He saw them take part in the launch of Buffalo's Sesquicentennial Celebration and the telethons to raise money for humanitarian assistance to Poland.[142]

In early 1982 Druba began to feel unwell and after a visit to the Veterans Administration Medical Center in Buffalo, he was diagnosed with leukemia. The aggressive cancer quickly overtook the nationally renowned conductor and on June 19, 1982, Carl E. Druba passed away.

9. Marylouise Nanna (1982-1983)

With the baton of Chopins in her hand for less than four months, Marylouise Nanna's tenure as the head of the choir is the shortest in the Society's history. Coming in to hold everything together while a permanent replacement for her friend Carl Druba could be found, Nanna left her mark on the choir by leading them in their 83rd annual concert, *A Salute to Buffalo on Their Sesquicentennial Year.* [143]

Born in Buffalo's Italian American Lovejoy neighborhood in the spring of 1937, Mary Louise Nanna's penchant for music could be found in her DNA. By day, her father, Peter, was a barber but at night he could be heard playing his mandolin. In her youth, Nanna's mother made a living playing the piano in the silent movie theaters of Buffalo, while her uncle, Jack D'Amico, was the leader of his own touring orchestra in the 1940s and 1950s. Of all her relatives, her jazz clarinetist uncle, Hank D'Amico became the most famous. As a band member, Hank could be found playing with Les Brown, Red Norvo, Tommy Dorsey, and the "King of Swing" Benny Goodman, while his recordings included tracks with Louis Armstrong, Ella Fitzgerald, and Bing Crosby.[144]

Attending School 43, Marylouise's talent and dedication to music was evident to all who heard her. At age twelve she took up the violin and was soon performing with the Junior Chromatic Club at the

---

[141] "Groups to Celebrate Pope's Anniversary." *Buffalo Courier-Express*, 24 Oct. 1981, pp. A-10.

[142] The Chopin Singing Society. *A Salute to Buffalo on Their Sesquicentennial Year! From the Chopin Singing Society.* Chopin Singing Society, 1982.

[143] The Chopin Singing Society. *A Salute to Buffalo on Their Sesquicentennial Year! From the Chopin Singing Society.* Chopin Singing Society, 1982.

[144] "D'Amico, Hank." *Discography of American Historical Recordings.* UC Santa Barbara Library, 2023. Web. 20 January 2023.

Twentieth Century Club and giving recitals at the International Institute.[145] When it came time for her to choose a high school, she enrolled at Mount Mercy Academy to study violin under Stanley King. At Mount Mercy, Marylouise continued to excel and in the summer of her freshman year attended the National Music Camp in Interlaken, Michigan.[146] By the next summer she was offered full scholarships to the Eastman School of Music in Rochester and Marywood College in Scranton, PA. Even while she was expanding her horizons beyond Western New York, Nanna never lost sight of her roots, still performing with her mother at community events like to Dante Alighieri Cultural Club of Buffalo's Christmas party.[147]

Choosing Marywood, Marylouise furthered her study of the violin and was part of the school's College Orchestra where she was often featured as a soloist.[148] As a senior, Nanna conducted her first major concert at the college, taking up the baton for the orchestra's 1959 spring concert.[149] Days after the May concert, it was announced that the violinist would be the recipient of a Fulbright grant to study music at the St. Cecilia Conservatory in Rome, Italy where she had the opportunity to take part in the Festival dei Due Mondi at Spoleto.[150]

After graduating cum laude from Scranton, she attended the Catholic University of America in Washington for her master's degree on a Woodrow Wilson scholarship. Of all her engagements in the nation's capital, the two most important would undoubtedly be playing at President Kennedy's Inaugural Gala,[151] and being the first woman to conduct the National Symphony Orchestra.[152]

In February of 1965, she returned to Buffalo and performed her first solo recital in the Mary Seaton Room of Kleinhans Music Hall and in the next year, she joined the Buffalo Philharmonic Orchestra under Music Director Lukas Foss. Over the course of the next half century, Nanna toured the globe, performed at Carnegie Hall, and appeared on over fifty recordings with the BPO.

While working with the philharmonic, Marylouise launched

---

145 "To Give Violin Recital." *Buffalo Evening News*, 18 June 1954, p. 34.

146 "Scholarship Won by Miss Nanna, Violin Student." *Buffalo Evening News*, 6 May 1954, p. 45.

147 "Carols, Other Christmas Music." *Buffalo Evening News,* 22 Dec. 1954, p. 4.

148 "Honors." *Buffalo Courier-Express*, 21 Apr. 1957, p. 27-A.

149 "Buffalo Student Will Conduct." *Buffalo Courier-Express*, 10 May 1959, pp. 28–8.

150 "Fulbright Award." *Buffalo Courier-Express*, 20 Mar. 1959, p. 6.

151 "Miss Nanna to Debut as Soloist." *Buffalo Courier-Express*, 7 Feb. 1965, p. 17.

152 "Ex-Fulbright Scholar at Music Hall Sunday." *Buffalo Courier-Express*, 7 Feb. 1965, p. 17.

several personal projects. In 1974 she started the Ars Nova Musicians Chamber Orchestra and in 1979 began the Viva Vivaldi Festival for the group.[153] While undertaking these endeavors Nanna was named music director of the Cheektowaga Community Symphony Orchestra, which in time would lead to her taking over Chopins in 1982. Later she would lead the Niagara Falls Philharmonic, the Genesee Symphony, and served as concertmaster under Christopher Keene for Artpark's summer 1985 opera season.

A mainstay of the Western New York musical world, Buffalo Mayor Anthony Masiello recognized her importance when he declared November 2003 "Marylouise Nanna month" with Ars Nova officially honored as "A Cultural Treasure of Buffalo."

While always at the forefront of Buffalo's musical community, Nanna's importance to the nation was highlighted with Julia D'Amico's 2007 documentary on the girl from Lovejoy, *La Maestra in the House*. As with many aging luminaries, the accolades of a life well lived began to rain down on Mary in the autumn years of her life. She was given awards and honorary degrees from local institutions, was inducted into the Buffalo Music Hall of Fame, and returned to one of the clubs that made her famous when she received the Charlotte Mulligan Award for outstanding achievement in music from the Twentieth Century Club of Buffalo. On December 2, 2020, Marylouise Nanna passed away.[154]

10. Ireneusz Lukaszewski (1983-1991)

With the passing of Carl Druba in 1982, Marylouise Nanna agreed to step in as musical director of Chopins until they could find a more permanent replacement. After an international search the group secured maestro Ireneusz Lukaszewski in 1983.[155]

Born in Poland in 1938, Lukaszewski graduated from the best conservatories in Gdansk and Poznan. His natural inclination and dedication to music earned him a teaching position at the Gdansk Music Conservatory as a professor, first place at international music competitions in Ireland, Italy, Bulgaria, and Austria, and multiple invitations to

---

[153] Putnam, Thomas. "Here's a Slice of Musical Treats." *Buffalo Courier-Express,* 25 Nov. 1979, pp. F-6.

[154] "Marylouise Nanna, 83, Ars Nova Founder and BPO First Violinist." *Buffalo News*, 5 Dec. 2020.

[155] Woolf, Jonathan. "Review: Lukaszewski Choral Music AP0252 [JW]: Classical Music Reviews." *MusicWeb*, MusicWeb.

the Vatican for papal performances.

While still living in Poland, Ireneusz started the Gdansk International Choral Meeting while acting as the fulltime conductor of the Baltic Opera and Philharmonic Ensemble. Lukaszewski also found the time to begin a prolific career as a composer, but it would be as conductor with the academic chorus of the Gdansk Medical Academy that Lukaszewski first got to meet members of Western New York's Polish community. In 1974 the chorus held a program at Alliance College while touring America in preparation for the Lincoln Center International Choral Festival. Presented with the rare opportunity to see singers from their homeland, a number of Buffalo Poles returned to their alma mater to take in the show.[156]

In the early 1980s as Poland imposed martial law, artists and musicians began a boycott in protest. It would be under these circumstances that the Chopin Singing Society extended an offer to Ireneusz to become their music director. Once established in Western New York, Lukaszewski took a position as director of church music at Corpus Christi and became a music faculty member at Villa Maria College.[157]

For nearly a decade Lukaszewski guided the choir musically, taking them to the Koszalin Choral Competition in 1985 where they received an award and enjoyed standing ovations at their other concerts in Poland. He eventually directed them to the Cardinal Hlond Trophy in 1989 as the top-scoring choir at the Hamilton, Ontario competition celebrating the 100th anniversary of the Polish Singers Alliance of America.[158] In time he went on to form a mixed choir at Villa Maria College and see several his compositions recorded.[159] After pulling away from Chopins in 1991, Ireneusz formed the Quo Vadis Choir. Eventually he slowly began retiring from his positions, departing Corpus Christi in 2007, and in time Villa as well.[160]

11. Thomas E. Witakowski (1991-2024)

Of the Society's eleven choral masters, Dr. Thomas Witakowski has held the baton of the Chopin Singing Society the longest at

---

[156] "Alliance College Hosts Gdansk Choir, April 30." *Independent*, 24 Apr. 1974, p. 11A.
[157] *The Cheektowaga-Chopin Gala Spring Concert*. 1991.
[158] "Chopin Singing Society Celebrates 90th Anniv." *Am-Pol Eagle,* 26 Oct. 1989, p. 7.
[159] Ireneusz Lukaszewski. "Choral Works." Augsburg Evangelical Church, Sopot, May 2011.
[160] Byrd, Christopher. "Dr. Ireneusz Lukaszewski's Last Mass as Organist for Corpus Christi Church." Broadway Fillmore Alive, 3 Feb. 2008.

over thirty years. Guiding the singers for nearly 25% of their life, Witakowski has done everything from leading the Chopinites on a tour of the southern U.S. and New England to guiding them through COVID and overseeing the singers during hundreds of concerts for Western New York's Polonia.

Born in Western New York in the middle of the 20th century, Witakowski proved to be bright at an early age. In school, Thomas was often ranked at the top of his class and graduated summa cum laude from John F. Kennedy High School.[161]

Enrolling at the University of Buffalo's school of music, Witakowski would make a name for himself in the institute's opera scene.[162] He would also independently study under one of Buffalo's great talents, Genia Las. Once finished with his undergraduate degree, Tom attended Indiana University Bloomington and its highly ranked Jacobs School of Music, eventually working towards a doctorate.[163] While in Indiana, Witakowski was a student of basso opera singer Nicola Rossi-Lemeni, spent a year at Warsaw University, and focused his studies on the works of Karol Szymanowski.[164] Tom also took his first step into the academic world, becoming an adjunct professor of music at Sinclair College in Dayton, OH. As a member of the community, Tom served as the music director of the Dayton Boys' Choir and was active with the city's Bach Society[165].

Returning from the Midwest, Witakowski soon became a fixture of Buffalo's musical and Polish communities. In 1989 he was one of the guest artists for the golden anniversary concert of the I.J. Paderewski Singing Society and in the next year became the musical director of the choir.[166] Outside of Polonia, Tom could be heard as a singer for the Clarence Summer Orchestra,[167] the Operabuffs,[168] and the Buffalo Choral Arts Society.[169] With the departure of Lukaszewski,

---

161 "Honor Roll Listed by Sloan School." *Buffalo Courier-Express*, 17 Feb. 1975, p. 20.
162 Putnam, Thomas. "UB's New Opera Group Out of Focus." *Buffalo Courier-Express*, 26 Mar. 1978, p. 16.
163 *Thomas Witakowski, Bass - Paul Homer, Accompanist: In Recital.* State University College of New York at Buffalo, 1993.
164 Witakowski, Thomas. "The Choral Works of Karol Szymanowski in their Historical and Cultural Context." *Indiana University*, 1994.
165 *Golden Anniversary Concert and Ball.* I.J. Paderewski Singing Society, 1989.
166 "Music Notes." *Buffalo News*, 9 Oct. 1990.
167 "Clarence Concert Assn. To Open Season Sunday." *Buffalo News*, 26 June 1990.
168 "Music Notes." *Buffalo News*, 13 Nov. 1990.
169 "Music Notes." *Buffalo News*, 29 Jan. 1991.

Witakowski was appointed musical director of Chopins in late 1991.[170] With this, Tom was musically heading two of Polish Buffalo's most important singing organizations, and the *Am-Pol Eagle* recognized this monumental task by giving him the award for the Citizen of the Year for Music.

In the following year, Witakowski would be named to the music faculty of Buffalo State College, becoming responsible for the choral and vocal programs of the music department in the Division of Performing Arts. In time he would see the Buffalo State College Chamber Choir through a tour of Eastern Europe and Spain and earn the respect of both his peers and students at the school.[171]

In 1995, Witakowski conducted the Paderewski choir for the last time with their 56th anniversary concert,[172] giving way to Peter Gorecki who took over the following year.[173] For the next thirty years, Tom focused on teaching and conducting Chopins, while still making time for other endeavors. He became the organist for St. Casimir Church, then Assumption Church, and finally Corpus Christi Church,[174] won a district championship with a local barbershop quartet,[175] took charge of the Amherst Chamber Ensemble, and was elected as the national director of the Polish Singers Alliance. He garnered several awards including a Biesada in his honor from the Polish Arts Club of Buffalo and a special recognition by the Polish American Congress, Western New York Division for his dedication to Polonia.[176]

At the end of 2016, Witakowski suffered a devastating, near fatal stroke. For the majority of patients, this health crisis upends the lives of those who suffer from it and forces major life changes. But with music therapy, modern medical science, his force of will, and the grace of God, Tom was directing the choir again and returned to teaching by the end of 2017.[177]

As the COVID-19 pandemic gripped the world, Tom, and the rest of the leadership were forced to cancel the singing society's

---

[170] "Honor Roll." *Buffalo News*, 3 Nov. 1991.
[171] "Buffalo State Choir Set for European Tour." *Buffalo News*, 18 May 1995.; The Chopin Singing Society. *Centennial Concert*. Chopin Singing Society, 1999.
[172] "Paderewski Singers Set Concert, Ball." *Buffalo News*, 24 Sept. 1995.
[173] "Paderewski Singers Set Concert, Ball." *Buffalo News*, 19 Sept. 1996.
[174] The Chopin Singing Society. *105th Annual Concert*. Chopin Singing Society, 2004.; "Assumption Welcomes Dr. Witakowski." *Am-Pol Eagle*, 12 Aug. 2009.
[175] The Chopin Singing Society. *103rd Anniversary Concert*. Chopin Singing Society, 2002.
[176] "Polish American Congress Holding Annual Dinner Sunday." *Buffalo News,* 24 Apr. 2014.
[177] Davis, Henry L. "A Stroke Patient's Musical Journey from Coma to Recovery." *Buffalo News*, 29 May 2018.

engagements. While the world ground forward, the Polish American Congress moved to recognize Witakowski's achievements by awarding him the Bronislaw Durewicz Memorial Award in 2021.[178] Through 2022 and 2023, the choir resumed a full schedule of events again. Dr. Witakowski went on sabbatical in the summer of 2023 and announced his new status as Director Emeritus during the Christmas season of 2023-4, a status he officially assumed after the choir's performance at the District 9 Koledy in Ontario which featured a reprise of "Ave Maria na Boze narodzenia," a piece he composed after his recovery which he "dedicated to the choirs of the Polish Singers Alliance of America, District IX, in gratitude."

12. Nicholas J. Steltzer (2024-)

A native of Geneseo, Nicholas John Steltzer began his extensive musical educational journey at the Eastman School of Music where he studied piano and organ at the as part of the Community Education Division. Since then, he has studied at the Cleveland Institute of Music, Temple University, Birmingham City University, and University of Washington in curricula covering sacred music, organ performance, and choral conducting.

While his work has brought him to St. James United Church of Christ in Havertown, PA, Saint Chad's Cathedral Birmingham in the United Kingdom and Messiah Lutheran Church of Auburn WA, his time at Monumental United Methodist Church in Portsmouth, VA would be especially noteworthy as he was named the inaugural appointee to the Lindauer Endowed Chair for Music and Arts. Moving to Western New York after the pandemic with his family, Mr. Steltzer took the position of organist at Christ United Methodist Church in Amherst. On the eve of the Chopin Singing Society's 125th anniversary he was named as their 12th Choral Master.[179]

Temporary Choral Masters

Franciszek Piorczynski (1902)

A native of Poland, Franciszek took up residence in Western New York in 1892. Living on Warner, he was choir master of Chopins

---

[178] "PACWNY to Install Officers, Directors, Honor Dr. Witakowski." *Am-Pol Eagle*, 31 Jan. 2021.

[179] Nicholas J Steltzer, 2020, nicholasjohnsteltzer.com

while a replacement for Michalski was sought.[180] He was the organist of St. Stanislaus Church in Rochester from 1907 until his death in 1919. While in Rochester, he was also the choir master of the Echo Singing Society.[181]

Franciszek L. Majerowski (1919)

Born and raised in Buffalo, Majerowski served as a fill in during the search for Leon Olszewski's replacement.[182] Educated in music at Canisius College and nephew of well-known Polish American priest Reverend Thomas A. Stabenau,[183] Franciszek soon took positions conducting the Fredro Singing Society as well as other choirs at community events.[184]

In April 1915, Majerowski was appointed to his first organist position when Father Gartska of St. John Kanty chose him to replace the late Thaddeus Balucinski.[185] By 1916 he was at the console of Transfiguration and was soon conducting the male section of the Harmonia Singing Society. [186] Franciszek also had the honor of debuting the Marr and Colton organ with a concert during the grand opening of the Clinton Strand Theater in November of 1923.[187] By the middle part of the decade Majerowski took a job in Chicopee, MA, but returned to Buffalo for a recital on the newly installed organ at Corpus Christi Church, whose pipes were specially designed to frame the stained glass window of St. Cecelia.[188]

From Massachusetts, Franciszek returned to New York eventually settling in the Five Boroughs where he passed away on June 1, 1939.[189]

---

[180] "Srebrny Jubileusz Tow. Spiewu Chopin." *Dziennik Dla Wszystkich*, 18 May 1924, p. 3.
[181] Lyon, Norman T. "History of the Polish People in Rochester." History of the Polish People in Rochester (3 of 5), GenWeb of Monroe County, 19 May 2018, mcnygenealogy.com/book/polish-3.htm.
[182] "Srebrny Jubileusz Tow. Spiewu Chopin." *Dziennik Dla Wszystkich*, 18 May 1924, p. 3.
[183] "Franc. Majerowski Znany Organista Nie Zyje." *Dziennik Dla Wszystkich*, 3 June 1939, p. 3.
[184] "Poles Do Honor to Lincoln and Own Kosciuski." *Buffalo Courier*, 23 Mar. 1914, p. 7.; "Parade to Precede Polish Celebration." *Buffalo Evening News*, 6 Jan. 1913, p. 7.
[185] "Appoints Church Organist." *Buffalo Courier*, 28 Apr. 1915, p. 9.
[186] "Polish Woman's Alliance Holds First Session." *Buffalo Evening News,* 26 Sept. 1916, p. 17.; "Harmonia Singing Society to Dine Returned Heroes." *Buffalo Courier*, 25 May 1919, p. 70.
[187] "Clinton Strand Theater to Open This Afternoon." *Buffalo Courier*, 11 Nov. 1923, p. 77.
[188] "New Corpus Christi Organ Will Be Played Thursday." *Buffalo Evening News*, 14 June 1928, p. 3.
[189] "Franc. Majerowski Znany Organista Nie Zyje." *Dziennik Dla Wszystkich*, 3 June 1939, p. 3.

Antoni Grzegorzewski (1919)

Grzegorzewski conducted the Chopin Singing Society temporarily after Olszewski.[190]

Walter A. Szwajda (1981)

Following the unexpected departure of Peter Gorecki, Associate Music and Choir Director Walter A. Szwajda took on the responsibility of guiding the singers until a permanent replacement could be found.

Wladyslawa Antoni Szwajda was born to Jan and Leonji Szwajda on the 23rd of June 1925. Raised in the shadow of Corpus Christi Church on Buffalo's East Side, the young Wally demonstrated an early aptitude for music. Before graduating from the University of Missouri at Kansas City Conservatory of Music, Szwajda first served with the Eighth Army Air Force in the European Theater. It was during the war that Szwajda gained some fame for his accordion playing. In time, Szwajda honed his squeeze box skills and performed under the moniker, Wally Anthony - King of the Accordion.[191]

Following university, Walter returned to Western New York and married Sophie Wojtowicz of Niagara Falls.[192] At this time he served as a music instructor,[193] but his entrepreneurial spirit would not rest. In September of 1964, Wally made the jump and started Wally Szwajda's Music Store & Studio at 2462 William Street in Cheektowaga.[194] For the next 35 years Szwajda would buy, sell, repair, rent, and teach all forms of musical instruments, but always had a particular fondness for the accordion.

Besides his store, Szwajda could be found behind the console of many of Polonia's church organs. Over the course of his life, Walter was the organist for Queen of the Most Holy Rosary, Corpus Christi, and St. Josaphat church.

Joining the Chopin Singing Society in the 1970s, Szwajda worked his way to the position of associate music and choir director.[195] It would be from this post that Walter would be thrust into the seat of temporary choral master when Gorecki quit in 1981. Guiding the

---

[190] "Srebrny Jubileusz Tow. Spiewu Chopin." *Dziennik Dla Wszystkich*, 18 May 1924, p. 3.
[191] "Walter A. Szwajda, Accordion Player, Store Owner." *Buffalo News*, 4 Nov. 2013.
[192] "Sophie Wojtowicz Weds at Church." *Niagara Falls Gazette*, 21 Nov. 1953, p. 8.
[193] "Prof. W. A. Szwajda." *Dziennik Dla Wszystkich*, 23 June 1953, p. 12.
[194] "Incorporations." *Buffalo Courier-Express*, 16 Sept. 1964, p. 34.
[195] The Chopin Singing Society. *80th Anniversary*. Chopin Singing Society, 1979.

singers as best he could through the rest of their schedule, Walter did not protest when it was decided to cancel the annual concert. For these efforts the *Am-Pol Eagle Newspaper* recognized Szwajda as the Citizen of the Year for Music in 1982.[196] It was also at Chopins that Wally met his second wife, Helen Bielak, after Sophie passed away in 1983.

Outside of Chopins, Walter was an active member of Leonard Post 6251 VFW, where he served as vice president,[197] and the Music Merchants Association of Buffalo.[198] On November 2, 2013, Walter A. Szwajda passed away and was interred at Saint Stanislaus Roman Catholic Cemetery in Cheektowaga, NY.[199]

Adrienne Tworek-Gryta (2006)

While Dr. Witakowski was teaching in Poland, Ms. Tworek-Gryta led the singers. A fixture in Buffalo's music scene Adrienne was known as a lyric-colaratura soprano who was regularly heard with the Buffalo Philharmonic Orchestra, the Ars Nova Musicians, and a number of other local groups. Before filling in for Witakowski, Tworek-Gryta reached much acclaim with the Society when she served as a guest soloist during their 1985 trip to Poland. The entire tour was known for the number of standing ovations they received at their engagements and the award at the Koszalin Music Festival they won. [200]

A graduate of the State University of Buffalo Tworek-Gryta made a name for herself while perusing her master's degree with her performances of the works of Monteverdi, Puccini, and Stravinsky. Appointed as an Adjunct Professor of Voice at Villa Maria College in 1982, Adrienne would additionally teach at Daemen College, as well as instruct at her own private vocal studio. She would later be featured on The Buried Treasures Ensemble's 1987 LP[201] and participate in the Des Moines Summer Festival of Opera. Back in Buffalo Adrienne led Chopin at the Mass celebrating the completed renovation of St. Stanislaus, the Society's Wigilia, and their section of the Polish Singers Alliance Christmas concert[202].

---

196 "*Am-Pol Eagle* Selects 'Citizens of the Year.'" *Buffalo Courier-Express*, 7 Feb. 1982, pp. A-6.
197 "VFW Post Elects." *Buffalo Courier-Express*, 8 June 1962, p. 6.
198 "Music Merchants Elect New Officers." *Buffalo Courier-Express,* 20 Jan. 1972, p. 21.
199 "Walter A. Szwajda, Accordion Player, Store Owner." *Buffalo News*, 4 Nov. 2013.
200 The Chopin Singing Society. *108th Annual Concert*. Chopin Singing Society, 2007.
201 "Buried Treasures Ensemble." Crystal Records.
202 The Chopin Singing Society. *124th Annual Concert*. Chopin Singing Society, 2023.

Andrew N. Kowtalo (2016-2017)

Andrew took over directing the Society in late 2016 and early 2017 as Dr. Thomas Witakowski recovered from his stroke.

A graduate of Bishop Timon-St. Jude High School and a voice student of Ms. Genia Las, [203] Andrew N. Kowtalo joined the Chopin Singing Society just before the turn of the last millennium.[204] As a skilled baritone, Kowtalo proved to be invaluable as a singer and a dedicated volunteer.

As early as 2001 Andrew's voice was featured at the Society's annual concert singing a duet with Witakowski on Hosa Dyna Polka and as one of four singers in a medley from Lehar's "The Merry Widow."[205] Kowtalo's voice would stand on its own at Chopin's 192nd birthday party where he was the soloist on "Precz z Moich Oczu."[206] In 2008 Kowtalo's dedication to the Society was recognized with his first election to its board of directors,[207] a position he held for a number of years. Andrew would further step up in 2016 when he took over the baton after Dr. Witakowski fell ill.

In his short tenure as music director, Kowtalo made several notable appearances with the singers. He guided the group during their performance on WBBZ's *Polka Buzz*, directed the singers at their 26th appearance at the USS Little Rock, and led the Society to fourth place at the 51st International Convention of the Polish Singers Alliance of America.[208] With Witakowski's recovery in the fall of 2017, Kowtalo returned to being a singer and featured soloist.[209]

Dr. Bradley Wingert (2023, 2024)

With Dr. Witakowski's sabbatical beginning in the summer of 2023, Dr. Bradley Wingert stepped in to lead the Chopin Singing Society as it kicked off its 125th anniversary celebration. A choral teacher for the Niagara Falls School District, adjunct professor at Canisius University and former adjunct professor at Niagara Community

---

203 "Congratulations Graduates." *Front Page*, 29 Jan. 1994, p. 11.; "Genia Las." The *Am-Pol Eagle*, *Am-Pol Eagle*, 25 May 2018

204 The Chopin Singing Society. *Centennial Concert*. Chopin Singing Society, 1999.

205 The Chopin Singing Society. *102nd Anniversary Concert*. Chopin Singing Society, 2001.

206 The Chopin Singing Society. *A Celebration of the 192nd Birthday of Frederic Chopin*. Chopin Singing Society, 2002.

207 The Chopin Singing Society. *109th Annual Concert.* Chopin Singing Society, 2008.

208 "Polish Singers Alliance of America Newsletter." Feb. 2018.

209 "After Yearlong Hiatus, WNYers Celebrate Chopin's Birthday." *Am-Pol Eagle*, 18 Mar. 2022.

College, Dr. Wingert was organist at St. Peter Church in Lewiston, NY, and then at Christ the King Church in Amherst, NY. He directs the Canisius University Chorale and Lewiston Choraleers. Dr. Wingert directed members of the Chopin and Kalina Singing Societies at the Polish Day Mass at Our Lady of Fatima Shrine in Lewiston and the 124th Anniversary Concert of the Chopin Singing Society held at St. Stanislaus Church.[210] Wingert would return as a temporary choral master with Witakowski's retirement in early 2024 when the choir joined with the voices of the Canisius University Chorale to celebrate the Chopin and Mickiewicz birthday bash at the University's Montante Center. He led the choir for Dyngus Day and the celebration of the 125th Anniversary Mass at St. Adalbert Basilica in April 2024.

[210] The Chopin Singing Society. *124th Annual Concert*. Chopin Singing Society, 2023.

Appendix III

Recordings

Title: Chopin Singing Society of Buffalo, NY
Year: 1975
Publisher: Chopin Singing Society
Catalogue Number: CHOPIN 5001
Length: 45:09 Minutes

Track Listing:
Side One
1. Processional – Arr. Peter Gorecki
2. Maki – St. Niewiadomski
3. Czesc Ci Polsko, Hold I Chwala – K. Kurpinski
4. Piesn O Warszawie – R. Rygiel
5. Tanga (Wiazanka) – Arr. Peter Gorecki. Soloists: Theresa Dybas, Louis Distel, Antoinette Osinski.

Side Two
1. Matulu Kochana – Arr. E. Liebling
2. Polesia Czar – A Wlast
3. Gdy Kochac, Kochac Raz – (Duet: Dybas-Distel) P. Gorecki
4. Battle Hymn of the Republic – Arr. P Wilhousky
5. My Melody of Love – H. Moyer
6. Dobranoc – P. Gorecki Soloists: Theresa Dybas, Louis Distel, Adam Malik, Victor Jarnot, Edward Krenglicki, Antoinette Osinski.

Rear Cover Text:

For members of the Chopin Singing Society of Buffalo, New York 1975 will always be remembered as the year during which the long-held dream of performing as a choral group in the land of their forefathers was fulfilled. This album, recorded during the group's concert in Warsaw's Philharmonic Hall, captures the love and affection of the Chopin members for their Polish brethren which they successfully transmitted to their audiences through the universal language of song. Stored in the hearts of the singers for two and three generations, these emotions seemed to burst forth and multiply with each offering, not only in Warsaw, but also in concert presentations in Rzeszow, Buffalo's Sister City, and in Czestochowa, the center of Poland's devotion to God.

While the 1975 Poland concert tour stands as one of the proudest moments in the 77-year history of the Chopin Singing Society, it by no means tells the entire story of this remarkable group. For several years the society had its own television series through which the musical heritage of the Polish people was shared with the entire Western New York community. And in March 1976 the Chopin group was honored with an invitation to participate as representatives of America's 12 million Polish Americans in Bicentennial activities in our nation's capital where they performed in the Kennedy Center and were received by First Lady Betty Ford at the White House.

This album is a tribute not only to members of the Chopin Singing Society, but also to the spirit of Poles everywhere. This spirit, exemplified through song, will live forever.

Virginia Angielczyk, Walter Bakos, Alexander Bakowski, Suzanne Bartos, Milton Bednarek, Estelle Beris, Genevieve Bertozzi, Kathleen Biedron, Phyllis Blonski, Eleanore Bogdan, Gertrude Butzek, Raymond Butzek, Arthur Chmielewski, Helen Crozson, Ludwik Distel, Regina Dobesiewicz, Barbara Dolak, Dorothy Dubnicki, Thaddeus Dubnicki, Theresa Dybas, Phyllis Elbers, Joanna Fintzel, Wallace Gardon, Zygmund Glebocki, Helena Gorecki, Lorraine Graziano, Zdislaw Grzeskowiak, Edward Halicki, Stanley Halicki, Cecelia Hark, Stanislaw Herc, Patricia Herko, Karol Idzik, James Jankowski, Victoria Jarnot, Richard Jesionowski, Marcia Kajdas, Frank Kania, Dorothy Kaniecki, Edward Kasprzak, Tessie Kaszubowski, Casimer Kedzierski, Betty Klapkowski, Teddy Konieczek, Edmund Krenglicki, Rita Kurkowski, Henry Kuzinowicz, Florence Levan, Adam Malik, Regina Mankowski, Virginia Maza, Anne McColl, Ann Mikoll, James Mikoll, Theodore Mikoll, Theresa Mikoll, Frederick Netzel, Irene Netzel, John Niedzialowski, Dorothy Nitkowski, Teresa Nowak, Melanie Nuwer, Henry Ogniewski, Antoinette Osinski, Lola Paravalos, Marie Ploch, Lee Pytlak, Louise Radecki, Maria Rafalski, Evelyn Rubach, Ceil Rucinski, Laura Rucinski, Stanley Rybczynski, Marianna Sadus, Irene Schunke, Irene Sielski, Victoria Skowronski, Betty Skrok, Sigmund Sloane, John Sniatecki, Ann Struzik, Leonard Struzik, Henry Superczynski, Edward Szarek, Geraldine Szemraj, Emily Trainer, Dorothy Wesolek, Francis Wilczak, Irene Wilczak, Walter Wrobel, Stella

Wrona, Michaeline Wyrobek, John Zabinski, Stanley Zagora, Helen Zawierucha, Henry Zawierucha, Genevieve Zielinski, Irene Zurkowski.

Title: From Poland with Song!
Year: 1977
Publisher: Mark Custom Records
Catalogue Number: MC 5537
Length: 48:20 Minutes

Track Listing:
Side One
1. Processionale – arr. P. Gorecki
2. Maki – St. Niewiadomski
3. The King and I – (Selections) R. Rodgers
4. Ukochany Kraj – T. Sypietynski
5. Piesn O Warszawie – R. Rygiel

Side Two
1. Tanga – arr. Peter Gorecki
2. Matulu Kochana – arr. E. Liebling
3. Polesia Czar – A Wlast
4. Battle Hymn of the Republic – Arr. P Wilhousky
5. My Melody of Love – H. Moyer

Rear Cover Text:

From Poland with Song! The Chopin Singing Society with the Warsaw Opera Orchestra under the direction of Peter Gorecki. Soloists: Theresa Dybas, Louis Distel, Adam Malik, Victoria Jarnot, Edward Krenglicki, Antoinette Osinski. Recorded in Warsaw National Philharmonic Hall.

The Chopin Singing Society of Buffalo, New York has emerged as one of our nation's most outstanding cultural organizations. They have spread their message of Polish song and heritage throughout the United States and Canada, as well as in their concert tours of Poland. Originally founded as a men's choir in 1899, the society today has 130 voices – all amateurs – although there is nothing amateurish about the beautiful music they make. The successes enjoyed by the group have not come by chance, but from the hard work and dedication of many people – singers, officers, directors, and countless

members and friends. In 1976, they presented a special bicentennial concert at the Kennedy Center in Washington, D.C., as well as performances at the White House. They also continue a series of one-hour television specials with the Buffalo Philharmonic. Share, now, the sense of the vast beauty and spirit of Poland and its people – in song!
The Chopin Singing Society 18 Kosciuszko St. Buffalo N.Y. 14212
Theodore V. Mikoll, President
Peter Gorecki, Music Director
Recording – Polish National Radio
Production Supervised by Vincent S. Morette and David Rutecki.
Album design – Bruce Marsh.
A product of Mark Custom Records, Clarence, NY 14031
Mfg. 1977.
Photos: Edward L. Kasprzak

Bibliography

Books

140 Years of Glory, Praise, and Wisdom. St. Stanislaus Bishop and Martyr Parish, 2013.

Adler, Selig, and Thomas Edmund Connolly. *From Ararat to Suburbia; the History of the Jewish Community of Buffalo*. Jewish Publication Society of America, 1960.

Album pamiatkowe i Przewodnik Handlowy: Osady Polskiej w miescie Buffalo, z dolaczeniem Okolicznych miejscowosci Ze Stanu New York, Wydane Staraniem i Nakladem Polskiej Spolki Wydawniczej, 1906

Alumni Directory. 1859/1928-... St. Bonaventure University, n.p, 1930.

The Appellate Division of the New York Supreme Court, Third Judicial Department: Over 100 Years of Judicial Service. 1998.

Barnes, Larry D. *A Polish Revolutionary in Batavia, His Wife and Descendants, and a House Divided: The Story of Henry Glowacki and His Family*. Larry D. Barnes, 2008.

Blejwas, Stanislaus A. *The Polish Singers Alliance, 1888-1998: Choral Patriotism*. University of Rochester Press, 2005.

Buffalo City Directory 1941

Canisius College Buffalo, N.Y. 1905-1906 Thirty Sixth Annual Catalogue. Canisius College, 1905.

Chenoweth, Eric. "Conference on AFL-CIO Foreign Policy." *AFL-CIO Support for Solidarity: Moral, Political, Financial*.

Chopin Singing Society - 80th Anniversary Program. Chopin Singing Society, 1979.

Chopin Singing Society 75th Anniversary, 1899-1974. The Society, 1974.

Diamond Jubilee, 1893-1968: Transfiguration R.C. Church, Buffalo, New York. Transfiguration Church, 1968.

Drabik, Michael. *The Aleksander Fredro Library and Singing Society*. Drabik, 1992.

Encyklopedia teatru polskiego. "Leonia Ogrodzka." *Encyklopedia Teatru Polskiego*, 2016.

Garfinkel, Marvin H. *Temple Beth El's First Century; Centennial Souvenir Book, 1847-1947*. 1947.

Golden Jubilee of St. Ladislaus Parish, 1920-1970: The Growth of a Community, St. Ladislaus Parish, 1970.

J. Fischer & Bro., New York. "Sylvia." A Nautical Knot or The Belle of Barbstapoole, 1911

Jablonski, Fred F. *Precious Blood Church; 75th Diamond Jubilee, 1899-1975*. Precious Blood Church, 1974.

Kobielski, Milton J. *Millennium of Christianity of the Polish People, 966-1966: Buffalo Diocesan Observance*. Millennium Committee of the Diocese of Buffalo, 1966.

Pamietnik 50-Cio Lecia Stowarzyszenia Domu Polskiego, 1905-1955. Dom Polski Association, 1955

Pamietnik Z Okazji Zlotego Jubileuszu 1897-1947, Polskiego Kola Spiewackiego, Buffalo, N.Y. Polskie Kola Spiewackie, 1947.

Pamietnik Zlotego Jubileuszu 1901-1951, Towarzystwo Spiewu Kalina, Buffalo, New York. 1951.

Pamietnik Zlotego Jubileuszu Kosciola Sw. Kazimierza, Buffalo, N.Y. Druk Dziennika Dla Wszystkich, 1940.

Pienkos, Donald E. *One Hundred Years Young: A History of the Polish Falcons of America 1887-1987*. East European Monographs; Distributed by Columbia University Press 1987. 129

Poetry and Prophecy: A Remembrance of Adam Mickiewicz. Polish Cultural Foundation, 2005.

Polish American Congress Western New York Division. *60th Anniversary Banquet*. Polish American Congress, 2004.

The Polish Arts Club Welcomes the Board of Directors of the Polish American Historical Association to Buffalo. Polish Arts Club of Buffalo, 2013.

Polish Singers Alliance of America 49th International Convention. Polish Singers Alliance of America, 2010.

Puddington, Arch. *Lane Kirkland: Champion of American Labor*. Wiley, 2005.

Rozek, Ben, and Norma Wujcikowski. "History." *Polish Falcons of America Nest #6 100th Anniversary Oct. 5, 1996*, Polish Falcons of America Nest #6, Buffalo, NY, 1996

Slawinska, Wanda M. "Dr. Francis Eustace Fronczak and Ignacy Jan Paderewski: The Enduring Friendship." The Polonian Legacy of Western New York: Stories of the Lives, Accomplishments, and Contributions of Four Prominent Polish-Americans, edited by Edward R. Szemraj, Canisius College Press, Buffalo, NY, 2005.

St. Augustine Parish Depew Diamond Jubilee 1909-1984. 1984.

Towarzystwo Czytelnia Polska w Domu Polskim Buffalo, New York 1889 1964. 1964.

Towarzystwo Spiewu Fryderyka Chopina 1899-1949. Tow. Spiewu

Fryderyka Chopina, 1949.
Welcome to the Polish Falcons of America Nest 6 Centennial 1896-1996. Buffalo, NY: Polish Falcons of America, 1996. Print
Zloty Jubileusz Parafii Sw. App. Piotra I Pawla. Depew, NY. 1947.

Newspapers and Magazines

Am-Pol Eagle (Cheektowaga, NY)
Argus (Albany, NY), 1865-1921
Buffalo Courier (Buffalo, NY) 1888-1926
Buffalo Courier-Express (Buffalo, NY), 1926-1982
Buffalo Criterion (Buffalo, NY)
Buffalo News (Buffalo, NY)
Buffalo Express (Buffalo, NY) 1878-1926
Cheektowaga Times (Cheektowaga, NY), 1946-2008
Clarkston News (Clarkston, MI)
Courier & Freeman (Potsdam, NY), 1861-1989
Daily News (Batavia, NY)
Dziennik Dla Wszystkich (Buffalo, NY), 1907-1957
Elmira Star Gazette (Elmira, NY)
Enterprise-Times (Lancaster, NY), 1898-1964
Evening Republic (Buffalo, NY), 1876-1885
Fairport Herald-Mail (Fairport, NY)
Finger Lakes Times (Geneva, NY)
Front Page (Lackawanna, NY), 1959-2020
Frontier Herald (Blasdell, NY), 1959-1966
German Citizen (Cheektowaga, NY)
Greenpoint Weekly Star (Brooklyn, NY), 1875-1968
Griffin (Buffalo, NY)
Hamburg Sun (Hamburg, NY)
Independent (Edinboro, PA), 1880-1977
Indianapolis Monthly (Indianapolis, IN)
Island Dispatch (Grand Island, NY)
Jamestown Post-Journal (Jamestown, NY)
Journal-Register (Medina, NY), 1970-2014
Lackawanna Herald (Lackawanna, NY), 1931-1941
Lackawanna Leader (Lackawanna, NY), 1936-1982
Lancaster/Depew Bee (Buffalo, NY)
New York Evening Post (New York, NY)
New York Times (New York, NY)
Niagara Falls Gazette (Niagara Falls, NY)

Orange Leader (Orange, TX)
Philadelphia Inquirer (Philadelphia, PA)
Polish American Journal (Boston, NY)
Rochester Democrat and Chronicle (Rochester, NY)
Sarasota Herald-Tribune (Sarasota, FL)
Times Record (Troy, NY) 1935-1988
Tonawanda News (North Tonawanda, NY), 1880-2015
Union-Sun Journal (Lockport, NY)
Washington Post (Washington, DC)
Wyoming County Times (Warsaw, NY), 1876-1973

Television and Radio Programs

Polish American Radio Program, (Buffalo, NY) WEBR
"Polonia: Western New York's Polish-American Legacy." WNED, 2005
What's My Line? (New York, NY) CBS, 1950-1967

Electronic Resources

"1929-1930 Stock Charts of the Great Depression Era." Online Stock Trading Guide, Online Stock Trading Guide, online-stock-trading-guide.com/1929-1930-stock-charts.html. Accessed 15 Jan. 2021

"About." *May Phang, Pianist*, mayphang.com/about.html. Accessed 3 Feb. 2023.

"Adam Mickiewicz Library and Dramatic Circle." Polonia Trail, Polish-American Congress WNY, 29 June 2016, poloniatrail.com/location/adam-mickiewicz-library-and-dramatic-circle

"Alfred Fabiniak - Sunday, May 15th, 2011." *Kolano Funeral Home*, May 2011 kolanofuneralhome.com/memorials/alfred-fabiniak/743798/obituary.php.

"*Am-Pol Eagle* Citizen of the Year Award." *Wikipedia*, Wikimedia Foundation, en.wikipedia.org/wiki/Am-Pol_Eagle_Citizen_of_the_Year_Award Accessed 5 May 2021

"Buffalo Memorial Auditorium." Polonia Trail, Polish-American Congress WNY, 29 June 2016, poloniatrail.com/location/buffalo-memorial-auditorium

Byrd, Christopher. "Dr. Ireneusz Lukaszewski's Last Mass as Organist for Corpus Christi Church." *Broadway Fillmore Alive*, 3 Feb. 2008, broadwayfillmorealive.org/2.0/2008/02/dr-ireneusz-lukaszewskis-last-mass-as-organist-for-corpus-christi-church/.

"CDC Museum Covid-19 Timeline." Centers for Disease Control and

Prevention, Centers for Disease Control and Prevention, cdc.gov/museum/timeline/covid19.html Accessed 15 Mar. 2023

"Chopin Singing Society." Polonia Trail, Polish-American Congress WNY, 29 June 2016, poloniatrail.com/location/chopin-singing-society

"Dow Jones - 1929 Crash and Bear Market." MacroTrends, Macrotrends LLC, macrotrends.net/2484/dow-jones-crash-1929-bear-market. Accessed 29 July. 2020

'D'Amico, Hank." *Discography of American Historical Recordings.* UC Santa Barbara Library, 2023. Web. adp.library.ucsb.edu/index.php/mastertalent/detail/107194/DAmico_Hank Accessed 20 Jan. 2023

"Kapalka, Jan." *Discography of American Historical Recordings*. UC Santa Barbara Library, 2022. Web. adp.library.ucsb.edu/index.php/mastertalent/detail/205221/Kapaka_Jan?Matrix_page=100000. Accessed 7 Mar. 2022

"Frederick Stanislaus Netzel (1914-1990)." Find a Grave, findagrave.com/memorial/216191677/frederick-stanislaus-netzel Accessed 30 Sept. 2020

"History of Polish Chair." *Detailed History of the Permanent Chair of Polish Culture*, Canisius College - Buffalo, NY, canisius.edu/node/2252.

Lyon, Norman T. "History of the Polish People in Rochester." History of the Polish People in Rochester (3 of 5), GenWeb of Monroe County, 19 May 2018, mcnygenealogy.com/book/polish-3.htm.

"Michael Joseph Stefanski." *FamilySearch*, familysearch.org/tree/person/details/LCJG-1NB.

"Michal Bilicki (1872-1908) - Find A Grave..." *Find a Grave*, 29 May 2017, findagrave.com/memorial/179822751/michal-bilicki

Noreck Ruppert, Barbara. "Stella Olszewska." *Grave Finder At St. Stans*, Grave Finder At St. Stans, 31 Dec. 2021, gravefinderatststans.com/details/?PersonID=2697.

"October 15, 1960 Weather History in Buffalo New York, United States." *Buffalo October 15, 1960 Historical Weather (New York, United States) - Weather Spark* weatherspark.com/h/m/20372/1960/10/Historical-Weather-in-October-1960-in-Buffalo-New-York-United-States Accessed 3 July 2021.

Oron, Aryeh. "Genia Las (Soprano, Mezzo-Soprano)." *Genia Las (Soprano, Mezzo-Soprano) - Short Biography*, Bach Cantatas Website, Sept. 2019, www.bach-cantatas.com/Bio/Las-Genia.htm.

"Peter Gorecki (1924-2011) - Find a Grave Memorial." Find a Grave, www.findagrave.com/memorial/226480883/peter-gorecki. Accessed 5 May 2021.

Pitas, Jeannine. "Photo Gallery: Slavic Soul at Corpus Christi Church." *Broadway Fillmore Alive*, 28 May 2016, broadwayfillmorealive.org/2.0/2016/05/photo-gallery-slavic-soul-at-corpus-christi-church

"Polish Army in France Recruitment Records - Page 32, R." Foundation for East European Family History Studies, Polish Genealogical Society of America, feefhs.org/resource/poland-army-recruitment-32 Accessed 13 Jan 2023

"Polish Falcons of America Nest 6." Polonia Trail, Polish-American Congress WNY, 29 June 2016, poloniatrail.com/location/polish-Falcons-of-america-nest-6/

"Polish Singing Circle." *Polonia Trail*, Polish-American Congress WNY, 29 June 2016 poloniatrail.com/location/polish-singing-circle

"Polish Union of America Building." Polonia Trail, Polish-American Congress WNY, 29 June 2016, poloniatrail.com/location/polish-union-of-america-building

"The Polish Village." *Polonia Trail*, Polish-American Congress WNY, 29 Jan. 2016 poloniatrail.com/location/the-polish-village

"Raymond A. Fabiniak's Obituary (2015) *Buffalo News*." *Legacy.com*, legacy.com/us/obituaries/buffalonews/name/raymond-fabiniak-obituary?id=4809056 Accessed 8 Oct. 2022.

Roberts, Richard. "The Financial Times: A Financial History of the Last 120 Years." Financial Times Historical Archive, Cengage Learning, 2010, gale.com/intl/essays/richard-roberts-financial-times-financial-history

Schuhrke, Jeff. "From Solidarity to Shock Therapy: The AFL-CIO and the Fall of Soviet Communism." *LAWCHA*, 22 Nov. 2022, lawcha.org/2022/11/22/solidarity-to-shock-therapy/.

"St. Adalbert's Basilica Complex." *Polonia Trail*, Polish-American Congress WNY, 29 June 2016 poloniatrail.com/location/st-adalberts-basilica-complex

"St. Michael's Roman Catholic Church." *Polonia Trail*, Polish-American Congress WNY, 29 June 2016 poloniatrail.com/location/st-michaels-roman-catholic-church

"St. Stanislaus, B. & M. Church." *Polonia Trail*, Polish-American Congress WNY, 29 June 2016 poloniatrail.com/location/st-

stanislaus-church
Staff. "Polish American Festival Held in Cheektowaga." *WGRZ.com*, WGRZ, 18 July 2016, wgrz.com/article/news/polish-american-festival-held-in-cheektowaga/71-275511888.
"Stroke Recovery: A Music Miracle." Catholic Health, 3 June 2018, facebook.com/MercyHospitalofBuffalo/videos/10155175318206511 Accessed 25 Nov. 2023.
Woolf, Jonathan. "Review: Lukaszewski Choral Music AP0252 [JW]: Classical Music Reviews." *MusicWeb*, MusicWeb, musicweb-international.com/classrev/2013/Jan13/lukaszewski_choral%20music_%20AP0252.htm. Accessed 4 Apr. 2023.

Recordings

"Buried Treasures Ensemble." Crystal Records.
"The Chopin Singing Society of Buffalo, NY." Chopin Singing Society, 1975.
"From Poland with Song!" Chopin Singing Society, 1977
Ireneusz Lukaszewski. "Choral Works." Augsburg Evangelical Church, Sopot, May 2011.

Event Programs

1990 Chopin Young Pianists Competition Finals. Chopin Singing Society, 1990.
25th Anniversary Celebration. The Dr. Martin Luther King Jr. Celebration Committee, 2004.
29th Annual Festival of Christmas Carols - "Koledy." Polish Singers Alliance District IX, 2009.
50th Anniversary Polish Singers Alliance of American Circuit IX 1937-1987. Polish Singers Alliance of American Circuit IX, 1987.
Annual Installation Banquet Frederick Chopin Singing Society 1899-1970. The Chopin Singing Society, 1970.
Buffalo Philharmonic Orchestra. *Pops Concert - December 6, 1968*. Thorner-Sidney Press, 1968.
Celebrating the 70th Anniversary of the Polish American Congress. Polish American Congress, 2014.
Cheektowaga Polish-American Festival Committee. *10th Annual Polish-American Arts-Festival*. Polish-American Festival Committee, 1988.
Cheektowaga Polish-American Festival Committee. *Polish-American Arts Festival*. 2000.

Chopin &Copernicus: The Art of Heaven. The Chopin Singing Society and the Polish Arts Club of Buffalo, 2023.

The Cheektowaga-Chopin Gala Spring Concert. 1991.

The Chopin Singing Society Concert. Niagara University, 1990.

The Chopin Singing Society. *41-Szy Koncert*. Chopin Singing Society, 1940.;

The Chopin Singing Society. *43-Ci Koncert Chopina*. Chopin Singing Society, 1942.

The Chopin Singing Society. *46th Annual Concert*. Chopin Singing Society, 1946.

The Chopin Singing Society. *48th Annual Concert.* Chopin Singing Society, 1947.

The Chopin Singing Society. *49th Annual Concert*. Chopin Singing Society, 1948.

The Chopin Singing Society. *50th Annual Concert*. Chopin Singing Society, 1949.

The Chopin Singing Society. *51st Annual Concert*. Chopin Singing Society, 1950.

The Chopin Singing Society. *56th Annual Concert*. Chopin Singing Society, 1955.

The Chopin Singing Society. *57th Annual Concert*. Chopin Singing Society, 1956.

The Chopin Singing Society. *58th Annual Concert*. Chopin Singing Society, 1957.

The Chopin Singing Society. *59th Annual Concert*. Chopin Singing Society, 1958.

The Chopin Singing Society. *60th Annual Concert*. Chopin Singing Society, 1959.

The Chopin Singing Society. *61st Annual Concert*. Chopin Singing Society, 1960.

The Chopin Singing Society. *63rd Annual Concert - Springtime in Poland*. Chopin Singing Society, 1962.

The Chopin Singing Society. *74th Annual Concert*. Chopin Singing Society, 1973.

The Chopin Singing Society. *75th Anniversary Concert*. Chopin Singing Society, 1974.

The Chopin Singing Society. *79th Annual Concert*. Chopin Singing Society, 1978.

The Chopin Singing Society. *80th Anniversary*. Chopin Singing Society, 1979.

The Chopin Singing Society. *81st Anniversary Concert*. Chopin Singing Society, 1980.
The Chopin Singing Society. *The 85th Anniversary Ball of the Frederick Chopin Singing Society*. Chopin Singing Society, 1985.
The Chopin Singing Society. *85th Anniversary Concert.* Chopin Singing Society, 1984.
The Chopin Singing Society. *88th Annual Concert*. Chopin Singing Society, 1987.
The Chopin Singing Society. *90th Anniversary Concert.* Chopin Singing Society, 1989.
The Chopin Singing Society. *94th Anniversary Concert.* Chopin Singing Society, 1993.
The Chopin Singing Society. *96th Anniversary Concert*. Chopin Singing Society, 1995.
The Chopin Singing Society. *97th Anniversary Concert*. Chopin Singing Society, 1996.
The Chopin Singing Society. *98th Anniversary Concert*. Chopin Singing Society, 1997.
The Chopin Singing Society. *102nd Anniversary Concert*. Chopin Singing Society, 2001.
The Chopin Singing Society. *103rd Anniversary Concert*. Chopin Singing Society, 2002.
The Chopin Singing Society. *104th Anniversary Concert*. Chopin Singing Society, 2003.
The Chopin Singing Society. *105th Annual Concert*. Chopin Singing Society, 2004.
The Chopin Singing Society. *106th Anniversary Concert*. Chopin Singing Society, 2005.
The Chopin Singing Society. *108th Annual Concert*. Chopin Singing Society, 2007.
The Chopin Singing Society. *109th Annual Concert.* Chopin Singing Society, 2008.
The Chopin Singing Society. *110th Annual Concert*. Chopin Singing Society, 2009.
The Chopin Singing Society. *111th Annual Concert*. Chopin Singing Society, 2010.
The Chopin Singing Society. *113th Annual Concert*. Chopin Singing Society, 2012.
The Chopin Singing Society. *115th Annual Concert*. Chopin Singing Society, 2014.

The Chopin Singing Society. *120th Annual Concert*. Chopin Singing Society, 2019.

The Chopin Singing Society. *124th Annual Concert*. Chopin Singing Society, 2023.

The Chopin Singing Society. *A Wigilia Celebration*. Chopin Singing Society, 1995.

The Chopin Singing Society. *A World of Music.* Chopin Singing Society, 2000.

The Chopin Singing Society. *A World of Music*. Chopin Singing Society, 2000.

The Chopin Singing Society. *Annual Concert - Federick Chopin Singing Society Featuring the Buffalo Philharmonic Orchestra March 25, 1972*. Chopin Singing Society, 1972.

The Chopin Singing Society. *Annual Installation Banquet Frederick Chopin Singing Society 1899-1971.* The Chopin Singing Society, 1971.

The Chopin Singing Society. *Bicentennial Concert*. Chopin Singing Society, 1976.

The Chopin Singing Society. *"Bon Voyage" Concert*. Chopin Singing Society, 1975.

The Chopin Singing Society. *A Celebration of the 192nd Birthday of Frederic Chopin*. Chopin Singing Society, 2002.

The Chopin Singing Society. *A Celebration of the 194th Birthday of Fryderyk Chopin with the Chopin Singing Society and Special Guest: Igor Lipinski*. Chopin Singing Society, 2004.

The Chopin Singing Society. *A Celebration of the 195th Birthday of Frederic Chopin: "Chopin in Paris."* Chopin Singing Society, 2005.

The Chopin Singing Society. *A Celebration of the 196th Birthday of Frederic Chopin*. Chopin Singing Society, 2006.;

The Chopin Singing Society. *A Celebration of the 198th Birthday of Frederic Chopin*. Chopin Singing Society, 2008.

The Chopin Singing Society. *A Celebration of the 199th Birthday of Frederic Chopin*. Chopin Singing Society, 2009.

The Chopin Singing Society. *A Celebration of the 200th Birthday of Frederic Chopin*. Chopin Singing Society, 2010.

The Chopin Singing Society. *A Celebration of the 201st Birthday of Frederic Chopin*. Chopin Singing Society, 2011.

The Chopin Singing Society. *A Celebration of the 203rd Birthday of Frederic Chopin*. Chopin Singing Society, 2013.

The Chopin Singing Society. *Centennial Concert*. Chopin Singing Society, 1999.

The Chopin Singing Society. *Chamber Series - Concert II*. Chopin Singing Society, 2002.

The Chopin Singing Society. *Chopin Chamber Series: Concert III*. The Chopin Singing Society, 2003.

Chopin Singing Society. "Chopin Singing Society Dyngus Day." 2016.

The Chopin Singing Society. *Chopin Singing Society in Concert St. John Kanty December 10, 1986*. Chopin Singing Society, 1986.

Chopin Singing Society. "Commemorating the Genius of Frederic Chopin." 2016.

The Chopin Singing Society. *"Encore" Concert*. Chopin Singing Society, 1975.

The Chopin Singing Society. *'Encore' Concert*. Chopin Singing Society, 1977.

The Chopin Singing Society. *Frederick Chopin Singing Society 65th Annual Installation Banquet*. The Chopin Singing Society, 1964.;

The Chopin Singing Society. *Frederick Chopin Singing Society Annual Installation Banquet, Saturday March 22, 1969*. The Chopin Singing Society, 1969.

The Chopin Singing Society. *Frederick Chopin Singing Society Annual Installation Banquet, Saturday March 22, 1969*. The Chopin Singing Society, 1969

The Chopin Singing Society. *Frederick Chopin Singing Society, Inc - Chopin Installation Banquet*. The Chopin Singing Society, 1963.

Chopin Singing Society. "Future Events." 2018.

The Chopin Singing Society. *In Concert - Chopin Singing Society - Slee Hall - December 14, 1983*. Chopin Singing Society, 1983.

The Chopin Singing Society. *Installation Banquet Frederick Chopin Singing Society 1899-1988*. Chopin Singing Society, 1988.

The Chopin Singing Society. *Installation Banquet*. Chopin Singing Society, 1996.

The Chopin Singing Society. *Jaselka*. Chopin Singing Society, 2000.

The Chopin Singing Society. *Koncert Choru Imienia Fryderyka Szopena*. Chopin Singing Society, 1977.

The Chopin Singing Society. *Lincoln's Day Double Header*, The Chopin Singing Society, 1964.

Chopin Singing Society. *The Many Faces of Poland - April 15, 1961*. 1961.

Chopin Singing Society. "Millennium Buffalo Presents Chopin Singing Society's 57th Annual Dyngus Day Celebration." 2018.

The Chopin Singing Society. *A Salute to Buffalo on Their Sesquicentennial Year! From the Chopin Singing Society.* Chopin Singing Society, 1982.

Chopin Singing Society. "Would like to Wish All of Polonia a Merry Christmas and a Happy Joyous New Year!" 2017.

Commemorating the Unveiling of the Chopin Memorial by the Chopin Singing Society: Humboldt Park, Buffalo, New York, June Seventh, Nineteen Twenty Five. The Society, 1925.

A Festival of Folk Songs and Dance - Oct. 15, 1960. Frederick Chopin Singing Society, 1960.

A Festival of Folk Songs and Dance - Nov 26, 1960. (Repeat Performance). Frederick Chopin Singing Society, 1960.

Festival Vigil Mass Book. Polish Heritage Festival, Inc., 2006.

First Anniversary of the Investiture of Pope John Paul II. Polish American Congress, 1979.

Fourth Concert Winter Pops. Buffalo Philharmonic Orchestra, 1961.

Fraternal Memorial Mass in Honor of the Living and Deceased Members of the Polish Roman Catholic Union of America. Polish Roman Catholic Union of America, 2006.

Gala Concert. Polish Singers Alliance of America, 2007.

Golden Anniversary Concert and Ball. I.J. Paderewski Singing Society, 1989.

Holy Mother of the Rosary Cathedral presents in concert: The Chopin Singing Society. Holy Mother of the Rosary Cathedral, 2015.

King Roger. Greater Buffalo Opera Company, 1992.

A Lenten Concert with the Chopin Singing Society. Annunciation Church, 2013.

Musical Interlude. The Polish Cultural Society of the Palm Beaches, 1994.

Operetka Sylvia Chor Chopina z Udzialm Choru Kalina Poniedzialek 10 Maja 1920. Chopin Singing Society, 1920.

Sacred Music 1988 Gala Concert to Honor the 10th Anniversary of the Elevation of Pope John Paul II. Polstar Publishing Corp., 1988.

St. Stanislaus Bishop and Martyr Parish Memorial Concert Honoring Pope John Paul II on the 1st Anniversary of His Death. St. Stanislaus Bishop and Martyr Parish, Buffalo NY, 2006.; *In Memory of Pope John Paul II*. Camerata Di Sant'Antonio, 2006.

Straszny Dwor. Greater Buffalo Opera Company, 1997.

Thomas Witakowski, Bass - Paul Homer, Accompanist: In Recital. State University College of New York at Buffalo, 1993.

Villa Maria Academy Parent's Guild. *"The Melody Lingers On" with the Chopin Singing Society for Immaculate Heart of Mary Academy*. Am-Pol Eagle, 1967.

WBEN-TV. *The Chopin Singing Society in a Special TV Concert - December 2, 1963*. Erie County Savings Bank, 1963.

WBEN-TV. *The Chopin Singing Society in A Special TV Concert - December 21, 1964*. Erie County Savings Bank, 1964.

WBEN-TV. *The Chopin Singing Society in A Special TV Concert - December 19, 1966*. Erie County Savings Bank, 1966.; WBEN-TV. *The Chopin Singing Society and The Matusz Polish Dance Circle in 100 Years of Polish Songs - March 21, 1967*. Adam, Meldrum & Anderson Co., 1967.

WBEN-TV. *The Chopin Singing Society in A Special TV Concert - December 3, 1962*. Erie County Savings Bank, 1962.

WBEN-TV. *The Chopin Singing Society in A Special TV Concert - February 20, 1963*. Erie County Savings Bank, 1963.

WBEN-TV. *The Chopin Singing Society in A Special TV Concert - January 28, 1963*. Erie County Savings Bank, 1963.

WBEN-TV. *The Chopin Singing Society in A Special TV Concert - January 24, 1966*. Erie County Savings Bank, 1966.

WBEN-TV. *The Chopin Singing Society in A Special TV Concert - March 25, 1963*. Erie County Savings Bank, 1963.

WBEN-TV. *The Chopin Singing Society in A Special TV Concert - March 15, 1965*. Erie County Savings Bank, 1965.

WBEN-TV. *The Chopin Singing Society in A Special TV Concert - November 12, 1962*. Erie County Savings Bank, 1962.

WBEN-TV. *The Chopin Singing Society in A Special TV Concert - October 26, 1964*. Erie County Savings Bank, 1964.

WBEN-TV. *The Chopin Singing Society in A Special TV Concert Celebrating the Polish Millennium - April 13, 1966.* Erie County Savings Bank, 1966.

Government Document

Local Board No. 51 - Wayne County. "D.S.S. Form 1 Registration Card - Vincent Eugene Kwiecikowski." Hamtramck, MI, 27 Apr. 1942.

"The Nation of Polonia:Polish/Russian: Immigration and Relocation in U.S. History: Classroom Materials at the Library of Congress:

Library of Congress." The Library of Congress
Naturalization Ceremony at Buffalo and Erie County Naval & Servicemen's Park U.S.S. Little Rock. United States Citizenship and Immigration Services, 2006.
President Wilson's Message to Congress, January 8, 1918; Records of the United States Senate; Record Group 46; Records of the United States Senate; National Archives.
Registration Card, Form 1 Number 36 - Zdzislaw Francis Krysztafkiewicz 1917.
Registration Card, Serial Number 1610 Order Number 1897 - Stanley Francis Kujawa 1918
"Trades and Professions Committees." *Report of Director of Publicity, Third Liberty Loan, April 1918*, by A. G. Bartholomew, Matthews-Northrup Works, Buffalo, NY, 1918, pp. 64–79.
U.S. Immigration and Naturalization Service Naturalization Ceremony at Buffalo & Erie County Naval & Servicemen's Park U.S.S. Little Rock. U.S. Department of Justice, 2000.
"United States 1950 Census," Entry for John A Kedzierski and Stella Kedzierski, 10 April 1950.
United States, Congress, Biden, Joseph R. *Continuation of the National Emergency with Respect to the Novel Coronavirus Disease (Covid-19) Outbreak: Message from the President of the United States, Transmitting a Continuation of the National Emergency with Respect to the Coronavirus Disease 2019 (Covid-19) Pandemic, Declared in Proclamation 9994 of March 13, 2020, Is to Continue in Effect beyond March 1, 2021, Pursuant to 50 U.S.C. 1622(d); Public Law 94-412, Sec. 202(D); (90 Stat. 1257).*

Archives

Adam Mickiewicz Library and Dramatic Circle, Buffalo, New York
Buffalo Mass Mob, Amherst, New York
Chopin Singing Society, Cheektowaga, New York
Polish American Congress Western New York Division, Buffalo, New York
Polish Singers Alliance of America, Cheektowaga, New York

Interviews

Peter Sloane, 8 Aug. 2023.
Michael Szafranski, 28 May 2023.
Mary Lou Wyrobek, 21 Sept. 2022.

Other Sources

Busyn, Helen. "Peter Kiolbassa: Maker of Polish America." Polish American Studies, vol. 8, Dec. 1951, pp. 65–84.

"Polish Independence to Be Explored at Symposium: Daemen University." *Polish Independence to Be Explored at Symposium*, Daemen University, 13 Sept. 2018,

Witakowski, Thomas. "The Choral Works of Karol Szymanowski in their Historical and Cultural Context." *Indiana University*, 1994.

Witul, Gregory L. "The History of Polish Americans in Cheektowaga." Cheektowaga Historical Museum, 20 Feb. 2014, Cheektowaga, NY, Cheektowaga Senior Center.

Index

Appendices are not included in this index.

Made in the USA
Columbia, SC
23 June 2024

37400412R00178